OWL

COMPARATIVE EUROPEAN POLITICS

Semi-Presidentialism in Europe

COMPARATIVE EUROPEAN POLITICS

Comparative European Politics is a series for students and teachers of
political science and related disciplines, published in association with the
European Consortium for Political Research. Each volume will provide an
up-to-date survey of the current state of knowledge and research on an issue
of major significance in European government and politics

OTHER TITLES IN THIS SERIES

Parties and Democracy: Coalition Formation and Government
Functioning in Twenty States
Ian Budge and Hans Keman

State formation, Nation-building, and Mass Politics in Europe
Edited by Peter Flora with Stein Kuhnle, and Derek Urwin

Politics and Policy in the European Community
(second edition)
Stephen George

Political Data Handbook: OECD Countries
Jan-Erik Lane, David McKay, and Kenneth Newton

Self-Interest and Public Interest in Western Politics
Leif Lewin

Government and Politics in Western Europe:
Britain, France, Italy, Germany
(third edition)
Yves Mény with Andrew Knapp

Localism and Centralism in Europe:
The Political and Legal Bases of Local Self-Government
Edward C. Page

Electoral Systems and Party Systems:
A Study of Twenty-Seven Democracies,
1945–1990
Arend Lijphart

Parties and their Members: Organizing for Victory
in Britain and Germany
Susan E. Scarrow

Learning Democracy: Democratic and
Economic Values in Unified Germany
Robert Rohrschneider

Semi-Presidentialism in Europe

Edited by

ROBERT ELGIE

OXFORD
UNIVERSITY PRESS

OXFORD

UNIVERSITY PRESS

Great Clarendon Street, Oxford OX2 6DP

Oxford University Press is a department of the University of Oxford.
It furthers the University's objective of excellence in research, scholarship,
and education by publishing worldwide in

Oxford New York

Athens Auckland Bangkok Bogotá Buenos Aires Calcutta
Cape Town Chennai Dar es Salaam Delhi Florence Hong Kong Istanbul
Karachi Kuala Lumpur Madrid Melbourne Mexico City Mumbai
Nairobi Paris São Paulo Singapore Taipei Tokyo Toronto Warsaw

with associated companies in Berlin Ibadan

Oxford is a registered trade mark of Oxford University Press
in the UK and in certain other countries

Published in the United States
by Oxford University Press Inc., New York

British Library Cataloguing in Publication Data
Data available

Library of Congress Cataloging in Publication Data
Data available

ISBN 0-19-829386-0

1 3 5 7 9 10 8 6 4 2

Typeset in Times
by Best-set Typesetter Ltd., Hong Kong
Printed in Great Britain
on acid-free paper by
Biddles Ltd.,
Guildford and King's Lynn

PREFACE

Semi-presidentialism is an increasingly popular form of constitutional government. Semi-presidential regimes can now be found in Western Europe, in Austria, Finland, France, Iceland, Ireland, and Portugal; in Central and Eastern Europe, including Bulgaria, Lithuania, Poland, Romania, Russia, and Ukraine; in Asia, in places such as Mongolia, South Korea, and Sri Lanka; and elsewhere in, for example, Guyana, Haiti, Angola, and Namibia.

By definition, all of these countries share a similar set of basic constitutional features, namely a directly elected fixed-term president and a prime minister who is responsible to parliament. However, the main observation to be made about them is that the exercise of political power varies greatly from one to another. For example, in some countries, particularly France, the president is usually the dominant political actor. In other countries, such as Finland, there is a sometimes uneasy balance of power between the president and prime minister. In yet others, notably Ukraine, the president and parliament share powers. Finally, in others still, including Austria, Iceland, and Ireland, the president is merely a figurehead and the prime minister dominates the decision-making process.

Overall, then, semi-presidentialism is a widespread form of government but the politics of semi-presidential government is extremely varied. It is precisely because of the very varied forms of political leadership which occur across these institutionally similar countries that some writers have dismissed the concept of semi-presidentialism. In fact, though, it is this variety which should attract the attention of the political scientist. Semi-presidentialism provides a perfect opportunity to study the general question of why political systems function in the way they do and to examine the relationship between particular constitutional arrangements and different forms of political practice.

This book examines the politics of semi-presidentialism in twelve European countries. Indeed, the only semi-presidential country which is omitted from this study is Portugal. In this case, it was most unfortunate that a proposed chapter was never submitted much to the disappointment of the editor and the publisher. Nevertheless, this book still provides the most comprehensive study of semi-presidential regimes, in Europe or more generally, that has been undertaken to date. It begins with an introduction which provides a background to the study of the concept and a framework for the analysis of semi-presidential regimes. In the chapters which follow, this framework is applied to the politics of individual European countries. In the conclusion the lessons of these chapters are reviewed and the future of semi-presidential studies is considered.

During the preparation of this book many debts have been incurred. In particular, I would like to thank the contributors for their enthusiasm and their patience. I would also like to thank them for their comments on the draft versions of the opening and closing chapters. As usual, though, responsibility for the end result lies purely with myself. In addition, I would like to express my warm appreciation to Dominic Byatt at Oxford University Press who has been extremely efficient and very encouraging thoughout the whole life of this project.

Finally, I would like to dedicate this book to Etain, whose support has been a source of great strength during the past couple of years, and to Matthew, because I can.

Robert Elgie

September 1998

CONTENTS

LIST OF FIGURES

LIST OF TABLES

ABBREVIATIONS

AWS	Solidarity Electoral Action (Poland)
BBWR	Non-Party Reform Bloc (Poland)
BSP	Bulgarian Socialist Party
CAP	Common Agricultural Policy
CPSU	Communist Party of the Soviet Union
CRG	Constitutional Review Group (Ireland)
DC	Democratic Convention (Romania)
DNSF	Democratic National Salvation Front (Romania)
EEA	European Economic Area
EFTA	European Free Trade Association
EMU	Economic and Monetary Union
FCMA	(Treaty of) Friendship, Cooperation, and Mutual Assistance (Finland-USSR)
FPÖ	Freedom Party (Austria)
GRP	Greater Romania Party
HDFR	Hungarian Democratic Federation in Romania
HU/CL	Homeland Union/Conservatives of Lithuania
LCDP	Lithuanian Christian Democratic Party
LCP	Lithuanian Communist Party
LCU	Lithuanian Centre Union
LDLP	Lithuanian Democratic Labour Party
LLU	Lithuanian Liberal Union
MRF	Movement for Rights and Freedoms (Bulgaria)
NLP	National Liberal Party (Romania)
NSF	National Salvation Front (Romania)
ÖVP	Austrian People's Party
PC	Centre Alliance (Poland)
PR	proportional representation
PRNU	Party for Romanian National Union
PSDR	Social Democratic Party of Romania
PSL	Polish Peasant Party
PZPR	Polish United Workers' Party
SD	Democratic Party (Poland)
SdRP	Social Democracy for Poland
SKDL	Finnish People's Democratic League
SLD	Alliance of the Democratic Left (Poland)

SLP	Socialist Labour Party (Romania)
SPÖ	Social Democratic Party of Austria
UDF	Union of Democratic Forces (Bulgaria)
UP	Union of Labour (Poland)
USD	Social Democratic Union (Romania)
UW	Freedom Union (Poland)
VdU	League of Independents (Austria)
ZSL	United Peasants' Party (Poland)

LIST OF CONTRIBUTORS

David Arter is Professor of Nordic Politics and Director of the Nordic Policy Studies Centre at the University of Aberdeen. He has just completed a detailed study of Scandinavian politics entitled *Politics and Policy-Making in the Nordic States* (Manchester University Press, 1998). His two previous books were *The Politics of European Integration in the Twentieth Century* (Dartmouth, 1993) and *Parties and Democracy in the Post-Soviet Republics* (Dartmouth, 1996). He writes regularly for *The Economist* on Scandinavia and is the Deputy-Chair of the Executive of the Finnish Institute in London.

Miro Cerar is Assistant Professor in the Law Faculty of the University of Ljubljana and an adviser on constitutional issues to the National Assembly of the Republic of Slovenia. He has published several articles in the fields of jurisprudence and constitutional law, including a recent book (in Slovenian) entitled *The Multidimensionality of Human Rights and Duties* (2nd edn., 1996).

Robert Elgie is Lecturer in Politics at the University of Limerick. He has published widely in the field of French politics, including *The Role of the Prime Minister in France, 1981–91* (Macmillan, 1993) and *Electing the French President: The 1995 Presidential Election* (Macmillan, 1997) as editor. He has also published in the field of comparative politics, notably *Political Leadership in Liberal Democracies* (Macmillan, 1996) and *The Politics of Central Banks* (Routledge, 1998) with Helen Thompson. He is currently writing a book with Steven Griggs for Routledge entitled *Debates in French Politics* and is editing a volume for Oxford University Press called *Divided Government in Comparative Perspective*.

Michael Gallagher is Lecturer in Politics at Trinity College, Dublin. He has published widely on Irish politics and is also the co-editor of *Candidate Selection in Comparative Perspective* (1988) and *The Referendum Experience in Europe* (1996).

Venelin I. Ganev is at the University of Chicago. He has published articles on various aspects of post-communist politics in numerous journals, including *The Journal of Democracy*, *The American Journal of Comparative Law*, and *East European Constitutional Review*. He is currently completing a dissertation on the dynamics of state-building in the post-communist period.

Gunnar Helgi Kristinsson is Professor in Government at the University of Iceland. He is the author of a book (in Icelandic) on the development of the Icelandic constitution, but his recent publications are mainly concerned with public policy and public administration, including an article in *West European Politics* (1996).

Wolfgang C. Müller is Associate Professor in Political Science at the University of Vienna. He has published widely on Austrian and comparative politics. His most recent book is *Policy, Office, or Votes? How Political Parties Make Hard Decisions* (Cambridge University Press, 1999), co-edited with Kaare Strøm.

Dainius Urbanavicius is a doctoral student in Public Administration at Kaunas Technological University.

Ania van der Meer Krok-Paszkowska is a research assistant in the Department of Political Science, University of Leiden. She has written several articles on the Polish parliament, including a recent article in *Journal of Legislative Studies*.

Tony Verheijen is Lecturer in Public Administration at the University of Leiden. He has published widely in the fields of public administration, constitutional law, and the European Union, including a book entitled *Constitutional Pillars for New Democracies* (1995).

Stephen White is Professor of Politics and a Senior Research Associate of the Institute of Russian and East European Studies at the University of Glasgow. His recent publications include *How Russia Votes* (1997) with Richard Rose and Ian McAllister and *Values and Political Change in Postcommunist Europe* (1998) with Paul Heywood.

Andrew Wilson is a Lecturer in Ukrainian Studies at the School of Slavonic and East European Studies in London. His publications include *Ukrainian Nationalism in the 1990s: A Minority Faith*

(Cambridge University Press, 1997) and *The Ukrainians: The Unexpected Nation* (Yale University Press, 1999). He also wrote the chapter on Ukraine in Ray Taras (ed.), *Postcommunist Presidents* (Cambridge University Press, 1997).

1

The Politics of Semi-Presidentialism

ROBERT ELGIE

This chapter provides an introduction to the concept of semi-presidentialism and establishes a framework for the study of the politics of semi-presidential regimes. In the first part of the chapter, the evolution of the concept of semi-presidentialism will be sketched, some of the main criticisms of the concept will be considered, a slight reformulation of the standard definition of the term will be proposed, and a list of semi-presidential regimes will be identified. In the second part of the chapter, a framework for the comparative study of semi-presidential regimes will be outlined. In this way, then, this chapter provides the basis both for the in-depth country studies of semi-presidentialism which follow and for the conclusion which examines the comparative experience of semi-presidentialism and addresses the issue of whether or not countries should adopt a semi-presidential form of government in preference to either presidential or parliamentary forms of government.

SEMI-PRESIDENTIALISM:
THE CONCEPT AND ITS CRITICS

In a popular context the term 'semi-presidential regime' was first used by the journalist and founder of the *Le Monde* newspaper, Hubert Beuve-Méry, in 1959 (reprinted as Beuve-Méry 1987).[1] At this time, though, the meaning of the term still remained rather vague and undefined. In an academic context the concept of semi-presidentialism was first elaborated by the French political scientist, Maurice Duverger. Duverger first employed the term in the 11th edition of his textbook on political institutions and constitutional law which appeared in 1970 (1970: 277). He treated the subject in slightly more detail in 1974 (Duverger 1974) and his first full-scale work on this theme appeared in 1978 (Duverger 1978). In France, then, the term was in regular use and was the subject of fierce debate by the end of the 1970s.

Elsewhere, interest in the concept took somewhat more time to develop. In 1980, the first article on the subject appeared in English written by Duverger himself (Duverger 1980). In 1983, an international conference was held on the theme of semi-presidentialism which included contributions from, amongst others, Portuguese and Finnish political scientists (published as Duverger 1986*b*). In 1984, the first major study based on Duverger's work appeared in Spanish by a South American academic (Nogueira Alcalá 1986). In the early 1990s there was a growing German interest in the concept as the process of democratization gathered pace in Eastern Europe and the former USSR. (See e.g. Bahro and Veser 1995; and Steffani 1995.) Overall, by the end of the 1990s, reference to the term has become widespread and politics textbooks increasingly include a section on semi-presidential regimes. Indeed, in 1997, Duverger's 1980 article was nominated and chosen as one of the most influential to have been published in the first 25 years of the history of the *European Journal of Political Research*.

The concept of semi-presidentialism, then, has well and truly come of age. Since its first formulation, though, it has evolved. Moreover, it has consistently been the subject of criticism. Indeed, both the confusion that has surrounded and continues to surround the concept and the criticisms that have been directed at it suggest that a reformulation of the term is required before the study of the politics of semi-presidential regimes can be undertaken.

The Evolution of the Concept of Semi-Presidentialism

The concept of semi-presidentialism has been the source of a certain confusion over the years. In particular, there is confusion surrounding both the definition of semi-presidentialism and the list of countries which should be classed as semi-presidential regimes. In part, this confusion is caused by the development of the concept in Duverger's own work. In part, it is caused by how the concept has been applied in the work of others.

In 1970 Duverger provided the first definition of semi-presidentialism. He stated that a semi-presidential regime was 'characterized by the fact that the head of state is directly elected by universal suffrage and that he possesses certain powers which exceed those of a head of state in a normal parliamentary regime. However, the government still consists of a cabinet formed by a prime minister and ministers who can be dismissed by a parliamentary vote' (1970: 277).[2] At this time, according to Duverger, the list of semi-presidential regimes comprised three Western democracies, Austria, Finland, and France, to which a fourth, Ireland, was added in the 12th edition of his textbook in 1971 (1971: 279). In 1974, though, Duverger altered the definition of semi-presidentialism somewhat, now stating that a semi-presidential regime exhibited three characteristics: '(1) the president is elected by universal suffrage ... (2) opposite him, there is a prime minister and ministers who can only govern with the confidence of parliament ... (3) the president can dissolve parliament ...' (1974: 122). At the same time Duverger also revised the list of semi-presidential regimes by both including Iceland and casting some doubt as to whether or not Ireland should in fact be classified as an example of such a regime (1974: 124). It is apparent, therefore, that up to this point at least there was a certain degree of confusion in Duverger's own mind concerning the concept of semi-presidentialism.

In fact, Duverger only arrived at both his final definition of semi-presidentialism and his stock list of semi-presidential regimes in 1978 (1978: 17). It was this 1978 definition which was effectively restated in his 1980 article and which, subsequently, has become the standard English-language definition of semi-presidentialism. This definition is as follows:

[a] political regime is considered as semi-presidential if the constitution which established it combines three elements: (1) the president of the republic is elected by universal suffrage; (2) he possesses quite considerable powers; (3) he has opposite him, however, a prime minister and ministers who possess executive and governmental power and can stay in office only if the parliament does not show its opposition to them. (Duverger 1980: 166)

Also according to Duverger, six countries should be classed as semi-presidential: Austria, Finland, France, Iceland, Ireland, and the then recently established Portuguese regime. Subsequently, Duverger has consistently maintained this definition[3] as well as the 1980 list of semi-presidential regimes, although constitutional developments particularly in Central and Eastern Europe and the former USSR have led him to acknowledge that certain countries, such as Poland and Romania, should now be added to the list (Duverger 1992: 901).

Since 1978, therefore, Duverger has been consistent in both his definition of semi-presidentialism and his classification of semi-presidential states. Since this time, however, other writers have adopted different definitions of semi-presidentialism and have identified different examples of semi-presidential regimes. For example, O'Neill uses the term 'semi-presidential' 'to refer to those executive systems where

(1) executive power is divided between a prime minister as head of government and a president as head of state, and where (2) substantial executive power resides with the presidency' (1993: 197).[4] This means that, for O'Neill, countries with directly elected but weak presidents, such as Austria, Iceland, and Ireland, should not be classed as semi-presidential, whereas countries with indirectly elected but strong presidents, such as Albania and (formerly) Czechoslovakia, should be classed as such. In a similar vein, Sartori states that a political system is semi-presidential if five properties jointly apply (1997: 130–1). These include the conditions that the president must be popularly elected, that the prime minister must be parliament-dependent, and that the president must share executive power with the prime minister. This means that, for Sartori at least, the list of semi-presidential regimes consists only of Finland, France, and, arguably, Sri Lanka. Furthermore, Linz argues, more succinctly, that semi-presidential systems are those which 'have a president who is elected by the people either directly or indirectly, rather than nominated by parliament, and a prime minister who needs the confidence of parliament' (1994: 48). For Linz, this means that Finland, France, and Portugal are the primary examples of semi-presidential countries.

It is apparent, then, that there has been and there continues to be a degree of confusion concerning the concept of semi-presidentialism. Different people mean different things by the term and different people classify different countries as examples of semi-presidential regimes. Needless to say, this causes problems both for the student of semi-presidentialism and, it may be argued, for the very appropriateness of the concept itself.

Criticisms of Duverger's Concept of Semi-Presidentialism

Even though reference to semi-presidentialism (however defined) has become widespread, there has always been and, indeed, there continues to be a certain amount of opposition to the concept. For example, in 1979 a leading French academic, Georges Vedel, stated that 'at best, a semi-presidential regime is only a convenient name given to a succession of contrary political practices closely linked to political changes' (*Le Monde*, 19–20 Feb. 1979). Similarly, Shugart and Carey found Duverger's use of the concept to be 'misleading' (1992: 230) and instead preferred to formulate the concept of 'premier-presidentialism'. It goes without saying that Duverger himself is very aware of these criticisms. Indeed, as we shall see, he is quite dismissive of some of them, particularly those which emanate from his French colleagues. At the same time, however, it is necessary to examine the objections to the concept of semi-presidentialism in order better to understand the meaning and implications of the term. In this context, four common criticisms of semi-presidentialism can be identified. The first two, it will be argued, are misdirected, whereas the final two raise issues which need to be addressed and which necessitate a slight reformulation of Duverger's definition.

i. The Terminological Criticism

One frequent criticism of semi-presidentialism concerns the term itself. Some writers simply object to Duverger's terminology. So, for example, Duhamel states that Duverger's use of the word is 'disputable' (1993: 158). In this context, there are two forms of this criticism. Some writers suggest that the term is satisfactory but that other terms are equally satisfactory, whereas others suggest that the term is unsatisfactory and should be substituted for a different term. Both objections, it might be argued, miss the mark.

The work of Linz and Stepan and Suleiman provides examples of the first terminological criticism. Both sets of writers accept the term 'semi-presidential' but argue that it is synonymous with the term 'semi-parliamentary' (Linz 1994: 48; Linz 1997; Stepan and Suleiman 1995: 394). For writers such as these, the term 'semi-presidential' is, thus, potentially misleading because it can be substituted by another term which is equally valid. In response, it might be argued that this criticism is insignificant. After all, what does it matter which term is used if the subsequent methodology is valid? Duverger argues, however, that it does matter and that the term 'semi-presidential' is the most appropriate one to use. In opposition to writers such as Linz and Stepan and Suleiman, he states that there is a significant distinction between the terms 'semi-presidential' and 'semi-parliamentary'. For him, this distinction is to be found in the essential difference between a presidential regime and a parliamentary regime. In the former there are two sources of popular legitimacy (presidential elections and legislative elections), whereas in the latter there is only one (legislative elections). To the extent that in semi-presidential regimes there are also two sources of popular legitimacy (presidential elections and legislative elections), then it is quite appropriate to call such regimes 'semi-presidential' (Duverger 1986b: 8).[5] For Duverger at least, then, it is clear that the terms 'semi-presidential' and 'semi-parliamentary' are not simply synonymous, that the term 'semi-presidentialism' is used to mean something quite specific and that it is the most appropriate term to use to describe the countries that Duverger wishes to examine.

The work of Shugart and Carey provides an example of the second objection to Duverger's terminology. They have argued that the term is misleading because the use of the prefix 'semi' implies that semi-presidential regimes are 'located midway along some continuum running from presidential to parliamentary' (Shugart and Carey 1992: 23). Consequently, they prefer to use the term 'premier-presidentialism' where no halfway house situation is implied. To a certain extent Duverger is guilty of bringing this criticism on himself. In an early work he stated that the Finnish system is a 'truly intermediate regime between a presidential and a parliamentary regime' (Duverger 1974: 131). However, this is not what Duverger now argues and, in any case, the logic behind Shugart and Carey's argument is muddled. Sartori, for one, is quite dismissive of their approach. He believes that the term 'semi-presidential' does not at all imply that such regimes are situated halfway along a presidential/parliamentary continuum. He points out that the prefix '*semi* is the Latin for "half", and—as any dictionary would show for hundreds of expressions—does not assume any continuum because it proceeds continuum-mania by well over two thousand years' (Sartori 1997: 137). Lijphart, too, springs to Duverger's defence, although his language is rather more understated. He notes that 'Duverger's concept of semi-presidentialism is multi-faceted and does not entail any inter-mediate distance between presidentialism and parliamentarism' (Lijphart 1997: 126). In this sense, then, Shugart and Carey's line of thought appears fundamentally flawed.

Overall, then, it does appear as if Duverger has reasonable grounds to argue that the term 'semi-presidentialism' means something quite distinct and that this term should be used in preference to alternative terms when examining the politics of particular countries.

ii. The Mixed Regime Criticism

Another common criticism of the concept of semi-presidentialism is that a semi-presidential regime is a mixed type of regime and, as such, is somehow intellectually out of place. Once again, it might be argued that this criticism is unfounded.

Some writers argue that semi-presidentialism implies a mixed regime type. As such, it does not constitute a 'pure' regime type, like presidentialism or parliamentarism, and so it does not have the same conceptual validity as these other more standard types of regimes. So, for example, Pactet argues that 'mixed regimes combine elements borrowed from presidential and parliamentary regimes, which with regard to the way that they function sometimes raises the problem of their coherence' (1995:153). Equally, Conac quotes de Tocqueville's objection to the very concept of mixed regimes and argues that semi-presidential regimes function either as presidential regimes or parliamentary regimes (1992: 817). Similarly, Vedel in a much-quoted article argues that the supposedly semi-presidential French Fifth Republic is not a synthesis of presidential and parliamentary systems (and in this sense a stand-alone regime type), but that it alternates between the two (*Le Monde*, 19–20 Feb. 1979: 2).[6] Indeed, the notion that semi-presidential states alternate between presidential and parliamentary phases is a further component of Shugart and Carey's objection to the term (1992: 23). In these ways, then, all of these writers object to the concept of semi-presidentialism because it is considered to be an impure, hybrid, or 'bastard' concept (Bahro and Veser 1995).

Again, Duverger is at least partly responsible for provoking this criticism. For example, in his 1980 article he stated that semi-presidential systems were 'intermediary between presidential and parliamentary systems' (Duverger 1980: 165). Even recently he stated that a semi-presidential regime is 'part presidential, part parliamentary' (Duverger 1991: 109). However, whether or not Duverger is culpable, it is certainly the case that he pulls no punches in his opposition to those who voice this criticism. For example, in one article he stated: 'the term semi-presidential regime is still boycotted by French jurists who continue to venerate only two sacred cows: the parliamentary regime and the presidential regime' (Duverger 1986c: 347). Similarly, in another he writes:

widely adopted in Portugal, accepted in Finland, used in Anglo-Saxon countries, the notion of a semi-presidential regime is still controversial in France . . . the majority of French constitutionalists (apart from the most serious of them) still maintain a fetishistic cult towards this dualistic vision [of parliamentary and presidential regimes] and consider anything which might complement it with a new model to be sacrilegious . . . (Duverger 1992: 901–2)

In fact, as Duverger implies, the mixed regime criticism is misdirected. There is no reason why a semi-presidential regime should be considered a mixed regime at all. Instead, as Pasquino states, semi-presidential regimes constitute a 'specific and separate' form of government (1995: 57). They possess their own 'appropriately devised institutional features' (Pasquino 1997: 129) and 'what is required for the construction of semi-presidential systems is an explicit, purposive and well designed act of

institutional and constitutional engineering' (ibid.). So, while it is certainly the case that Finnish constitution-builders did not state that they
were creating a semi-presidential regime in 1919, that the Fifth Republic's founders were ignorant of the term in 1962, that the Bulgarian constitution states that the regime is parliamentary, and so on, it is also the
case that the political institutions in these countries and others were
arrived at purposefully and that collectively they constitute a specific
and separate regime type. It follows, then, that 'Presidential systems
cannot simply, so to speak, lapse into semi-presidential systems nor can
parliamentary systems jump into semi-presidential systems' (Pasquino
1997: 129). As such, semi-presidential countries do not alternate between presidential and parliamentary regimes. On the contrary, these
countries simply exhibit various forms of political practice within the
same basic constitutional structure and, in this sense, within the same
regime type. In this way, semi-presidential regimes are just as 'pure' as
presidential or parliamentary regimes which also exhibit equally varying
forms of political practice at different times (see below).

iii. The Ambiguity of the Direct Election Criterion

In contrast to the two previous objections, a relatively minor but
nevertheless cogent criticism of semi-presidentialism stems from the
wording of Duverger's standard definition.

The first element of Duverger's definition states that 'the president of
the republic is elected by universal suffrage'. For some, this wording is
problematic because it implies that the president is directly elected. And
yet, certain countries which Duverger classifies as semi-presidential
appear not to meet this criterion. Most notably, this was said to be the
case for Finland where the president was chosen by an electoral college
prior to the reform of the country's electoral system in 1988. For
example, Stepan and Skach argue that 'from 1925 to 1988 the Finnish
president was not so much directly elected but indirectly chosen by
party blocs' (1993: 5). Similarly, Shugart and Carey state that 'Given its
party-centred character, [the election of the president] was not much
different from election in parliament' (1992: 213). It should be added
that a similar criticism might be levelled against the Irish case. Here,
there is a long tradition of parties conspiring to nominate an agreed
presidential candidate (see Chapter 6). In this situation, the election
is dispensed with altogether and the candidate is elected unopposed.
Consequently, some Irish presidents have assumed power without
having been directly elected at all which, again, might be seen to cause
a problem for Duverger's analysis.

For Duverger, this criticism is largely irrelevant. For example, he acknowledges that prior to the 1988 reform the Finnish president was only elected indirectly and concedes that the nature of the electoral system was such that it led to 'an election by notables much more than a popular election' (Duverger 1978: 58). However, he also insists that election by notables is not the same as election by parties as in a parliamentary system (ibid.) and that the Finnish system resembled the US system where strictly speaking the president is also elected by an electoral college (Duverger 1978: 64). So, Duverger saw nothing in Finland's (pre-reform) electoral system which was essentially incompatible with its status as a semi-presidential regime. Equally, he saw nothing in the Irish propensity towards uncontested elections which might threaten its status either (Duverger 1978: 86).

While this may be a reasonable line of argument, it must also be acknowledged that there is at least some degree of ambiguity in this aspect of Duverger's definition and that this ambiguity needs to be addressed. So, for example, in his definition of semi-presidentialism Sartori prefers to adopt a more stringent criterion. He states that an essential characteristic of a semi-presidential regime is that the president 'is elected by a popular vote—either directly or indirectly—for a fixed term of office' (Sartori 1997: 131). Indeed, he insists on this wording at some length because he considers that US and (pre-reform) Finnish-style indirect elections closely resemble Latin American-style direct elections particularly in that all are increasingly susceptible to what he calls 'video-politics' or the opportunity for political outsiders to bypass the party system and manipulate television in the pursuit of votes. Thus, he prefers to reword Duverger's original definition so as not to risk excluding countries like Finland from the list of semi-presidential regimes. To avoid confusion, this seems to be a sensible solution. It is appropriate, therefore, to adopt Sartori's approach.

iv. The Problem of Presidential Powers

The final problem with the concept of semi-presidentialism is also derived from the wording of Duverger's standard definition. This time, the problem stems from the second element of the definition which states that in a semi-presidential regime the president 'possesses quite considerable powers'. This wording provokes writers to make one or other of two objections: either that the concept of semi-presidentialism is incoherent and should be ditched altogether or that the concept is coherent but that Duverger's list of semi-presidential regimes should be revised. The first objection, it might be argued, is unfounded, but the second does suggest that there is a problem with Duverger's definition which needs to be addressed.

The first objection of this sort is made by those writers who focus on Duverger's standard list of semi-presidential regimes. These writers note that the list contains some countries with very strong presidents and others with very weak presidents. This, they suggest, undermines the whole concept of semi-presidentialism because it lumps together countries which are too dissimilar. For example, Nogueira Alcalá states that from a purely legal point there are indeed six West European semi-presidential regimes (1986: 134). However, he also states that from a political point of view the term 'semi-presidential' leads to a 'misleading appreciation' of the Austrian, Icelandic, and Irish cases where there are weak presidents and argues that it is clearer and 'more exact' to classify all six countries as having a 'dual executive with a presidential corrective' (Nogueira Alcalá 1986: 135). Similarly, Cohendet states that Austria, Iceland, and Ireland are parliamentary, that Portugal is only intermittently semi-presidential, that Finland was for a long time an exceptional case because of its proximity to the USSR and that the only real example of a semi-presidential regime is France (1993: 74–5). Consequently, she prefers to distinguish between monist birepresentative parliamentary regimes (in which there are two sources of popular authority but only one controlling power, presidential or prime ministerial), such as Austria, France, Iceland, and Ireland, and dualist birepresentative parliamentary regimes (in which there are two sources of popular authority and two controlling powers, presidential and prime ministerial), such as Finland and Portugal (Cohendet 1993: 77). Finally, Shugart and Carey respond to this problem by distinguishing between premier-presidential regimes, which indicates the primacy of the prime minister as well as the presence of a president with significant powers, president-parliamentary regimes, which establish the primacy of the president and the dependence of the cabinet on parliament, and parliamentary (with president) regimes, where the popularly elected head of state is simply a figurehead (Shugart and Carey 1992: 18–27).

Duverger has always been quick to reply to this line of argument. His standard defence is to point out that similarly diverse political practices occur in other more uncontroversial regime types. For example, in 1978, he argued that, despite the fact that the German and Italian systems work so differently, 'everyone puts [them] in the same category: parliamentary regimes' (Duverger 1978: 18). He then goes on to add: 'It is no more (or less) artificial to place France, the Weimar Republic, Finland,

Austria, Iceland, Ireland and Portugal in another category: semi-presidential regimes . . .' (ibid.). More recently, Duverger has reiterated this argument, stating that parliamentary regimes are just as diverse as semi-presidential regimes: 'you only have to compare the institutions in London with those in Rome to be aware of this' (1991: 113). By 1992 Duverger was once again comparing the German and Italian systems, concluding that 'parliamentary regimes demonstrate just as much heterogeneity [as semi-presidential regimes]' (1992: 902).

For Duverger, then, the fact that political practice in the six West European semi-presidential regimes is so diverse does not mean that the concept of semi-presidentialism is undermined. Instead, it is simply a reflection of the fact that countries with the same basic constitutional structure can operate in a variety of different ways. In this respect, Duverger's argument is sound. There is indeed just as much diversity amongst parliamentary regimes as semi-presidential regimes. Indeed, it might be added that there is just as much diversity amongst presidential regimes as semi-presidential regimes. For example, the US operates very differently from Mexico and yet both countries are unequivocally classed as presidential. Therefore, the fact that there is indeed a variety of political practice across semi-presidential regimes does not undermine the fundamental validity of the concept itself.

The second objection of this type is made by those writers who take Duverger's definition literally and who then proceed to reconstitute the list of semi-presidential countries. They accept the validity of the concept of semi-presidentialism but note that it only includes countries which have presidents who possess 'quite considerable powers'. They then proceed to eliminate countries with weak presidents from the list of semi-presidential regimes. So, for example, when identifying semi-presidential regimes Mainwaring states that 'what matters is whether [presidential] offices are largely symbolic or, conversely, whether the office holders wield considerable power' (1993: 203). On the basis of this logic, he argues that there are just two stable semi-presidential democracies, Finland and France (ibid. 205). On the basis of a similar logic, Stepan and Skach also noted only two examples of semi-presidential regimes, France and Portugal (1993: 9). Equally, Ieraci named just one, France (1994: 63). These writers, then, accept that there is such a thing as a semi-presidential regime but classify only those countries with relatively strong presidents as examples of such a regime. As a result, the list of semi-presidential countries varies from one writer to another according to each writer's subjective judgement as to what constitutes a 'relatively strong president'.[7]

In contrast to the previous objection, it might be argued that there is some justification for this line of argument but, it might also be argued, this does not mean that the list of presidential regimes should be redrawn. It is certainly the case that the wording of Duverger's definition invites people to eliminate from the list of semi-presidential regimes those countries whose presidents do not possess 'quite considerable powers'. As things stand, therefore, writers such as Mainwaring, Stepan and Skach, and Ieraci are interpreting Duverger's definition quite logically and consistently. And yet, it might also be argued that there is a basic problem with their approach. This is because it allows different writers to provide their own interpretation of the powers of presidents and to draw up their own preferred list of semi-presidential regimes on the basis of this interpretation. In other words, it allows the classification of regime types to become an essentially subjective exercise. (See the argument in Elgie 1998.) However, this subjectivity should be avoided because it poses problems for the study of comparative politics. The very reason for establishing concepts such as presidentialism, parliamentarism, and semi-presidentialism is so as to be able to compare similar regime types more accurately. So, if different writers are able to draw up their own subjective list of semi-presidential regimes, then it follows that those writers will not be comparing like with like and so the basis of the comparison is weakened. (This point will be considered in more depth in the last chapter.)

This suggests, then, a problem with the interpretation of Duverger's definition. This problem is caused by Duverger's stipulation that a semi-presidential regime must exhibit a president who possesses 'quite considerable powers'. In order to eliminate this problem, what is needed is a definition of semi-presidentialism which excludes the opportunity for subjective classifications of semi-presidential countries and establishes a clear-cut list of semi-presidential regimes. This can only be achieved if Duverger's definition is slightly reformulated. Only then will it be possible to arrive at an unambiguous list of semi-presidential regimes which promotes the objective study of comparative politics (Elgie 1998).

Reformulating the Concept of Semi-Presidentialism

It has been demonstrated both that the concept of semi-presidentialism has been the subject of a degree of confusion over the years and also that the criticisms of both the first and second elements of Duverger's standard definition are to an extent justified. Thus, it is necessary to reformulate the concept of semi-presidentialism so as to dispel the confusion and take account of these criticisms. To this end, therefore, the following reformulation will be proposed:

A semi-presidential regime may be defined as the situation where a popularly elected fixed-term president exists alongside a prime minister and cabinet who are responsible to parliament.[8]

This is a purely constitutional definition of the concept.[9] Moreover, it is a definition which simply indicates the ways in which the head of state and head of government come to office and how they remain in office. It does not make any assumptions about the actual powers of these two actors. This is also a clear and straightforward definition of semi-presidentialism which has the advantage of remaining very close to Duverger's standard definition.[10] Moreover, it has two further advantages. First, it takes account of Sartori's point that the first element of Duverger's definition is potentially misleading. It does so by replacing the implication that a directly elected president is needed for a semi-presidential regime with the notion that a popularly elected president is required, meaning a president who is directly elected or is elected in a 'direct-like' manner. So, countries such as pre-reform Finland can unequivocally be classed as semi-presidential regimes. Secondly, it omits altogether the second element of Duverger's definition which refers to presidential powers. This means that the problems caused by this reference are removed. As such, countries with weak presidents, such as Austria, Bulgaria, Iceland, and Ireland, can unequivocally be classed as semi-presidential alongside countries with strong presidents, such as France and Russia, as well as countries with some sort of limited presidency, such as Finland, Poland, and Portugal. In this way, then, semi-presidentialism emerges as an example of a pure type of regime which exists alongside other such pure types, most notably, presidential regimes and parliamentary regimes (Elgie 1998).

On the basis of this definition, a list of regimes which can unambiguously be classed as 'semi-presidential' can be established (see Figure 1.1).[11] This list includes the six West European countries that Duverger has consistently identified as being semi-presidential. It also includes the large number of countries in Central and Eastern Europe and the former USSR which adopted a semi-presidential form of government after 1989 or 1991. It includes the two most frequently discussed examples in South and South-East Asia, Sri Lanka and South

Robert Elgie

Africa	Americas	Asia/ Middle East	Central and Eastern Europe	Former-USSR	Western Europe

Angola
Benin
Burkina
  Faso
Cape Verde
Gabon
Ghana
Madagascar
Mali
Namibia
Niger
Togo
	Dominican
	  Republic
	Guyana
	Haiti
		Lebanon
		Maldives
		Mongolia
		South
		  Korea
		Sri Lanka
			Bulgaria
			Croatia
			Macedonia
			Poland
			Romania
			Slovenia
				Armenia
				Azerbaijan
				Belarus
				Georgia
				Kazakstan
				Kyrgyzstan
				Lithuania
				Moldova
				Russia
				Ukraine
				Uzbekistan
					Austria
					Finland
					France
					Iceland
					Ireland
					Portugal

FIG. 1.1. Examples of semi-presidential regimes by region

Korea, respectively. Finally, it includes a large number of semi-presidential regimes in Africa and a small number in the Americas. Overall, if a head count of regime types in democratic political systems were to be conducted, it would find that semi-presidentialism is more widespread than presidentialism (although less so in Central and South America) and is perhaps only slightly less widespread than parliamentarism (although more so in Central and Eastern Europe and countries of the former USSR).

By definition, semi-presidential regimes share the same basic constitutional structure. They all have presidents who are elected in a direct or direct-like manner and they all have prime ministers and cabinets who are responsible to the legislature. As has already been indicated, though, in practice semi-presidential countries operate in many different ways. The constitutional power of presidents, prime ministers, and cabinets varies just as the political power of presidents, prime ministers, and cabinets varies. Most notably, constitutionally strong presidents are sometimes politically weak and constitutionally weak presidents are sometimes politically strong. Presidents sometimes dominate prime ministers. Prime ministers sometimes dominate presidents. Sometimes neither one dominates the other. In order to examine the politics of semi-presidentialism, therefore, it is necessary to establish a framework which captures the variety of political practices from one country to another. This is the aim of the next section.

THE POLITICS OF SEMI-PRESIDENTIAL COUNTRIES

Duverger has frequently reiterated that 'the purpose of the concept of semi-presidential government is to explain why relatively homogeneous constitutions are applied in radically different ways' (1980: 177). For Duverger, then, the concept of semi-presidentialism is as much an heuristic device as a description of a particular set of constitutional arrangements (Duverger 1986*d*: 8; 1986*c*: 349; and 1982: 193). For him, the principal advantage of such a device is that it 'permits the construction of an analytical model which allows the in-depth explanation of how these regimes function . . .' (Duverger 1986*d*: 14). Moreover, also according to him, 'it is not only a question of explaining past and present incarnations of semi-presidential regimes but also predicting their future incarnations . . .' (Duverger 1978: 89–90). The basis of this analytical model is the identification of the appropriate set of variables which account for why semi-presidential regimes operate in such different ways.

Those who have followed Duverger have frequently identified their own set of variables. For example, Bartolini states that factors exogenous to the institutional system need to be identified in order to account for why countries with the same constitutional features operate in practice so differently (1984: 225). For him, four factors are important: the politico-cultural origins of the regime in question; the process by which presidential and parliamentary candidates are selected; the relationship between presidential and parliamentary electoral systems; and the relationship between the president and party-system coalition-building (ibid. 226–7). In a similar vein, Linz argues that 'it is impossible to analyze the performance of a bipolar regime independently of the larger political system . . .' (1994: 51) and in this respect he singles out two factors which are particularly important, the party system and the 'complex historical situation' (ibid.). Equally, in his analysis of semi-presidential regimes Pasquino focuses on two variables, the electoral system and the party system (1995: 59).

It is apparent from this list that there is at least some degree of consensus as to the factors which most appropriately explain the variety of practices to be found in semi-presidential regimes. As might be expected by now, though, the list of factors which Duverger himself identifies has varied over the years.[12] In general, however, Duverger's list reinforces this consensus. For the most part, Duverger considers three variables to be of particular significance: the constitutional powers of the major political actors; the events surrounding the formation of the regime; and the nature of the parliamentary majority and the relationship between the president and the majority. Each of these variables will briefly be considered.

The Constitutional Powers of the Major Political Actors

As noted above, by definition semi-presidential regimes all operate within the same basic constitutional procedures. Over and above these procedures, though, the constitutional powers of presidents, prime ministers, and parliaments vary. This variety helps to account for the diversity of semi-presidential politics.

For Duverger, variations in constitutional powers can be captured by reference to three general types of situations. The first type is where the president is merely a 'controlling force' (Duverger 1980: 177). In this situation, the president simply acts as the guardian of the constitution and may have the right, for example, to refer laws to the constitutional court and propose a constitutional referendum. The second type represents an intermediate situation in which the president enjoys these controlling powers and also has the unilateral right to dismiss the prime minister (ibid.). The third type is where the president is a 'governing' force (Duverger 1980: 178). In this situation, the president 'shares in the running of the country, in collaboration with the prime minister and the cabinet' (ibid.).

Even though Duverger distinguishes between these three types of constitutional situations, he also takes great pains to emphasize that constitutional rules and political practice do not always coincide. In some cases presidents who would appear to be in a position only to operate as a controlling force in fact operate as a governing force and in other cases the opposite is true. It would be wrong to conclude from this, though, that Duverger believes constitutional powers to be irrelevant to the practice of semi-presidential regimes. Indeed, he clearly states that 'the constitution plays a certain part in the application of presidential powers' (Duverger 1980: 179). Nevertheless, he also states that constitutional factors remain only 'secondary compared to the other parameters' (ibid.).

In this way, therefore, in order to understand the comparative politics of semi-presidential regimes and the reasons why such regimes operate so differently, it is appropriate to outline the constitutional powers of presidents, prime ministers, and parliaments. It is necessary to know whether the president can dismiss the prime minister, dissolve the legislature, appoint government ministers, assume emergency powers, and so on. Collectively, these powers indicate both the *de jure* balance of power between the various political actors and they also usually provide at least a hint (and sometimes more) of the *de facto* relationship between them as well.

The Events Surrounding the Formation of the Regime

The second factor which helps to explain the variety of semi-presidential regimes concerns the historical, or politico-cultural, context within which the regime was created. It is hardly surprising that this factor should be invoked to explain the variety of semi-presidential regimes because, necessarily, each country's context is unique. This contextual factor, then, helps to engender national differences that persist over time and which can distort the operation of the set of *de jure* constitutional rules.

Each country operates within a given geographical area, against the background of a particular historical situation and according to the dynamics of a specific constitutional foundation. Nevertheless, certain similarities can be traced from one country to another. Three common types of context can be singled out. The first type concerns the situation where a semi-presidential regime is adopted for purely symbolic reasons. This may occur, for example, when the adoption of semi-presidentialism is associated with the process of national self-determination. For example, if prior to independence the head of state was a foreign monarch, then the subsequent creation of a semi-presidential regime with a popularly elected president may be motivated by the desire to reinforce the democratic credentials of the new regime rather than the desire to install a powerful head of state. In these cases, then, semi-presidentialism may coincide with a weak presidency. The second type concerns the situation where a semi-presidential regime is adopted for reasons of governability. This may occur, for example, when a semi-presidential regime is adopted following the collapse of, say, a parliamentary system of government. Here, there may be a desire to create a strong leadership figure who will give direction to the new regime and prevent a repeat of the previous situation. In these cases, semi-presidentialism may coincide with a strong presidency. The third type concerns the situation where a semi-presidential regime is adopted during the transition to democracy. Here, one of several motivations may be present. For example, the presidency may be tailor-made for the leading figure in the democratization process, so creating the conditions for a strong president. Equally, the presidency may be designed so as to prevent one person from assuming too much power, so creating the conditions for a weak president. Alternatively, the establishment of the regime may be the product of a 'fudge'. In this case, the powers of president, prime minister, and parliament may be shared. Whatever the situation, the context surrounding the creation of the regime creates the opportunity for a great variety of political practices to occur across the set of semi-presidential countries.

In his work, Duverger stresses the importance of the 'combination of tradition and circumstances' (1980: 180) in the evolution of semi-presidential systems. Moreover, Duverger stresses not just the importance of, as it were, the moment of constitution-building but also the conventions of political practice that endure thereafter. As Duverger states, countries develop a 'factual tradition' (ibid.). They initiate rules, norms, and procedures which subsequently become fossilized. In this context, the presidency of the first incumbent of the presidential office is often very important. If the first president is a figurehead, then the chances are that a figurehead presidency will become the norm. By contrast, if the first president is an authoritative decision-maker, then, the likelihood is that a working presidency will be established. Whatever the outcome, it is apparent that events surrounding the formation of the regime are central to an understanding of the politics of semi-presidentialism.

The Nature of the Parliamentary Majority and the Relationship Between the President and the Majority

Since the first formulation of the concept Duverger has stressed that party political factors are fundamental to the operation of semi-presidential regimes. For example, in 1971 he stated that 'the structure of parties and the relationship between them is more important than constitutional powers' when explaining why semi-presidential regimes function so differently (Duverger 1971: 116). By 1978 Duverger had settled on his standard formulation of this variable stating that the mechanics of semi-presidential regimes vary according to the nature of the parliamentary majority and the relationship between the president and the majority.[13]

The nature of the parliamentary majority can take a number of forms. The first case concerns the situation where there is an absolute parliamentary majority. Here, various scenarios present themselves. On occasions there may be a monolithic majority, implying that a single party enjoys a majority of seats in the legislature. On other occasions there may be a coalition majority with one dominant party, meaning that the position of the dominant party is strong but less so than in the previous situation. On yet other occasions there may be a balanced coalition majority, suggesting that power is shared between the majority parties in parliament. On all occasions the government's position is likely to be safe but only in the first scenario is the problem of inter-party bargaining likely to be absent. The second case concerns the situation where there is only a relative or quasi-majority in parliament. In this case, one party has more seats in parliament than any other but lacks an overall majority. Here, the position of the leading party may either be quite secure if it takes an 'unholy alliance' of political opponents to combine to bring the government down or it may be perilous if there is an alternative government waiting in the wings. The final case concerns the situation where there is no parliamentary majority at all. Here, the seats in parliament are shared between a large number of small parties and governments are supported by unstable and shifting coalitions.

Just as the nature of the parliamentary majority can take a number of forms, so too can the relationship between the president and the majority. For example, the president may be the leader of the majority or she or he may simply be a member of the majority. Equally, the president may be from the opposition or, alternatively, she or he may be a completely neutral figure altogether. By themselves, these various situations tell us very little about the type of semi-presidential regime which is likely to ensue. Instead, they only help to explain the differences between semi-presidential regimes when each is combined with the various forms of parliamentary majority that can occur. So, for example, Duverger argues that a president who is the leader of a monolithic majority will emerge as an absolute (republican) monarch (1980: 186). By contrast, a president who is simply the member of a party which only has a relative parliamentary majority will operate as a symbolic figurehead leader (ibid.). Overall, in his classic work on semi-presidentialism Duverger identified 17 separate situations which may arise by combining the various forms of the parliamentary majority and the various relationships between the president and the majority (ibid.). Thereafter this number was reduced (Duverger 1982: 230), but the basic argument remained the same, namely that the politics of semi-presidentialism varies as a function of party political factors.

CONCLUSION

This book examines the politics of semi-presidentialism. In particular, it examines the politics of European semi-presidentialism focusing on the experience of a large number of semi-presidential regimes in Central and Eastern Europe, Western Europe, and the former USSR. In this context, the main question which is being asked is the following: why do countries which share the same basic institutional structure operate so differently in practice? As we have seen, Duverger's work on semi-presidentialism provides a framework with which we can begin to answer this question. As such, in the chapters which follow particular attention will be paid to the constitutional powers of political actors, the circumstances surrounding the creation of the regime, the nature of the parliamentary majority, and the relationship between the president and that majority. At the same time, though, other factors will also be shown to be important in particular countries and these will be identified when and where appropriate. In the conclusion we will consider what the experience of semi-presidentialism tells us about the academic debate concerning comparative institutional engineering and the pros and cons of presidential, semi-presidential, and parliamentary regimes.

NOTES

1. Duverger himself acknowledges that Beuve-Méry was the first to use the term (1992: 901).
2. Except where noted all translations are by the author.
3. Most recently, see Duverger 1996a: 501.
4. In a more recent work, O'Neill provides an expanded but essentially similar definition of semi-presidentialism (1997: 217).
5. More contentiously, Duverger has also recently claimed that the reformed Israeli system should be classed as a 'semi-parliamentary' regime because, here, the source of popular legitimacy is solely legislative (1996b: 117–19).
6. Interestingly, the origin of this argument appears to have been misunderstood by certain eminent scholars. Vedel's observation was meant to be taken as a direct criticism of the concept of semi-presidentialism. In reply, Duverger quotes Vedel and provides a counterargument (1980: 186). The fact that, first, in his reply Duverger acknowledges Vedel's article to be 'brilliant' and, secondly, that Duverger's counterargument is written in (or was at least translated into) a rather incomprehensible form of English seems to have fooled various people into thinking that Duverger was arguing that the Fifth Republic should be considered as a synthesis of presidential and parliamentary systems. This is not the

case. So, Linz is actually agreeing with Vedel's criticism of Duverger and not with Duverger's own point in his discussion of semi-presidentialism (1994: 52). The same is also true for Lijphart (1992: 8), and Shugart and Carey (1992: 23). In the case of Shugart and Carey, this misunderstanding would seem to question their whole rationale for dismissing Duverger's formulation of semi-presidentialism (ibid.).

7. Some writers, such as Stepan and Skach (1993: 6) and Lijphart (1992: 8), state that Duverger himself makes this argument when he declares that whereas '[t]he constitutions of Austria, Iceland and Ireland are semi-presidential . . . [p]olitical practice is parliamentary' (Duverger 1980: 167). In fact, Duverger does not makes this argument at all. Indeed, in this very quotation he clearly states that these countries are semi-presidential even if they are all examples of semi-presidential regimes with weak heads of state and strong heads of government which is similar to the situation in many parliamentary systems. So, it may well be that, as Duverger stated on another occasion, '*practice* [in Austria, Iceland, and Ireland] is closer to that of parliamentary regimes than *the other* semi-presidential regimes' (my italics) but this does not mean that Duverger is actually classifying these countries as parliamentary (Duverger 1986*d*: 8).

8. This definition is very similar to the one adopted by Linz above. Somewhat strangely, though, Linz states that countries such as Austria, Iceland, and Ireland should not be classed as semi-presidential when, according to his own definition, they clearly should.

9. In his 1980 article, Duverger stated that his definition was 'defined only by the content of the constitution' (1980: 166). However, as was demonstrated above, Duverger's stipulation that in semi-presidential regimes presidents had to possess quite considerable powers somewhat undermined this statement and certainly confused the issue.

10. This contrasts with O'Neill's reformulation of the term (see above) which is very different from Duverger's definition and which stretches the concept beyond breaking point.

11. This list includes regimes which are only slightly democratic.

12. See e.g. the following: Duverger 1978: 120–36; Duverger 1980: 177–86; Duverger 1992: 903; and Duverger 1996*a*: 514–17.

13. In his 1980 article Duverger indicates that these are two separate variables but the analysis is the same (1980: 182–5).

2

Austria

WOLFGANG C. MÜLLER

Since the constitutional reform of 1929 Austria comes under the rubric of semi-presidentialism as defined in this volume. Alongside the chancellor (prime minister), who is fully responsible to parliament, there is a directly elected president, who appoints the government and can dismiss it. While the president can, on the government's proposal, dissolve parliament, he himself enjoys an office with, in practical terms, very limited accountability.[1]

Nevertheless, Austria is generally considered as a parliamentary system by leading comparativists. Linz places Austria among those countries (together with Finland and Iceland) which 'have worked fundamentally as parliamentary systems even though they have some of the characteristics of semipresidential systems' (1994: 49). Sartori also rejects classifying Austria as a semi-presidential system (1997: 126) because presidents are 'strong only on paper' and 'count for little or nothing' (1994: 106), resulting in 'at most, façade presidentialism' (ibid.). Stepan and Skach label Austria 'not de facto semipresidential, since "political practice is parliamentary" ' (1994: 135 n. 15). Lijphart goes even further; according to him Austria is 'unambiguously parliamentarian' (1994: 95). These authors by and large echo what specialists on Austrian politics have observed since long ago (Pelinka and Welan 1971: 151–3; Steiner 1972: 111–13; Welan 1986; Müller 1996, 1997).

Indeed, it is parliamentary elections rather than presidential ones which decide about the distribution of political power in Austria. Governments are formed after parliamentary but not after presidential elections. The cabinet's routine offer of its resignation to each newly elected or re-elected president as a rule has been turned down. In practice it is no more than an act of politeness and is by no means meant to be more. The major actors in government formation are the political parties. The presidents have largely confined themselves to ratifying the deals struck by their leaders. While government formation gives the president at least formally an active role, he is hardly involved in the government's day-to-day business. And in the post-war period the president has never used his strongest competences, dismissing government and dissolving parliament. Although a close observation reveals fine variations in the weight and impact of the presidency over time, it is fair to say that this pattern has been stable over the whole post-war period.

By 1998 Austria had 58 years experience with a semi-presidential setting (1929–34 and 1945–98). Eight presidents have served under these rules. While this chapter concentrates on the post-war period, the inter-war years are important for understanding the gap between the large constitutional powers and the limited role the presidents actually have played. First, it was then that semi-presidentialism was introduced. As will be demonstrated below, Duverger is right in arguing that the events surrounding the formation of the regime are important for its actual working (Duverger 1980). A second but related factor is the unlucky role played by the first president who enjoyed the enlarged powers of the 1929 constitutional amendment. In several respects it was important in shaping the president's role from the negative side.

This chapter draws on the literature on the Austrian presidency, original archival work, and interviews with political actors.[2]

THE HISTORICAL LEGACY OF INTRODUCING SEMI-PRESIDENTIALISM

The direct election and formal powers of the Austrian president which account for the country's classification as semi-presidential were introduced in 1929. The presidency already had been created in 1920, when the constitution was enacted. After the breakdown of the Habsburg empire in 1918 first a collective, the council of state (Staatsrat), had assumed the position of head of state. In the 1918–20 period, the president of parliament had acted as head of state. In 1920 a figurehead presidency was established as a political compromise between the Social Democrats (who would have preferred to have had no presidency, with the president of parliament remaining head of state) and the Christian Socials (who would have preferred a strong president) (Welan 1986: 11–14). The position of the Social Democrats was shaped by their experience in the Habsburg empire which had never been fully democratized, allowing the emperor to dissolve parliament in 1914 and resorting to authoritarian rule. Accordingly, a strong president would have implied the dangers of caesarism and monarchism. The Christian Socials were less afraid of a head of state who might exploit such powers than of unconstrained majority rule of the left which seemed a quite realistic prospect when the constitution was drafted. Rather they considered a strong (non-socialist) president as a safeguard against a left majority in parliament.[3]

The compromise was a figurehead president. There was no direct election by the people but a secret election by the federal assembly (Bundesversammlung), the joint meeting of both houses of parliament (the directly elected Nationalrat and the Bundesrat, consisting of representatives of the Land diets). The president's term was four years and any incumbent was limited to two subsequent terms. In order to prevent a restoration of the Habsburgs via the office of president, on the demand of the Social Democrats members of ruling houses or former ruling houses were excluded from it by the constitution. The president's formal powers were strictly contained both in their scope and the president's capacity to act. It is particularly interesting to note that the president was not involved in government formation and that he had neither dissolution power vis-à-vis the government nor parliament. Consequently, the first president, Michael Hainisch, once commented that his handkerchief was the only thing he could stick his nose into (Weissensteiner 1982: 62).

The presidency remained an issue of controversy after the enactment of the constitution. Practically all elements of the political right criticized the existing constitutional framework from anti-party and anti-parliamentary points of view. While the radical right, the paramilitary Heimwehren, aimed at establishing an authoritarian regime, the other parties of the right aimed at sweeping constitutional reform with the aim of strengthening the central government vis-à-vis the Länder and the executive vis-à-vis parliament. According to their reform programme, further constitutional amendments were to be eased by replacing the requirement of a two-thirds parliamentary majority by a parliamentary majority and subsequent referendum. The constitutional court was to be depoliticized. In the words of one of the main advocates of these reform proposals their enactment would contain 'party rule' (_Parteienherrschaft_) and allow 'true democracy' (_wahre Demokratie_) (Seipel 1930). In practice, the reform proposal aimed at weakening those institutions on which the Social Democrats had relied since their retreat from government in 1920: the parliament, with its strong minority rights, federalism, allowing 'red Vienna' to unfold, and the constitutional court, the (liberal) decisions of which occasionally had outraged the non-socialist parties. Two failed attempts to elect a new government in 1929 and the bankruptcy of one of the major commercial banks, underlined the need for effective government and served as fuel for this discussion. The threat of violence, as upheld by the Heimwehren throughout the constitutional reform process, made the Social Democrats (whose votes were required for a two-thirds majority in parliament) willing to compromise (Berchtold 1978; Matzka 1985). The 1929 constitutional reform introduced the direct election of the president and gave him the powers to appoint and dismiss the government and to dissolve parliament. Although these are important powers, this compromise left many demands of the political right unfulfilled.

But what were the practical consequences of the president's new powers in the inter-war period? His right to dissolve parliament was used only once. In 1930 the Christian Social president Wilhelm Miklas appointed a minority government led by his party and on its proposal dissolved parliament before the cabinet had to face it. While the Christian Socials expected a victory, the election turned out a disaster. They lost seven seats, falling back behind the Social Democrats.

President Miklas could make no sense of his other new powers (or did not want to do so). In 1933 he failed to make an attempt to resolve the crisis which had emerged over the subsequent resignation of all three presidents of parliament, leaving the parliament 'self-blocked'. This situation was a gift to the government, some of whose members had already made plans for replacing parliamentary government by an 'authoritarian government'. The government declared that parliament had dissolved itself and continued establishing an authoritarian regime which was completed in 1934 after a short civil war. If president Miklas had acted as the guardian of the constitution, he would have dismissed the government, appointed a new one and, on the latter's proposal, formally dissolved the Nationalrat. Although it is doubtful whether the government would have allowed the president to do this, it is clear that he failed to make any attempt to use his powers in this crisis situation. Likewise, in 1938, when the government surrendered unconditionally to Hitler, the president's resistance remained half-hearted (Goldinger 1982).

The anti-democratic mood and extra-parliamentary pressure which had surrounded the constitutional reform of 1929, and the experience with the actual use or abuse of the president's new powers did not encourage the desire for 'strong' presidents in the post-war period. This is all the more true since it was the Social Democrats who nominated the successful presidential candidates until 1986. Indeed, in an internal memorandum for the first post-war president, Karl Renner, SPÖ chairman, Adolf Schärf, argued that the constitutional position of the Austrian president would be very similar to that of the English king. Despite the fact that president Renner and his successor, Körner, whom Schärf also provided with this memorandum, were Schärf's party comrades, the SPÖ chairman argued against a further strengthening of the president's powers (Kollmann 1973: 361–2; Stadler 1982: 301–3).

The Social Democrats' position initially reflected a convenient correspondence of principle and the expectation that they would not hold the presidency permanently. In the long run, however, the behaviour of the presidents established a constitutional convention which became a reference point in presidential elections. Most candidates indeed promised to follow the patterns the previous presidents had established. However, the two most recent presidents, Kurt Waldheim and Thomas Klestil, indicated their willingness to change these conventions, declaring in their campaigns that, once elected, they would be 'active presidents'.

CONSTITUTIONAL POWERS AND THEIR PRACTICAL RELEVANCE

Direct Election and Accountability

The president is directly elected by the people.[4] In order to be elected a candidate needs more than half of the valid votes. If no candidate gets a majority, a second ballot is held between the two front-runners no later than 35 days after the first. This happened three times, in 1951, 1986, and 1992 (see Table 2.1 below).

The president's term is six years. A re-election for one subsequent term is possible, allowing for a continuous term of 12 years. A further candidacy—after a break (i.e. a different president)—is possible from a constitutional point of view, but has not yet occurred (and, given the typical age of the presidents (see Table 2.1 below), it is quite unlikely).

The president can be removed from office only by a complicated procedure which contains considerable risk for those who initiate it. It requires a referendum majority (50 per cent plus one vote of those who participate) to get rid of the president. The referendum is called by a majority (50 per cent plus one vote) of the federal assembly. The federal assembly in turn is summoned for this specific task by a decision of the Nationalrat which requires a two-thirds majority (with a 50 per cent quorum). Once the Nationalrat has made this decision, the president is

TABLE 2.1. *Austrian presidents and party politics, 1945–1998*

President	Age at time of election or re-election	Nominating party	Electoral support		Date entered office	Date left office	Party composition of government[c]	Date of change in government's party composition[d]	Parliamentary base of government (in % of seats)[e]
			First ballot	Second ballot					
Dr Karl Renner	75	SPÖ	—[a]	—	20 Dec. 1945	31 Dec. 1950[b]	ÖVP–SPÖ–KPÖ	20 Dec. 1945	100
							ÖVP–SPÖ	20 Nov. 1947	87.3–97.6
Theodor Körner	78	SPÖ	39.2	52.1	21 June 1951	04 Jan. 1957[b]	ÖVP–SPÖ		87.3–94.5
Dr Adolf Schärf	67	SPÖ	51.1	—	22 May 1957	22 May 1963	ÖVP–SPÖ		94.5–95.2
	73	SPÖ	55.4	—	22 May 1963	28 Feb. 1965[b]	ÖVP–SPÖ		95.2
Franz Jonas	66	SPÖ	50.7	—	09 June 1965	09 June 1971	ÖVP–SPÖ		95.2
							ÖVP	19 Apr. 1966	51.5
							SPÖ		49.1
	72	SPÖ	51.1	—	09 June 1971	24 Apr. 1974[b]	SPÖ	21 Apr. 1970	50.8
Dr Rudolf Kirchschläger	59	SPÖ	51.7	—	08 July 1974	08 July 1980	SPÖ		50.8–51.9
	65	SPÖ	79.9	—	08 July 1980	08 July 1986	SPÖ		51.9
Dr Kurt Waldheim	65	ÖVP	49.6	53.9	08 July 1986	08 July 1992	SPÖ–FPÖ	24 May 1983	55.8
							SPÖ–FPÖ		55.8
Dr Thomas Klestil	59	ÖVP	37.2	56.9	08 July 1992	08 July 1998	SPÖ–ÖVP	21 Jan. 1987	76.5–85.8
							SPÖ–ÖVP		63.9–76.5
	65	(ÖVP)[f]	63.5	—	08 July 1998		SPÖ–ÖVP		67.7

[a] Elected in the Bundesversammlung (the joint meeting of both houses of parliament) with 204 of 204 valid votes (one unvalid vote).

[b] Died in office. According to the constitution, the chancellor acted as president until the new president was elected and sworn in.

[c] The chancellor's party is listed first. In all cases it has been the strongest parliamentary party.

[d] Date when new government officially assumed office.

[e] This column contains a new line when the government's status changes between majority and minority (which happened only once). Less important changes are reported only by the range of the majority.

[f] President Klestil claimed not to be a party candidate in his re-election. Indeed, he refrained from getting the support of MPs for his candidacy and rather collected support signatures from citizens. As a consequence of this, he was listed only second on the ballot sheet. However, Klestil could draw on the help of the ÖVP party organization in collecting these support signatures and providing other resources.

no longer allowed to exercise his powers. The referendum *de facto* leaves the voters with a choice between the president and parliament. If the voters opt for the removal of the president, the removal procedure is completed and a presidential election is called. If, however, the voters reject the president's removal, this means the automatic dissolution of the Nationalrat, followed by a parliamentary election. At the same time the referendum also counts as a re-election of the president for another six-year term. This rule is qualified by the provision that the total presidential term must not exceed 12 years. Thus, in practical terms, the president can be considered unremovable. No attempt has ever been made to remove a sitting president by engaging his political accountability.

Likewise, no one has ever tried to engage the president's judicial accountability, which is quite limited and also difficult to realize. The president is accountable only for violations of the constitution but not ordinary laws. In this case the constitutional court would judge on the indictment of the federal assembly. The federal assembly's decision would require the presence of at least half of the members of each chamber and a two-thirds majority. The federal assembly would be called by the chancellor on the demand of either the Nationalrat or the Bundesrat (which decide by majority and a quorum of one-third). If the constitutional court found the president guilty, this in any case would mean removal from office, in particularly severe cases also his temporary loss of political rights.

When the president cannot fulfil the duties of the office, the chancellor acts as deputy. In 1977 a constitutional amendment introduced exceptions to this rule. If the president's disability is longer than 20 days, if he dies in office, or if the referendum procedure for his removal has been started, the three presidents of the Nationalrat as collegial body take over the president's functions. They decide by majority.

Constraints on Presidential Powers

The constitution gives the president important powers, however, it severely constrains their use. According to Article 67, all acts of the president require a proposal by the cabinet or a cabinet minister who is entrusted by the cabinet if the constitution does not explicitly say otherwise. All acts of the president need to be countersigned by the chancellor or the minister in charge.

In exercising his powers, the president can rely only on a very modest bureaucracy. Presidential resources are part of the government's budget. Thus, presidents depend on the government's and parliament's goodwill. In 1950 the president's staff totalled 32 people, in 1970 44 people, in 1980 57 people, and in 1996 73 people. The more recent increase in presidential staff is due to attempts of presidents Waldheim and Klestil to recruit personal trustees and increase their staff in order to play the role of 'active' presidents. However, due to budgetary restraint, the increases have fallen short of the presidents' ambitions.

Government Formation

According to the constitution, the government is appointed by the president. It is he who appoints the chancellor and at the chancellor's proposal the other cabinet members plus the secretaries of state (junior ministers). The constitution contains no restriction whatever as to who should be invited to form a government and of which components it should consist. However, *de facto* the president has little room for manoeuvre. Once formed and sworn in, the cabinet must present itself to parliament (the Nationalrat) within one week from assuming office (Article 70). In so doing, it avoids going through an investiture vote. However, on this occasion and at any time afterwards the government can be removed by a vote of no confidence (Article 71). Thus, Austria falls within the rubric of 'negative' parliamentarism (cf. Bergman 1993), meaning that the burden of proof rests with the opposition. To unseat a government requires a quorum of at least 50 per cent and a majority of those MPs who are present.

The president will therefore refrain from appointing a cabinet which is opposed by a parliamentary majority. In situations of single-party majorities, the president has no leeway (Welan 1997: 48). Parliamentary majorities of single parties have existed in the 1945–9, 1966–70, and 1971–83 periods. During more than two-thirds of the post-war period, however, this has not been the case. When no party has a parliamentary majority and alternative majority coalitions could be formed, the constitutional setting would allow the president to become the architect of coalition formation (cf. Koja 1994), as has occasionally been the case in Finland. However, this has not been the case in post-war Austria (Müller 1997). Rather the constitutional convention has become established that the president appoints the leader or 'chancellor candidate' of the largest parliamentary party as a *formateur*.[5] Up until now the largest party (and with one exception also the person who was first officially designated chancellor candidate by the president) has always succeeded in forming a viable government. No government has had to face a vote of no confidence when it first presented itself to parliament. The presidents thus have been largely restricted to ratifying what the parties agree on. In so doing they often find themselves pre-empted by public declarations of the parties or even pre-electoral commitments.

With a single exception—president Renner's refusal to reappoint a minister who was under the suspicion of corruption in 1949 (Kreisky 1986: 431)—presidents have also accepted the parties' monopoly for choosing the cabinet members.

It would be wrong, however, to consider the president as not constraining government formation. President Theodor Körner in 1953 out lined the type of government he wanted—again a grand coalition of the Austrian People's Party (ÖVP) and SPÖ—at the beginning of the party negotiations. He intervened during the negotiations when the ÖVP insisted on including the League of Independents (VdU) in the government. According to the ÖVP proposal the government would have consisted of ÖVP, SPÖ, and VdU, leaving out only the tiny Communist Party. Although still under liberal leadership, the VdU was a party which appealed mainly to former Nazis and protest voters. In several meetings with ÖVP and SPÖ politicians, president Körner stated that the VdU would not be conducive to the maintenance of public order (*staatserhaltend*) and, under the circumstances, he would never accept one of its representatives in government. A public statement by the president was worded more diplomatically but contained the same message (Kollmann 1973: 372–4). Eventually the grand coalition of the ÖVP and SPÖ was renewed.

It remains a question as to what the ÖVP really wanted to achieve by proposing to include the VdU. It should be seen against the background that the SPÖ had made substantial gains in the 1953 election, winning more votes than the ÖVP (but—due to the electoral system— it had one seat less). It was clear that the SPÖ would demand considerable concessions on the part of the ÖVP in the coalition negotiations. There are two readings of the ÖVP proposal. In the first one, the inclusion of the second non-socialist party in government was the first step towards forcing the Social Democrats out of government. Once the VdU had got credibility by being a party of government, the ÖVP would aim at a non-socialist coalition government. In the second reading, the VdU was just a bargaining chip of the ÖVP. Rather than being interested in the VdU's government participation (which in the short term would have reduced its own share of the cake), the ÖVP wanted to extract concessions from the SPÖ for giving up this idea. Anticipating the president's and Social Democrats' reaction, the ÖVP could blame them for the VdU's exclusion from government and maintain good relations it. While the SPÖ leaders firmly believed in the first version, the leaders of the VdU tended to believe in the second. In any case, the ÖVP 'won' the coalition negotiation, making only minor concessions despite the SPÖ's major gains.

However, the president's influence on government formation should not be overestimated even in this episode. While it has generally been recognized, its nature has never been specified and perhaps often has not been properly understood. Since the 1953 presidential intervention is generally considered the one in which the president was most decisive, it is worth constructing a counterfactual for this case (cf. Tetlock and Belkin 1996). In so doing, I proceed from the assumption that the ÖVP's first preference really was a three-party coalition. Only the Social Democrats' continued participation in government would have made it a smooth transition and would have legitimized the VdU's government participation. This option was excluded already by the Social Democrats' refusal to negotiate a three-party coalition. Strictly speaking, no presidential intervention was necessary to prevent this outcome. If the ÖVP's second preference was a coalition with the SPÖ (the actual outcome), again no presidential intervention was necessary. In this scenario it would have been the Nash equilibrium: neither the ÖVP nor the SPÖ could have struck a better deal. If, however, the ÖVP's second preference was a coalition with the VdU, the president's intervention might have mattered.

It is here, that I turn to the counterfactual. What would have happened if the ÖVP had insisted on bringing the VdU into government? Together the ÖVP and VdU controlled a parliamentary majority of 53.3 per cent (88 of 165 seats, while the SPÖ held 73 seats and the Communists 4). If the president had rejected this coalition, the only realistic alternative was to appoint an SPÖ minority government. However, this would have been immediately removed by a vote of no confidence. The president's only possibility of avoiding this, would have been the dissolution of parliament. But would the elections have produced a different majority situation? Probably not. On the one hand, voting behaviour was still relatively stable and there had never been a left of centre majority in parliamentary elections. On the other hand, the gains the SPÖ had made in the elections immediately preceding this situation might have already exhausted its potential. In this scenario, the president eventually would have been forced to appoint an ÖVP–VdU coalition. Moreover, his authority would have been undermined.

Against the background of this scenario, the president would have backed down and appointed an ÖVP–VdU government.

However, although it is the less likely scenario, it cannot be ruled out that the dynamics of the situation might have produced an alternative election outcome, leaving the ÖVP and VdU without a majority. Given the anti-system role of the Communists, this would not have led to a government of the left but rather to an SPÖ-led grand coalition. And this would have precisely been the SPÖ's campaign strategy, while the president would have expressed his support for any kind of grand coalition. Thus, remaining firm vis-à-vis the president also would have included a certain amount of risk for the ÖVP.

Returning to the real case, the president's intervention was relevant in two respects. First, it lent additional weight to the SPÖ's rejection of a three-party coalition and made the SPÖ's commitment that it would not serve in this kind of coalition more credible. Secondly, it increased the ÖVP's costs (or at least its risk) involved in a change of coalition partners. If the ÖVP's calculation of its cost-benefit ratio was not already clear, the president's resistance may well have been relevant in tipping the balance. This logic also applies to the other cases of presidential intervention, to which I turn now.

In 1959 the SPÖ again had more votes but one seat less than the ÖVP. According to an unpublished manuscript in the private papers of president Schärf,[6] the ÖVP leader, Julius Raab, proposed the inclusion of the Freedom Party (FPÖ), the VdU's successor, in cabinet when he first met the president in order to become appointed *formateur*. Raab had stated that the inclusion of the FPÖ should be contemplated already before the election (Engelmann 1962: 656). Schärf reminded Raab that both major parties had promised to continue their cooperation in the campaign and that the inclusion of the FPÖ would violate their electoral promises. The sources I have checked, which include the minutes of the SPÖ party executive and a rather detailed account by FPÖ chairman, Friedrich Peter (1986), of his contacts with the two major parties, reveal no further hint at an attempt of including the FPÖ in the government coalition in 1959. It is hard to say whether the president's critical attitude eliminated a serious option of one of the major players in the coalition game or whether it was just an attempt by the *formateur* to repeat the 1953 game. The president, in any case, proved important for maintaining the grand coalition government in 1959. This is because the negotiations between the ÖVP and SPÖ soon ran into troubles. It was only due to the intervention of president Schärf that they could be completed successfully.

In 1962/3 president Schärf urged the SPÖ and ÖVP leaders to complete their extraordinary long coalition negotiations and stressed that they had a mandate from the voters to continue with the grand coalition government (Müller 1995). In the presidential campaign of 1963, which led to his re-election, for electoral reasons Schärf stated that he would not exclude any of the parliamentary parties from government participation (Piringer 1982: 83). At this time, however, an SPÖ–FPÖ coalition had become a feasible alternative. Schärf personally still considered the grand coalition government to be the best choice and informally did everything he could to discourage SPÖ politicians from abandoning it.

Another important presidential decision in the context of government formation was the appointment of the SPÖ's minority government by president Franz Jonas after the parliamentary elections in 1970. This was the first (and only) minority government of post-war Austria. Negotiations between the SPÖ (which had won a plurality of seats) and the ÖVP (which had lost its majority) had ended in stalemate and *formateur* Bruno Kreisky had reported back to the president that a minority SPÖ cabinet would be viable. The president accepted this proposal and appointed the Kreisky I cabinet (cf. Fischer 1993: 63–6 and 71–6). Alternatively, Jonas could have insisted on the formation of a majority cabinet. This, in turn, would have required further negotiations between the SPÖ and ÖVP—the only coalition not ruled out by precommitments. It fits with the dominant pattern of presidential non-interference in the party-political game that Jonas refrained from doing so. By appointing the Kreisky I cabinet, president Jonas ratified the tacit consensus between the SPÖ and FPÖ. It allowed the minority government to survive and indeed to pass major legislation.

Presidents Kurt Waldheim in 1986 and Thomas Klestil in 1995 publicly expressed their preference for a grand coalition of the SPÖ and ÖVP. At the time of their statements alternative coalitions had not yet been excluded from the agenda. Nevertheless, these interventions were hardly more than a 'tail wind' for the most likely solution of beginning negotiations. If the parties had not been willing to arrive at an agreement, the presidents' preferences would have failed to materialize.

In addition to the presidents' influence during the formation of government coalitions they have also been helpful in overcoming problems between the coalition parties during the government's term and thus have contributed towards maintaining coalition governments (Kollmann 1973: 361–2 and 375–9). Presidents Körner (in 1952) and

Schärf (in 1960) rejected the resignation of cabinets over problems of agreeing the budget. Likewise, although unsuccessful, president Klestil tried to help solve the budget crisis in 1995. The SPÖ–ÖVP government had not been able to agree on a budget for 1996 and eventually called early elections after having been in office for just one year. This was the solution to a government crisis which was prescribed by the coalition agreement and was also the classic pattern in post-war Austrian politics. Although the president could not prevent the government's resignation and elections, he nevertheless might have been of considerable influence in this context. According to rumours, which have been fuelled by brief remarks by the president during his re-election campaign in 1998, president Klestil prevented a change of government without calling an election in 1995. Allegedly, the ÖVP leader's preferred alternative was a minority government of his party. It would have included experts proposed by the FPÖ which, in turn, would have tolerated the cabinet. Notwithstanding the actual details, Klestil's behaviour through this government crisis had been characterized as 'completely correct' by SPÖ chairman and chancellor Franz Vranitzky.

Government Dismissal

The president can dismiss the chancellor or the entire government (Article 70), without needing a proposal. These powers have never been used in the post-war period.[7] It is also the president who dismisses individual ministers, but this requires a proposal by the chancellor. In practice, the presidents have routinely followed the chancellors' proposals, which, in turn, have been based on intra-party decisions of the party which had nominated the minister.

Dissolution of Parliament

The president can dissolve parliament (the Nationalrat), leading to a parliamentary election. Presidential dissolution requires a proposal by the government and is constrained by the clause that the president can dissolve only once for the same reason (Article 29[1]). Both constraints are not really serious ones from a constitutional point of view. Given the president's capacity in the creation and dismissal of government, it should be easy to get a government proposal, and the fact that there is no way to verify the president's reasons considerably reduces the relevance of the second constraint. Nevertheless, this provision has never been used after the president's unlucky dissolution in 1930.

Foreign Policy

The constitution boldly states: 'The Federal President represents the Republic internationally' (Article 65). Constitutional lawyers have interpreted this clause differently. In the most extensive interpretation (Koja 1993), the president has a constitutional monopoly for Austria's formal representation in acts under international law. Accordingly, the chancellor or the foreign minister can only represent the country in a formal sense on the president's delegation. Based on this particular view, president Klestil claimed that he should represent Austria in the European Council, the European Union's highest body, when Austria became a member in 1995. The chancellor disagreed and eventually the president gave in, however, maintaining the claim that he only has delegated this task to the chancellor.

What may have eased president Klestil's concession is the material side of foreign policy-making. Here, even advocates of a strong president agree that the constitution gives precedence to the government and parliament. All foreign policy acts of the president require a proposal of the cabinet or a cabinet minister who is entrusted by the cabinet. Thus the president is not allowed to initiate foreign policy. Rather he has to wait for a proposal which he can only accept or reject (Koja 1993: 631). This would hardly be practicable while sitting in international bodies. Consequently, president Kirchschläger has stated that 'foreign policy is made by the government, not by the president'.

This indeed has been the rule since 1945. Although some presidents have occasionally deviated slightly from the government's policy (cf. Stadler 1982: 301–2; Kollmann 1973: 379–85), by and large they have loyally supported it and indeed have been assets in foreign relations. The incumbent president Klestil is perhaps the best example of both. On the one hand, he has been helpful in restoring the country's international reputation after the 'Waldheim years' and has supported Austria's EU integration both by his international activities and domestically. On the other hand, Klestil has taken positions concerning neutrality and NATO membership which are controversial within government, lending his weight to the side of the People's Party.

Commander-in-Chief

The president is the commander-in-chief (Article 80). According to the dominant constitutional interpretation, this function is one which he can exercise without a proposal from the government (Ringhofer 1977:

25–6; Welan 1992: 72; Koja 1997). However, the constitution constrains the president by introducing the 'right of disposal' (*Verfügung*) over the army, which makes the commander-in-chief largely a ceremonial figure. The right of disposal is reserved to the minister of defence save insofar as the armed forces law (*Wehrgesetz*) explicitly reserves it to the president. This law leaves only unpleasant duties to the president, namely to call in soldiers for extraordinary service and to delay their transfer into reserve, but does not give him any role leading the military forces. While according to the most extensive interpretation of the constitution the president's commander-in-chief powers are dominant and allow the president to give orders to the defence minister (Koja 1997: 20), this interpretation has been virtually without practical relevance. Although presidents have occasionally tried to increase their role in defence matters by making reference to their commander-in-chief status, they have not achieved much. Indeed, subsequent presidents have had to struggle with government to get information about defence matters (Körner) and to get a minimum staff (one military officer) to deal with defence matters (Schärf) (Kollmann 1973: 385 ff.). Since these achievements, the president is relatively well-informed about defence matters, but the commander-in-chief function has remained an 'empty shell', as president Kirchschläger has put it.

Appointment Powers

The president not only appoints the government but also civil servants, military officers, and judges (Article 65). The latter include those who serve in the administrative and constitutional courts. While presidents have delegated the bulk of appointments to the government or individual ministers, they have maintained their right to make appointments in senior positions (those in the two highest service classes). All of these appointments have to be agreed unanimously by the cabinet before they are formally proposed to the president. Although the president cannot act without proposal, he is not bound to accept it. Indeed, all presidents have used their right to check these proposals and occasionally have rejected them. In the late 1960s, for instance, president Jonas rejected the ÖVP government's proposals for the president of the administrative court and the ambassador to West Germany. More common than outright rejections are non-decisions or substantial delays in making decisions on the part of the president. Nevertheless, only a small number of appointments are affected in these ways. More important is the 'law of anticipated reaction'. In order to avoid a presidential *refus*, government members who anticipate problems with the president tend to sound him out before making a formal proposal. Problems of getting the president's approval are likely if the appointment to be made is controversial, for instance, by passing 'natural' candidates and/or pushing the minister's party comrades. The president is likely to learn about these cases by informal means and to check the papers carefully.

The incumbent president, Thomas Klestil, has been identified as having given up his predecessors' traditional self-restraint in influencing civil service appointments, trying to check political parties (Welan 1995*a*: 491). Indeed, Klestil has rejected ministerial proposals for appointing school directors. However, Klestil differs not by the fact that he rejects government proposals. While he may do so in terms of frequency (although no hard data is available), he certainly publicizes his rejections more. While previous presidents as a rule did not want the cabinet members to lose face and handled these matters privately, Klestil takes pride in checking the power of the parties. When Klestil violated another convention, namely that the president appoints the first of the parliament's three ranked candidates for vacant positions in the constitutional court, parliament struck back. A 1994 constitutional amendment abolished the requirement of proposing more than one candidate to the president (*Bundesgesetzblatt* 1013/1994).

Verification of the Constitutional Enactment of Laws

The president verifies the constitutional enactment of federal laws (Article 47). It is the president's signature which completes the law-making process and it is a necessary requirement for laws passed by parliament to come into force. Constitutional lawyers and presidential candidates have often discussed the extent to which this gives the president a veto power over legislation (Jahnel 1987; Korinek 1990). The dominant interpretation is that the president does not verify the constitutionality of the laws' content. This task is reserved to the constitutional court in the case of an appeal. Indeed, should the president intervene, this body, which is most qualified to make the judgement, could not become involved because there would be no law to be appealed. Rather than the constitutionality of the laws' content, the president verifies that the process of law-making has followed the constitutional requirements. These include parliamentary quorum and majority requirements. Given the sheer number of laws and the complexity of constitutional interpretation, as president Kirchschläger (1992: 207–8) has pointed out, the president is able to sign laws as long as they do not involve a total revision of the constitution (which would require a referendum) or raise specific and obvious doubts about the constitutionality of the law-making process. Such a case certainly had existed in 1934, when the government drew on a rump parliament (purged from its opponents) to enact a completely new constitution. Again, president Miklas made no attempt to stop the government. Fortunately, in post-war Austria the constitutional provisions about the law-making process have been strictly observed. Consequently, the president has never refused to sign a law (Welan 1997: 60). He has signed even in cases where there have been severe doubts about the constitutionality of their content and even if the president himself shared these doubts. President Waldheim (1996: 132), however, has hinted that he had tried to pre-emt such situations by contacts with the government before parliamentary decisions. In any case, the president is obliged to sign if there is no constitutional reason for not doing so.

Emergency Powers

The president also has emergency powers. He can issue law-changing decrees in order to prevent 'irreversible damage to the public' (Article 18) in times where the Nationalrat is not in session and cannot be summoned in good time. However, the president's emergency powers are strictly contained. Emergency decrees require a proposal by the government which, in turn, must be agreed with the main committee of the Nationalrat, which is a permanent one. The decrees need to be countersigned by the government and must be voted on by the Nationalrat within four weeks. Welan has characterized this constitutional clause as 'simply impracticable' (Welan 1986: 37). Indeed it has never been used.

THE PRESIDENCY AND PARTY POLITICS

Presidential Elections and Party Politics

The direct election was the only aspect of the presidency which came close to being changed in the post-war period. To begin with, due to a transitory regulation, the president had never been directly elected in the inter-war period (Goldinger 1982: 101–4). For practical reasons, this pattern was followed in 1945. According to Schärf, the leaders of the SPÖ and ÖVP had agreed in 1948 to abolish the direct election on a permanent basis, but the ÖVP leaders did not succeed in getting this proposal accepted by their party (Schärf 1955: 270–1). In 1951, when the election of a new president was due, the ÖVP had changed its mind and advocated an election by the federal assembly, i.e. both houses of parliament, in which it held a majority. However, the two major parties could not agree on a candidate; hence, the first direct election was held. Surprisingly, the candidate of the Social Democrats won.

In 1957, when the next presidential election came up, the ÖVP renewed its proposal to return the presidential election to the federal assembly. After the SPÖ's victory in the previous presidential election, the ÖVP now made the offer to vote for an SPÖ candidate if the SPÖ in turn would agree on a constitutional amendment (Kreisky 1988: 360). The Social Democrats rejected this proposal. In contrast to direct election, in which the number of votes decides, in any indirect election the electoral system would have given a considerable bias in favour of the ÖVP (Schärf, n.d.). Before 1970, this was true even for the Nationalrat. Of particular importance, however, was the representation system in the Bundesrat (which over-represents the small and ÖVP-dominated Länder). When the Social Democrats rejected the proposal to return the election to the federal assembly, they felt that they did not stand a realistic chance of ever gaining a majority there due to the ÖVP's advantage in the Bundesrat.[8]

Presidential elections are held close to the end of the term of a sitting president or after his death. It has been a deliberate policy of the parties not to hold presidential elections and parliamentary elections together. Although presidential elections have a strong and increasing element of personality, they contain several features which strengthen the party element. While the office as such and its non-partisan image may invite independent candidates, parliamentary parties enjoy a number of advantages when it comes to filling it. First, a candidacy requires the support of 6,000 voters (who have to sign for the candidate in a not uncomplicated procedure). This can be compensated by the signatures of five MPs to the Nationalrat (*Bundesgesetzblatt* 339/1993). While candidates without party support have to devote a considerable amount of time and effort to collecting the signatures, candidates of established parties have a head start. Secondly, no public finance is available for presidential candidates. This is quite a contrast to the generous system of public party finance which exists at all levels in Austria and again it is an advantage for those candidates who can rely on established parties (or have other access to resources). Estimates of the major parties' presidential campaign expenditures in the last decade have been up to 100 million Schillings (roughly 7.1 million ECU) per election. Thirdly, no free television spots are provided for presidential candidates and they cannot purchase television time from the national television station. However, political parties may and actually do use their free television time to broadcast spots for their candidates. Finally, in the case of a second ballot, the groups which have nominated the two front-runners have the right to exchange their candidates between the two ballots. Although this has never happened, this rule makes more sense for political parties than for individual candidates. As a consequence of the dominant position of political parties in structuring politics in general and these rules in particular, only candidates of one of the two major parties have won the office of president. Only the 1998 presidential elections showed first signs of an erosion of the parties' monopoly on the presidency. While the incumbent tried hard to distance himself from his past as party candidate, three challengers, winning a total of 27 per cent of the vote, did not have a party background.

How, then, have the presidential elections related to parliamentary elections? The presidency and the chancellorship have been held by the same party only in the 1970–4 period. In the 1974–86 period, the president was an independent who had been nominated by the SPÖ which was the only or major government party. Divided government in the strict sense, with the party of the president not being included in government, has existed only for 4.5 years, in 1966–70, when the SPÖ was in opposition while Franz Jonas was president, and in 1986–7, when the ÖVP was in opposition while Kurt Waldheim was president. Rather, elections have tended to produce 'divided government' in the sense that the offices of chancellor and president were held by candidates of different parties—always the SPÖ and ÖVP.

This pattern was first established by a deal of the party leaders in 1945.[9] Although making Karl Renner, the founder of the Second Republic and much acclaimed head of the provisional government from April to November 1945, president seemed a natural choice, the presidency was part of the coalition negotiations. While the parties quickly agreed on Renner, this position was taken into account when the balance sheet was drawn up, resulting in a smaller share of the Social Democrats in cabinet positions. Since 1951 direct elections were held. In 1951, 1957, 1963, and 1965, the SPÖ candidates were elected president. At this time the SPÖ was the junior partner in a grand coalition with the ÖVP, which held the office of chancellor and the most important cabinet positions. Indeed, the SPÖ fought the presidential elections with slogans which called for a balance of power between the major parties. By 1970, the situation had changed. The SPÖ had replaced the ÖVP as the strongest party, forming single-party governments from 1970 to 1983 and being the senior partner in coalition governments since then, first with the FPÖ (1983–6), and with the ÖVP since 1987. Now it was the ÖVP's turn to employ the power balance rhetoric. Nevertheless, the SPÖ candidate, Franz Jonas, won the 1971 election. However, this result needs qualification. Jonas was the incumbent president and, given this fact, he won only by a narrow margin.[10] Moreover, at the time of Jonas's re-election—June 1971—the SPÖ still lacked a parliamentary majority. Its popular minority government seemed particularly vulnerable to presidential dismissal, especially since the ÖVP had criticized Jonas's decision to appoint a minority government. Moreover, the ÖVP presidential candidate, Kurt Waldheim (in his first attempt to win the presidency), had stated that minority governments were not a normal state in a Western democracy and had declared his preference for a grand coalition government during his campaign (Schausberger 1982: 300).

When Jonas died in 1974, however, the SPÖ had a parliamentary majority. In contrast to the ÖVP, which fielded a popular party politician, the SPÖ decided to nominate a non-partisan, Rudolf Kirchschläger (Welan 1995b). A judge and later a diplomat, he had served as foreign minister in the SPÖ government, but was a practising Catholic. Kirchschläger won the election and presided over the country at a time when Pope Paul VI referred to Austria as 'an island of the blessed'. In 1980, when Kirchschläger ran again, the ÖVP did not present a candidate and he was re-elected with 79.9 per cent of the valid votes. In 1986, when Kirchschläger's second term came to an end, the Social Democrats were still in government, now in a highly unpopular coalition with the FPÖ. This time it was the ÖVP which presented a diplomat who had served as non-partisan foreign minister (1968–70) and general secretary of the United Nations, Kurt Waldheim. In contrast, the SPÖ fielded a genuine party politician, Kurt Steyrer, the minister of health. The campaign soon became dominated by Waldheim's past. It caused a deep division in Austrian society and severely damaged the country's image abroad (Gehler 1995; Pelinka 1995). Nevertheless, Waldheim was elected. While maintaining the Kirchschläger tradition of having a non-partisan president, Waldheim's election also returned to the tradition of 'divided government' in the sense that the presidency was not held by a nominee of the chancellor's party. Waldheim decided not to run for a second term in 1992 when it turned out that he remained internationally isolated. The 1992 presidential elections continued the 'divided government' pattern. The junior government party nominated Thomas Klestil, who was considered an outsider at the beginning of the campaign. Nevertheless, he was elected in the second ballot against the most popular SPÖ minister, Rudolf Streicher. In 1998 he was re-elected with neither the SPÖ nor the FPÖ putting up a candidate.

It would be misleading, however, to see the outcome of presidential elections exclusively from the point of view of party competition and the voters' preference for 'divided government'. The personalities of the candidates have always been important and since the 1970s the relevance of this factor has considerably increased. In particular, the candidates' detachment from parties and their image in terms of party-political 'neutrality' has been important. Since 1974 the candidate who has won, although always supported by one of the major parties, has been less a 'party man' than his main competitor. This applies to the two non-partisan presidents (Kirchschläger and Waldheim) and it also applies to the incumbent president, Thomas Klestil. Although Klestil has been a member of and was an unsuccessful parliamentary candidate for the ÖVP, he was less a 'party man' than his opponent (in 1992). Moreover, Klestil did his best to distance himself from political parties and actually made checking the government parties his main campaign message ('power needs control').

While the two major parties aimed to win the presidency, they also pursued other goals in presidential elections. Some of these were also relevant in respect of coalition building in the parliamentary arena. In this vein, the nomination of a joint presidential candidate of the ÖVP and FPÖ in 1957 was another attempt at non-socialist cooperation. If this candidacy had been successful, it might well have led to a government coalition of these parties. In any case, the president would no longer have been an obstacle to this type of coalition. The decision of both the SPÖ and FPÖ not to field candidates in 1998 also included coalitional considerations. While none of them had a realistic chance of getting its candidate elected against the incumbent, the (previously) ÖVP-nominated Thomas Klestil, a candidacy might have had an impact on inter-party cooperation and the president's goodwill. An FPÖ candidacy might have reinforced cooperation between the two government parties—the SPÖ and ÖVP—particularly if the SPÖ had abstained from the presidential election. An SPÖ candidacy, in contrast, would have driven a wedge between the two government parties and might have made future ÖVP–FPÖ cooperation more likely, in particular, if the FPÖ would have supported Klestil's re-election.

Likewise, parties without chance of winning (the Communists, VdU, FPÖ, Greens, and Liberal Forum) have participated in presidential elections to pursue goals other than winning office. They believed that voters who once voted for one of their candidates were more likely to vote for the party in the future or wanted to use the publicity given to the presidential candidates for making party propaganda.

The Relations between the President and the Parties

Presidential elections have been much more partisan than the presidential office. All presidents have stressed their commitment to the country rather than party. Accordingly, the presidents have never held party leadership functions. According to Welan, the president's non-partisan role is already implied in the constitutional incompatibility of the presidency with any other public office, which courageously is interpreted to include also party office (Welan 1997: 30). This, however, would still allow for a Gaullist kind of semi-detached party leadership (cf. Duverger 1984). Nevertheless, it has not happened. Several reasons account for this.

To begin with, the parties have not normally nominated their most powerful leaders, but rather 'elder statesmen' (until 1971). Since 1974 successful candidates have been political insiders without a power base. The only exception was the candidacy of the SPÖ's chairman Schärf in 1957. He was pushed and pulled by his younger party comrades, who wanted to take over his party and government positions. Schärf stood for election in order to postpone his retirement from politics by gaining presidential office (Müller 1995). For all of the presidents it was their last political office. Indeed four of them died in office. The presidents' age and sometimes bad health have not been conducive to great activism and the ambition to change things. Indeed, after a long and faithful service for party and/or country, they have been interested in maintaining a 'low temperature' in domestic politics, the smooth working of the machinery of government, and friendly international relations. In this respect, the incumbent 'active' president does not distinguish himself from his 'passive' predecessors.

Being above party and not intervening in day-to-day politics is also the public role prescription for the president. According to representative surveys conducted between 1974 and 1997, Austrians have consistently demanded a non-partisan president or a president above parties (Welan 1997: 17–19). In 1992 this was 'very important' for 67 per cent and 'quite important' for 22 per cent of respondents; in 1997 it was 'very important' for no less than 72 per cent of respondents. Presidents who are concerned about their popularity, for intrinsic or instrumental (re-election ambition) reasons, have a strong incentive to behave accordingly.

Finally, I will reconsider the actual behaviour of presidents from a party-political perspective. The question is: Have they used their powers in a partisan way?

As mentioned above, the strongest powers of the president—dissolution of parliament and dismissal of government—have never been used in the post-war period. For one thing, there was no crisis situation in post-1945 Austria which would have justified such behaviour. Moreover, as I have argued above, it has become a widely accepted norm that the president should not act in a partisan manner. Thus, French-style dissolutions of the 1981 and 1988 type in Austria would be considered as a violation of the president's duties. The situation in which such a scenario was most likely to unfold was Kurt Waldheim's election to president in 1986. It had been preceded by a heated campaign which had poisoned the climate between the leading government party—the SPÖ—and the newly elected president (Gehler 1995). Moreover, opinion polls and the presidential election itself indicated that the SPÖ had lost its plurality in the electorate to the ÖVP—the party which had nominated Waldheim. Nevertheless, the new president did not dissolve parliament and in his memoirs he denies having considered this option seriously (Waldheim 1996: 124).[11] Likewise, there is no hint at any attempt by the ÖVP to get the president to dissolve parliament.

The president has also a strong position in government formation and maintenance. I have discussed the president's impact on this in some detail in the previous section. Here, it is sufficient to evaluate this behaviour. Was it 'above party' or have presidents acted as partisans? The answer is straightforward in the cases of Waldheim and Klestil, who both expressed support for grand coalition government. The alternatives would have been governments with their nominating party—the ÖVP—as the senior rather than the junior partner. While the impact of these presidents on the actual outcome of government formation has been marginal, it certainly has not been partisan. The situation is more complex in respect of presidents Körner, Schärf, and Jonas. Körner and Schärf actively intervened in the party game, supporting grand coalition government. The alternative would have been a government which would have allowed their own party—the SPÖ—less influence. Nevertheless, these presidents certainly acted according to what they considered to be best for the country and there is no evidence that they misrepresented the median voter. This became particularly clear when president Schärf did his best to contain the anti-grand coalition wing in his own party in the early 1960s. Finally, how should Jonas's behaviour be evaluated? In contrast to his predecessors, he did not intervene actively. Rather he ratified the outcome of the party political game. This, in 1970, was favourable to his party—the SPÖ. The crucial question is a counterfactual: Would he have behaved in the same way if the ÖVP (rather than the SPÖ) had proposed a minority government which could have relied on tacit parliamentary support after a major electoral victory? Probably the president would have been less willing to do so. He might have demanded another round of negotiations, pressing both major parties to make concessions. If, however, the parties had remained firm, Jonas would probably have appointed an ÖVP minority government too. All this suggests that holding the presidency is an advantage for parties in government formation situations, but the limits of what a president can and will be willing to do are clearly drawn.

Finally, have the presidents used their influence in day-to-day politics in a partisan manner? Have they tried to shape foreign policy and government appointments according to their party's point of view? Have they tried to throw their weight behind their own party in other matters by publicly supporting party positions? Again the answer is that holding the presidency is an advantage for parties, but not a major one. However, none of the presidents has grossly violated the public expectation of neutrality in party-political terms and certainly no president has acted against his own convictions for reasons of party discipline.

CONCLUSION

In this chapter I have argued that the legacy of the creation of semi-presidentialism has indeed influenced its working in practice. In addition to the conditions of constitution-making, the very different behaviour of incumbents has shaped the presidency both in negative (inter-war period) and positive (post-war period) terms.

The formal powers of the president can be captured in the following analogy. While the president is well suited for a 'nuclear strike' (the powers to dissolve parliament and to dismiss and appoint government), he is not well equipped for 'conventional warfare' (depending on government proposals for and the countersignature of his acts). Dissolution and dismissal powers have not been used in the post-war period. While these powers were potentially relevant to back the presidents' interventions in government formation situations, it is fair to say that the president has never been the decisive force in government formation. Rather presidents have largely confined themselves to ratifying the outcome of elections (in majority situations) or party negotiations (in minority situations). Likewise, presidents have used their other formal powers unobtrusively and have largely refrained from making controversial statements in day-to-day politics. In short, they have tried to live up to the 'above party' image of the office. All this self-restraint has served one purpose—to have moral authority and not just formal powers in the case of crisis situations. While crisis situations which would have called upon the president to make use of his strongest powers have not occurred in the post-war period, I have hinted at several critical moments in which the president was more than the 'state notary'. Thus the office may be properly characterized as the 'authority in reserve' presidency.

NOTES

1. Since the office of president has been held only by men so far, I will refrain from the usual 'he or she' references.
2. The interviews include the last two former presidents (Rudolf Kirchschläger and Kurt Waldheim), the last four former chancellors (Josef Klaus, Bruno Kreisky, Fred Sinowatz, and Franz Vranitzky) and more than 50 cabinet ministers and party leaders.
3. The presidency was just one and certainly not the most important controversy in constitution-making. The related issues of federalism, the powers of the second chamber (the Bundesrat), and the status of Vienna were more critical to the Social Democrats and Christian Socials. The presidency was most important for the third major political camp, the German nationals.
4. Active voting rights are identical to those for the parliament. Voting can be made obligatory by Land laws. Candidates must have a minimum age of 35 years. Members of ruling and former ruling houses are still not allowed to run.
5. All presidents have followed this rule and at least three of them have positively acknowledged its existence. Schärf did so in 1959, when he rejected his own party's desire to win the nomination for chancellor on the basis that it had won more votes than the People's Party. Presidents Kirchschläger and Waldheim (1996: 128) have acknowledged this convention in interviews and memoirs.
6. Adolf Schärf, 'Bundespräsident', unpublished manuscript, Nachlaß Schärf (KK15), Verein für Geschichte der Arbeiterbewegung, Vienna.
7. Only one president is alleged to have considered dismissing a sitting government. This was Kurt Waldheim who was obviously unhappy with the government's handling of commissioning a report on his past from international historians. While it is true that Waldheim had discussed his constitutional power

of dismissal with a law professor in this context, he categorically rejects having seriously considered actually making use of it (personal interview, 1996).

8. An SPÖ majority in the Bundesrat indeed did not occur before the late 1960s. Since the early 1980s, the SPÖ has again fallen back behind the ÖVP in the Bundesrat, while still enjoying a substantial advantage in the Nationalrat.

9. The People's Party had an absolute majority in parliament. Theoretically, it could have formed a single-party government. With regard to the presidency, it needed the support of the Social Democrats to move the election into the federal assembly.

10. Jonas had an advantage of 5.6 per cent over the candidate who finished second, compared to 14.8 per cent for Schärf in 1963, 63.0 per cent for Kirchschläger in 1980, and 50.0 per cent for Klestil in 1998. However, Kirchschläger and Klestil did not face a candidate of the second major party when running for re-election.

11. To provide a full record of events, it should be mentioned that chancellor Fred Sinowatz resigned the day after the presidential election, to be followed by Franz Vranitzky, who had a less strained relationship with Waldheim. Sinowatz's resignation, however, was not triggered by the fear that the new president would dismiss him on assuming office. Rather Sinowatz aimed at (and succeeded in) destroying the momentum of the People's Party attempt to recapture the status of the strongest party by giving the government a new and popular head.

3

Finland

DAVID ARTER

In the 1970s Finland, in the person of Urho Kekkonen, possessed an 'all-powerful president'—to adapt Maurice Duverger's terms—actively supported by, and enjoying the confidence of the Soviet Union, whose style of 'preventative diplomacy', that is his concern to avoid an adverse reaction in the Kremlin, involved the discussion and resolution of all significant domestic Finnish questions with the Soviet Union. However, since Kekkonen's retirement through ill-health in 1981—at the age of 81!—a process of piecemeal constitutional reform has strengthened the core concept of parliamentary government at the expense of the old quasi-monarchical elements in the Finnish political system. The constitutional modernization process has been propelled by a concern to avoid the possibility of a recurrence of the 'enlightened despotism' of the Kekkonen era. At the same time, the collapse of the Soviet Union has betokened a less personalized and less hierarchical handling of Finno-Soviet relations. Recent constitutional changes have also enhanced the involvement of the prime minister and government in the performance of the federative (foreign policy) function. Above all, the institutional adaptation required by membership of the European Union (EU) has emphasized the bicephalous character of the Finnish political executive in a way reminiscent of inter-war practice. Furthermore, if a by-product of EU membership has been to elevate the position of the government and especially the prime minister, so the standing of the cabinet vis-à-vis parliament has been consolidated in the performance of the legislative function by the abolition of such distinctively Czarist elements as the system of qualified majority rules. Political factors, notably the ability of the party system to deliver stable majority coalitions, have worked in the same direction.

In a recent polemic in the national daily *Helsingin Sanomat*, the political scientist, Matti Wiberg, underlining the residual prerogative powers of the office, argued vigorously for the abolition of the whole institution of the presidency, claiming, *inter alia*, that in practice the head of state is not above the daily round of politics and remains a powerful backstage operator (Wiberg, in *Helsingin Sanomat*, 2 Apr. 1998). His consciously tendentious submission was not without support (Eero Silvasti, in *Helsingin Sanomat*, 7 Apr. 1998). The Finnish president is certainly not (yet) a ceremonial figurehead and the present incumbent, Martti Ahtisaari, has sought to direct foreign policy on the wider world stage. However, with parliament having recently accepted the main findings of the Nikula Committee's report and restricted the president's involvement in the process of coalition-building, as well as vesting the government with powers jointly to manage foreign policy, it is clear that Finland is en route to becoming an orthodox parliamentary democracy. The head of state has lost his exclusive charge of the federative function; his involvement in the legislative process is limited and exceptional; and even his executive powers—particularly his powers of appointment—have been restricted in recent years.

CONSTITUTION-MAKING 1917–1919: A MONARCHICAL REPUBLIC?

Facilitated by the Czar's October Manifesto in 1905, the shift from anti-quated Diet of Estates to a unicameral 200-member parliament, or Eduskunta, elected on the basis of universal and equal suffrage in 1906, meant that mass democracy was achieved at a stroke in the Grand Duchy of Finland over a decade before the achievement of independence from St Petersburg. However, it turned out in practice to be a façade democracy since, as in Russia, the Czar as head of state repeatedly dissolved the Eduskunta. Parliamentary practices and the principle of parliamentarism were not established and, with general elections virtually an annual occurrence, both popular interest in politics and electoral turnout declined. Nonetheless, in 1916, the Social Democrats gained the only absolute majority of parliamentary seats ever gained by a single party in a Finnish general election. A low turnout helped their cause.

The abdication of Nicholas II and the collapse of Czarism in Russia early in 1917 raised the tricky question of Finland's constitutional status as a Grand Duchy of the Romanov Empire—and more particularly the issue of who governed—but a mixture of indeterminacy and prevarication on the part of the provisional government in St Petersburg combined to frustrate Finland's desire for clarification of its legal position. At the provisional government's insistence, new elections were staged

in Finland in October 1917 at which the Social Democrats lost their
absolute majority. Indeed, seizing the opportunity afforded by Lenin's
Bolshevik revolution in the Russian capital, it was a non-socialist coalition (Senate) which unilaterally declared Finnish independence on 6
December 1917 against the backdrop of an expected German victory in
the First World War.

The Finnish civil war of winter–spring 1918, a cameo version of events
in Russia, left a legacy of deep division between the two Finlands—Red
and White. When it was over, not only the numerical strength, but
also the legitimacy of parliament, had been severely reduced. Of the
200-member Eduskunta elected in October 1917, only 84 were present
when parliament reconvened on 15 May 1918, the day before the White
victory parade. Moreover, out of 92 elected Social Democrats, 40 had
fled to Russia, while no less than 50 had been taken prisoner by the
Whites, of whom five had been executed immediately (Jussila, Hentilä,
and Nevakivi 1995: 112). Ironically, too, the victorious Whites were
themselves divided over the form of government to adopt.

Support for monarchism had grown on the political right during
the civil war and sections of the White élite expressed their deep
disappointment with the Finnish people. An extreme monarchist
complained to the commander-in chief, Ludendorff, during a visit to
the German military command, that 'everything would perhaps be
fine if only we had a nation that was a little more politically mature'
(Vares 1993: 334–5). The origins of the Red rebellion, the monarchists
insisted, lay in the fact that the populace was not ready for democracy
and that the transition to universal and equal voting had been a step
too far. Indeed, plans were laid in right-wing circles in spring 1918
to restrict franchise rights which would have been granted on the
basis of wealth and social status (estate!) (Jussila, Hentilä, and Nevakivi
1995: 114). Some of the most extreme conservative ideas emanated
from the Swedish People's Party, the organ of the national language
minority. Estlander, for example, demanded an end to the (barely
extant) principle of parliamentarism and the introduction of a corporate (estate-style) system of representation (Vares 1993: 339). There
were, it is true, various shades of Finnish monarchism at a time when
in 1918 monarchy was the rule in Europe and republicanism the exception. By and large, however, it can be said that in spring 1918 monarchism was supported by high-status conservatives and/or those for
whom the foreign policy of Germany sufficed. Equally, a monarch without German backing was not regarded as sufficient. Only the backing
of the German Kaiser was held to be strong enough to stabilize Finnish

society and protect the Finnish state against Russia and the Scandinavian form of monarchy, for example, was thought to be too weak to achieve these ends. Rather, the monarchists held that respect for authority should be restored and that Finland should possess a strong executive power.

Over the summer and early autumn of 1918 the monarchist majority pressed hard to achieve its goal. In June the government led by J. K. Paasikivi put before parliament a proposal for a monarchical constitution and, although this was approved, the republicans (in the centre-based Agrarian and Progressive parties) succeeded in preventing the measure being declared 'urgent' and, hence, one that could be enacted in the lifetime of a single parliament. In short, it was voted over an election. The monarchists then changed tack, arguing that since the 1772 monarchical constitution (dating back to the period when Finland was linked to the Swedish crown) had not been rescinded, parliament should take steps to elect a monarch. The government was encharged with this task. Fatefully, on 9 October 1918, the Eduskunta elected a German prince, Karl Friedrich of Hesse, King of Finland, precisely the same day as the Germans approached the Entente powers for an armistice.

The German defeat scuppered the monarchists' plans, obliged Finland to seek a rapprochement with the West and (since Britain made it a condition of recognizing Finnish independence) led to a new general election in March 1919. The Social Democrats emerged as the largest group with 80 MPs, only twelve less than in 1917, despite the fact that they had been able freely to operate only a matter of months and, with the Agrarians gaining 16 seats, the republicans made up three-quarters of the MPs in the new Eduskunta. Republicanism was also supported by the small Progressive Party, along with the national daily *Helsingin Sanomat*. As promised, Britain recognized Finnish independence on 6 May 1919 and the same month the Castrén government put before parliament a bill introducing a republican constitution. The two most contentious issues turned out to be the powers of the head of state and the presidential electoral system. The former monarchists on the right favoured a president-dominant system, whereas the former Reds in the Social Democratic camp canvassed a parliament-based model. The Eduskunta's Constitutional Affairs committee came up with a compromise according to which the president would be chosen on the basis of an electoral college and would acquire significant powers, although the first president would be elected by parliament (Jussila, Hentilä, and Nevakivi 1995: 118–19). Ultimately, after some right-wing recalcitrance, a republican form of government was adopted on 21 June 1919 by the overwhelming margin of 165–22. Parliament subsequently chose between two leading candidates: K. J. Ståhlberg, a high-ranking lawyer and consistent republican, and the former White leader and monarchist sympathizer C. G. Mannerheim. The latter was naturally vehemently opposed by the Social Democrats. As the columnist in the party organ *Suomen Sosialidemokraatti*, Sasu Punanen put it: 'Better [an unknown fictitious person such as] Jahvetti Turpeinen from [the small town of] Tuusniemi than Mannerheim' (Virkkunen 1978: 17–18). Ståhlberg was comfortably elected, but with sections of the White Finnish élite openly critical of him, his position was initially very weak. (For a list of Finnish Presidents since 1919, see Figure 3.1.)

The form and content of the new constitution represented a compromise which undoubtedly favoured the former monarchists on the right (Conservatives and Swedish People's Party) over and above both the republican centre (Agrarians and Progressives), which did not have a clear picture of the institutional balance they wanted in the new constitution, and the advocates of a purely parliament-based system in the Social Democrats. The latter were in general influenced by Rousseau's notion of popular sovereignty and in 1917 adopted a constitutional model based on the predominance of parliament. The Social Democratic critique of the semi-presidentialism advocated in bourgeois circles followed much the same lines as Marx's critique of Louis Napoléon Bonaparte in 1852. In the event, however, parliament did not become the supreme organ of state. Instead, alongside it and to

Name	Term
K. J. Ståhlberg	1919–26
L. K. Relander	1926–31
P. E. Svinhufvud	1931–7
K. Kallio	1937–40
R. Ryti	1940–4
K. G. Mannerheim	1944–6
J. K. Paasikivi	1946–56
U. K. Kekkonen	1956–81
M. Koivisto	1982–94
M. Ahtisaari	1994–

FIG. 3.1. Finnish presidents, 1919–1998

an extent in competition with it, the president was granted independent decision-making powers, including the right to intervene in the legislative process.

For Ståhlberg, the first president and leading proponent of semi-presidentialism, the most significant foreign influence was the American presidential system, although, ironically, the Finnish republican constitution of 1919 displayed marked monarchist tendencies. The president in short assumed many of the powers of the former Czar, including the direction of foreign policy and the dissolution of parliament. In the latter context, a strong president was viewed, especially by the former monarchists, as a counterweight to a leftist-dominated assembly of the likes of the one elected in 1916. Similar checks on the will (tyranny!) of the majority had been built into the 1906 Orders of State in the form of a nexus of qualified majority rules designed not least to protect the property rights of the Establishment classes.

The monarchical elements in the 1919 Finnish constitution should not, however, be exaggerated. First, the head of state lost the unconditional right to veto legislation. Parliament, albeit a qualified majority of members, was vested with the (theoretical) right to determine the constitutional arrangements of the institutions of state. True, the head of state could through the use of his suspensive veto postpone by several years such amendments and changes. Secondly, the highest executive body in governing matters was divided into two and the head of state's body of advisers got its own constitutionally prescribed sphere of competence. This was in contrast to the Grand Duchy era when the Czar had simply delegated to the Senate (the domestic government in Helsinki) the executive powers vested in him by the constitution. Equally, while the supreme executive body in some matters was the president and in others the cabinet, the most important political matters—except some central economic questions—remained with the president (Jyränki 1971: 30).

Summing up, the 1919 constitution empowers the president to appoint governments, present bills to parliament, ratify measures, appoint senior officials, convene extraordinary sessions of parliament, open and close Eduskunta sessions, and head the armed forces. Crucially, too, Article 33 states that 'the relations of Finland with foreign powers shall be determined by the president'. When Article 33 is taken in conjunction with Article 2 which is in two parts—'Legislative power shall be exercised by parliament in conjunction with the President of the Republic' and 'Supreme executive power shall be vested in the President of the

Republic'—it can be seen that the president exercises legislative, executive, and federative powers in John Locke's sense of the control of
relations with other states. In addition, the second part of Article 2
stipulates that 'for the general government of the state there shall be a
Council of State comprising the prime minister and the requisite
number of ministers' (Arter 1987: 79–117).

When viewed in a contemporary light, the Finnish constitution of
1919, with its dual executive and modified version of the separation of
powers principle, represented a unique formulation. Yet as Antero
Jyränki has noted, the constitutional rules governing the powers of parliament, the president and cabinet and their interrelations were written
in a form which allowed for many interpretations (1981: 46). The way
the inter-war presidents interpreted their foreign policy direction
function, set out in Article 33, is a case in point.

During the drafting of the constitution there was not a thorough discussion of the way foreign policy would in practice be conducted. Article
33 was mechanistically adopted from the Swedish Gustavian model of
ruler-centred foreign policy direction which, on the whole, had been well
suited to the general conditions in the Grand Duchy (Kalela 1993: 226).
Ståhlberg did not pursue the conduct of foreign policy in a monarchical style, but neither did he resign himself to being a mere figurehead.
Giving a broad interpretation to the second paragraph of Article 33 that
'all communications to foreign powers or the diplomatic representatives
of Finland abroad must be made through the minister to whose competence the management of foreign affairs belongs', Ståhlberg assumed
the practice either of making his decision in the presidential sitting of
the cabinet on Friday morning, on the basis of the foreign minister's proposal, or otherwise relying on the foreign secretary's cooperation in his
decision (Kalela 1993: 226). This was in line with a ruling of the Constitutional Committee of the Eduskunta in 1919 that the foreign secretary bears responsibility for taking care of foreign matters. Furthermore,
Ståhlberg agreed to meet with representatives of foreign states only
when the foreign minister was present and refused to enter into private
correspondence with Finnish ambassadors abroad (Komitea mietintö
1994: 467–8). Curiously, Ståhlberg did not engage in a single overseas
visit during his term of office (Arter 1987: 86). It was not until the advent
of P. E. Svinhufvud (1931–7) that the president stressed his personal
right to determine the nation's foreign policy and, still more than
his two predecessors, Finnish security under Svinhufvud was grounded
on assumptions of German strength, even after Hitler came to power
(Jyränki 1981: 222).

THE SHIFT TO A PRESIDENT-DOMINANT SYSTEM, 1940–1987

Throughout the independence period the presidential office has been very small. 'The presidency', Paasikivi once retorted, 'is a bloody awful post—only two adjutants and that infernal Porilaisten march' (the latter played on the innumerable ceremonial occasions). At present there is an unofficial presidential cabinet of only four policy advisers, three specializing in foreign affairs—the secretary-general and two persons seconded from the foreign ministry—together with a legal adviser. The institutional resources of the presidency in short are very limited. Unlike France during much of the Fifth Republic, moreover, the president has not rested on a parliament majority; if anything, just the reverse since the absence of a cohesive *majorité*, and a party system which until the 1960s did not facilitate stable coalitions, strengthened the hand of the president in government-building. In the two decades after the war, a series of presidential 'caretaker' cabinets comprising civil servants (experts) and/or non-partisan public figures testified to the lack of inter-élite consensus in the parliamentary arena and the need for stop-gap solutions. True, after 1966, Kekkonen succeeded in harnessing the three main parties of the centre-left (Centre, Social Democrats, and Communists) in a relatively durable presidential majority, although with members of these so-called Popular Front governments frequently at odds with one another, Kekkonen had still to fall back from time to time on short-lived cabinets of experts. Incidentally, the Finnish head of state is by convention a *pouvoir neutre*—above the clash of competing party factions—and resigns his party membership on assuming the highest office.

Despite the limited manpower resources at his disposal, the real powers of the Finnish president grew at the expense of government and parliament in the period after the Second World War, particularly during the long era of Urho Kekkonen (1956–81) when presidentialism was particularly evident in the federative sphere. The extent of the personalization of foreign policy management and its concentration in presidential hands was already evident from the outset of the Winter War with the Soviet Union in autumn 1939. There were two main causal factors in this development. First, the crisis management conditions of war between 1939–44 led the head of state to take personal charge of the conduct of foreign policy. Significantly, Risto Ryti (1940–4) was the first president to engage in bilateral discussions with the head of a foreign power when he met Hitler in 1942. This was during the so-called

Continuation War against the Soviet Union (1941–4) when Finland fought as a 'co-belligerent' with Nazi Germany. As noted, between the wars formal decisions were made by the president, but routine foreign policy was handled by the foreign secretary or prime minister or both. For example, the Agrarian Kyösti Kallio (1937–40), a monoglot, made as a condition of his standing for the highest office that the multi-lingual Rolf Holsti would continue to handle foreign affairs.

Secondly, after the Second World War, the supreme importance of foreign policy in the context of developing and maintaining amicable relations with the Kremlin considerably enhanced the status and powers of the head of state. Finland's post-war position was precarious—these were the so-called 'danger years'—and Paasikivi accepted concessions to Moscow as inevitable. He was almost certainly articulating Soviet demands in insisting before the March 1945 general election that several wartime politicians—those associated (rightly or wrongly) in the Russian mind with the enlistment of German aid—should not submit themselves for re-election. Those mentioned as *personae non gratae* included four Agrarians, three Conservatives, four Social Democratic, and all the [neo-fascist] Patriotic People's Party delegates and despite their remonstrations, none of them stood—Paasikivi's threat of resignation proved a sufficient sanction. From the earliest post-war years, in short, the dividing line between foreign and domestic policy was extremely blurred and the president (enjoying the confidence of the Kremlin) was able to exert significant influence in ensuring that internal events did not damage amicable Finno-Soviet relations. These were anchored in the February 1948 Treaty of Friendship, Cooperation, and Mutual Assistance (FCMA) with the USSR which became the cornerstone of Finnish foreign policy until 1991. Indeed, reference came to be made to *official foreign policy*—the Paasikivi–Kekkonen line—named after the two post-war presidents and based on wholehearted support for the FCMA.

Although in practice Paasikivi took all the important decisions himself, he did seek to conduct foreign policy through the government and with the assistance of his foreign minister. However, Juhani Suomi has shown how Kekkonen, during his first year as president in 1956, took three decisions that diverged from Paasikivi's practice (Kalela 1993: 227–8). First, he personally took command of the top foreign ministry officials, bypassing the foreign secretary. His power in short extended to influencing the preparation of measures. True, there was by no means agreement on all matters between the president and senior foreign ministry officials and to a surprising extent Risto Hyvärinen and Max

Jakobson succeeded in influencing Kekkonen's decisions (Jakobson, in *Helsingin Sanomat*, 31 Oct. 1996). Secondly, he did all he could to prevent the foreign secretary being, or becoming, a strong politician. Ahti Karjalainen was the exception. Indeed, Kekkonen delegated to Karjalainen powers to negotiate with the Kremlin to secure Soviet assent for Finland's association agreement with the European Free Trade Association (EFTA) in autumn 1960 (Hämäläinen 1997: 37–9). Thirdly, Kekkonen deliberately set out to limit the role of the prime minister in foreign policy, particularly in *Ostpolitik*. Following the official visit of K. A. Fagerholm in June 1957, it was fourteen years before a Finnish prime minister (Ahti Karjalainen) visited Moscow and he was the last prime minister to do so during Kekkonen's time as president until 1981 (Rumpunen 1997). Often, the prime minister and foreign secretary were not fully cognisant of the president's plans or the activities of cabinet officials.

Furthermore, Kekkonen's role in the resolution of two crises in Finno-Soviet relations—the so-called Night Frost Crisis in autumn 1958 and the Note Crisis in autumn 1961—enabled him to keep foreign policy separate from other politics as an area reserved for the president and also to use the foreign ministry as his personal instrument. The personalized and authoritarian styles of Paasikivi, Kekkonen, and to a large extent Mauno Koivisto (1982–94) were complemented by the extremely hierarchical nature of the Soviet system—in which senior personnel took relatively minor decisions—which both encouraged and facilitated 'sauna summitry'. So, too, did the strong Soviet cultural preference for 'the devil you know', that is, dealing with people they knew for better or for worse. This would account for the multitude of unofficial visits Kekkonen made to Moscow which in turn should be set against the backdrop of the peculiar Soviet system in which the party leadership was the real government and relations with other countries were handled by the international department of the CPSU, not by the foreign ministry.

It was during his third term as president between 1968–74 that Kekkonen's direction of foreign policy was at its most personalized and authoritarian. In contrast to inter-war practice, Kekkonen was in fact criticized for meeting Soviet leaders without the presence of a minister or even a secretary. Certainly on holiday trips to the USSR he engaged in bilateral talks with the Soviet leadership at which KGB officials usually acted as interpreters (Kekkonen clearly had no control over the translation) and Vladimir Stepanov, the head of the KGB in Finland, was always present. This meant that the KGB was abreast of all the latest developments in Finno-Soviet relations. Evidence of Kekkonen's autocratic style can be gained from the way in June 1968 he proposed (unsuccessfully) to Brezhnev changes in the national frontier—the concession of part of Lapland in return for the reacquisition of the Viipuri area in 'conceded Karelia' and Finnish recognition of the two Germanies—not in his capacity as head of state, but as a 'private citizen'. It was not even mentioned in Kekkonen's detailed 16-page report on the trip and was not known to the prime minister at that time, Mauno Koivisto (Suomi 1996: 55–66). Indeed, Koivisto has admitted that on subsequently reading of the whole episode in the Juhani Suomi biography, his gut reaction was to say that 'if I had ever said anything critical of Brezhnev I will never do so again . . . !'.

Equally, this individualized management of Finno-Soviet relations and the confidence he enjoyed 'in high places' bestowed on Kekkonen autocratic powers as the sole arbiter and mediator of the national interest. The corollary of Kekkonen's preventative diplomacy and his quasi-despotic position was his readiness to subordinate the entire parliamentary system, public word, and even historical writing to the needs of a policy designed to maintain the confidence of the Soviet leadership and to avoid military consultations under Article 2 of the 1948 FCMA with the USSR. The most blatant victim of this 'Finlandized' management style was the National Coalition (Conservative) Party, which was excluded from government between 1966 and 1987 despite significant gains at the polls in 1970 and 1979. After the Night Frost Crisis, Kekkonen clearly believed that in order to direct foreign policy he had also to control domestic policy. By the late 1970s, Paavo Kastari was moved to write that 'foreign policy constitutes the Archimedian point on the basis of which the president can direct Finnish internal affairs to a hitherto unknown degree' (Kastari 1977: 151).

Thus, Kekkonen played an active role in coalition-building. His role in the Popular Fronts of the late 1960s and the exclusion of the Conservatives has already been mentioned. Moreover, in November 1975, Kekkonen used the media to declare a state of national emergency and within a single day ended a two-month post-election stalemate by contriving a broadly based Government of National Unity (the Conservatives were excluded) under Martti Miettunen specifically to deal with rising unemployment. On occasions, Kekkonen also channelled the prestige of the presidential office into the search for the resolution of domestic industrial conflict. By the time of protracted negotiations on a third incomes policy agreement during the autumn of 1970, both the majority wing of the [divided] Communist Party in parliament and the

Communists in the trade-union movement had joined the hardline [neo-Stalinist] faction in refusing to countenance continued economic stabilization. When, as a result, talks became badly bogged down, the president intervened. First he sent a letter to seventeen leading interest groups expressing concern at the delay in reaching agreement and requesting consultations to clarify the situation. Then, when talks between the central employers' organization, SAK, and peak blue-collar federation, STK, finally collapsed, Kekkonen produced a compromise proposal during a powerful speech on radio and television which he urged the labour-market organizations to accept 'in the national interest' (Arter 1981: 229).

The episode points to a number of general conclusions regarding Kekkonen's relations with the major domestic policy actors. First, the presidential intervention was a final option to save the embryonic incomes policy system. Kekkonen did not suddenly impose himself on the negotiations, but was urged to do so by the labour-market leaders when deadlock was reached. He did so fully cognisant of the fact that he was exceeding his constitutional remit. Secondly, Kekkonen kept in close touch throughout with the cabinet, Bank of Finland, interest-group leaders, the state coordinator, and, above all, the national expert on incomes policy. The last-mentioned were instrumental in producing the compromise package which, adopted by Kekkonen in his television appearance, was eventually signed by all the leading labour-market organizations. Lastly, it was symptomatic of the widespread support for an incomes policy system that the president's intervention was widely commended. Kekkonen's action presaged future incursions into the industrial relations field. Most notably in November 1976, he broke an illegal strike of railway traffic controllers (signalmen etc.), stating in quite unprecedented fashion that he would refuse to ratify any parliamentary bill meeting their claims for a reduction in the retirement age. Again, the president's move was very much a last resort when the efforts of the state coordinator failed.

In addition to his pro-active part in shaping governing coalitions and promoting broad-based solutions in the corporate channel, Kekkonen personally enforced a system of press self-censorship in relation to coverage of Soviet matters. It was significant that a joint communiqué, agreed with Kekkonen in connection with the Soviet president Podgorny's visit to Finland in 1973, stated that the media should work 'positively to influence the development of friendly relations between the two states' (Salminen 1996: 17). In all these things (except nominating the prime minister), Kekkonen clearly exceeded the formal constitutional powers of the presidency. Moreover, the president's powers to appoint senior officials—extending down to university professors!—created a deferential elite in the upper echelons of the civil service, while there developed competition between politicians and political parties for the favours of Moscow and/or Kekkonen. These were the years of compulsory consensus politics and the position of the legislature in particular was marginalized by developments. Furthermore, the qualified majority rules worked in a paradoxical way. Until their abolition in 1992, these rules enabled one-sixth of MPs to prevent constitution-level legislation being declared 'urgent' (and, thus, capable of being enacted in the lifetime of a single parliament) and one-third of MPs to vote bills over a general election. Since there has been a premium on forming governments that were numerically strong enough to direct the economy, this raised the threshold of minimality for winning coalitions above that elsewhere in Western Europe. In order effectively to govern, governments had perforce to include three of the four big parties—that is to be large coalitions—and have the backing of two-thirds, i.e. 133 delegates, in the 200-seat Eduskunta. Yet, as Dag Anckar has observed, designed to provide the political minority with safeguards against the governing majority and to weigh the legislative balance in favour of parliament, the qualified majority provisions, in promoting large coalitions, tended in practice to have the opposite effect (1992: 151–90).

Yet, although by the 1970s it seems legitimate to speak of an 'all-powerful Finnish presidency', and Kekkonen's influence behind the scenes was extensive, the head of state in Finland, unlike his American counterpart, has never functioned as a legislator in the sense of instigating and overseeing a major policy programme. His New Year address may seek to be 'tone-setting', expressing concern about levels of unemployment, evidence of veiled racism, or the incidence of social exclusion, but it simply cannot be compared in substance or intent with the State of the Union message in the United States.

FROM PRESIDENT-DOMINANT TO PLURALIST FOREIGN POLICY-MAKING, 1987–1998

A series of constitutional reforms during the second term of Mauno Koivisto's presidency (1988–94) strengthened the position of the government vis-à-vis the president. Indeed, Koivisto was elected in 1982 with an express commitment to reverse the authoritarianism of the Kekkonen era and introduce more parliamentary practices. It took him five years, however, to achieve the undisputed authority needed to effect a series of constitutional amendments which cumulatively prevented a recurrence of the worst excesses of the Kekkonen era.

The head of state was limited to a maximum of two consecutive terms of office, that is twelve years. The American-style electoral college system—a popular ballot selecting a 301-seat electoral college—was 'democratized', since Koivisto was adamantly opposed to the possibility of so-called 'black horses' (persons who had not stood as a candidate in the first round) being entered at the second round of electoral college voting. By 1994 the president (Ahtisaari) had been chosen on the basis of the two-stage direct elections used in France. The president was prevented from dissolving parliament and calling new elections except following an approach by the prime minister and the president was prevented from dismissing a government which enjoyed the confidence of parliament. This had been the fate of the Karjalainen II coalition in autumn 1971, which was forced out of office by Kekkonen despite possessing majority backing in the Eduskunta. In short, the position of the parliamentary executive was reinforced and the prime minister at the time, Esko Aho (1991–5), was able to write in the early 1990s that 'when the governmental system functions normally, the president can remain in the background' (Aho 1993: 83–98). This has been the case. All the coalition governments since 1982 have been broad-based majorities that have run their full course and neither coalition-building nor maintaining the coalition in office have been problematical.

Equally, first European Economic Area (EEA) and then EU membership have emphasized the bifurcation of the Finnish political executive, significantly enhancing the government's capacity to run, and the Eduskunta's ability to influence and scrutinize European policy. The EEA application in 1990 blurred the dividing line between foreign and domestic policy and led to demands for governmental involvement in, and parliamentary scrutiny of, European policy. In the context of EEA membership, a constitutional amendment was passed in the form of Article 33a which stipulated that 'Parliament shall participate in the national preparation of decisions . . . and the Council of State [government] shall determine the content of the national preparation of a decision to be made by an international organ [in this case the EEA]'. President Koivisto's reaction to this was favourable, although it should be borne in mind that the EEA agreement did not include agriculture, environmental policy, aspects of regional policy, and, above all, foreign and security policy. At the time (before the disintegration of the Soviet

Union), it appeared to offer Finland many economic benefits—
including access to the single internal market and non-applicability to
the sensitive area of agriculture (national subsidies were higher than
CAP levels)—without the political costs of involvement in a putative
political union that appeared to risk compromising Finnish neutrality
and amicable relations with the Kremlin.

Article 33a, however, was rapidly overtaken by events and Finland's
imminent membership of the EU. A committee was set up under the
chairmanship of Seppo Tiitinen, the chief secretary of the Eduskunta,
and consequently in December 1994, Article 48 of the Parliament Act
was amended to imply *de facto* government responsibility for all EU
policy:

The Eduskunta's Foreign Affairs Committee shall, on request and otherwise
when circumstances warrant, receive a report from the government on relations
with foreign powers and information on matters concerning the common
foreign and security policy of the European Union.

The Foreign Affairs Committee could not, of course, receive such a
report if the prime minister did not personally attend meetings of the
European Council. This was the Tiitinen committee's recommendation
and the Aho government proceeded to introduce legislation accordingly. However, the amended Article 48 was ultimately approved on the
basis of an initiative from the Eduskunta's Constitutional Committee
when the minister of justice, Anneli Jäätteenmäki, withdrew the government proposal following opposition from the president. Indeed, just
before Christmas 1994, president Ahtisaari entered a dissenting statement to the cabinet's decision to approve the amended Article 48 on
the basis of the majority will of parliament. In short, following a highly
fractious episode between the two arms of the political executive, parliament elevated the prime minister above the president as Finland's
senior figure in EU affairs. When following the general election in
March 1995 the Aho non-socialist coalition was voted out of office, the
incoming government under Paavo Lipponen reached a pragmatic compromise with the president: the prime minister would always attend
meetings of the European Council, while the president could attend
when he so wished.

Four months before Finland's EU application in March 1992, the collapse of the Soviet Union betokened the need for a less personalized
and less hierarchical handling of Finno-Soviet relations, although
Koivisto practised caution to the last. When in the early 1980s, on
coming to the highest office, a journalist requested him to describe the

substance of Finland's foreign policy in three words, the president retorted 'hyvät suhteet naapureihin' (good relations with our neighbours) and he remained faithful to this maxim until the final disintegration of the USSR. His statement that the violent events in Vilnius in February 1991 were 'an internal Soviet matter' both incensed and embarrassed many Finns who felt that their nation should have given its support to the cause of Baltic independence. In any event, the end of the Cold War spawned a legislature which viewed semi-presidentialism as aberrant and anachronistic and sought 'normalization', that is the establishment of an orthodox parliamentary democracy. The generational factor was crucial since the younger parliamentarians in particular reacted strongly against the dark-age elitism of the Kekkonen era and favoured a conventional parliamentary system.

Further steps in this direction were recommended by the *Constitution 2000* committee, chaired by the Green MP (now Chancellor of Justice), which in June 1997 produced a unanimous report on a new constitution which will come into force on 1 March 2000, the first day of the next presidential term. Its primary aim of further 'strengthening the parliamentary features of the governmental system' was achieved in two ways. The choice of the prime minister will shift from being the exclusive preserve of the president to become the responsibility of the Eduskunta and the parliamentary party groups in particular. Moreover, Article 33 will shortly be amended to read 'the president directs foreign policy in cooperation with the government' (the original Nikula wording 'together with the government' was not approved by the cabinet as a whole). The *Constitution 2000* committee also proposed that the preparation of EU decisions would formally be shared between the government and parliament.

Summing up, two conclusions appear in order. First, the result of EEA and subsequently EU membership, along with the attendant institutional adaptation, has been to emphasize the bicephalous character of the Finnish political executive. Put simply, the blurred dividing line between domestic and foreign policy—especially in relation to the European Union—has elevated the position of the prime minister and government in relation to the president. The president directs foreign policy through the government and the foreign and security policy cabinet committee in particular; the prime minister directs EU policy (the first and third pillars) through the EU cabinet committee. By dint of his forceful advocacy of Finnish membership of economic and monetary union (EMU), moreover, Lipponen emerged as probably the dominant foreign policy opinion leader during his term as premier.

Secondly, not only has the impact of EU membership been to emphasize the dual nature of the Finnish political executive, it has also significantly enhanced the capacity of the legislature to influence and scrutinize foreign policy. The Grand Committee, originally designed as a 45-strong Council of Elders and vesting the Eduskunta with modified unicameralist features, has been reduced to 25 members and deals with EU first and third pillar questions. The Foreign Affairs Committee, which comprises 17 members, deals with pillar two. All in all, in the words of Jaakko Kalela, the secretary-general to the president: 'In the extent of its efficiency and pluralism, the present system of foreign policy-making has no counterpart in Finnish history, or indeed in many other countries' (1996: 43).

TOWARDS A CEREMONIAL PRESIDENCY?

In bringing our discussion to a conclusion, several main points are worth recapitulating. First, Article 33 of the 1919 Finnish constitution grants the head of state federative powers to direct relations with foreign states, although between the wars foreign policy management was of a semi-presidential character with the foreign minister actively involved in decisions. The crisis caused by losing two wars against the Soviet Union and the subsequent need to maintain amicable relations with the Kremlin elevated the office of the presidency in the post-war period. Under the presidencies of Paasikivi and particularly the long-serving Kekkonen, foreign policy was separated off from other policy areas as a presidential *domaine réservé* using the foreign ministry as his instrument. Kekkonen's powers in short extended to influencing the preparation of foreign policy measures. The styles of Paasikivi, Kekkonen, and indeed, Koivisto moreover, were personalized and authoritarian and there is a strong case for describing the highest office under Kekkonen in the 1970s as an 'all-powerful presidency' *à la* Duverger. Certainly during Kekkonen's time it was customary to refer to the 'official foreign policy'.

Secondly, as a reaction to 'Kekkocracy' the parliamentarization of the non-federative powers of the presidency proceeded apace during Koivisto's second term of office between 1988–94. Furthermore, the Finnish applications for EEA and subsequently EU membership led, via Article 33a and the amendment to Article 48 of the Parliament Act, to the president's constitutional monopoly of foreign policy direction being broken. When Ahtisaari succeeded Koivisto there was a battle (royal!) between the president and government for control over European Union affairs and in particular who was to represent Finland in European Council (summit) meetings.

Thirdly, there is clearly a potential conflict between Articles 33 and 33a of the constitution and the equivocal wording of the Nikula committee's reformulation of the entire paragraph, giving the president and government joint management powers, does nothing to clarify a division of labour. Those concerned to defend the status quo of the bicephalous management of European policy argue that the present allocation of responsibilities (effectively confirmed by Nikula) enable the prime minister to devote time to domestic policy matters, while the president is able to engage in valuable state visits, *inter alia*, to promote foreign trade. Were it not for European Council meetings, they contend, everything would work perfectly well. However, there are those (particularly younger generation) Eduskunta members, as well as academics like the aforementioned Wiberg, who wish to see the parliamentarization of the foreign policy-making process taken to its logical conclusion, the government given exclusive federative powers and the president reduced to a symbolic figurehead. The Centre Party MP, Juhani Korkeaoja, a member of both the Eduskunta's Constitutional Affairs and Foreign Affairs standing committees, has publicly advocated a ceremonial presidency along the lines of Germany and Iceland, while the political scientist, Teija Tiilikainen, has predicted that, as the EU proceeds further towards a common foreign and security policy and national sovereignty in foreign relations is conceded to supranational authorities, the president's power base will simply disappear (*Helsingin Sanomat*, 27 Feb. 1998).

Fourthly, while the prerogative powers of the president in domestic politics—the nomination of the prime minister, dissolution of the Eduskunta, the vetoing of legislation, etc.—were not designed to give the head of state significant policy influence, and the Finnish president has not been a legislator in the manner of his American and French counterparts, presidential influence in domestic matters should not be underestimated. It has been most evident in the sphere of coalition-building, aided in some measure by the polarized nature of the Finnish party system and its concomitant government instability. Thus, Kekkonen's role in incorporating the Communist-dominated Finnish People's Democratic League (SKDL) into a series of so-called Popular Front centre-left coalitions after 1966 was decisive. Conversely, there was the exclusion of the Conservatives who languished in the political wilderness between 1966 and 1987. But beyond the realm of government formation, both Kekkonen and Koivisto used the prestige of the presidential office to resolve conflict between the main economic policy actors. Although Ahtisaari has restricted himself to backing the government in the negotiations towards broad incomes policy agreements, one of his first initiatives on assuming office was set up a committee to come up with a blueprint for reducing (mass) unemployment.

The conditions for a strong presidency no longer exist. Although now directly elected, the head of state is restricted to two consecutive terms of office; his formal powers are much reduced; stable, broad-based government has been the norm in Finland for over three decades; and, above all, the Friendship, Cooperation, and Mutual Assistance Treaty with the Soviet Union is no longer the cornerstone of Finnish foreign policy. In contrast, the threat of joint military consultations under Article 2 of the latter hung like a sword of Damocles over Kekkonen and as a consequence of the supreme importance of the president's task of maintaining amicable Finno-Soviet relations the dividing line between foreign and domestic policy was like a line drawn on water. It could not be drawn. All this is behind Finland and as Erkki Pennanen concluded recently:

The Finnish dual executive is based today on nothing more than historical factors. It is no longer a question of fear of Finland's eastern neighbour, but of getting stuck in the rut of a psychological dependency on a ruler who appears above the daily round of party politics. The forces of change should not, however, be underestimated. An increasing number of Finns believe that the election as president of a presentable woman is quite conceivable! (Pennanen, in *Helsingin Sanomat*, 6 Apr. 1998)

4

France

ROBERT ELGIE

The Constitution of the Fifth French Republic was adopted by referendum in September 1958. Article 6 of the Constitution stated that the President of the Republic would be elected by an electoral college comprising nearly 80,000 people, consisting mainly of parliamentarians and representatives of local government. Meanwhile, Article 20 stated that the prime minister was accountable to the National Assembly and Articles 49 and 50 made it clear that if the prime minister was defeated in a vote of confidence, then there was no option but to resign. By virtue of these characteristics, then, the original text of the 1958 Constitution unequivocally established a parliamentary regime. However, in October 1962 the Constitution was amended by way of another referendum. Article 6 was changed to allow for the direct election of the president by universal suffrage. At this point, therefore, the Fifth Republic was transformed into a semi-presidential regime.

As one writer has nicely put it, if the 1962 constitutional amendment granted the president no new powers, then 'it did afford him an important new *power*' (Wright 1989: 13), namely popular legitimacy. Prior to the 1962 reform the president was a major political actor. For the most part this was due to the personal characteristics of the first incumbent of the office, Charles de Gaulle. After the 1962 reform, though, the *presidency* was a major political actor. The president's capacity to influence the system was institutionalized. Presidential elections became the focal point of the regime. The president's campaign promises became the manifesto which the government was mandated to implement. And yet, since this time the extent of presidential power has still varied. The nature of the French semi-presidential system is such that the president cannot exercise power without the help of the prime minister. As a general rule, in the early years of the system prime ministers were willing subjects and presidents reigned supreme. Increasingly, though, presidents have been obliged to appoint political enemies as prime minister and presidential rule has been openly challenged.

In this chapter, the relationship between the president and the prime minister in the Fifth Republic will be explored. In the first section, an overview of presidential/prime ministerial relations will be provided. In the second section, the constitutional situation, the founding context of the 1962 reform, and the relationship between the president and the parliamentary majority will be discussed. In the conclusion, the wider context of presidential/prime ministerial relations will be considered and the changing parameters of executive leadership generally will be discussed. In these ways, the contemporary nature of the Fifth Republic's semi-presidential system will be established.

PATTERNS OF POLITICAL LEADERSHIP

The Fifth Republic is characterized by a twin-headed executive, or executive dyarchy, in the sense that the president and prime minister are both important figures in their own right. However, the Fifth Republic can best be classed as a hierarchical dyarchy (Massot 1993) in that on occasions leadership responsibilities have been incumbent upon the president and at other times they have rested with the prime minister. Broadly speaking, the presidency was strongest during the early years of the regime, whereas prime ministerial government has occurred at regular intervals since the mid-1980s.

The president is a powerful political actor. This is particularly true in the domain of 'high' politics. The president is France's most prominent international spokesperson, leading the French delegation at summit meetings, maintaining close bilateral contacts with the world's most powerful leaders and receiving transcripts of reports from French embassies overseas. Successive presidents have maintained control over defence policy issues, arising out of the president's responsibility for France's nuclear deterrent. They have also been active in foreign affairs, consistently asserting France's independence from the two superpowers in the 1960s and 1970s and then promoting the country's interests in the post-communist system. They have also shaped both France's policy towards the European Communities/Union and the policies of the institutions at the European level as well. Overall, this influence in the realm of 'high' politics has led successive presidents to speak and appear as if they incarnated France itself. Consequently, the presidential verb is always a grandiloquent one and the presidential portrait has a regal aspect. (For a list of presidents and prime ministers since 1958, see Figure 4.1.)

President	Prime minister
Charles de Gaulle (1959–69)	Michel Debré (1959–62)
	Georges Pompidou (1962–8)
	Maurice Couve de Murville (1968–9)
Georges Pompidou (1969–74)	Jacques Chaban-Delmas (1969–72)
	Pierre Messmer (1972–4)
Valéry Giscard d'Estaing (1974–81)	Jacques Chirac (1974–6)
	Raymond Barre (1976–81)
François Mitterrand (1981–95)	Pierre Mauroy (1981–4)
	Laurent Fabius (1984–6)
	Jacques Chirac (1986–8)
	Michel Rocard (1988–91)
	Edith Cresson (1991–2)
	Pierre Bérégovoy (1992–3)
	Edouard Balladur (1993–5)
Jacques Chirac (1995–)	Alain Juppé (1995–7)
	Lionel Jospin (1997–)

FIG. 4.1. Presidents and prime ministers in France, 1958–1998

If presidents have been careful to cultivate their role in 'high' politics, they are also obliged to delve into the domain of 'low' politics too. The rationale for this is straightforward. Presidential elections are won and lost on 'bread and butter' issues: the economy, social policy, cultural matters, and so on. Presidential candidates fight elections on the basis of a platform which addresses these issues. Consequently, once elected, presidents have a quasi-contractual responsibility to ensure that their election promises are kept. They also have an electoral incentive to do so because their chances of re-election are affected by the perception of their performance in this respect. Presidents, then, have to show an interest in basic policy matters. At the same time, though, they tend to intervene only obliquely in this domain. Rarely, if ever, have they taken personal charge of domestic policy-making. More frequently, they have preferred to encourage or chide the government by way of a carefully chosen phrase in a interview or a visit to a symbolically important location. The result is that the media army of Elysée-watchers is constantly on the lookout for presidential titbits, deciphering the president's words and decoding the president's image.

At the same time the prime minister is also a powerful political actor. In contrast to the president, whose administrative support structures are light, the prime minister is at the head of an extensive set of governmental, administrative, and information services. The policy-making process cannot function without these services. Consequently, the prime minister occupies the most strategically important position within the system when it comes to the nitty-gritty business of policy preparation and implementation. The result of this position is that the prime minister is inextricably linked with the day-to-day conduct of the government's business. Outside 'cohabitation' (see below) the president will have a considerable personal interest in whether or not the government's policy decisions are successful, but it is the prime minister whose political future is most immediately associated with the administration's short-term policy performance.

The prime minister is also closely associated with the work of parliament and with the conduct of legislative elections. The president takes no part in the parliamentary process. The prime minister, though, has both to defend the government's record there and to ensure a majority for the government's policies. Once again, this means that the prime minister is associated with the everyday business of government. The prime minister becomes the most public representative of the government's policies. In addition, the prime minister usually leads the government's troops in the general election campaign. The president will sometimes decide the timing of the election and may appear on television and urge people to vote for his supporters. It is the prime minister, though, who criss-crosses the country's constituencies in the search for votes. It is also the prime minister who is most closely in contact with the party organizations which support the government. Again, the president may sometimes arrange the set, but the prime minister is the one who is on stage for the performance.

In this way, then, the Fifth Republic is an amalgamation of both presidential and prime ministerial responsibilities. In this sense, there is a twin-headed executive. As one prominent writer has noted: 'Governing, at the end of the day, is the process of drawing up and implementing policy. These two aspects are inseparable. If this definition is accepted, it must be admitted that the President of the Republic and the Prime Minister govern France together' (de Baecque 1976: 165). The same writer has also stated that 'it is by the common action of the head of state and the head of government that the executive discharges its responsibilities' (de Baecque 1986: 283). Another prominent writer has argued that 'there is an extraordinary complexity in the relations between the head of state and the head of government. If the normal situation is indeed that there is a certain hierarchy which guarantees presidential pre-eminence, it is also the case that . . . the President cannot do without a Prime Minister . . . [T]he sharing of roles, in other words a dyarchy, is also a necessity' (Massot 1993: 174). As this last quotation suggests, though, even if the essence of the French semi-presidentialism system is an executive dyarchy, it is a hierarchical dyarchy in which power is usually skewed more in favour of one political actor than another.

For the most part, the political balance has been on the side of the presidency. In this respect, the most powerful presidents are generally to be found in the early years of the Fifth Republic. The first president, Charles de Gaulle, was a particularly dominant figure. He benefited from an unrivalled personal authority derived from his wartime record and subsequent opposition to the unloved Fourth Republic (1946–58). In the first years of the Fifth Republic he confined himself largely to foreign and defence policy-making and to the resolution of the Algerian war with the prime minister assuming responsibility for domestic affairs. After the granting of Algerian independence, though, de Gaulle increasingly intervened in this area too. De Gaulle's successor, Georges Pompidou, was also a strong political figure. Although he lacked de Gaulle's political stature, he was equally keen to ensure that he left a personal imprint on the policy-making process. Indeed, for at least one writer, the Fifth Republic under Pompidou was even more presidentialized than under de Gaulle (Décaumont 1979). In addition to the early years of the Fifth Republic, the first period of François Mitterrand's presidency from 1981 to 1986 provides the other main example of a powerful president. The president swept the left into power for the first time in the history of the Fifth Republic and the government embarked on an ambitious programme of policy reforms which the president oversaw. The two prime ministers during this period were both intimately involved in the policy-making process, but ultimately were still subordinate (Elgie 1993).

Since the first two presidents of the Fifth Republic (and with the exception of the early Mitterrand years), the presidency has been less powerful but has still been the most prominent figure in the political system. For example, in 1974 the election of the first non-Gaullist president, Valéry Giscard d'Estaing, marked a departure from the then norm of the Fifth Republic. For some, Giscard's presidency confirmed the presidentialization of the system. As one writer noted: '[t]he French are scarcely aware of the fact, but their President is,

by a long way, the most powerful chief executive in the West . . .'
(A. Duhamel 1980: 23). In fact, though, Giscard's hold on power was
weaker than his two predecessors. He fought a phoney war with his
first prime minister, Jacques Chirac, before the latter resigned in protest.
He then allowed his second prime minister, Raymond Barre, whom
Giscard introduced to the public as 'the best economist in France', to
manage, poorly as it turned out, the country's economic and social
affairs while the president confined himself mainly to foreign, defence,
and European policy. A similar pattern characterized the first period of
the second Mitterrand presidency (1988–93). In 1988 Mitterrand was
easily re-elected but was then immediately obliged to appoint one of his
long-term rivals, Michel Rocard, as prime minister. Mitterrand and
Rocard were uneasy bedfellows and the president hastened the prime
minister out of office in 1991. In his place, Mitterrand appointed Edith
Cresson who proceeded to break all records for prime ministerial.
unpopularity. By the time Cresson had been replaced by Pierre
Bérégovoy the president had long since become preoccupied with the
development of the European Union to the exclusion of most other
issues.

The first period of Jacques Chirac's presidency also fits into this category (1995–7). The return of a Gaullist to the Elysée Palace did not see
a return to the presidential hegemony of the de Gaulle and Pompidou
years. The Gaullist party was no longer monolithic and the president
was faced with a much more fragmented set of power structures than
was previously the case (Elgie and Wright 1996). And yet, with the
support of a loyal prime minister, the people still expected the president
to keep his electoral promises and solve the country's problems. Chirac
responded but not in a way that the public appreciated. For example, in
October 1995 he bowed to various pressures and personally announced
that France was unequivocally committed to the Maastricht criteria.
This, though, seemed to be a reversal of his election position and
satisfied neither his own supporters nor those who opposed him. In this
way, the early part of Chirac's presidency indicates that the president
was still the ultimate reference point but the independent decision-
making capacity of the office was more limited than before (see the conclusion to this chapter). When the president tried to reassert both his
and the government's authority by dissolving the National Assembly in
March 1997, the result was an unexpected but devastating defeat for the
president's supporters.

In general, then, the Fifth Republic's dyarchy has operated to the
advantage of the president. On three recent occasions, though (1986–8,

Cohabitation

1993–5, and 1997–), this has not been the case and a period of political 'cohabitation' has occurred. 'Cohabitation' is the situation where a president from one political party holds office at the same time as a prime minister from an opposing political party. During 'cohabitation' the balance of power tilts towards the prime minister. This is because presidential control is at least partly based on the support of a loyal parliamentary majority. It is the presence of such a majority which has allowed successive presidents to appoint the prime minister of their choice. However, when the majority opposes the president, then the president no longer enjoys such a luxury. In this situation, it is the prime minister who, with the backing of the parliamentary majority, assumes responsibility not just for policy coordination and implementation, as usual, but for policy initiation as well.

During 'cohabitation' there is in general terms a relatively clear division of responsibility between the president and the prime minister. In the domain of domestic policy, it is the prime minister who takes the lead. It is the prime minister's programme which serves as the government's plan of action and the prime minister decides which elements of that programme will be legislated. By contrast, the president's role is minimal. The president can criticize the government's plans and has certain powers to delay the passage of legislation. However, the president loses any *de facto* power to veto legislation or even to influence it in any way. By contrast, in the domain of foreign, defence, and European policy the president does maintain a certain degree of control. Prime ministers usually try to shape strategic policy decisions by making international speeches or proposing plans for reform. Nevertheless, the president is still treated as the main spokesperson for French interests abroad and reserves the right to oversee the overall direction of policy in this domain.

Within this general context, the particular relationship between the president and prime minister has varied somewhat from one period of 'cohabitation' to another. During the first period (1986–8), prime minister Chirac was responsible for taking all key domestic policy decisions. For example, he personally decided which of the state-controlled television channels should be privatized and he was responsible for the most difficult arbitrations in the budgetary policy-making process (Elgie 1993). At the same time, though, president Mitterrand was a constant thorn in his side. Mitterrand established himself as a clear opponent of the prime minister's domestic programme even if he was unable to alter the content of the government's policies. By contrast, in the realm of foreign and defence policy-making the president maintained an influence, insisting, for example, that France's short-range nuclear arms were not 'tactical', battlefield weapons, but were part of a wider, 'strategic' whole (Howorth 1993: 158). During the second period (1993–5), prime minister Balladur was as influential as Chirac had been previously, determining France's position during the GATT world trade negotiations and deciding the manner in which the July 1993 constitutional amendment, limiting the right of political asylum, was adopted. On this occasion, though, Mitterrand's position was weaker than before. The right's victory in 1993 was much greater than in 1986 and the president's room for manoeuvre was reduced accordingly. He was also weakened by age (he was 76 in 1993) and illness. Consequently, even in foreign and defence policy-making, the president was less influential than before. For example, Balladur assumed responsibility for sending French troops to manage the security and humanitarian problem in Rwanda. During the third period (1997–), prime minister Jospin's influence has been as great as might by now be expected but president Chirac has had considerable difficulty in carving out a coherent role for himself. Even though Jospin heads a multi-party coalition, his party, the Socialist party, is the dominant force and so the prime minister is in a position to shape the policy process perhaps to an even greater extent than 'cohabitation' prime ministers previously. By contrast, Chirac is a spent force. He is now only a point of 'reference' for his own Gaullist party supporters and he is blamed for the electoral defeat by the right as a whole. As usual, he has distanced himself from the government's domestic policy and has tried to maintain an influence in foreign, defence, and European policy. These efforts, though, do not hide the fact that he is a lame-duck president who wields scarcely more power than the aged and infirm president Mitterrand at the end of his term of office.

Evidence suggests, therefore, that the Fifth Republic's executive dyarchy has not been characterized by a single mode of political leadership. Even though overall there has been a propensity towards presidential government, the pattern of political responsibilities has always been a function of the particularities of presidential/prime ministerial relationship that have occurred at any one time. Moreover, evidence suggests that in recent years the general tendency towards presidential government has itself been weakened and that the opportunity for prime ministerial government has become more marked. In the next section, the factors which help both to establish these basic tendencies and to create the particularities of the relationship will be considered.

FRENCH SEMI-PRESIDENTIALISM IN CONTEXT

Constitutional Powers

As noted in the introduction to this chapter, to the extent that the 1962 reform conferred no new powers on the president, then it is still the basic text of the 1958 constitution which sets out the respective positions of the president and prime minister. The essence of this text is twofold. First, it establishes the conditions for a strong executive. Secondly, within the executive it provides both the president and the prime minister with a set of constitutionally defined powers.

The Fifth Republic was deliberately designed to be the antithesis of its immediate predecessor, the Fourth Republic. By common consent, the Fourth Republic suffered from chronic governmental instability. There were twenty-five governments in the twelve-year history of the regime. As a result, one of the main motivations of all of the founding parents of the Fifth Republic was the desire to create the conditions for executive stability. For example, when presenting the new constitution to the Council of State in August 1958, Michel Debré noted that 'the purpose of this constitution . . . is, first and foremost, to try to reconstruct the governmental authority without which there is neither State nor democracy, that is, as far as we are concerned, neither France nor Republic'. To this end, the powers of parliament were weakened, leading one observer to note that '[u]nder the new régime the Parliament of France, once among the most powerful in the world, became one of the weakest' (Williams 1968: 21), and the powers of the executive were strengthened. The 1958 constitution, then, establishes a framework for executive dominance over parliament.

Within the executive, the 1958 constitution provides both the resources for presidential influence and the basis for prime ministerial government. The president has a number of specific constitutional powers. For example, the president names the prime minister (Article 8) and appoints a certain number of civil and military figures (Article 13) as well as three members of the Constitutional Council including its president (Article 56). The president can dissolve the National Assembly, although not more than once a year (Article 12); can oblige parliament to reconsider a bill, although only within 15 days of the bill being passed (Article 10); can submit a bill to the Constitutional Council for consideration (Article 61); can assume all law-making powers in the case of a national emergency (Article 16); and is charged with the responsibility for negotiating and ratifying treaties (Article 52). In addition, the president also has one very general prerogative. Article 5 states that the president is charged with seeing that the constitution is respected, with ensuring, by his arbitration, the regular functioning of public authorities and the continuity of the state and with guaranteeing national independence, territorial integrity, and the respect for international treaties. As one writer notes, this article 'constitutionalizes the spirit of the presidential function' (Ardant 1987: 38) but it does so at the expense of 'contributing to the blurring of the president's place in the institutional structures' (ibid.). In other words, Article 5 encourages the perception that the president is above the political process but at the same time it can also legitimize almost any intervention that the president might wish to make.

The prime minister also has a set of constitutional powers. In this respect, three articles are particularly important. Article 20 states that the government decides and directs the policy of the nation, that it has the administration and the armed forces at its disposal, and that it is accountable to the lower house of the legislature, the National Assembly; Article 21 states that the prime minister is in general charge of the government's work and the implementation of laws; and Article 8 states that the prime minister has the right to propose the names of government ministers to the president for approval. So, the prime minister is placed at the head of a government, the members of which he or she has chosen and which is collectively responsible for the day-to-day realization and implementation of public policy. In addition to these articles, the prime minister has a further set of powers in relation to parliament by virtue of being head of government. The prime minister has the right to issue decrees in the areas in which parliament is not permitted to legislate (Articles 21 and 37); to request an extraordinary session of parliament (Article 29); to initiate legislation (Article 39); to accelerate the legislative process (Article 38); and to call for a vote of confidence in the government (Article 49). Lastly, the prime minister can also submit a bill to the Constitutional Council (Article 61) and can make various civilian and military appointments (Article 21).

In addition to the individual powers of the president and prime minister, there are also certain powers which are quite explicitly shared between the two institutions. For example, with a few notable exceptions, such as the right to dissolve the National Assembly, the prime minister must countersign all presidential decisions (Article 19), which in theory at least gives the prime minister the right to veto all but a few presidential actions and which can be particularly important during periods of 'cohabitation'. By contrast, though, the president has to sign all decrees that are considered in the Council of Ministers (Article 13), which somewhat restricts the role of the prime minister and which, again, is potentially most significant during periods of presidential/prime ministerial conflict. Similarly, Article 21 states that the prime minister is responsible for national defence but Article 15 declares that the president is the head of the armed forces. Equally, even though the prime minister is at the head of a government which decides and directs the policy of the nation, it is the president who chairs the Council of Ministers, the French equivalent of the cabinet (Article 9). Finally, the president can call a referendum on any bill but only on the proposition of the government collectively (Article 11) or the prime minister personally (Article 89).

It is apparent, then, that under the 1958 constitution the executive is expected to lead and both the president and the prime minister are required to perform key leadership functions. The result, though, according to one contemporary observer at least, was that 'one cannot avoid being struck by the vast amount of ambiguity' which is contained in the constitution (Hoffman, 1959: 332). Similarly, according to another observer, the distribution of executive power means that '[t]he central question of any constitution—who rules?—is fudged' (Wright 1989: 12). In other words, it is the 1958 constitution which is primarily responsible for creating the finely balanced constitutional dyarchy. In general terms, the prime minister is charged with guiding and coordinating all matters which concern the immediate governance of the country, whereas the president is given the task of overseeing and protecting the long-term interests of the regime. This general division of labour neatly corresponds to the basic pattern of presidential responsibility for 'high' politics and prime ministerial control over domestic decisions. And yet, this general division of labour represents only half the picture. The overlap between presidential and prime ministerial powers is so great that there is ample scope for either institution to control the policy-making process when the necessary conditions are in place and for both institutions to fight for control when they are not.

The Founding Context

The text of the 1958 constitution sets the scene for the Fifth Republic's executive dyarchy. At the same time, though, the founding context of the 1962 reform helps to account for the presidentialized nature of the decision-making process for much of the Fifth Republic. In this respect, there are two important elements to the founding context: the experience of presidential decision-making in the period immediately prior to the 1962 reform and the events surrounding the passage of the reform itself.

First, the circumstances leading up to the 1962 reform were significant. Even though the 1958 constitution established a balanced executive dyarchy, in practice political power was soon presidentialized. In September 1958 when the General first outlined the constitution he stated that the president would be a 'national arbiter, far removed from political bickering'. In the same speech, though, he also stated that the constitution would allow the country to be 'effectively governed by those to whom it gives the mandate and to whom it grants confidence . . .'. De Gaulle believed that the people had given him a mandate by agreeing to the 1958 constitution in the September referendum and that this mandate had been confirmed as a result of both his election by what he considered to be a wide-ranging electoral college in December 1958 and then subsequent referendums which were held in January 1961 and April 1962 on Algerian self-determination. For these reasons, de Gaulle felt free to interpret his role quite liberally. The result was that by the time of the 1962 constitutional reform, the president was already the country's dominant political reference point not the prime minister. In this way, the precedent of presidential government had been set even before the reform was passed and the practice of presidential pre-eminence was simply institutionalized by way of the constitutional amendment.

Secondly, the precise circumstances surrounding the 1962 reform were also significant. Events unfolded as follows. On 22 August 1962 there was an assassination attempt on de Gaulle's life. On 12 September de Gaulle announced that a referendum would be organized on the direct election of the president. On 20 September it was announced that Article 11 of the constitution would be used to hold the referendum. On 26 September a government minister resigned in opposition to the reform. On 1 October the Council of State advised the government that the referendum proposal was unconstitutional. On 6 October the government was defeated in the National Assembly and the prime minister tendered his resignation. On 7 October de Gaulle announced that parliament would be dissolved and that there would be a legislative election. On 28 October the referendum was approved by 61.8 per cent of those voting. On 18 and 25 November the parties of the governing coalition made big gains in the legislative election such that the government enjoyed an overall parliamentary majority. The significance of these events lies in the fact that they ensured that the debate surrounding divisive constitutional issues was overshadowed by the debate concerning the very future of the regime and the president's place within it.

In the period from August to October there were two main constitutional issues. The first concerned the reform itself. In 1848 the Second Republic introduced the direct election of the president. However, the first directly elected president, Louis-Napoléon Bonaparte, then engineered a *coup d'état* in 1851, so discrediting the concept for many years thereafter and leading to indirectly elected presidents in the Third and Fourth Republics. Indeed, as late as 1958 there was still no question of installing either a presidential or semi-presidential regime during the constitutional deliberations and in September 1962 the left was opposed to de Gaulle's reform as were many elements of the centre-right. Indeed, a wide-ranging 'cartel des non' was formed to campaign for a 'no' vote at the referendum. Against this background, it may be the case that de Gaulle had previously avoided proposing such a reform for tactical reasons (Rudelle 1984: 689) and it is certainly the case both that the granting of Algerian independence in early 1962 raised one obstacle to the reform (voters in Algeria would otherwise have been eligible to vote) and that France's acquisition of a nuclear capacity in 1961 meant that the president's responsibilities were now of a completely different nature than before. Nevertheless, it is quite apparent that de Gaulle was in a minority when he put forward the amendment and that many people were vehemently opposed to it.

The second constitutional issue concerned de Gaulle's use of Article 11. This article then stated that the president could organize a referendum on any issue relating to the 'public powers'. For most people, including the lawyers in the Council of State and the Constitutional Council, the direct election of the president was not such an issue. In this way, then, de Gaulle was not only proposing a controversial reform, he was also proposing it in a constitutionally controversial manner.

These constitutional issues, however, were overshadowed by the effects of the governmental, legislative, and presidential crises with which the system was faced. The governmental crisis was caused, first, by the resignation of a senior minister and, second, by the forced resignation of the prime minister following the loss of a vote of confidence in the National Assembly. (This remains the only time that the government has been brought down by the legislature under the Fifth Republic.) Its main effect was to remind people of the executive instability of the Fourth Republic which, supposedly, the people had sanctioned by voting so overwhelmingly for the new regime in 1958. The legislative crisis was caused by de Gaulle's decision to dissolve parliament rather than simply appoint a different prime minister who might have been acceptable to the existing National Assembly. In this way, de Gaulle upped the political ante and challenged his opponents. The presidential crisis was caused by de Gaulle's indication that he would resign if the referendum were defeated. This was a favourite presidential tactic and this time, as before, it had the desired effect of personalizing the crisis. The net effect of these crises was to deflect attention away from the ins-and-outs of the various constitutional niceties and to force both politicians and voters alike to think not just in terms of whether or not they were in favour of the reform *per se* and the way in which it was being proposed, but whether or not they were in favour of the government, the regime, and the General himself (Lagroye 1992).

For both reasons, then, the 1962 reform represented more than simply a minor constitutional victory for those who happened to support a particular reform. Instead, it also represented the point at which support for the political system of the Fifth Republic and its proclivity towards presidential politics was crystallized. In this sense, the context of the 1962 reform should be seen as a fundamental part of the process which institutionalized both the Fifth Republic itself and the practice of presidential government within it. It did so by reinforcing the popular expectation that presidential government was the 'normal' way for the Fifth Republic to function, by establishing the presidential election as the focal point of the political process and by providing de Gaulle's successors with at least the opportunity to assume his political mantle. Only over time have the conditions which caused this propensity towards presidential government been weakened.

Presidential/Party Relations

At this stage, then, we can assert that there is a basic constitutional balance between the president and the prime minister but that the context of the 1962 reform reinforced the already established tendency towards presidential pre-eminence. It is apparent, though, that, since this time, there have been different modes of presidential/prime ministerial relations. In short, presidential pre-eminence is conjunctural. In other words, the president's ability to influence the decision-making process varies according to the prevailing political situation. As such, presidential power should be treated not as an independent variable but as a dependent variable. In this respect, Duverger has argued that the power of the president is dependent upon two factors: the nature of the parliamentary majority and the relationship between the president and that majority (Duverger 1996*a*: 511). For the most part the president has benefited from the conjunction of political forces but increasingly this has not been the case.

As noted in Chapter 1, Duverger states that various elements determine the president's party power (Duverger 1978: 122). First, there is the issue of whether there is an absolute majority in the legislature, whether there is only a quasi-majority, or whether there is no majority at all. Secondly, there is the issue of whether the majority comprises either a single party, a coalition of parties in which one party is dominant, or a coalition in which the various parties are equally strong. Thirdly, there is the issue of whether the president leads the majority, is opposed to the majority, is simply a member of the majority, or is a neutral figure. The various combinations of these elements correspond to different degrees of presidential power. All other things being equal, when the president is the leader of a single-party majority, then the potential for presidential power is at its greatest. By contrast, when the president is opposed to a single-party majority, then the potential for presidential power is at its weakest. In between these two extremes, there is a variety of scenarios. In this respect, both Duverger (1996*a*: 519–74) and Keeler and Schain (1996) have identified three basic modes of presidential/parliamentary relations. By contrast, Olivier Duhamel has proposed seven such modes in the period from 1958 to 1993 (1995: 125). For the purposes of this exercise a similar number of modes will be examined, although these vary from the ones proposed by Duhamel (see Figure 4.2).

	Absolute majority			Quasi-majority	No majority
	One-party	Imbalanced coalition	Balanced coalition		
Presidential and parliamentary majorities coincide	1968–73 1981–6	1962–8 1973–4 1974–8	1995–7 1978–81	1988–93	(1958–62)
The majority opposes the president		1997–	1986–8 1993–5		

FIG. 4.2. Modes of presidential/parliamentary relations in France, 1958–1998

The first set of scenarios occurs when the presidential and parliamentary majorities coincide. As noted above, this is the most common scenario under which the Fifth Republic has operated and it corresponds to the various periods when presidents have been at their strongest or when they have at least been the most prominent figures within the executive. In the first case, the president has enjoyed the support of an absolute majority in the legislature and has either led a one-party government or a coalition in which the president's party has been far stronger than any other. This helps to account, then, for the strength of the presidency during much of the de Gaulle presidency, the Pompidou presidency, and the first period of the Mitterrand presidency (1962–74 and 1981–96). In the second case, there has been a variety of situations. At times, the president has enjoyed the support of an absolute majority in the legislature but has led a coalition in which the president's party was the weaker of the coalition partners. This was the situation during the early years of the Giscard presidency (1974–8). At other times, the president has enjoyed the support of an absolute majority but has led a coalition in which the president's party has been only one of two more or less equal partners. This was the situation during the later years of the Giscard presidency (1978–81) and during the first period of the Chirac presidency (1995–7). At yet other times still, there has only been a quasi-majority in parliament, even though it has supported the president. This was the situation during the first period of Mitterrand's second term in office (1988–93). In these ways, then, the nature of the parliamentary majority and the relationship between the president and the parliamentary majority helps to account not just for the general tendency towards presidential leadership in the early years of the Fifth Republic but also more generally for the varying degrees of presidential leadership since 1958.

The second set of scenarios occurs when the presidential and parliamentary majorities are opposed to each other. Again, as noted above, this has occurred on three occasions during the Fifth Republic. Even on these occasions, though, an examination of the precise configuration of these two factors helps to differentiate between the various experiences of 'cohabitation'. On the first two occasions during the Chirac and Balladur premierships (1986–8 and 1993–5), the prime minister enjoyed the support of an absolute majority in the legislature (Chirac only just, Balladur overwhelmingly so) but led a coalition in which the two coalition partners were of relatively equal strength. During these times, the prime minister was strong but was still obliged to accommodate the demands of his coalition partner. By contrast, on the third occasion during the Jospin premiership (1997–), the prime minister has enjoyed the support of an absolute majority and has led a government in which his party was by far the largest component. During this time, the prime minister has still been obliged to accommodate the demands of his partners in the 'plural' coalition, but has also benefited from both the strength of the Socialist party and the dispersed forces of the other coalition groups. Once again, therefore, the combination of the nature of the parliamentary majority and the relationship between, this time, the prime minister and the parliamentary majority helps to account for the varying degrees of prime ministerial leadership during the Fifth Republic.

CONCLUSION—THE CONTEMPORARY NATURE OF FRENCH SEMI-PRESIDENTIALISM

There are various approaches to the study of presidential power in the Fifth Republic (Elgie 1996). The framework that Duverger has provided represents one such approach. The strength of this approach lies in the fact that it demonstrates why the president has consistently been the major political actor in the system but also why presidential power is fragile. It does so by underscoring the point that the president operates within a twin-headed executive system and that the key variable within the system is the parliamentary majority and the president's relationship with it. And yet, it is also necessary to place both the presidency and the prime ministership in their wider political context. The French semi-presidential system is built up of a series of overlapping relationships. These include the relationship between the president and the prime minister and the relationship between the president, prime minister, and parliamentary majority. They also include, though, other relationships. They include the relationship between the executive and wider state structures; the relationship between the political elite and the people; and the relationship between France, Europe, and the world generally. As the nature of these relationships changes so too does the power of the executive as a whole and within it the respective powers of the president and prime minister (Elgie and Wright 1996).

In this respect, the recent evolution of these relationships has challenged the basic authority of the French executive. For example, France has generally become less state-centred. Some elements of the state have been privatized. Other aspects of state control have been offloaded onto independent administrative agencies. State planning in general has been downgraded and the language of evaluation, consumer charters, and new public management has become the norm. At the same time, the gap between the people and the people's representatives has widened. Fewer people are now willing to trust politicians. More people are likely to vote for 'unconventional' parties. More people are ready to engage in social protests which bypass normal party organizations. Fewer people are happy to defer to traditional political authority structures. Equally, France's relationship with both its European and world partners has changed. French governments risk losing control, or at least being seen to lose control, of policy-making functions in many fundamental areas. Budgetary policy choices have been restricted. Monetary policy choices have been curtailed. World trade negotiations threaten broadcasting policy. European regulations curb competition and industrial policy. In all of these ways, the state in France has become as hollow as the state in many other established liberal democracies. As a result, those who are responsible for governing have less and less government with which to carry out their essential tasks (Rhodes 1996).

The changing nature of governance in France affects the place of the president and prime minister in the system and the analysis of their powers. In the past, French policy was made at least relatively independently. Within France the state was strong. Within the state, the executive wielded the levers of power. Within the executive, then, the battle between the president and the prime minister was the main battle for political power. In this context, the text of the constitution was significant, the precedent of presidential government was essential and the nature of the parliamentary majority was crucial. Now, though, with the decline of independent policy-making, the weakening of the state, and the challenge to the position of the executive, the battle between the president and the prime minister looks increasingly peripheral. True, the constitution sets out the rules of the political game, the public still expects the president and the government to achieve results and the composition of the parliamentary majority continues to determine the basic contours of presidential and prime ministerial influence. Even so, the position of the president and the prime minister within the wider system is undoubtedly less influential now than it was previously.

In this way, then, the changing nature of French governance needs to be integrated into an account of the nature of French semi-presidentialism. It helps to explain why the earliest presidents of the Fifth Republic were generally the strongest. It also helps to explain why recent presidents have failed to meet popular expectations and why periods of 'cohabitation' have become increasingly frequent as the public has become more and more fickle. At the same time, though, Toinet is certainly correct both to emphasize the limits to the current expressions of French 'malaise' and to place it in its appropriate historical context (Toinet 1996). The system is not yet ungovernable and the past is not always a better place. Indeed, the high level of public support for the Jospin government in its first year suggested that political leaders who confront the new terms of the debate and provide appropriate responses can still engage in successful statecraft. In this context, the competition between the president and the prime minister is still an essential element of French politics. The relationship between the two components of the twin-headed executive is still a defining feature of France's semi-presidential system.

5

Iceland

GUNNAR HELGI KRISTINSSON

In 1992–3 president Vigdis Finnbogadottir came under pressure not to countersign legislation confirming Iceland's membership of the European Economic Area. A refusal of this kind would have forced a referendum on the issue, but not on its own prevented the legislation from taking effect. Having given the issue some consideration, the president turned down the appeal, explaining that she could not be expected to go against the wishes of a democratically elected assembly. Although Finnbogadottir herself had been returned to office in 1988 by 94.6 per cent of the votes, she did not consider her mandate comparable to that of the legislature.[1] Finnbogadottir's interpretation of her role was in no way unusual in the Icelandic semi-presidential system. Rather, it was typical of the way the role of the president is interpreted. The obvious contrast to de Gaulle's interpretation of the French presidency in the 1960s—indicating that his mandate was superior to that of the National Assembly (Duverger 1980: 171)— is illustrative of the world of difference that separates the two semi-presidential systems.

The Icelandic president, as Duverger points out, 'plays a strictly parliamentary game' (ibid. 168). The office was created with the establishment of a republic in 1944 to take over the functions of the Danish monarch, which were largely ceremonial by that time. Many of the articles in the constitution dealing with the presidency are in fact transcribed from the constitution of 1918, when Iceland was still a kingdom, modelled on earlier Icelandic and Danish constitutions. Hence, it is customary in Iceland to regard the form of government as a parliamentary one, essentially similar to the Danish one, despite the different ways heads of states come into office.

The president is selected in direct popular elections, where the candidate receiving the largest number of votes gets elected. For a number of reasons, this is not interpreted as a strong political mandate. Presidential elections are not party political contests and major candidates usually stay clear of controversial political issues. Once elected, a president can usually stand unopposed for as many terms as he or she wishes.[2] Moreover, the election law has no majority provisions or thresholds against the election of a president by a minority.[3] President Vigdis Finnbogadottir, for example, first came into office in 1980 on the basis of a mere 33.8 per cent of the popular vote. The common perception of the president is that of a figurehead and symbol of unity rather than a political leader.

Political power in Iceland lies above all with parliament and a government responsible to it. Parliament, the Althingi, is relatively strong since the time it stood as the symbol of national aspirations against a foreign government in the nineteenth century. Governments as a rule are coalitions of two or three parties, and none of the parties is really in a predominant position in the coalition system. The government as such is not a strong collective body, nor does the prime minister have substantial powers within the government. Governmental decision-making takes place essentially through negotiations of the parties involved in the coalition at any given time. Within the parties, the parliamentary party is usually the decisive instance, but the strength of the party leadership vis-à-vis the parliamentary party depends among other things on the skill and experience of the party leader.

Despite the apparent powerlessness of the Icelandic president, the fact that the office holder does possess a direct popular mandate cannot be ignored altogether. The text of the constitution is in some respects ambiguous with regard to the powers of the president. While no president so far has attempted to play on this ambiguity, the theoretical possibility exists for the presidency to play a more assertive role, in a manner that no monarch probably could. Thus, the fact that the president is elected by popular vote contributes to an on-going political and theoretical interest in the office and its potential.

The present text explores the actual and potential powers of the Icelandic presidency in the light of Duverger's concept of semi-presidential government. It will be argued that traditional interpretations of the Icelandic constitution have overlooked the distinctiveness of semi-presidential government. The powerlessness of the presidency is less a fact of law than of politics. An attempt will also be made to account for why the presidency has developed in the manner of a powerless figurehead rather than an effective political leader.

THE PRESIDENCY AND POLITICAL LEADERSHIP IN ICELAND

General consensus exists on the fact that the presidency—whatever its potential—in fact exercises little or no political leadership functions in Iceland. Among semi-presidential systems, Iceland is undoubtedly among those where the president has least power. To account for the development of the presidency we shall adopt Duverger's approach, analysing the events surrounding the formation of the regime, the constitutional powers of the president, and majority formations in parliament. (See Duverger 1980, and Chapter 1 this volume.)

Formation of the Regime

The Icelandic struggle for independence, which began in the nineteenth century, was not a republican one, in the sense of being aimed specifically at the monarchy. Overall, the independence movement was surprisingly little concerned with the form of government which should succeed Danish rule. Most likely, a miniature version of the Danish system was widely taken for granted as the likely successor of Danish rule, with or without a Danish monarch.

Once parliamentarism was established in Iceland in 1904, along with home rule, a major root of friction between the Althingi and the Danish Crown was removed. Disagreements continued over issues concerning the constitutional relations between the two countries, but the king and his role were usually not a matter of much controversy. The Union Treaty with Denmark in 1918 established Icelandic sovereignty, but maintained a number of links between the countries, especially with regard to foreign affairs and related issues. It also confirmed the existence of a joint monarch. The Treaty stated that renegotiations of its terms could take place after 1940, and could be terminated unilaterally if three years of negotiations failed to produce a new agreement.

During the inter-war period, broad agreement prevailed among Icelandic politicians that the Union Treaty would be terminated in accordance with its own provisions. This did not necessarily mean the abolition of the monarchy, which rested on different foundations. Politicians wanted to hold separate the issue of the Union Treaty and that of the monarchy, since the latter was potentially more controversial than the former, and could endanger the consensus which was considered necessary on the Union issue. Towards the end of the 1930s, however, it became increasingly clear that the movement towards independence would be considered incomplete without the abolition of the monarchy along with the termination of the Union Treaty.

After the occupation of Denmark in 1940 by Germany, the Danish king and government became unable to fulfil the terms of the Union Treaty. Iceland—occupied by Allied forces shortly afterwards—reacted by transferring the functions of the monarch to the Icelandic government. The following year Althingi declared its intent to terminate the Union Treaty and establish a republic. At the same time a regent—elected by a majority in the Althingi—took over the functions of the king. In 1944 a republic was established with a new constitution, which dealt extensively with the presidency and appears in its discussion of both legislative and executive power to associate them strongly with the president.

The Althingi has been an unusually strong parliament ever since the introduction of home rule and parliamentarism in 1904. The executive, by contrast, has been relatively weak, and subject to case-by-case interventions from parliament (Kristinsson 1996). It was never the intention of the Althingi to create a strong presidency which might undermine its supremacy and parliamentary rule. It wished primarily to maintain the established functions for the Head of State. The idea of a strong president probably had little following, and it was widely felt that it should in any case not come under consideration except as part of a more thorough revision of the constitution. Such a revision was not considered a good idea at the time of the separation from Denmark, since it might endanger the broad consensus of opinion which prevailed on the separation. The Althingi resolved in 1942 to make only such minimal changes to the constitution which were necessitated by the termination of the Union with Denmark. Hence, the articles dealing with the powers of the presidency in the new constitution were to a large degree similar to those in the previous constitution dealing with the powers of the monarch.

The previous constitution, adopted in 1918, was essentially the product of constitutional developments in nineteenth-century Denmark (Kristinsson 1994).[4] The articles on the powers of the monarch were interpreted in accordance with the development towards parliamentary rule (established in Denmark in 1901), which essentially circumscribed the powers of the king, although the text of the constitution might suggest otherwise in some respects. When the republican constitutional bill was first presented to the Althingi, it intended the president to be elected by the Althingi (in up to three rounds, to secure a majority). This

was thought sufficient given the largely ceremonial and symbolic functions of the office. It was only at a later stage, when this met with a fairly
negative response from the electorate, that provisions for the direct
election of the president were introduced into the constitutional bill.
To require an electoral majority for the office, however, was considered
unnecessary, since it was not intended to share effectively in political
power. Nor were there any provisions for a vice-president.[5]

General revision of the constitution never took place.[6] The presidency
has co-existed peacefully with parliamentary rule primarily because
those occupying the office have never attempted to infringe on the
powers of parliament and parliamentary government. The five presidents who have occupied the office have probably had political ambitions to a varying extent on behalf of their office. Some of them have
attempted to influence political developments while others have
appeared more or less without political ambition. The most successful
of them, president Asgeirsson (1952–68), was influential in a personal
capacity and behind the scenes, rather than through the use of his constitutional powers against the established political forces. Thus, the
emergence of a semi-presidential regime in Iceland was in no way
influenced by the doctrines of presidentialism. It was a pragmatic
response to complex political circumstances, and never intended to
infringe on the predominant status of parliament in the Icelandic
political system.

Constitutional Powers

Duverger maintains that a notorious contrast exists between the legal
powers of the Icelandic president as stated in the constitution and political practice (Duverger 1980: 178–9). The extent to which the constitution grants political power to the president is debated among
constitutional authorities in Iceland, but the consensus of opinion seems
to be that they are not substantial. With minor exceptions, it is conventional among legal experts to interpret the constitution in accordance
with Danish parliamentary practice and the regime of parliamentary
monarchism which existed in Iceland in 1904–44.

Several articles of the constitution appear to give substantial powers
to the president. It states, among other things, that the Althingi and
the president share legislative power, that the president convenes
the Althingi, can adjourn its sessions and dissolve it, in which case a new
election must take place. Moreover, it states that the president appoints
ministers, decides their number and division of tasks, that the president

appoints state officials, concludes agreements with other states, and has the right to put bills to parliament. Nowhere does the constitution explicitly state that a parliamentary form of government shall prevail, although tradition as well as some of its articles are interpreted to that effect (Schram and Johannesson 1994: 24).

These articles on the powers of the president are usually interpreted in the light of Article 11, which states that the president is not responsible for governmental actions, and Article 13 which states that government ministers execute the powers of the president. Government ministers are legally responsible for executive actions and the presidential signature is insufficient for legislative or executive decisions to take effect without the countersignature of a government minister. In the light of this, and the tradition of parliamentarism, the constitution is interpreted to the effect that ministers in all normal circumstances are in charge of the powers which the text of the constitution invests in the presidency (ibid. 110).

A thorny issue concerns the controlling powers of the president. Iceland does not have a specific constitutional court and the president has no role in deciding the constitutionality of legislation. The Supreme Court can in individual cases decide to ignore normal legislation on the basis of unconstitutionality, but there is no recourse in the Icelandic legal system to legislative review, where the courts specifically address the constituionality of legislation. Article 26 of the constitution, however, states that the president can refuse to countersign legislation. In that case, the legislation in question takes effect nonetheless, if signed by a government minister, but has to be put to a referendum, which decides the issue. This, of course, is irrelevant to the question of constitutionality, but nonetheless could be interpreted as a control against the possibility of Althingi abusing its legislative powers.

In actual fact, no president has ever refused to countersign legislation. Most likely, such a move would bring on a constitutional crisis, and throw the president into direct conflict with the government and parliament. Given an unchanged political landscape, it is difficult to imagine circumstances where such a situation might arise, and some jurists even argue that the president on his own does not have the right—Article 26 notwithstanding—to withhold his signature. Thus, Vilhjalmsson argues that since government ministers execute the powers of the president according to the constitution, the same must necessarily apply to Article 26, and the president has no independent right to a refusal. He points out that such an interpretation is consistent with the interpretations of Norwegian and Danish jurists of their respective constitutions concerning the veto powers of the Head of State (Vilhjalmsson 1994).[7]

The flaw in Vilhjalmsson's argument is that it fails to recognize that the Icelandic form of government is not a parliamentary monarchy, but a semi-presidential system, where the president has a direct mandate from the people. Indeed, the constitution of 1944 specifically modified the veto powers of the president as compared to those of the king precisely because an elected president might not feel as constrained in their use as a hereditary monarch would. The presidential signature would in fact have been quite unnecessary, were it not intended as a possible control on the powers of parliament.

Icelandic presidents themselves have undoubtedly believed in their constitutional right of refusing to countersign legislation. The fact that none has ever used it has more to do with political realities than the literal interpretation of the constitution. When president Vigdis Finnbogadottir at one point delayed giving her signature for less than three hours, as a symbolic protest against a particular legislative action, the minister in question stated that he would have resigned had there been any further delay. The president can hardly take on the political establishment without sacrificing his status as the symbol of national unity and political neutrality at the same time. This can occur only in the most extraordinary of circumstances. Thus, the president is a reserve controller rather than an instrument of routine political control.

Speculatively, a similar line of argument could be adopted concerning some of the other powers of the president as well. In a period of political crisis it is conceivable that the presidency would play a more active role than it does under normal circumstances. This applies, in particular if parliament were unable for longer periods of time to produce working majorities.

Parliamentary Majorities

No party has ever held an effective majority of seats in the Althingi since the 1920s. Icelandic politicians, however, are firm believers in the merits of majority governments, and the country is normally governed by coalition governments with a majority in the Althingi. Only three minority governments have been in power since 1944: two may be considered caretaker governments and none sat in power for as much as a year.

The president can play a certain role in the process of coalition formation. After a parliamentary election, the president decides who gets the mandate to lead coalition negotiations, and in what order, if the first ones fail. Formally, the president has an entirely free hand in this. Given the parliamentary form of government, however, a government formed without the confidence of parliament would not last long. In practice, the president gives the mandate to lead the negotiations on government formation to the individual he considers most likely to form a majority government. To test the ground among the parties, the president has discussions with the party leaders, prior to his decision on who is to get the mandate. Other considerations may enter into the president's decision—like the one of not appearing to favour or disfavour one of the parties—but his primary concern remains that of getting the job done.[8] Party political neutrality can be tricky, but presidents so far have managed more or less to avoid serious public criticism of their role in the coalition formation process. Privately, presidents may have strong opinions on the type of government they wish for, but such considerations as a rule do not affect their decisions in an obvious manner. The major example of a president influencing the formation of a government was in 1958–9, when the Social Democrats first formed a minority government and subsequently a coalition with the centre-right Independence Party which lasted until 1971. The president had an impact primarily behind the scenes, and only much later has his role in the coalition formation become clear.

The overriding emphasis on majority coalitions in Icelandic politics is an interesting phenomenon which requires some discussion. The Scandinavian countries have been governed by minority governments for long periods of time, and minority governments were in fact not uncommon in Iceland prior to the Republic: such governments were in power approximately half the time during the inter-war period.

To explain the strong focus on majority coalitions in Iceland, two factors appear to be of particular relevance. One is the fact that the Icelandic parties are eager office seekers, partly because a governing position grants access to various material benefits and patronage. Minority governments do not guarantee sufficient sharing of the spoils of power to satisfy the political community. More interesting in the present context is the fact that the presidency has contributed significantly to the emphasis on majority governments in Iceland. To understand how this has come about it is necessary to look back to 1942.

Early in 1942 the grand coalition which had reigned since 1939, excluding only the communists, crumbled and a major government crisis evolved. After two parliamentary elections in 1942, the parties still failed to form a government. The regent—who later became the first president of the country—decided to form a non-partisan government. This came as a surprise to many politicians, who were not accustomed to such interventions from the head of state. Many of them—especially the leadership of the powerful Independence Party—were annoyed, feeling that the political parties should have been given more time to form a government. In a very divided parliament, however, the political parties could not even agree upon bringing down the non-partisan government, and it sat until the autumn of 1944. Relations between parliament and the non-partisan government were strained all the time, and parliament made a point of humiliating the government on a number of occasions.

The experience of the non-partisan government was not one which the political parties wished to repeat. Whenever negotiations on coalition formation among the political parties have become protracted the spectre of a non-partisan government has encouraged the parties to speed up the process. The seriousness of the threat is apparent from the fact that on a few occasions the president is known to have started preparations for the formation of such a government. Such an intervention by an hereditary monarch would be highly unlikely.

Under normal circumstances the president takes little or no part in the work of government. The non-partisan government was a partial exception to this and to some extent the first president, Björnsson (regent 1941–4, president 1944–52) may have had a conception of the presidency slightly different from his successors. Björnsson tried to intervene in politics on a number of occasions and even called (unsuccessfully) for a constituent assembly early in 1944 to address the issue of a new constitution and the dissolution of the union with Denmark. He generally followed the work of the government closely, and meetings in the Council of State—where the president meets the government—were often around 30 per year. Subsequent presidents have adopted the practice of countersigning legislation outside the Council of State while being kept informed of the work of the government in a more informal setting by the prime minister. Formal meetings of the Council of State take place only a couple of times each year. They are an entirely formal occasion, devoid of political significance. Björnsson's successors have thus normalized the relationship between the office of the president and the political parties by accepting the role of neutral by-standers, who can at best have a certain impact behind the scenes through cooperation with the politicians rather than in conflict with them. It was above all Asgeirsson who moulded the presidency in this manner, but the non-political role of the president was taken still further by Eldjarn (1968–80) and Finnbogadottir (1980–96). Unlike Björnsson and Asgeirsson, Eldjarn and Finnbogadottir had little political experience. They were elected as cultural personalities, emphasizing the symbolic aspects of the office. Grimsson (1996–), on the other hand, is more in the tradition of the older presidents, being a former professor of political science, a seasoned parliamentarian, and formerly party leader and minister of finance.

Duverger's three factors seem very relevant in accounting for the development of the Icelandic presidency. The events surrounding the formation of the regime show that the presidency was intended primarily to take over the functions of the monarch without creating a new locus of power or upsetting the pre-existing balance of power. That the new office had a potentially greater amount of power than the monarch previously was unintended but unavoidable. The constitution, as such, guarantees the president very little powers under normal conditions, with regard either to governing the country or controlling those who do. On both accounts, however, the presidency may be regarded as a reserve power, which can be activated in unusual situations or periods of crisis.

THE PRESIDENCY AND THE POLITICAL FORCES

As we have seen, the powers ascribed to the presidency in the constitution are such that on their own they are insufficient for the president to play a major role in Icelandic politics. But of course, the issue of the real powers of the president is only partly a legal issue. The constitution would easily allow the president to exercise effective political leadership, were this in accordance with the wishes of the major political forces. A president, who was at the same time the leader of a majority party, could—to take an example—function as the effective political leader of the country with the Council of State replacing ministerial meetings (where the prime minister chairs) as the effective government. In this sense, the relationship of the president to the political forces is an important issue.

The Icelandic presidency has developed as a non-partisan and mainly non-political office. The president is a political outsider, committed to party political neutrality, even when he has a political background. This is not a constitutional requirement, but a strong norm related to the office.[9] To depict the relationship of the presidency with the political forces, we shall explore two themes: the impact of presidentialism in Icelandic politics, on the one hand, and presidential elections, on the other.

Presidentialism in Iceland

Presidentialism never enjoyed a broad political following in Iceland. Nonetheless, the ideas of presidentialism have occasionally had an impact within some of the established parties and on parties challenging the established party system. It was especially during the early years of the republic that presidentialism had a certain appeal. At that time the ideas of presidentialism existed as minority views within three of the four established parties, the Independence Party, the rural Progressive Party, and the Social Democratic Party. Presidential government was among the main issues in an attempt to split the Independence Party in 1953, when the Republican Party received 3.3 per cent of the national vote, but failed to obtain parliamentary seats.

The case for presidentialism during the 1940s was put most eloquently by Gislason, a left-winger within the Social Democratic Party, who later became its chairman. Gislason maintained that, while parliamentary government might have been a natural part of the politics of the nineteenth century, such close relations between parliament and the executive were not a good idea in the politics of the twentieth century. Close relations between the two, he maintained, gave parliament and the political parties far too much weight in executive decisions concerning public investment and finance and contributed to a spoils system in public employment. To establish a strong executive, capable of long-term policy-making without undue interference from parliament, he suggested among other things the abolition of parliamentary government and the introduction of presidentialism. Along with other reforms the net result of such a change would be to secure a clearer division of powers within the political system—implicitly suggesting a smaller role for parliament—and a reduction in parliamentary log-rolling and patronage (Gislason 1945).

Unlike Gislason—an economist by profession—major lawyers among the political elite defended parliamentarism. Benediktsson maintained that the amount of progress in the country since the introduction of parliamentarism indicated that there was no reason to 'assume that we have been on the wrong track or that our methods in general have been at fault' (Benediktsson 1965). Another legal canon, Johannesson, opposed presidentialism on the following grounds:

A clear division of labour between the legislative and executive powers is certainly valuable. But dividing the state is not an objective in itself. Individual components of the state are not opposites, but branches on the same tree. The theory of the threefold division of the state emerged under social circumstances very different from those that prevail today. In a modern society it seems desirable, or even unavoidable, that parliament and government work together in many ways. A theory, however good it may be, should not stand in the way of such cooperation. (Johannesson 1954)

The lawyers, like the political elite of which they were powerful members, adhered to an organic view of the state where the state functioned as the agent of the common national interest and the popular will. That the exercise of state power might become perverted and turn against those it was intended to serve was not a consideration which featured prominently in this view. The opposite view, that presidentialism and a separation of powers between the legislature and the executive were desirable, was related to a more negative evaluation of the Icelandic political system. This, however, remained a dissident view, which existed primarily on the fringe of Icelandic politics.

The demand for increasing presidential powers was taken up on a few occasions during the 1960s and 1970s by minor parties trying to break the mould of the Icelandic four-party system. Usually, it was aimed at what was considered the excessive power of the established political parties. The major attempt to put presidentialism—or something very similar to that—on the agenda of Icelandic politics was made in 1983 by the Social Democratic Alliance. The Social Democratic Alliance was a splinter group from the Social Democratic Party, led by Gylfason, son of the aforementioned Gislason. According to the Social Democratic Alliance, parliamentarism should be abolished and the prime minister elected separately.[10] The Althingi would not be directly involved with the functions of the executive, although it would have to approve the budget. Otherwise is should concentrate on its legislative and control functions. This was part of a campaign which was populist in some degree and aimed at reducing various forms of corruption and excessive party power, which allegedly characterized Icelandic politics. The party received 7.3 per cent of the vote in the parliamentary election of 1983, but gradually declined after the untimely death of its leader, and most of its leading personnel eventually rejoined the Social Democrats. The success of the party in the election of 1983 probably had more to do with the popularity of its main leader, Gylfason, than genuine support for the ideas of presidentialism.

Support for presidentialism in Iceland has been based on an analysis of the parties or parliament as too strong and excessively involved in the work of the executive. A strong president has been proposed as a possible counterweight. Even if the analysis were correct, however, some doubts may be raised as to the effectiveness of the proposed remedy. Presidentialism by itself does not circumscribe the powers of a strong parliament or abolish log-rolling and patronage. Some of the alleged deficiencies of the Icelandic system, as has been pointed out, are in fact much more apparent in the US presidential system than the parliamentary ones of Northern Europe.

It is instructive to note, nonetheless, that the debate in Iceland has been conducted exclusively on the merits of parliamentarism vis-à-vis presidentialism. The pros and cons of semi-presidential government have received scant attention by the political forces. In fact, an awareness of the distinctiveness of this form of government—as a form of government *sui generis*—is more or less non-existent among politicians and academics alike. The significance of the Icelandic form of government and its potential consequences are thus probably less clear to politicians and academics than is usually assumed.

The Choice of a President

A perceptive member of Althingi in 1944 opposed the popular election of presidents on the following grounds:

It seems to me that the election of a powerless president, like the bill prescribes, cannot be a genuine national election. He is not expected to have a political platform, and can therefore not pose as a political leader. And I must ask: how is an election campaign to be conducted among the electorate where this is not the case. Obviously, candidates can emerge more than one and more than two, so that a contest is likely to take place. . . . But it is obviously unfortunate to hold presidential elections which can only evolve around the personality of the president. Of course it may be argued that we should follow the example of the United States and expect the president to be a political leader with a certain amount of power as a consequence of that. But so long as we have not made up our minds about this, it seems to me obvious that the president should, as planned by those who originally wrote the bill, be elected by parliament. (Möller, 1944, *Althingistidindi*, B, 88)

The first popular election of a president in Iceland took place in 1952. The first inhabitant of the office, Björnsson, was originally elected regent by the Althingi on account of his diplomatic experience, which was considered important during the formative years of the Republic. He was at the time more or less the only Icelander experienced in dealing with representatives of foreign states, having served as Iceland's only ambassador during the inter-war period. The president was elected for the first time by the Althingi at the historic place of Thingvellir on the day the republic was formed in 1944. A popular election was to take place the following year. While Björnsson was to a certain extent controversial among politicians, none felt it tactical to challenge him, and he actually never had to enter a popular contest until he died in office early in 1952.

It seems clear that when faced with a presidential election in 1952, political leaders in Iceland had not fully made up their minds whether they wanted a party political contest for the presidency or not. Nor were they clear on whether they wanted a politically experienced president or not. In the end, three candidates ran for president, two were seasoned politicians, while one, a respected clergyman, had little political experience. Behind the candidacy of the clergyman stood the two largest parties in the country, cooperating at the time in a coalition government. In the parliamentary election of 1949 the two parties, the Independence Party and the Progressive Party, pulled 64 per cent of the vote between them, and they controlled a substantial share of the popular press. They ran a fierce campaign against the candidate who was considered the greatest threat to their chosen one. The candidate in question, Asgeirsson, was a member of Althingi for the SDP, but ran a nonpartisan campaign, with an *ad hoc* organization, under the slogan, 'the people chooses the President', which was clearly aimed at the attempt by the two parties to pre-empt the election. Asgeirsson won by 48.3 per cent of the votes against 45.5 per cent for his closest competitor (the one supported by the two parties).

In this first popular election to the office, several of the characteristics of presidential elections in Iceland were already apparent. In the first place, it was clear that the parties do not control the presidential vote. After the humiliation of 1952, in fact, the parties have never officially taken sides in presidential elections in Iceland.[11] Such elections have been contested by *ad hoc* organizations around individual candidates. Secondly, presidential elections are personal contests rather than political ones. Candidates run on personal merit rather than a political platform, and while there is undoubtedly a strong political pattern in the support for candidates, their personal appeal is at least as important. Finally, the candidate was chosen in 1952 which was least to the liking of the largest party, the Independence Party. The same was the case in other presidential elections, in 1968, 1980, and 1996. While too much should perhaps not be read into this fact, it may indicate that voters attach some importance to the role of the president as a reserve controller and a counterweight against the politically powerful.

Presidential candidates emerge through an entirely informal process where rumours, personal signs of interest, and the dedication of supporters play a crucial role. The only formal requirement to enter the race is the signed recommendation of at least 1,500 voters. Like so often in personality contests, the campaign is often vicious and personal, but the candidates themselves always maintain a polite posture. Rumours and stories often play a significant role, many of them gross and entirely untrue. Yet, after the election, every president so far has managed to acquire the degree of respectability and popularity to ensure that it is still considered customary not to run against a sitting president.

The president is a political outsider in the sense that he is chosen on personal rather than on political grounds and not expected to play a political role. Nothing in the Icelandic constitution prevents the election of a political president, if the electorate and the major parties so wished. In that case, the president could assume a number of different roles, depending on political circumstances. It is even conceivable that he could play an effective governing role, if there was political support for that.[12] This is not a likely scenario, given the strength of tradition concerning the presidency and the unlikelihood of a single party gaining majority. Nor is a scenario where the president on his own uses his or her powers to govern without support from the political parties likely. But it is not unthinkable, during a parliamentary crisis.

CONCLUSION

Icelandic lawyers have tended to interpret the powers of the president as essentially limited or even no greater than those of a monarch under parliamentary government. This interpretation is compatible with the traditions associated with the office and is likely to hold so long as the party system remains stable and effective parliamentary majorities can be formed in parliament.

We maintain, however, that the generally perceived powerlessness of the presidency does not follow from the letter of the constitution as much as from political practice. Lawyers have scanned the constitution in search of presidential prerogatives: powers of which the president holds monopoly. But if the president were to assume the role of a political player, instead of a political outsider, the constitution allows him a considerable scope for manoeuvre, whatever the intentions originally of the constitution makers. The fact that the president has a popular mandate and a number of constitutional openings could—given the right circumstances—turn the semi-presidential form of the constitution into its real content. The following alternative roles of the president seem compatible with the constitution given the right circumstances:

1. So long as the president chooses to remain a political outsider, without political ambitions, he will essentially remain a figurehead. This will be his primary role, whatever the situation with regard to majority formations in parliament. The president in this role can be regarded as a reserve controller, but is unlikely to take any initiative which causes political concern or provokes criticism of his actions. This is—with minor exceptions—the traditional role of the president in Iceland. The role of a political outsider was especially prominent during the presidency of Eldjarn and Finnbogadottir.[13]

2. A second role which the president may choose is that of a non-partisan player. Such a president has political ambitions, without being willing to sacrifice his non-partisan position and cordial relations with different types of political leaders. Among Icelandic presidents, Björnsson came closest to this position, but it can be assumed that the other two presidents with substantial political experience, Asgeirsson and Grimsson, may not be far removed from it either. The amount of influence such a president actually can exercise essentially depends on his relationship with the political parties and the situation with regard to majority formation in parliament. In case of a parliamentary crisis such a president can form a non-partisan government and exercise political leadership functions to a certain degree, as Björnsson showed as regent in 1942–4. The emphasis by the parties on majority coalitions has foreclosed this possibility during most of the post-war period. Nonetheless, Asgeirsson showed that even under a majority coalition a skilful president can have a certain amount of political impact.

3. The third role a president could choose is that of a party political player. In such a case the president would belong to a political party and adhere to a particular political programme. Various possibilities exist in such a scenario. Such a president need not be an effective leader, for example if he were not among the main leaders of his party, in which

case he would remain a figurehead. Similarly, if his party were in opposition, his role would be that of a controller rather than an effective part of the government. But a party political president could also become an effective leader, if his party were in a majority in parliament or a predominant party in government. This has never happened in Iceland and may not be particularly likely. But the point is that there is nothing in the constitution which prevents such a development.

The power of the presidency in the Icelandic semi-presidential system depends to a very large extent on political factors, although the constitution is by no means insignificant. In fact, our analysis of the Icelandic presidency seems to support Duverger's contention that three factors shape the development of the presidency in a semi-presidential system: the events surrounding the formation of the regime, the constitutional powers of the president, and the relations of the president with the predominant powers in parliament.

The Republic of Iceland was created to put an end to the relationship with Denmark rather than to create a new form of government. Political expediency rather than constitutional principles guided the constitution makers at the initiation of the new regime in 1944. It seems beyond dispute that the intention of parliament at the time was to create a presidency with functions essentially similar to that of a monarch in a parliamentary democracy. This intention has shaped the traditions of the Icelandic presidency.

The constitution, thus shaped by the force of circumstances, is—nonetheless—compatible with widely different political roles for the presidency. On its own, the presidency does not have access to substantial powers. Such powers that the presidency has are primarily applicable in exceptional situations, such as in a parliamentary crisis or if the Althingi were to grossly misuse its legislative authority in the judgement of the president. There is, however, nothing in the constitution to prevent a much more politically active presidency, if this had sufficient support among the parties and the electorate.

A strong emphasis on majority coalitions by the political parties has been a major factor preventing the president from playing a more active political role. The emphasis on majority coalitions is in fact partly brought on by the presidency itself through the possibility of non-partisan government. In a more fragmented party system or one more divided by issues of great principle, majority formation might not have been as easy. In that case, there might also have been greater scope for manoeuvre by the president.

NOTES

1. The statement is reprinted in Vilhjalmsson 1994: 610–11.
2. The single exception being the election of 1988 when Vigdis Finnbogadottir was opposed by a fringe candidate.
3. Even though it should be relatively easy to secure a majority, e.g. by adopting the Irish election method of selecting a president, see Hardarson 1997. Such a move might have the consequence of strengthening the mandate of the president.
4. The first constitution, 'given' to Iceland by the Danish king in 1874, was in most respects similar to the Danish one. The constitution of 1918, however, followed the Danish model even more closely.
5. If the president for some reason is unable to attend the duties of his office, they are taken care of jointly by the prime minister, president of the Supreme Court, and the speaker in Althingi.
6. Various changes have been made to the constitution (1959, 1984, 1991, and 1995), but none concerning the presidency.
7. For the opposite legal opinion on this point, see Lindal 1992.
8. Prior to 1978, however, the party furthest to the left was never given the mandate.
9. President Grimsson, for example, felt it necessary in 1996 to resign from his old party, having been elected president.
10. A prime minister in a non-parliamentary regime, elected separately by popular vote, is functionally equivalent to presidential government, and discussed as such in the present context.
11. That the humiliation was substantial there seems little doubt. In fact, frictions within the Independence Party in the election campaign of 1952 contributed to an important degree to an internal party crisis in the 1980s!
12. In this context it may be mentioned that among those who considered entering the race for the presidency in 1996 was the prime minister, David Oddson, leader of the largest political party, the Independence Party.
13. Note, nonetheless, Eldjarn's threat of forming a non-partisan government in 1980, as well as Finnbogadottir's flirtations with the refusal to countersign legislation.

6

Republic of Ireland

MICHAEL GALLAGHER

The Irish presidency is usually seen as one of the weakest in any liberal democracy, certainly as the weakest presidency to be filled by direct election. Shugart and Carey, scoring directly elected presidents according to the powers they possess on a range of criteria, award the Irish presidency precisely zero points out of 40, rating it as weaker than all bar the Bulgarian presidency (1992: 155). Sartori says the Irish president 'truly has very little power', and prefers to see Ireland as a parliamentary system *pur sang* rather than as an example of semi-presidentialism (Sartori 1997: 97 n. 1; at 138 n. 7 he says that the Irish president does not have any particular power, so 'there is nothing to resurrect').

This chapter will not be arguing that these characterizations are necessarily wrong, but, inevitably, they raise their own questions about the nature of the Irish presidency. Is it really as weak as it seems, and, if so, is this because of written or unwritten constraints? Is the presidency weak at all times, or has it been in the past—or could it be in the future—more significant under some circumstances than others?

POLITICAL LEADERSHIP IN IRELAND

The search for the fount of political leadership in Ireland would certainly not begin with the president, and indeed might not take in that office at all. The Irish political system is based very much on the Westminster model. Although in some important respects it deviates from that model (for example, it has a proportional representation electoral system, a written constitution, judicial review, and much experience of coalition government), the central role of the government in the political process is unquestionable and largely unquestioned (cf. Ward 1996).

Within this overall framework of executive dominance, there is scope for some variation according to circumstances. Parliament might be a little more effective vis-à-vis government during periods of minority government, or at times when the ever-changing committee system is in one of its more productive modes (Gallagher 1996). Within the government, the Taoiseach (prime minister) is more likely to be dominant during periods of single-party government than in coalitions (Farrell 1996; O'Leary 1991). It would be fair to say, though, that no one looks to the president for political leadership; the lack of demand for leadership from that quarter is a powerful constraint on any president who might harbour dreams of supplying some.

THE CONTEXT OF THE PRESIDENT'S ROLE

We shall consider two factors that have a strong influence upon the role of the president: the formation of the regime, and the provisions of the constitution. We shall then go on in the next section to examine relations between the president and other political actors.

Formation of the Regime

Ireland was, not entirely willingly, a component part of the United Kingdom until the Irish Free State secured independence in 1922, and many aspects of its governmental system show the strong imprint of British influence. Independence was secured under the terms of the Anglo–Irish Treaty signed in December 1921, and this Treaty contained a number of provisions inserted at British insistence that were unwelcome to the Irish negotiators (see Farrell 1988: 24–6). One of these concerned the head of state, the Governor-General of the Irish Free State, who the British insisted must be designated the 'Representative of the Crown' in Article 60 of the new state's constitution. Although the powers of this office were limited indeed, it was objectionable to many as a symbol of the limitations on the sovereignty of the new Irish state, and in 1936, after several years of being scaled down, the office was abolished entirely (Sexton 1989).

The following year an entirely new constitution came into being. The 1937 constitution, which remains in force, marked part of the process of asserting the Irish state's independence by sloughing off features that could be seen as imposed by Britain in the 1921 Treaty settlement. For this reason, it was essential symbolically that the new constitution be brought into existence by the Irish people themselves, and accordingly a referendum took place, on 1 July 1937, in which the people voted by 57 per cent to 43 per cent to adopt it.

The current office of President of Ireland was 'one of the most conspicuous innovations' of the 1937 constitution (Hogan and Whyte 1994: 83). Its rare combination of direct election and an almost complete lack of real political power can be understood in terms of the circumstances of the time. The political marginality of the president needs little explaining; it was consistent with pre-1937 practice and with the largely unquestioned Westminster model of government. It is the direct election of the president that requires explanation, and this owes partly to the same spirit that animated the referendum on the constitution. It was not enough that there should be a head of state provided for under an Irish constitution; it was important that it be made quite unambiguous that this head of state was chosen by the Irish people themselves.

The other important aspect of the origins of the presidency concern the suspicions aroused about the office when it was unveiled. The 1937 constitution was drawn up by the Fianna Fáil party, which had been in government since 1932 under the leadership of Eamon de Valera. The main opposition party, Fine Gael, believed that the presidency could be used by de Valera to achieve dictatorial power; he might, they thought, have himself elected president and then get his compliant government to bestow excessive power on him (Gallagher 1988: 77–8). Perhaps to allay such fears, de Valera went to some lengths to choose as the first president someone who was patently not going to abuse the office. He proposed to Fine Gael that Douglas Hyde be nominated to the position, and when Fine Gael agreed, there were no further nominations and Hyde became president without the need for a contest. Hyde was in his late seventies, a Protestant nationalist, not associated with any political party, who had played a leading part in the cultural and language revival movement. His presidency set a tone for the office, a tone that was dignified, elderly, non-party, and 'above politics' (for his presidency, see Dunleavy and Dunleavy 1991: 392–429). If, instead, when the first president was to be elected, all the main parties had nominated heavyweight political candidates and the president had been elected on a partisan platform, the subsequent development of the office might conceivably have been quite different.

Provisions of the Constitution

When the Dáil (the lower, directly elected house of parliament) debated the new constitution in 1937, the office of president engendered considerable discussion. Eamon de Valera, the prime minister and main progenitor of the 1937 constitution, declared that the role of the president was 'to guard the people's rights and mainly to guard the constitution', maintaining the 'mastery' of the people between elections (*Dáil Debates*, 67: 40 and 51, 11 May 1937). 'Nobody would propose getting the whole people to elect a person unless it was proposed to give him substantial powers', he declared (*Dáil Debates*, 67: 38, 11 May 1937).

Given the expectations raised by such statements, the actual powers conferred on the president by the constitution are a distinct anti-climax. In fact, the president is given only two powers of any real significance. The first relates to the promulgation of legislation; every bill passed by the two houses of parliament goes to the president for signature, and the president must either sign it into law within a week (Article 25.2.1) or refer it to the Supreme Court for a judgment on whether it is compatible with the constitution (Article 26). Unlike the comparable right of the Icelandic president to refer bills to a referendum, this modest controlling power over legislation is not a dead letter; it is in fact the only presidential power to have been used to date.

The second significant presidential prerogative concerns the dissolution of the Dáil and the calling of a general election. Under usual circumstances this is a matter solely for the Taoiseach, who 'advises' the president to dissolve the Dáil. However, in certain circumstances the president may refuse to dissolve the Dáil; specifically, the president may refuse to do this if the 'advice' comes from a Taoiseach 'who has ceased to retain the support of a majority in Dáil Éireann' (Article 13.2.2). The constitution does not elaborate on precisely how the question of whether the Taoiseach has ceased to retain the support of the Dáil is to be tested, nor does it spell out when and why a president might decide to refuse a dissolution to such a Taoiseach.

The absence of further details in the constitution invites speculation. Clearly, a Taoiseach who has been defeated in a confidence vote has 'ceased to retain the support of a majority' in the Dáil, but could the president refuse a request to dissolve in other circumstances, for example if the government has simply been defeated on an item of legislation? There seems little doubt that this is the case. A precedent was established in 1944, when the government was defeated in a vote on a minor issue in parliament: both de Valera, then Taoiseach, and the president of the day, Douglas Hyde, accepted that this was a situation in which the president had the right to refuse a dissolution (Dunleavy and Dunleavy 1991: 428). In other situations, too, a president might reasonably conclude that a Taoiseach has 'ceased to retain the support of a majority' in the Dáil. Circumstances might arise, and indeed have arisen, in which a coalition government breaks up and the defecting party announces its intention to vote against the government in a confidence motion. If all the world knows that the government faces imminent defeat in such a motion, it seems inappropriate to require that a president, faced with a dissolution request from a Taoiseach who manages to reach the presidential residence before the vote is actually taken, has to act as if unaware that the ground on which the Taoiseach stands is about to be taken from under his or her feet.

Why, then, might a president refuse to agree to a request for a dissolution in these circumstances? Such refusal would make most sense if there is reason to believe that a new government, with a reasonable prospect of stability, could be formed from the existing Dáil, of a different partisan complexion or even of the same complexion but under a different leader. It is known that, in 1944 when this situation first arose, the key factor in the president's decision to grant the request was his belief that no stable government could be formed from the existing Dáil (Dunleavy and Dunleavy 1991: 428).

The other four presidential powers are minor in comparison, and only the first—and that in largely ceremonial circumstances—has ever been employed. First, the president may convene a meeting of either or both houses of the Oireachtas (parliament), under Article 13.2.3. The other three arise in the case of disputes between the Dáil and the Seanad, the indirectly elected upper house of parliament. Two are minor, relating to the appointment of a committee to decide whether a particular bill is a 'money bill' (in which case the Seanad's scope for action is reduced), and to whether a bill is so urgent that the Seanad's time to consider it should be reduced (Articles 22.2 and 24.1). The third is a controlling function; in the case of a bill that has been passed by the Dáil but rejected by the Seanad, one-third of the members of the Dáil and a majority of Senators may petition the president to refer the bill to a referendum, whereupon the president has complete discretion as to whether to do so (Article 27).

The president serves a maximum of two seven-year terms. He or she may be removed from office if the Supreme Court declares the president to be 'permanently incapacitated' (Article 12.3.1), or through the process of impeachment for 'stated misbehaviour' (Article 12.10), a term not further elaborated in the constitution. The impeachment process is not easily launched. A proposal to impeach the president must be supported by two-thirds of the members of one house of parliament, whereupon the other house investigates the charge; if two-thirds of the investigating house support a proposal that the charge has been sustained and that the misbehaviour is such as to render the president 'unfit to remain in office', the president is thereby removed from office. Removal of the president through impeachment, then, requires broad political consensus in favour of this step.

Four other provisions of the constitution are worth noting. First, the president is not answerable to any court for the way in which he or she discharges the responsibilities of the office (Article 13.8.1; see Hogan and Whyte 1994: 95–6). Secondly, one striking restriction placed on the president is laid down in Article 12.9, which states that the president may not leave the state without the consent of the government. This provision, taken on its own, might convey the impression that the president is decidedly subordinate to the government, with the status of a functionary who may not go off duty without permission. Thirdly, the president is empowered to address a message to the nation or to parliament at any time on any 'matter of national or public importance', but any such message must have received the approval of the government (Article 13.7). Fourthly, the constitution declares that 'the supreme command of the Defence Forces is hereby vested in the President' (Article 13.4), though the next article goes on to state that the exercise of this 'supreme command' shall be regulated by law, and de Valera, when explaining this section of the constitution when the Dáil discussed it, said that this command 'is only nominal' (Hogan and Whyte 1994: 91 n. 6). Indeed, the point was colourfully made on one occasion that despite possessing this 'supreme command', the president does not have the power even to order a soldier to pour a bowl of soup (Professor John Kelly, *Dáil Debates*, 293: 187, 21 Oct. 1976).

Most of the presidential functions, with the exception of the discretionary power to refuse a dissolution to a Taoiseach who has ceased to retain the support of a majority in the Dáil, can be exercised only after consultation with the Council of State, though the final decision is the president's alone. The Council of State contains a number of present and former senior political and judicial office holders (Article 31.2), plus up to seven people appointed by the president.

Summing up this list of presidential roles and functions, it can be seen that they come nowhere near to giving the president any kind of executive power. The president may not veto or introduce legislation, has no power over the budget, and has no role in government formation. The president's only significant powers are not initiating but controlling ones, concerning the referral of bills to the judiciary and the ability, in certain circumstances, to deny a prime minister a dissolution of parliament.

THE PRESIDENT IN POLITICS

The Election of the President

As has been noted, the direct election of the president was an important aspect of the new office when it was established, affirming that the Irish people had the right to choose their own head of state. The president is elected in a nationwide vote, but the nomination procedure is very restricted. To stand for the office, any candidate (other than a current or past president, who can nominate himself or herself) must be nominated either by (i) 20 members of the houses of the Oireachtas, or (ii) four county or major city councils (Article 12.4.2). The election is held under the alternative vote, under which voters can rank order the candidates, and, unless one candidate has received a majority of first preferences, the count proceeds by successive eliminations of the lowest-placed candidates and the redistribution of their votes to the other candidates according to the next preferences marked on the ballot papers (for the alternative vote, see Farrell 1997: 45–50).

In practice, only the largest three parties, Fianna Fáil, Fine Gael, and Labour, can expect to have as many as 20 members of parliament, and moreover these three parties dominate every local council, so this procedure gives them a key gatekeeper role. Five 'elections' have been uncontested. Twice the parties have agreed upon a candidate among themselves, thus depriving the electorate of any choice: in 1938 there was all-party agreement on the selection of the elderly Douglas Hyde as the first president, and in 1974 the parties agreed to nominate a leading judicial figure, Cearbhall Ó Dálaigh. On three other occasions, too, the people have been deprived of any choice: in 1952 and 1983 the parties, partly because they did not want to expend their energies on an electoral contest for a relatively unimportant position, were happy to allow the incumbent to nominate himself unopposed for a second term, and in 1976 the government, following a clash with President Ó Dálaigh that had led to his resignation, offered no nominee for the resulting vacancy, thus allowing the opposition party's candidate to fill the post.

The first five contested elections, those of 1945 to 1990 inclusive, bore out the view that the major parties formed a cartel that could deny a presidential nomination to all but their favoured candidate(s). On each occasion Fianna Fáil ran a candidate, who was opposed by a Fine Gael candidate in 1959 and 1966; by a Fine Gael candidate who was also backed by Labour in 1973; by both a Fine Gael candidate and an independent (who was nominated by some Labour and minor party parliamentarians) in 1945; and by both a Fine Gael candidate and a Labour-backed independent in 1990. A report by a Constitutional Review Group (CRG) in the mid-1990s took the view that the nomination requirements 'are too restrictive and in need of democratization', recommending either a reduction in the number of parliamentarians needed to validate a nomination or, perhaps, the option for a certain number of registered electors to nominate a candidate, though it was concerned about the practical difficulties of validating such nominators (Constitution Review Group 1996: 29).

Some of these assumptions about the over-restrictive nature of the nomination process were called into question by the 1997 election. For the first time, two independent candidates succeeded in being nominated by the county council route. The major parties did not use their strength on the councils to vote against these independents, either out of embarrassment at being seen to deprive someone of their chance to put themselves before the people or because of a belief that these independent candidacies might benefit their own candidate. For the most part, the major party councillors in these cases did not vote on the proposed nominations, with the result that some of the nominations were made by a handful of minor party or non-party councillors, with the majority of councillors abstaining. Any change to this aspect of the nomination process might stipulate that nomination by a council require the support of a majority of all councillors, not just a majority of those voting.

Until the 1990s, parties tended to nominate elderly politicians for whom acceding to the presidency marked in effect retirement from active politics. As Table 6.1 shows, three of the first four presidents had reached pension age when they became president. Seán T. O'Kelly was slightly younger, but he had gone as far as he could go in government; he was deputy prime minister but 'was not widely considered Taoiseach material' (Lee 1989: 239). Hillery, the sixth president, would still have had a future in national politics, but his acceptance of his party's nomination to the presidency was seen as abandonment rather than furtherance of his political aspirations. Five of the first six presidents went into retirement after leaving the presidency; the sixth, Childers, died in office.

TABLE 6.1. *Presidents of Ireland, 1938–1998*

President	Year	How became president	Age	Party	Background
Douglas Hyde	1938	Sole nominee	78	Ind.	Academic, Irish language enthusiast
Seán T. O'Kelly	1945	Elected 1945 Sole nominee 1952	62	FF	Government minister 1932–45
Eamon de Valera	1959	Elected 1959 Re-elected 1966	76	FF	Prime minister 1932–48, 1951–4, 1957–9; Leader of FF 1926–59
Erskine Childers	1973	Elected	67	FF	Government minister 1951–4, 1957–73
Cearbhall Ó Dálaigh	1974	Sole nominee	63	FF	Judge. Former Attorney-General in FF governments 1946–8, 1951–3
Patrick Hillery	1976	Sole nominee 1976 and 1983	53	FF	EC Commissioner 1973–6. Government minister 1959–72
Mary Robinson	1990	Elected	46	Lab.	Academic lawyer. Defeated Labour parliamentary candidate 1977 and 1981
Mary McAleese	1997	Elected	46	FF	Academic lawyer. Defeated FF parliamentary candidate 1987

Source: Coakley and Gallagher 1996: 274–8.

The 1990 election was seen as changing much of this. Although Fianna Fáil nominated a veteran politician, Labour's nominee, Mary Robinson, was not only the first woman to stand for the presidency but also considerably younger than the presidential norm (O'Sullivan 1991). She also became the first president to move on to another job after serving her time in the office, becoming the United Nations High Commissioner for Human Rights in 1997. Her presidency was widely seen as very successful; for example, in a 1995 opinion poll, 86 per cent of respondents hoped that she would seek a second term when her first expired (Marsh, Wilford, King, and McElroy 1996: 256). In 1997, each of the three major parties selected a woman, and of the five candidates only one, an MEP since 1984, had ever been elected to any public office. The criteria for the job, it seemed, had changed; being a veteran male politician, almost a requirement in earlier contests, was now a major handicap.

Presidential elections themselves are a mixture of party-based and personality-driven contests. On the one hand, the conventional wisdom is that candidates need the backing of a party organization to be elected. Indeed, with the exception of 1990, every contested election has been won by the candidate of Fianna Fáil, Ireland's largest party. In 1990 the winner, Mary Robinson, was selected and backed by the Labour party, although she was at pains throughout to stress that she was running as an independent, having left Labour in 1985. On the other hand, in an electorate whose party identification, always low, seems to be declining further, the possibility of an independent without party backing prevailing is not a complete impossibility, assuming that such a person manages to leap the hurdle of nomination in the first place. There have been three independent candidates in elections thus far. In 1945 Patrick McCartan won 20 per cent of the votes, and in 1997, while Derek Nally's campaign fizzled out into ignominy at the polls (a mere 5 per cent), Rosemary Scallon, better known (at least in Ireland) as the 1971 Eurovision winner Dana, took 14 per cent, over twice as many as the Labour candidate.

The political parties take a strong interest in capturing the presidency not because the office represents the 'commanding heights' of the landscape but, to pursue the orographic metaphor, simply because it is there. Winning a national contest boosts a party's morale; faring poorly has the opposite effect. After Labour's surprise success in 1990, the party was very upbeat, and went on to achieve unprecedented success at the next general election, in 1992. In contrast, Fine Gael's dismal performance at that election led to the ousting within days of the party leader, and the 7 per cent vote of the Labour candidate in 1997 was soon followed by the resignation of the party leader, who had handpicked the candidate. However, winning the presidency is most certainly a sideshow compared with gaining power through success at a general election, and Duverger's claim that the direct election of the president structures the party system by leading to 'the polarisation of the citizens around the two large parties' (Duverger 1986*a*: 72) is, to say the least, far-fetched.

Those who want to wield power, or indeed to be politically active, do not want to be president. Mary Robinson while president used to tell visitors, perhaps only partly in jest, that she had received a seven-year sentence, and if she behaved well, far from receiving remission, her sentence would be doubled (Siggins 1997: 161). President Hillery seems to have looked on the role in this light; approaching the end of his first term he was looking forward to doing something more fulfilling and made his views known to the political parties. When one party leader asked him whether there was anything he wanted, he replied, 'All I want is out' (Carroll, in *Irish Times*, 3 Aug. 1991, 2). In the event, his sense of duty led him to bow to the entreaties of the parties, whose finances could not sustain an election campaign at the time, and accept a second seven-year stretch. Hillery seemed an unenthusiastic president from the start, telling a journalist shortly before he took up his post in 1976 that 'At the moment I'm going into a vacuum that's hard to explain' (Kerrigan 1983: 49).

Party is certainly a strong influence on voting behaviour. In 1997 both the winner and the runner-up were the first choice of around 70 per cent of their respective supporting parties (Marsh 1999). In 1990 the relationship was even stronger: the winner was backed by 86 per cent of supporters of the parties backing her, and the runner-up by 76 per cent of his party's supporters (Gallagher and Marsh 1993: 75). At the same time, election campaigns are not straightforward party contests. Candidates, even when nominated and backed by a party, increasingly stress their independence and resist attempts by their supporting party to fly the party flag. The candidates hope thereby to broaden their appeal beyond the party faithful, but it can be resented by the party, which feels that the candidate is treating their organizational support as if it were a free lunch. Tensions between the candidate and the supporting party were noted both for the successful Robinson campaign in 1990 and the unsuccessful campaign of the Fine Gael candidate, Mary Banotti, in 1997 (O'Reilly 1991: 61–4; Marsh 1999).

Although, then, party allegiances are a significant influence on voting behaviour, presidential elections inevitably have a strong element of personal popularity contest about them, given the low stakes in policy terms. The candidates themselves, unable—because they cannot make any—to talk about the policy changes they might like to bring about, are compelled to resort to projecting themselves as likeable, sensible people who could be trusted to symbolize the nation in its own eyes and who would convey a good impression of the country abroad. Since they can make no political promises, they are inevitably driven back on completely apolitical platforms that lack any substance.

In 1990, it was said that 'all three candidates promoted the same basic theme—An Open Presidency. Many of their speeches were indistinguishable, making the same general statements about promoting

Ireland, giving minority groups recognition, making the Office and the Áras [the president's house] more accessible' (O'Reilly 1991: 84). Things were much the same in 1997. The campaign literature of the winner, Mary McAleese, said:

I' have a dream for the eighth Presidency of Ireland which I hope you will recognize as your dream too. It is a dream for a Presidency which will meet the future with hope and confidence. I want to be a President who will bring a cool head to protecting the Constitution and a warm heart to each person whom the Constitution exists to defend, a President who can show each person that he or she is utterly respected and valued. When you come to choose Ireland's next President I hope you will decide that you and I can meet the future together.

The appeals of the other candidates were equally bland. The runner-up stressed her 'proven ability and experience' to fulfil the 'ambassadorial, symbolic and constitutional roles' of the office, while the Labour-backed candidate declared that 'Adi Roche wants to build a Presidency of the People—a Presidency that every member of our community can share in and be proud of'. Even if it could be argued that many party platforms these days are not much less vague, parties do at least usually issue manifestos addressing various policy issues. In the case of the presidential candidates, the broad platitudes are all there is.

Presidents and Their Powers

As we have already noted, most of the few powers that the constitution grants to the president of Ireland have lain unused. This does not mean that presidents have been less active than they should have been; when it comes to most of the minor powers, the president is merely one link in a sequence, and the events that would be required to trigger presidential activity have not occurred. For example, the president has never been petitioned by the requisite number, or indeed any number, of TDs and Senators to refer a bill to a referendum. The president has on occasion summoned parliament either for purely ceremonial reasons or to hear a government-approved 'message' of a general nature, but there has been no question in these cases of the president crossing swords with the political establishment.

The president's use, or potential use, of the two main powers—the right, under specified circumstances, to refuse a dissolution to a Taoiseach, and the right to refer bills to the Supreme Court—have been more significant. No president has ever refused a dissolution to a

Taoiseach, although on several occasions the request for a dissolution
has come from a Taoiseach who has clearly 'ceased to retain the support
of a majority in Dáil Éireann'. Since this power to deny the Taoiseach
a general election would clearly constitute major intervention in the
political process, it is worth examining the four cases where this power
has come closest to being exercised.

First, in 1944, when the government was defeated on a fairly minor
matter, the Taoiseach, de Valera, sought a dissolution. As we have seen,
de Valera accepted that this was a situation where the president had discretion to deny him a dissolution, but the president decided, after some
thought, to grant the dissolution (Ward 1994: 290). Secondly, in January
1982, the government was defeated on its budget, and the Taoiseach,
Garret FitzGerald, sought a dissolution. The opposition Fianna Fáil
party made known its hope that the president would turn down the
request, declaring its own readiness to form a government, and even
trying to telephone the president to 'remind' him of his power to turn
down FitzGerald's request (a course of action that featured as a controversy in the 1990 presidential campaign—see O'Reilly 1991: 101–44).
However, the president agreed to the dissolution. Thirdly, in 1989,
Charles Haughey, while remaining in office as a caretaker Taoiseach
pending the election of a new Taoiseach, asserted that he had the right
to seek a dissolution, and rashly stated that 'the accepted wisdom' was
that no president would ever refuse a request from a Taoiseach for a
dissolution, adding that he knew the views of several presidents on the
matter, an assertion that triggered a wave of contrary opinion (Casey
1992: 73).

The fourth case, and the crunch that shows that this presidential
power is not a dead letter, arose in November 1994. The coalition government of Fianna Fáil and Labour collapsed, and the Labour TDs
announced their intention to support an opposition motion of no
confidence in the Dáil, which the rump Fianna Fáil government was
certain to lose. The president, Mary Robinson, made a point of calling
in the chairperson of the Bar Council for a consultation, presumably to
seek confirmation that she would have the power to refuse a request for
a dissolution if one were made, and although she did not publicly state
her position, it has been said that she 'has let it be known that she would
have refused a dissolution in November 1994 had one been sought by
the then Taoiseach' (Hogan, in *Irish Times*, 21 Oct. 1997). The Taoiseach,
accordingly, resigned but did not seek a dissolution, which paved the
way for the first ever change of government without an election, as the
Labour party linked up with two former opposition parties to form a

new coalition (Garry 1995). This incident seems to have definitively established that the president's power to refuse a dissolution to a Taoiseach is not confined to situations where the Taoiseach has lost a confidence motion. In other words, the president seems to have some discretion, albeit not absolute discretion, in deciding when this power may be exercised (Gallagher 1988: 85). Political actors, then, must take account of this presidential power, which can thus be effective even without having to be wielded. It may be this that former president Patrick Hillery had in mind when he said, rather cryptically, of his powers that 'the most important use of these powers was sometimes not to employ them at all', while acknowledging that not everyone was impressed with what he termed 'such considered inaction' (Hillery, in *Irish Times*, 12 Nov. 1997).

The other main power, the Article 26 power to refer a bill to the Supreme Court for a judgment on its constitutionality, was employed on twelve occasions up to the end of 1997. On six occasions, the Supreme Court found the bill constitutional, and on the other six it found that the bill, or sections of it, were unconstitutional.

While this power can be seen as the most effective of those possessed by the president, it is a double-edged one, and needs to be used sparingly. For one thing, a bill considered by the Supreme Court on a presidential referral and cleared by it can never again be constitutionally challenged, under Article 34.3.3. Thus, whatever the subsequent course of constitutional jurisprudence, and whatever new arguments, facts, or aspects of the actual operation of the piece of legislation may later come to light, the bill is protected for all time. For this reason the Supreme Court itself has pointed to the undesirability of presidential referrals, and it has been suggested that the Article 26 procedure is appropriate only in cases that raise 'a pure question of constitutional interpretation' (see Casey 1992: 267–71). Another problem with this presidential power is that whereas in the normal course of events the constitutionality of a law can be challenged only by an individual with a specific case to argue, in an Article 26 referral hypothetical suppositions can be conjured up and a bill might be found unconstitutional because of a possibility that might never arise in practice (Hogan, in *Irish Times*, 21 Oct. 1997).

Relations between Presidents and Political Actors

As we have seen, the presidency has evolved as a basically non-partisan office. Presidents do not behave, in office, as party politicians, and concepts such as 'cohabitation' and 'divided government' are not part of the lexicon of Irish politics. Presidents are not expected, by either the public or the political class, to play an active political role, or to use their office as a base from which to support or thwart government plans. Nevertheless, relations between presidents and governments are not always harmonious.

These relations are well shielded from the public gaze. The quasi-monarchic nature of the office means that many of the questions that could legitimately be asked about party politicians would appear intrusive if put to or raised about the president. Little information is disclosed on communication between president and government. For example, under the constitution (Article 28.5.2) the Taoiseach is obliged to 'keep the President generally informed on matters of domestic and international policy'. In 1976 it emerged that the Taoiseach, Liam Cosgrave, had visited President Ó Dálaigh only four times in the previous two years (*Dáil Debates*, 294: 429–30, 23 Nov. 1976). He had visited the previous president, Erskine Childers, about once a month, but Cosgrave's briefings contained 'little more than could be gleaned from the newspapers' (Young 1985: 190). Subsequent questions on this subject have tended to be answered rather primly, as if the questioner were prying improperly into a private and intimate matter. In 1980 the then Taoiseach Charles Haughey refused to give details of his meetings with the president on the grounds that this would not be 'in keeping with the dignity of the office of President' (*Dáil Debates*, 325: 563–5, 9 Dec. 1980; see also Garret FitzGerald, *Dáil Debates*, 345: 3–5, 19 Oct. 1983). The president in question, Patrick Hillery, later said that this communication could be done as well by telephone as by a meeting, and although the Taoiseach of the day would come up 'now and again', he said like Childers that 'sure everything they'd be telling you, you knew already from the papers' (Carroll, in *Irish Times*, 5 Aug. 1991, 10).

It appears that, behind the scenes, there has been more tension between presidents and governments than might be supposed, arising more from a presidential desire to expand the scope of the office than from straightforward political clashes. The second president, Seán T. O'Kelly, has been described as 'not the easiest of presidents for a government to deal with; he could be obstinate and unreasonable at times' (Keogh 1994: 163). Eamon de Valera's presidency, for all but the last four months, coincided with Fianna Fáil governments, leaving little apparent scope for political clashes, yet this presidency is seen by some as an intriguing story that remains to be written. His successor as Taoiseach and leader of Fianna Fáil, Seán Lemass, suspected one of his own ministers (by coincidence Erskine Childers, the future president) of privately passing political information to de Valera (Horgan 1997: 197). In the period 1969–73, when the Fianna Fáil party was split over the issue of Northern Ireland, it seems that de Valera, while president, may have played a part behind the scenes in striving to maintain the unity of the party (Boland 1977: 13; Coogan 1993: 686–7; Dwyer 1980: 146).

De Valera's successor, Erskine Childers was elected in 1973 after a campaign in which he had spoken of widening the scope of the office and establishing his personal 'think tank'. After what have been described as 'warning growls' from politicians he was compelled to rein in his schemes, and he apparently contemplated resigning in frustration just a few weeks after his election (Chubb 1978: 28–9; Young 1985: 169–92; FitzGerald 1991: 254).

Tense relations with the government were most apparent in the case of the fifth president, Cearbhall Ó Dálaigh. Matters came to a head late in 1976 when Ó Dálaigh quite reasonably referred a security bill to the Supreme Court for a judgment on its constitutionality. The Minister for Defence, addressing a group of soldiers, described the president in a phrase sanitized by the media to 'a thundering disgrace', and when the Taoiseach did not insist on the minister's resignation, Ó Dálaigh resigned. Although no one defended the minister's abuse of the president, it appears that there was some feeling within the government that, given the serious security situation at the time, the president should not have exercised his controlling function on this occasion (Collins 1996: 187). It later emerged that relations between the president and the government had been bad for some time. Although Ó Dálaigh's background was in Fianna Fáil, and the government was a coalition of Fine Gael and Labour, the Minister for Foreign Affairs in the government later blamed the difficulties not on political differences but on Ó Dálaigh's lack of political experience and judgement, describing Ó Dálaigh as 'difficult and even eccentric' and as 'temperamentally less disciplined' than his predecessor (FitzGerald, in *Irish Times*, 20 Sept. 1997; his article was followed by a vigorous defence of Ó Dálaigh by O'Flaherty, in *Irish Times*, 29 Sept. 1997).

There seem to have been no problems between governments and Ó Dálaigh's successor, Patrick Hillery, who had a strong sense of the constraints of the office, which he felt it would be inappropriate to challenge. Mary Robinson's presidency (1990–7) was far more high profile, and indeed during her electoral campaign in 1990 she had spoken startlingly of confronting the government; she said she would be able to look the Taoiseach in the eye and 'tell him to back off if necessary' because she would have been directly elected by the people and he hadn't (Siggins 1997: 157). She soon retreated from this position, but once in office governments of all complexions had occasion to be unhappy with her actions. Sometimes the government blocked her plans, for example in 1993 to co-chair a group established to consider the future of the United Nations and in 1991 to deliver a lecture on the BBC (for accounts of her presidency, see O'Regan, in *Irish Times*, 10 Sept. 1997; Siggins 1997: 161–83; Sykes 1997: 57–62). The strongest disagreement occurred in 1993, when against the clear wishes of the government she visited Northern Ireland and shook hands with Gerry Adams, the leader of Sinn Féin, the political party linked to the IRA, at a time when the IRA was engaged in a campaign of violence. The government press secretary recorded in his diary that the Minister for Foreign Affairs was 'livid' at her action (Duignan 1995: 107–8). In April 1995 further government displeasure was reported after Robinson expressed concern about the 'genuine fears' of Northern Ireland unionists about a policy document agreed by the British and Irish governments (Siggins 1997: 170–1). The tension was primarily between the president and the leadership of the Labour party, which had supported her when she ran for the office in 1990, and cannot be seen as a manifestation of 'divided government'. It was interpreted by some as arising from Labour resentment at her determination to emphasize her independence of the party rather than from policy disagreement. Overall, though, relations between Robinson and successive governments were good, and her high opinion poll ratings quelled any temptation for governments to confront her too bluntly.

Enlarging the Office

As it has evolved, then, the Irish presidency is a predominantly ceremonial role, though its political aspects make it more than merely ceremonial. It could be enlarged in either or both of two ways: by stretching the existing powers of the office, or by bestowing additional powers on the office.

The precise boundaries of the Irish presidential role are not defined—though, clearly, many areas are off-limits. Thus, the answer to the kind of 'what if the president goes mad?' question once beloved of British constitutional writers is unambiguous: Article 12 of the constitution provides for the removal of a president who is incapacitated or who behaves in a manner that parliament believes renders him or her unfit for office. Yet there are grey areas. Whereas President Hillery (1976–90) always accepted without demur the government's view of the limits of the office, his successor, Mary Robinson, said that she had expanded the barriers: 'there were a number of what they said were precedents which had no particular basis and I had the equipment as a constitutional lawyer to know that boundaries had been set which weren't really the constitutional framework' (Carroll, in *Irish Times*, 26 July 1997: 3).

The greyest area concerns what the president may say and to whom. Although the content of presidential 'messages to the nation' must be approved in advance by the government, it does not follow that any presidential utterance must secure this clearance. Past practice seems to have varied: the fourth president, Erskine Childers, sent all his scripts to the government for prior approval, to find them returned in a heavily amended form, whereas his successor, Cearbhall Ó Dálaigh, apparently refrained from submitting his scripts to the government at all (Brady, in *Irish Times*, 3 Dec. 1976: 14). Presidents might push at the boundaries of the office by using their many engagements to indicate their views on issues on the political agenda, while being at all times constrained by the political cultural expectation that the president will not enter the party political arena. Open criticism of government policy would be widely felt to contravene the bounds of the office, but there are subtler ways for a president to step onto the political pitch. A president might, for example, let his or her views be known in advance of a referendum (Ireland is one of Europe's most frequent users of the referendum), or express views similar to those of the opposition on some contentious issue. In these circumstances, impeachment might seem a draconian response with potentially heavy political costs for the government that seeks to invoke it—quite apart from the fact that, given the two-thirds majorities in both houses that the impeachment process requires, a successful impeachment would require the support of at least part of the opposition in the first place.

Between the bland utterings that everyone sees as acceptable, and the grave misbehaviour that would be seen by both politicians and people as meriting impeachment, there exists an extensive but largely uncharted terrain that some future president may choose to explore. The answer to the question 'How far can a president go before being impeached?' is unknown. While this possibility, or problem, was unlikely to arise in the past, when presidents were nearly always retired politicians who had been socialized into the view that presidents did not rock the boat, it is less unlikely to emerge in the future given the changing profile of presidents (cf. Table 6.1).

Beyond the possibility of greater outspokenness, there is little scope for a more activist presidency. A president who set out to thwart the government of the day, either out of personal malice or in furtherance of the opposition's political agenda, would lack even residual powers to deploy to this end. The only relevant power would be that to refer bills to the Supreme Court for a judgment on their constitutionality, but a president who routinely referred bills in order to delay the government's legislative programme would be generally seen as abusing the office.

As for explicitly adding to the powers of the office, an opinion poll once suggested vague and general support for the idea (Marsh and Wilford 1991: 143), but it is rarely mooted. The presidency was considered by the CRG, which stressed the desirability of the president's being seen as 'above politics' (CRG 1996: 25–34). It opposed any increase in presidential powers, observing that this might involve the president in 'party politics' and would also create a problem of accountability given that the president is not answerable to parliament or the courts. The power usually mentioned when this subject arises is a role in government formation, similar to that of the head of state in many other European countries. The president has no such role, and the CRG did not favour creating one. Instead it advocated the German-style constructive vote of no confidence, under which a motion of no confidence in an existing Taoiseach would have to specify a successor. This, coupled with fixed-term parliaments, would, it felt, effectively remove the president from any role in the dissolution of parliament, let alone in government formation (for a critical discussion, see Ward 1996: 46–51). Other suggestions, such as allowing the president rather than the government to select judges, have fallen on stony ground.

CONCLUSION

Ireland clings onto a place in the 'semi-presidential' category by its fingertips. Were it not for the direct election of the president, no one would propose placing it in that category, and given the actual role played by the president since 1938, a 'centi-presidential' model might seem more appropriate for Ireland than a semi-presidential one. Nonetheless, and accepting that the role of the president occupies a minor space in an essentially parliamentary system of government, the president does have two significant controlling powers—to refuse a dissolution in certain circumstances, and to refer bills to the courts for a test of their constitutionality—and, even though the first of these has never been used, its very existence has had a political impact especially in 1994. The high esteem in which the office is held enables the president to use fully those powers that she or he does possess. Criticism of a president for exercising his or her discretionary powers is virtually unknown, and would rebound against any politician engaging in what would be seen as inappropriate behaviour.

The Irish presidency is weak primarily because the written constitution accords it few powers. This position is reinforced by the evolution of the office as one characterized by dignity and an 'above politics' aloofness, a political cultural norm that would constrain any president tempted to use the moral authority bestowed by direct election to claim a mandate to speak out on controversial issues. The president, indeed the presidency, is held in high esteem, but only as long as the occupant's behaviour conforms to the people's expectations concerning the office. The bounds of the office have not been tested in the past, partly because most presidents have been retired politicians fully socialized into a non-activist perception of the office. The changing profile of presidents and presidential candidates raises the possibility that these bounds may be tested more frequently in future.

7

Bulgaria

VENELIN I. GANEV

The semi-presidential regime in Bulgaria is of recent origin. An absolute novelty in the political history of the country, it was established in July 1991, when a Great National Assembly[1] adopted a new constitution. Article 1 of the constitution proclaims that 'Bulgaria shall be a republic with a parliamentary form of government'. The emphasis on 'parliamentary' was clearly intended to dispel any doubts about the subordinate role of the president, who 'shall be elected directly by the voters for a period five years' (Article 93). Even though the framers of the constitution deliberately created a dual structure of the executive branch, the text of the fundamental law envisages a mode of distribution of prerogatives which is heavily skewed in favour of the legislature and a cabinet accountable to the deputies.

It would be difficult, however, to sustain a claim that a general pattern of leadership is beginning to emerge under Bulgarian semi-presidentialism.[2] On the one hand, Bulgaria has only had two presidents under its new constitution—Zhelyu Zhelev (1991–7) and Petar Stoyanov (1997–) and, therefore, any attempt on the part of students of Bulgarian politics to manufacture nomothetic statements which may be instantly employed in comparative analysis should be rightfully dismissed as a hollow hubristic exercise. On the other hand, transient equilibria were often swept away by unforeseen events, and in the aftermath of dramatic clashes, institutional arrangements crystallized in unpredictable forms. The closest to a valid generalization which may be ventured in the light of the evidence is that, while parliament enjoys supremacy over law-making and the government remains the primary site of executive decision-making, the *rapports* between these two institutions and the presidency have varied dramatically, with the influence of the head of state running the gamut from almost complete exclusion to a palpable ability to shape agendas. The carefully crafted institutional structure did not translate itself into a more or less permanent configuration of power where a 'figurehead' president is consistently upstaged by a dominant prime minister.

The purpose of this enquiry, then, is to identify and analyse the ways in which constitutionally designed patterns of institutional interaction shift in response to changes in the social and economic environment. Even though an attempt will be made to cast the arresting sequence of episodes which left their indelible mark on the inner workings of Bulgarian semi-presidentialism, this is not a chronicle of events. Rather, the analysis is conceived as a chronology of *the successive problems* with which political actors had to cope. As the Bulgarian polity evolved, the knotty plot underpinning semi-presidentialism, this 'new political system model' (Duverger 1980) blossomed into a fully-fledged political play structured around a set of familiar subplots: varieties of relationships between the presidency and parliamentary majorities; 'spasmodic' interventions of presidents eager to tip the balance of power in their favour; accepted procedures for 'sorting out' conflicts between the autonomous components of the institutional framework; resolving controversies which stem from the 'dual democratic legitimacy' enjoyed by presidents and parliaments representing opposing political forces. What makes the study of Bulgaria theoretically engrossing is that these leitmotifs are inextricably intertwined with the characteristic themes of the study of 'transitions to democracy': the emergence of rules and procedures where the arbitrary rule of party leaders reigned supreme; delineation of various stages in the consolidation of the party system; engineering the edifice of a viable system of separation of powers; the quest for institutional means to avert acute political crisis. Admittedly, an in-depth inquiry into the Bulgarian experience with semi-presidentialism would hardly yield definitive truths about the relationship between semi-presidentialism and democracy. It may provide, however, a firmer grasp of the polyphonic fashion in which these 'problématiques' play out in a post-communist context.

THE CONSTITUTIONAL BALANCE OF POWER

The Bulgarian constitution of 1991, like every other constitution, bears the imprint of the concrete historical circumstances under which it was created. More specifically, two types of strategic considerations undergirded the construction of the modern Bulgarian presidency: evaluation of the recent past and opportunistic calculations about the next elections.[3]

In 1990 the country had just emerged from a long period of communist oppression. Dictator Todor Zhivkov, who spent 35 years at the helm of party and state, was deposed on 10 November 1989, but the memory of the disasters which his authoritarian rule had inflicted on the country was still very much alive. Both the ex-communists (whose party was soon renamed Bulgarian Socialist Party, or BSP) and the fledgling opposition (most opposition parties were united in an umbrella coalition, the Union of Democratic Forces, UDF) were painfully aware that unbridled executive power is the hallmark of all oppressive regimes and determined to take all precautionary measures against a possible recrudescence of authoritarian leadership. Simply put, in the early 1990s there was no constituency supporting the idea of a strong, personalized presidency.

In the beginning of 1990, Round Table Talks were held between communist officials and the opposition, and they paved the way to the first multi-party elections (see Kolarova and Dimitrov 1996). At this early stage of the negotiations, the question of the presidency loomed large as an extremely contentious issue; what also became clear was that the rancorous debates reflected not impartial visions of well-balanced governmental structures, but tangible partisan interests. After a series of open and behind-the-scenes negotiations, which were often marked by dramatic reversals of positions and gridlock, all parties agreed on three things. First, as a temporary measure, the existing constitution was amended by the last all-communist parliament and the State Council (the highest executive body) was transformed into a presidency. Secondly, the new president shall be elected by the National Assembly. Thirdly, the future design of the presidential institution would be hammered out by a Great National Assembly, which would also adopt an entirely new constitution.[4] Soon thereafter, Petar Mladenov, the leader of the BSP, was elected president, and general elections were scheduled for June 1990.

The elections were won by the BSP, which captured an absolute majority (it controlled 211 out of 400 seats). However, soon thereafter Mladenov resigned and after prolonged negotiations the leader of the UDF, Zhelyu Zhelev, was elected president (see Elster 1993/4). As the work on the new constitution progressed, the BSP grew increasingly aware that its political fortunes were sinking, and hence their approach to the presidency was premissed on the expectation that this was an office which they would not be able to control after the next round of elections. Trimming the prerogatives of the presidency, therefore, became one of their overriding objectives. Conversely, while the opposition certainly did not entertain any thoughts of an 'imperial presidency', it was bent upon extending the power of an institution which they hoped to dominate.

Predictably, then, the Bulgarian version of semi-presidentialism embodies a compromise which made possible the coalescence of a two-thirds majority requisite for the passage of the constitution. BSP agreed to a popularly elected presidency, which was almost certain to be captured by incumbent Zhelyu Zhelev. But on virtually all other issues, BSP's blueprint for limited presidential powers prevailed.

While historical circumstances obviously affected the design of the presidency, it would be an exaggeration to maintain that the political context has a significance which transcends the episode of constitution-making itself. There was no popular consensus regarding the proper form of political leadership which might have imparted a particular dynamic on the newly created institution. Neither was there a charismatic individual to articulate an enduring vision of a powerful presidency. The cast of the semi-presidential regime was a by-product of political—and not ideological—considerations (see also Elster 1997: 236), and the peculiar outlines of the mould were to be determined by the outcome of future partisan struggles. At least in the Bulgarian case, the historical background has no import other than the way it affected the process of framing the provisions of the fundamental law. For better or worse, a deeply ingrained vision of the exact role of a president in democratic politics was a component which the Bulgarian political tradition did not possess.

The president can be re-elected only once and is assisted by a vice-president. The president has virtually no control over the government. Article 99 of the constitution provides that 'following consultations with parliamentary groups', the president must entrust the mandate to form a government to a prime minister designate nominated by the largest parliamentary faction. Should this individual fail to form a government within seven days thereafter, the president should give the mandate to a prime minister designate nominated by the second largest faction in the assembly, who also has seven days to fulfil the task. In case of a new failure, the mandate should be passed on to a candidate nominated by one of the smaller factions (and the president may choose with which smaller faction to negotiate). And if this third attempt to form a government is also futile, the president may dissolve parliament, appoint a caretaker government, and schedule new general elections. The president is not authorized to disband parliament under any other circumstances.

In practical terms, this procedure leaves the president with no authority over nominations. The process of 'consultations' is simply a formality which amounts to little more than party leaders informing the president to whom the mandate should be given; the only thing the president can do is temporize—the president is not bound by a specific deadline (as we shall see, on at least one occasion this circumstance proved to be important). Once entrusted with a mandate, the nominee is free to select ministers without consulting the head of state. And once elected by parliament, neither the ministers nor the prime minister can be dismissed by the president.

The president is deprived of law-making prerogatives, having no 'decree power', and the constitution does not allow for the passage of 'enabling acts' whereby legislative power is conferred on executive bodies.[5] The president has a veto power, but it is very weak: the veto can be overturned if more than half of all deputies vote against it, which leaves the president helpless against absolute majorities or large coalitions.

The president has limited power to appoint and dismiss, and the prerogatives in this respect are outlined both in the constitution and other legal acts. As a commander-in-chief, the president has the authority to make appointments in the higher command of the military forces and to bestow high military ranks (Article 100). On a motion from the government, the president can also appoint and dismiss ambassadors and to fill other important diplomatic positions (Article 98.6). The president appoints four of the twelve members of the Constitution Court (four are elected by parliaments and four are selected on a joint session of the Supreme Administrative Court and the Supreme Court of Cassation, Article 147). In addition, the president also has standing to petition the Court. Several laws passed since the adoption of the constitution expanded the power of the office to appoint and dismiss. For example, the president was granted the authority to appoint the head of the National Investigative Service and several members of the Board of Directors of the Bulgarian National Bank.

The president can address the nation, but cannot call referenda. He can declare 'a state of emergency' only if 'the National Assembly is not in session and cannot be convened' (Article 100.5). Otherwise, the president can only introduce in parliament a motion demanding a declaration of emergency, but the authority to issue the requisite declaration falls squarely within the ambit of parliamentary power (Article 84.12) (see Ganev 1997*a*).

Within the prerogatives vested in the institution, the president may issue decrees, which have to be countersigned, although some types of decrees are exempt from this requirement (Article 102). The president also presides over the Consultative National Security Council, a body whose functions are not specified in the constitution, but which, as we shall see, played an important role at several critical junctures of Bulgaria's recent history.

This survey warrants the conclusion that the Bulgarian presidency is designed as a fairly weak institution. The head of state is excluded from important spheres of executive decision-making and as a result has no direct leverage over social and economic policy. There is virtually no sphere in which the presidency can, at least *de jure*, impose its will unilaterally. While not purely ceremonial, its functions are rather limited, a circumstance which attests to the intention of the 'founding fathers' to relegate it to a secondary role in Bulgarian political life (Elster 1993: 192).

PRESIDENTIAL/PARLIAMENTARY RELATIONS

Presidential Interventions (1991–1994)

During the first three years of its existence, the semi-presidential regime in Bulgaria experienced dramatic fluctuations and sudden reversals. Conceived as a sturdy institutional scaffolding, the constitutionalized configuration of power at times displayed the magic qualities of a malleable magma which would cool into unpredictable shapes only to melt again under the heat of political struggles. Predictably, the ebb and flow of the president's 'partisan powers', or his ability to steer policy making which stems from 'his standing vis-à-vis the party system'[6] were the crucial factors determining both the scope of the president's personal influence and the institutional reach of the presidency. But other factors also played a significant role, thus complicating further the arduous task of throwing analytical light on these dramatic events.

The first general elections after the adoption of the new constitution were held in October 1991 under a d'Hondt-type PR electoral system with a 4 per cent threshold, which has remained a permanent component of the Bulgarian political system. The elections produced an assembly which was symmetrically fractured. The UDF captured 110 of all 240 seats, the BSP won 106, and the remaining 24 seats went to the political party of ethnic Turks, the Movement for Rights and Freedoms (MRF). Hence, the fate of all future governments was to be decided by the MRF, which controlled the swing vote—and also had built up a particularly warm relationship with President Zhelev. Initially, the MRF decided to support the UDF, which paved the way for the formation of a government headed by Philip Dimitrov, the Chairman of the UDF.

Only months later, in January 1992, Zhelev won his contest for the presidency against a die-hard communist opponent, Velko Vulkanov. At least for a fleeting moment, it appeared that the presidency and parliament, both dominated by democratic forces, would combine their forces to overcome the catastrophic problems bequeathed to the fledgling democracy by the *ancien régime*. Soon thereafter, however, the relations between Zhelev and his former party began to deteriorate and by the autumn of 1992 Dimitrov's government was ousted from power. In the Western literature these events are usually cast as a morality play which depicts a noble president valiantly defending democracy from the excesses of a clique of 'totalitarian anti-communists' (Brown 1994: 113). In addition to being ludicrously simplistic, such accounts are marred by a more general defect, which Ray Taras labels 'the tendency to focus on individuals rather than institutions' (Taras 1997a: 16). As a result, they obscure the importance of institutional and structural factors which played a major role all throughout this period. A close-up look at these factors may help us better comprehend the structure of opportunities that allows presidents to embark upon ambitious projects seemingly irreconcilable with their 'weak' position, and to identify the causes of their success and failure.

As 1992 wore on, President Zhelev began to voice his dissatisfaction with the Cabinet, pointing in particular to the 'lack of reforms'. Prime minister Dimitrov wasted no time returning the charges, accusing Zhelev of abandoning his own party and betraying his constituents. In early September 1992 Zhelev held a press-conference on the lawn in front of his presidential residence in Boyana, near Sofia. During the press conference Zhelev repeatedly attacked the UDF, accusing it of 'waging a war against everybody in this country'.[7] Several days later the head of the National Intelligence Service, Brigo Asparukhov, who was a close associate of Zhelev at that time and was directly subordinated to him, announced that his office had uncovered a link between some members of the UDF government and an attempted illegal shipment of weapons to Macedonia in defiance of the UN-imposed sanctions against former Yugoslavia.[8] Dimitrov flatly denied any wrongdoing and announced that he would ask parliament for a vote of confidence (at the time of writing, no evidence substantiating Asparukhov's claim has surfaced, despite the fact that his sensationalist revelations triggered several rounds of parliamentary and criminal investigations).

The crucial vote was preceded by intense 'consultations' between President Zhelev and the leader of the MRF Ahmed Dogan, and when it finally came, MRF switched sides and joined the jubilant ex-communists in toppling the government. Acting in accordance with Article 99 of the constitution, Zhelev entrusted the mandate to form a government first to the UDF, whose efforts to form a new government were stalled by the MRF, and then to the BSP, whose nominee was declared ineligible because he held a dual citizenship (French as well as Bulgarian). When MRF's turn to take the mandate finally came, Dogan announced that his party's candidate for prime minister was Ljuben Berov—Zhelev's personal economic adviser, whose loyalty to the president was his sole political asset. Undeterred by the fact that Berov was obviously hand-picked by the president, the BSP decided to support his candidacy. Thus, in December 1992 a new Cabinet under Berov was installed. Even in the surreal world of post-communist politics, this government was something of an anomaly: it ruled Bulgaria, which is usually stereotyped as a country seething with 'nationalist' passions, on behalf of an ethnic minority party, and was supported by a coalition which brought under the same umbrella ethnic Turks and the BSP, the very same party which subjected the Turkish minority to horrific ethnic persecution and violent discrimination in the 1980s (see Ganev 1995: 49–53).

Zhelev's behaviour towards the UDF is quite in keeping with a general trend of presidential interventions observable in a handful of post-communist countries. In a fine essay, Thomas A. Baylis characterizes the presidents' strategy in the following way: 'Their sense of national responsibility and their own distinctive legitimacy, as well as, in differing degrees, their ego involvement, leads them to seek ways of converting their assets of prestige into "real" power over policy' (Baylis 1996: 306). Tactical deployment of personal influence with a view to removing a political opponent and installing an ally is an integral part of this strategy. But did this intervention precipitate a shift of 'real' power towards the presidency?

Initially, it seemed that 'yes' would be the correct answer to this question. Prime minister Berov announced that he would work in close collaboration with the presidency. Zhelev himself untiringly repeated that the presidency was the veritable institutional fulcrum for change. The assorted policies which the president championed were put high on the government's agenda. But the honeymoon did not last long.

Berov and his ministers quickly realized that their future hinged on the votes of the BSP and MRF—not on the approval of the president. And since both parties, especially the BSP, were implacably hostile to any reforms, the government soon faced a dilemma: press forward with Zhelev's agenda, or listen carefully to the instructions of its parliamentary supporters. The result was quite predictable: Berov exited the orbit of presidential influence and became completely subservient to the demands of the heterogeneous parliamentary majority. Zhelev's relentless pleading for more reforms passed unheeded and one by one his initiatives—including his pet project, the restitution of agricultural land—were effectively killed. In April 1994 Zhelev finally announced that Berov's government was 'harmful for Bulgaria', but this time he could not mobilize his allies to bring down the Cabinet. Berov stepped down only in September 1994, when the BSP felt confident that its grip on power—especially outside the big cities—was sufficiently firm to ensure an electoral victory.

What appeared as a successful foray into constitutional spheres from which the president is scrupulously barred (such as ministerial appointments and legislative initiative), turned out to be an ill-conceived project which soon ran out of steam. What conclusions about the functioning of the Bulgarian semi-presidentialism can be derived from this incident?

The true dimensions of presidential failure and success may be adequately grasped if two commonsensical distinctions are kept in mind.

The first distinction is between splitting a hostile coalition and building up a new one. Zhelev did indeed persuade the MRF to change horses in mid-stream; but he never replaced the coalition which crumbled with a presidential alliance. A diffused agreement to support Berov held sway over a number of deputies, because on six separate occasions the government survived no-confidence motions filed by the UDF. At least some measure of party discipline seemed to prevail. Rather than a 'régime des partis', this was a form of parliamentary partnership called by Duverger a 'regime of shifting majorities' which falls somewhere between coherent majorities and unstructured partisan anarchy (Duverger 1986*d*: 15). The kind of relationship between parties was as important as their number and internal discipline: the lack of commitment to any specific policy objectives rendered futile the president's effort to spark off the process of reform through a rearrangement of the existing power equilibrium. In the absence of a pro-reform consensus in parliament, Zhelev's behind-the-scene operations floundered rather quickly on the reefs of BSP's anti-reform obduracy. To the extent that the disintegration of the largest parliamentary group caused a vacuum, this situation was beneficial to the second largest group, not the presidency. To use Tony Verheijen's succinct formulation, 'the BSP found its way back to power without having to take government responsibility' (1995: 138). Rather than a Frankenstein, Zhelev installed a marionette only to discover that someone else would be pulling the strings.

The second distinction is between smoothing the way of a close associate to power and steering the politics of the government in a particular direction. Zhelev was fairly successful in pushing through his candidate. But, contrary to his expectations, this manoeuvre established a 'connectedness' between the presidency and the government which was tenuous at best. The two institutions were de-linked as soon as the instructions coming from the head of state conflicted with the demands of the deputies as well as 'the small requests' of shady businessmen with whom Berov's ministers were quick to strike a *rapport*.

This turn of events brings into sharp relief the shortcomings of a strategy frequently embraced by presidents bereft of parliamentary support: the instalment of a government composed of putative experts. Zhelev welcomed Berov and his ministers as 'experts' who would 'rise above' petty partisan controversies and embrace the cause of 'the common good' (Crampton 1997: 229). In Bulgaria, this idea served little more than as a veil of legitimacy drawn over Zhelev's attempt to gain dominance over the executive branch. In this context, it is perhaps necessary to mention that Berov's persona exuded the unmistakable odour of mediocrity. More importantly, however, it is crucial to understand that all these 'experts' are, in fact, agents forced to operate in the political thicket and soon learn how to behave accordingly. Disregard the inconvenient appeals of the president and count the votes on the eve of the upcoming no-confidence motion—this is the 'expertise' which they have to master as long as they are willing to play the game of politics.

One additional problem with theoretical implications might also be considered here: how does the effort to gain access to executive power by way of a mentor/protégé relationship affect both the presidency and the personal influence of the president? An interesting asymmetry seems to transpire in this respect: relying on a loyal, figurehead prime minister may enhance the power of the incumbent, but undermine the strength of the presidency. Joseph Schumpeter once remarked that 'the prime minister in a democracy might be likened to . . . a general who [is] so fully occupied with making sure that his army will accept his orders that he must leave strategy to take care of itself' (1950: 287). Giving to that powerful view a somewhat unexpected twist, one may argue that Zhelev, while busy making sure that Berov behaved properly, might have missed the opportunity to establish the patterns of interaction which would lend credence to future presidents' claims that 'precedent is on their side'. When conflict arrived, Zhelev had two choices: either treat it as a personal problem between himself and Berov, or as an institutional problem to be resolved through delineation of competencies. Zhelev obviously preferred the first option, and it seems that in such situations time spent revitalizing a sagging personal relationship is time lost for the building of the institution. Had Zhelev chosen the second alternative, he might have used his residual influence over the government to win institutional victories for the presidency, especially in such an early period when the contours of the system of power-sharing are arguably blurred on the edges. To appoint a favourite may be good for a president in the short run—it is a mixed blessing for the presidency in the long run.

The diminished intensity of 'partisan powers'—in other words, Zhelev's abdication from the leadership of the UDF and his drift towards other parliamentary forces—is certainly a factor of paramount importance which should be never lost sight of. But there is an additional factor which should be also included in any equation purporting to explain Zhelev's failure: the weakness of the presidency as an administrative unit.

In a perceptive analysis of the role of the British prime minister, Richard Rose points out that in Britain 'the office exists before the individual' (1980: 43). This was not the case with the Bulgarian presidency, both in the constitutional sense and in the very practical sense of knowing which secretary is in charge of the faxes and where the key for the file cabinets is kept. And while the machinery necessary for the functioning of the presidency was relatively easy to acquire, bureaucratic coherence and administrative efficiency proved much harder to accomplish.

In a very palpable sense, the presidency is an administrative unit which has to handle daily tasks in a routine manner. It appears, though, that Zhelev considered it more as a habitat populated by his personal friends who could resolve problems by talking them over (Gurkovska 1996 and Popov 1996). The president was surrounded by a fading group of former dissidents who in fact isolated both himself from other social actors and themselves from society in general. Perceiving the running of the presidency as a continuation of the old camaraderies in a new context, Zhelev never made an effort to discipline his advisers and make sure that they did not make statements which might be damaging for the institution. And he never established a working bureaucratic apparatus to process information and generate policy proposals. Always capable of expressing his concern for the reforms in captivating, eloquent phrases, Zhelev neglected the task of building up the institutional wherewithal which would allow the presidency to keep pushing forward vital pro-reform projects. And abstract concerns expressed during public appearances were rarely followed by concrete, informative policy decisions distributed among those interested in policy change.

The lack of administrative coherence and access to reliable information made it impossible for the presidency to sustain campaigns over time. There is no way to prove conclusively that, had the presidency been a more efficient institution, the outcomes of the political clashes would have been different. But the presence of an efficient, well-informed, and intelligent team capable of providing logistical support would surely have increased the capacity of the president to expand his influence.

Zhelev's interventions from 1991 to 1994 attest to the limits of 'spasmodic' action, a term which Duverger uses to depict one of the permanent attributes of presidential power under semi-presidentialism. The famous French scholar derives this 'spasmodic' quality from the analysis of the constitutional prerogatives and the general lack of 'power of decision' which cannot be compensated by emergency powers or the power to appoint and dismiss (Duverger 1980: 171). I would emphasize the spasmodic character of interventions which are opportunistic and conjunctural and akin not to 'constitutional prerogative' but to everyday struggle for domination under volatile political conditions. And the ebbs and flows of this struggle should sensitize us to the unescapable ambiguity inherent in categories such as 'weak' and 'strong' presidencies. Certainly, there are things which a president under a semi-presidential system cannot do without destroying the delicately wrought institutional structure, as well as things which he can do on a regular basis in the absence of explicit constitutional authorization. And then, there are also things which a president can do—but only once. The first two years of Zhelev's presidency were marked by actions which fall into that elusive category. Relying on his personal influence, he did split an existing majority and did arrange for the instalment of a prime minister of his choice. But he never created a 'presidential majority' and failed to energize pro-reform policies. Once he cut himself adrift from the UDF and embarked upon the risky pursuit of an evanescent opportunity to unite the executive branch under his leadership, Zhelev discovered that his sticks posed only a minor threat and that his carrots were a vegetarian nicety in the carnivorous world of political survival.

Bitter Conflicts, Ambivalent Outcomes: The Presidency Under Siege (1994–1996)

In an effort to explicate the characteristic traits of semi-presidentialism, Giovanni Sartori points out that the 'problem of sorting out a dual authority structure . . . is *the* distinctive feature of the specimen' (1997: 134). It is imperative, therefore, that explorations of concrete semi-presidential regimes show how the conflicts between a president and a hostile parliamentary majority are resolved within a system of power-sharing without inflicting damage on the overarching constitutional framework. Furthermore, it is necessary to demonstrate that even in times of adversity the presidency retains its 'autonomy potential' as a component unit of the executive branch (ibid. 132). What are the parameters of this autonomy? What prerogatives and mechanisms can a president resort to in order to sustain it? These are the questions to be addressed in the following paragraphs.

In the short history of Bulgarian semi-presidentialism, the period 1994–6 stands out as a textbook example of a 'cohabitation' which sets a president against both an assembly and a government completely dominated by an antagonistic political force. In the December 1994 general elections the BSP regained its absolute majority in parliament (where it now controlled 125 of all 240 seats) and formed a government headed by Zhan Videnov, an unrepentant communist adamantly opposed to any pro-market reforms.[9] Accordingly, president Zhelev had to make an adjustment. Rather than attempting to energize a lethargic and fractured parliament, he had to deal with an assembly where iron-fist discipline was imposed on the absolute majority by a leadership bent upon settling scores with all political opponents, including the president himself.

One of the first steps Videnov undertook as a prime minister was to ban a representative of the presidency from taking part in the sessions of the Cabinet. The president's requests for information about draft legislation were consistently turned down. Even rather commonsensical requests for some planning of public events in which both president and prime minister were scheduled to participate were denied. All presidential vetoes (except one)[10] were overturned without discussion, some of them several hours after they were imposed. Despite Zhelev's admonitions, the process of reforms was reversed, and Bulgarian foreign policy took a decisively anti-Western turn, with China and Vietnam accorded more attention than Germany and the United States.

The form which the confrontation between the BSP-controlled institutions and the presidency assumed confirms Sartori's hypothesis that conflicts between presidents and anti-presidential majorities play out differently in presidential and semi-presidential systems. At no point was the functioning of the political system beset by 'gridlocks' and 'stalemates' and nothing approximating a war of institutions ever erupted. What transpired was an 'oscillation' of power towards the government (Sartori 1997: 123). Of course, one might add that this scenario became possible only because a background condition was present—a condition which Sartori neglects and Shugart and Carey highlight (1992: 56)— namely that conflicts over the interpretation of key constitutional provisions pertaining to separation of powers are minimal and a degree of clarity exists with regard to proper mechanisms for resolving constitutional disputes. Nonetheless, Sartori's general observation that while presidentialism is stalemate-prone, semi-presidentialism has gridlock-avoiding mechanisms built into it, is applicable in the Bulgarian case as well (see Ganev, forthcoming).

The emphasis on the rapid expansion of governmental power, however, should not obfuscate the fact that the problem of resolving conflicts still remained. The president was indeed put on the defensive— but he never gave up the effort to use his limited prerogatives to forestall the onslaught of the BSP. In this context, the process of 'sorting out' refers to a set of formal and informal strategies whereby one component of the executive exercises its domination while the other attempts to realize its 'autonomy potential' even though its impact is inevitably circumscribed.

Zhelev used some of his prerogatives to carve out pockets of decision-making where he could prevail. A very important asset in this respect was his power to appoint and dismiss high-ranking military officers. Somewhat surprisingly, Zhelev scored important victories on the 'military front' and successfully wrestled the army away from communist influence.

What exactly follows from the fact that the president is commander-in-chief of the armed forces has never been quite clear. Even in established democracies this is a murky area not susceptible to precise regulations, with tensions between presidents, ministers of defence, parliamentarians, and the military brass recurring in ever-changing forms (see Linz 1994: 57–9). In a post-communist state like Bulgaria such conflicts were bound to occur even more often. Zhelev had repeatedly

claimed that this constitutional provision bestowed upon him broad prerogatives to shape personnel policies and the overall defence strategy.
Of course, Videnov was not persuaded by such arguments and
announced that the presidential influence in the army would be curbed
(see 'Bulgarian Update', in *East European Constitutional Review*, vol. 4,
no. 3 (1995)). In retaliation, Zhelev blocked several military appointments proposed by the BSP. In the autumn of 1995 he again refused to
appoint BSP-backed officers to a variety of positions within the military
and objected to a governmental decree resuscitating an institution
which served as a conduit of communist power in the past, the Inspec-
torate of the Ministry of Defence.

An important resource for Zhelev in this struggle was the errors committed by his opponents. Other than stacking the ranks with its own
cadres, the BSP displayed little interest in the problems of the army,
which was dramatically underpaid and in a dire financial situation. All
Zhelev needed to do in this situation was demonstrate some sympa-
thy—and give the high-ranking military officials the opportunity to use
their meetings with the president as a forum where they could articulate their grievances.[11]

The other display of 'autonomy potential' of the presidency was
Zhelev's reliance on judicial review to overturn BSP-sponsored legislation which clearly violated the constitution. The statistics do not present
a very impressive picture—the president filed three petitions with the
Court in 1995 and four in 1996.[12] But in fact, his involvement was much
more active. The Court may solicit the opinion of parties which are not
directly involved in the case, and the justices would regularly ask the
president to file an amicus brief even when he was not a petitioner. Such
briefs were filed only on three occasions in 1992 and 1993, but in 1995
and 1996, when the struggle between the president and the BSP reached
its climax, the Court asked for eleven and eight briefs, respectively.
Moreover, on several occasions the president abstained from filing a
petition simply because the laws he deemed unconstitutional were
already protested by the opposition. In such cases, even though not
directly involved in the proceedings, Zhelev would make public statements in support of the petition and against the *diktat* of the
majority. At least so far, the impact of judicial review on the conflicts
between president and government has been to boost the power of the
president.

On the two occasions when decrees of the president have been
protested before the Court, the justices have affirmed their constitutionality (Decision 9/93 and Decision 11/94). In two other cases, the

Court offered an interpretation which was quite favourable to the presidency. In the first case, the justices ruled that the president may be given the authority to appoint the head of the National Investigative Service (Decision 6/93). In the second decision, which is probably unique in the history of judicial review, the Court had to interpret the phrase 'The president shall be the embodiment of the unity of the nation'. The practical issue behind this grandiose hermeneutical enterprise was whether the president could express his political preferences during an electoral campaign, or whether such actions would amount to a dereliction of his duty to uphold national unity. The Court held that the president is entitled to express his political views during electoral campaigns and that such behaviour does not violate the fundamental law (Decision 25/95).

Finally, the Court blocked two efforts on the part of the BSP to curtail the powers of the president. The BSP inserted a provision within the Standing Orders of Parliament mandating that all candidates for ambassadorships nominated by the president should be subject to parliamentary hearings and approval; this provision was struck down by the justices (Decision 4/95). In a similar fashion, the Court declared void a declaration of parliament stipulating that all presidential decrees pertaining to judicial appointments should be subject to the ministerial countersignature requirement, i.e. to a ministerial veto (Decision 13/96).

The fact that judicial review became an important element of 'sorting out' conflicts related to the 'flexible dyarchy' which informs the functioning of semi-presidential systems had a powerful impact on the Bulgarian polity. In view of the fact that the president appoints one-third of the justices, cynics may be entitled to the opinion that the decisions of the Court will be little more than, to paraphrase Robert Michels, 'constitutional embellishments of political struggles'.[13] But it is also undeniable that Zhelev's tactical use of judicial review cleared the pathway towards one of the strategic objectives of semi-presidentialism, cogently characterized by Gianfranco Pasquino as 'translating personal ambitions into systemic goals' (1997: 135). Imposing limits on majority tyranny is undeniably an integral element of Bulgarian political practices. While it is too early to talk about a 'juridicization' of Bulgarian politics,[14] it seems that anticipations of the Court's reactions are beginning to shape the behaviour of politicians.

Finally, Zhelev also tried to 'sort out' his conflicts with the BSP by bringing his case to the public. Public appeals may betoken an implicit admission of defeat—but they may also be considered as a continuation of institutional conflict with other means. In a series of televised and publicized addresses, Zhelev unleashed relentless criticisms against the BSP and persuasively argued that citizens should look at what parliament and the government were doing if they wanted to figure out where the causes for the disastrous downturn of the Bulgarian economy and the deep socio-economic crisis lay. How much he accomplished is a matter of dispute, but one may safely assert that his rhetoric provided some impetus to the process of general disenchantment with the BSP which finally led to the ex-communists' political defeat.

Evidence culled from the analysis of Bulgarian semi-presidentialism warrants the conclusion that confrontations between presidents and prime ministers are likely to be resolved differently under a system of flexible dyarchy than in a presidential system. There was no gridlock or attempts to forcefully remove opponents from the political scene. Under the terms of a tension-prone 'cohabitation', president Zhelev had to forsake his ambition to govern. But, to use an expression which Ezra Suleiman coined to depict the behaviour of French presidents facing similar predicaments, he 'exercised "power" in a way appropriate to the new situation' (1994: 150). Paradoxically, in these adverse conditions the autonomy potential of the presidency began to emerge more graphically than in earlier periods when wielding personal influence seemed to be Zhelev's preferred mode of political engagement. Even though he could make political appointments on a very small scale and could never turn this prerogative into a tool for promoting partisan influence,[15] he did rely on it as a pulsating source of political influence. And he contributed to the brisk transformation of judicial review from an imported novelty into a potent instrument for enforcing what Guillermo O'Donnell has felicitously dubbed 'horizontal accountability', i.e. accountability which runs across 'a network of relatively autonomous . . . institutions that can call into question' transgressions of established rules (1996: 100).

The foregoing enquiry suggests that the ubiquitous question 'Who possesses "real" power under semi-presidentialism?' may provoke one-dimensional answers which fail to capture fully the dynamics of institutional interaction. While issues of domination and acquiescence are certain to remain in the limelight, categories such as 'sorting out of conflicts' and 'development of autonomy potential' offer additional insights which should be incorporated in the analysis of semi-presidentialism. Stripped of parliamentary support, a president may see his influence diminish dramatically; but he can turn available rules and procedures into building blocks bricking out meddlesome governments from certain spheres of power. Likewise, presidential reactions which reflect the presidency's autonomy potential do not simply preserve a status quo, they transform the institutional framework into which political conflict evolves thus eventually subverting the dominant role of ostensibly untouchable majorities. More quickly than their counterparts in other systems, political actors bound to follow the arcane script of semi-presidentialism are destined to experience the uncertainties of victory and the ambivalence of defeat.

The Presidency Revitalised (1996–1997)

What is the impact of direct presidential elections on the political system? What is likely to transpire if presidential elections in a semi-presidential system take place in the midst of parliament's term and the opposition candidate wins a landslide victory? What roles might an incumbent president play in times of acute constitutional crisis? These questions may seem only loosely connected within a theoretical agenda for the study of semi-presidentialism; however, they converged on a single theme which dominated Bulgarian politics in 1996–7: the demise of the neo-communist regime of the BSP. The oscillations of institutional power pulsated with the energy of animated civil society, the sorting out of conflicts suddenly became subservient to the dynamic of electoral preferences, and the skilful usage of the subtleties of flexible dyarchy by a dexterous incumbent spelled the peaceful end of a disastrous rule. In what follows, I will try to present an analytical framework which will make all these themes clearly audible in their connectedness and distinctiveness.

The second presidential elections were scheduled for November 1996 and, as they grew nearer, Bulgaria found itself strapped in the abyss of ever worsening socio-economic crisis (see 'Bulgarian Update' section of the *East European Constitutional Review*, vol. 4 (1995), vol. 5 (1996), and vol. 6 (1997)). Painfully aware of the fact that a victory of the BSP would have tragic consequences for Bulgarian democracy, several opposition parties—including UDF, MRF, and a conservative alliance named People's Union—agreed to hold American-style primaries in order to nominate a joint candidate and prevent possible fragmentation of the opposition vote.

How this formula was hammered out is also worth mentioning. It was first conceived by an independent think-tank, the Centre for Liberal Strategies,[16] and once thrown into the public sphere, it became the focal point of intense civic deliberations. Pressure from below played as significant a role in motivating opposition parties to enter negotiations as self-interested elite manoeuvring. In the literature on Eastern Europe

Bulgaria is routinely stereotyped as a country where civil society is weak. The fact that agents of civil society were able to recast the terms of political debates and change the structure of political incentives attests to the superficiality of such stereotypes.

The negotiations resulted in the nomination of two candidates: incumbent president Zhelyu Zhelev and UDF Deputy Chairman Petar Stoyanov. The primaries were held on 1 June and were an astounding success: more than 20 per cent of all eligible voters showed up at improvised polling stations, with citizens under the age of 35 being especially active (Kristev 1997: 76–80). Stoyanov defeated Zhelev by a 2 : 1 margin, whereupon Zhelev announced that he would honour the agreement and exited the presidential race.

At first glance, these events may appear simply as a re-enactment of a well-known and quite predictable phenomenon: majoritarian elections create incentives for coalition-building. But, in the Bulgarian case, the gist of the story is quite different: it does not have to do so much with the number of parties involved as with the kind of party structures which began to emerge. Prior to the primaries, virtually all opposition parties maintained a ghost-like presence outside of the big cities, and even in the urban centres their cells were dominated by upward-looking cadres more interested in gaining the attention of the national leadership than representing local interests. The primaries, in contrast, were organized by local activists who perceived the presidential elections as their last chance to turn things around and help their communities.[17] The primaries were the opening from above which stimulated the emergence of deeper and stronger opposition structures from below, a turn of events which confirmed Stephen Holmes's hypothesis that 'open competition for the presidency may provide a much better education in democracy than backstage bargaining' (1993/4: 39). Originally conceived as a procedure for solving inter-party conflicts, the primaries precipitated a veritable social movement and consolidated the party system in general. Not surprisingly, in November 1996 Stoyanov, with the support of the allied opposition, won the second presidential elections, defeating BSP candidate Ivan Marazov by a 20-point margin.

At this point, another problem emerged which, as Shugart and Carey have argued (1992: 57–8), is quite relevant to the study of semi-presidential systems: what is likely to happen if presidential and parliamentary elections do not coincide and the former produce a winner who faces a sitting cabinet and an assembly composed of his principal opponents? An obvious way to resolve the situation would be for the president to invoke his more recent electoral mandate and dissolve parliament (this is what Mitterrand did in France in 1981 and 1988.) But what are his options in a semi-presidential system which, like the Bulgarian one, does not allow presidents to dismiss parliament? This situation has received scarce attention in the literature.

Theoretically, two types of claims are conceivable in this context. The first would be for the president to invoke the obvious shift in electoral preferences in order to demand more power for the presidency. In a semi-presidential system where spheres of competence are clearly delimited and not in favour of the presidency, such a demand would smack of a *coup d'état*. The second claim would be that the sitting parliament no longer represents the will of the people and should disband itself. And it is this second argument which Stoyanov used immediately upon his election. When the possibility of oscillation within the established configuration of power is limited, then the plea for reuniting the dual democratic legitimacy of parliament and presidency into the hands of a single political force is the more likely alternative.

Thus, it appears that, while the actual power of the presidency is quite restricted, its symbolic power is significant. Winning the presidency in 1996 did not open to the opposition the doors to genuine executive power, but it lent legitimacy to their claims that the sitting parliament and government should step aside. In and of itself, the election of Stoyanov did not constitute a dramatic shift of executive power; but it did create what Robert Elgie has called 'an opportunity for institutional disequilibria to occur' (Elgie 1996: 289) and put the BSP-controlled institutions on the defensive.

As the situation deteriorated in December 1996, dissent arose within the BSP ranks, which finally led to Zhan Videnov's resignation on 21 December 1996. But the expectations that some real change might be in the offing were dashed when the BSP announced that Videnov's team would continue working on important economic legislation until a new BSP Cabinet was installed. In no uncertain terms, the BSP leadership made it clear that the party's domination over all aspects of the national political life would continue. Meanwhile the national currency was in a free fall and the average pension slid to a pitiful $4 a month. After four years of gradual and socially sensitive reforms, Bulgaria was in a worse shape than war-torn Bosnia.

Against the background of this economic disaster and neo-communist intransigence, daily mass demonstrations against BSP's rule began in Sofia and soon the whole country was engulfed by waves of civic protest. When the BSP nominated Minister of Internal Affairs Nikolai Dobrev as a prime minister designate, President Zhelev, who was about to step down on 21 January and be replaced by Stoyanov, announced that he would not issue a decree granting to Dobrev the mandate to form a government, asserting that since Stoyanov would work with the government, the prerogative to issue such decrees should be his. He also pointed out that the constitution does not set a deadline. This delay was crucial, because as time passed the pressure on the BSP increased exponentially.

On 21 January Petar Stoyanov was sworn in and immediately he took the centre stage, where he was to remain for the following months. Since the very first moments of his term, the new president demonstrated political skill and savvy hardly ever seen in post-communist Bulgaria. In his first speech as a president he declared that the dissolution of the present parliament and the scheduling of new elections were the only viable alternative to violence and explosions of popular discontent. But he also announced that he would fulfil his duty and issue a decree conferring to Dobrev a mandate to form a government.[18] All throughout these heady days Stoyanov relentlessly argued that solutions to the looming crisis should be sought within the procedures outlined in the constitution. He never broached the prospect of a presidential rule or invoked the murky demon of emergency powers. Elections, the ultimate expression of popular will, and not emergency measures ought to lead Bulgaria out of the crisis. Meanwhile, he reassured the public that should parliament be dissolved in accordance with Article 99, he was capable of forming a caretaker government. This position of the president resonated with the demands of the protestors, who wanted new elections and not changes in the constitutional order.

On 29 January, Stoyanov issued the long-awaited decree and thus Dobrev had seven days to complete his task. None of the other parties were interested in forming a Cabinet which would have to work with a parliament dominated by unrepentant former communists, so there were two options: a new BSP government, or dismissal of parliament and new elections. On 4 February, with Dobrev's mandate about to expire at midnight, Stoyanov summoned the National Consultative Security Council, a body which, although mentioned in the constitution, had no delimited range of authority and operated on an *ad hoc* basis. All leading politicians were there, including Videnov and Dobrev. After four hours of negotiations, Stoyanov announced to the jubilant crowds that Dobrev was returning his mandate and new elections would be held in April.

This incident shows that the dexterity of incumbent presidents may transform the presidency from an institution under siege into a font of captivating leadership. The fact that the conflict was resolved after deliberations presided over by the president marked the emergence of the presidency as a new centre of power with which all political actors had to reckon. And Stoyanov's determination to maintain the integrity of the constitution and not to allow its principles to be suspended by means of *ad hoc* 'pacts'[19] or extraordinary measures turned the presidency into a pillar of the political order around which public trust began to coalesce. Thus, several days thereafter the president appointed a caretaker government, and this government accomplished so many successes in such a short time that even BSP-affiliated politicians heaped accolades on it. During the brief period when the president found himself in complete control of the executive branch, Bulgaria made the decisive breakthrough which had eluded it for so many years. Among Bulgarians from all walks of life, Stoyanov is credited with handling an explosive situation in a statesmanlike manner and winning a victory for Bulgarian democracy.

A broad coalition led by the UDF won the general elections held in April 1997 and a new government was formed, headed by UDF Chairman Ivan Kostov. While the period of 'cohabitation' is definitely over, steady new patterns of relationship between the presidency and the other political branches are yet to emerge. Petar Stoyanov is widely recognized as a national leader both by the new majority and the opposition and he had reasserted his domination over several domains of executive decision-making (including national defence and some aspects of foreign policy). Several of the ministers he appointed to the caretaker government continued to serve under Kostov without severing their contacts with the presidency. A relatively new vehicle through which presidential power may be enhanced is the establishment of *ad hoc* executive bodies authorized to deal with particular financial and economic tasks (such as financial stabilization or the repayment of the foreign debt). In these bodies representatives of the presidency sit side by side with officials appointed by the government, which gives the president a say in decision-making as well as access to important information. How this scenario will be played out in the future remains to be seen.

In what sense are these events relevant to the study of semi-presidentialism? To begin with, they show that popular elections confer power which matters. Irrespective of the scope of his constitutional prerogatives, democratic legitimacy gives the president considerable leverage.[20] Furthermore, an oscillation is likely to occur when popular elections are held amidst the term of parliament. Lost elections tend to aggravate intra-party conflict and erode even homogenous majorities. The configuration of forces in parliament remains the same, but the virus of doubt eats away the confidence of the majority. It also appears that the procedure of Article 99, which may look quite cumbersome, in fact can rather quickly lead to the dismissal of parliament. In a situation of popular protest against a sitting government, smaller parties have little incentive to form a government and lots of incentives to snatch away pieces of the dissolving erstwhile majority. Hence, if the majority fails to form a government, the result most likely will be new elections. Finally, whether an oscillation would occur and its scope depend in no small measure on the qualities of the incumbent. Stoyanov, whose behaviour displayed self-confidence unblemished by arrogance and energy unmarred by hastiness, earned the trust of civil society and transformed the presidency into a source of veritable leadership.

CONCLUSION

Every semi-presidential regime is a body of principles and rules animated by the agency of political actors and fully comprehensible in its dynamic evolution and societal effects. The Bulgarian experience so far may be interpreted as a sign that the rules of the constitution are sufficiently clear to provide a compass for institutional action and that the overall impact of the establishment of a semi-presidential system is the consolidation of Bulgarian democracy. Presidential power has proven susceptible to significant shifts, which may at times appear as fathomless permutations, but are actually shaped by peculiar combinations of structural factors (such as the coalescence or dissolution of pro-president majorities in parliament or the president's limited access to executive decision-making) and sudden ruptures within the political landscape (among which the swirls of personal rivalry and eruptions of public protest figure prominently). These shifts have not occurred at the expense of constitutional principles and the permutations never resulted in an institutional meltdown. The Bulgarian case, then, lends credence to Duverger's sweeping claim that semi-presidentialism is 'a system which has now become the most effective means of transition from dictatorship towards democracy in Eastern Europe and the former Soviet Union' (Duverger 1997: 137). And while further research is perhaps necessary before this claim is transformed into a scholarly argument, the foregoing analysis warrants at least some provisional conclusions. Rendering inherently implausible monocratic claims to power, semi-presidentialism stimulates political actors to sort out their differences and negotiate the parameters of their respective autonomy. In this form of contention, the quest for institutional allies is more important than rhetorical claims to possession of sovereign authority. Moreover, strategies for institutional expansion under a semi-presidential regime are not aimed exclusively at appropriation and reappropriation of a limited number of pre-set prerogatives—political actors bent upon acquiring additional authority will be apt to create new institutional resources, which may then be used for the purpose of better governing. As the rise of judicial review in Bulgaria demonstrates, sometimes the alliances of the weak have an impact which outlasts the policies of the strong. Thus, a robust democratic framework may emerge as an unintended consequence of intense struggle for domination. Finally, the fact that the popular mandate to rule is conferred on different actors, inevitably infuses their rhetoric with strong democratic overtones; to couch one's arguments in terms of democratic legitimacy in a contest with rivals similarly endowed is only possible if the overarching idea of democratic rule is explicitly recognized.

Arguably, these achievements of semi-presidentialism may have a deeper cause, perhaps an ineffable change of values, or may be attributed to a series of conjunctural factors which have eased the path of Bulgarian democracy. And it is not far-fetched to maintain that the same result might have been accomplished under the terms of a different institutional arrangement. These conundrums will undoubtedly haunt scholars bent upon dissecting the multi-layered relations between complex variables. Meanwhile, one thing remains certain: six years after it was introduced, semi-presidentialism in Bulgaria has evolved into a stable form of democratic government.

NOTES

1. In the Bulgarian historical tradition, the 'Great National Assembly' is a special popularly elected representative body authorized to adopt new constitutions. The Great National Assembly which adopted the Constitution of 1991 was elected in the first multi-party elections after the disintegration of the one-party system, held in June 1990.
2. For an argument that, notwithstanding all rifts and fluctuations, there has been 'a general tendency towards presidential government in the Fifth Republic', see Elgie 1996: 287.
3. The best account of the context in which the constitution was created is to be found in Kristev 1996.

4. For an insightful analysis of this and other topics related to the political outcomes of the Round Table Talks, see Peeva 1997.
5. On 'decree power', see Shugart and Mainwaring 1997: 44–7. On 'enabling acts', see Kirchheimer 1967.
6. On 'partisan powers', see Shugart and Mainwaring 1997: 13.
7. A transcript of the press conference is now published in Zhelev 1995.
8. Hereafter I draw on Ganev 1993/4: 62–4.
9. On Videnov and the BSP in general, see Ganev 1997b: 133–5.
10. The only veto which survived was on the national coat of arms. While Zhelev's arguments against it were rather solid—the BSP-sponsored Coat of Arms had nothing to do with Bulgarian history and bore an awkward resemblance to the logo of Renault automobiles—the fate of the veto was determined by the fact that a faction within the BSP was beginning to fight Videnov and they chose the symbolic issue of the Coat of Arms to vent their discontent.
11. How successful that strategy has been became clear in January 1997, when the mass demonstrations against the rule of the BSP erupted and the thought of using violence against the demonstrators was apparently entertained by some of Videnov's ministers. After a meeting with Zhelev, the Chief of the General Staff declared that the military would not get involved in any 'measures to restore order' and that the crisis was political and should be sorted out by politicians.
12. He filed two in 1992, two in 1993, and three in 1994. See statistical data in Vargova 1997: 562–82.
13. In his classic book, *Political Parties*, Robert Michels talks about the 'ethical embellishments of social struggles' (ch. 2) and explains why the ambition to ground one's political aspirations on moral principles will become all-pervasive in a mass democracy. In post-communism, where claims about the 'common good' are redolent of the perverted practices of Marxist dictatorship and 'the right to speak for the people' is shared between various political actors, the claim to 'defend the constitution' is a convenient rhetorical device for justifying one's political strategy.
14. On the concept of 'juridicization', see Stone 1992.
15. On how the power to appoint is used in strong presidential systems, see Geddes 1995.
16. For the original statement of the idea, see Kjuranov and Kristev 1996.
17. The following observations are based on numerous interviews with opposition activists which I conducted in the summers of 1996 and 1997. I wish to thank Milcho Spasov for his invaluable help and unwavering support all throughout this project.
18. The full text of Stoyanov's speech is published in *Democraticheski pregled*, Spring 1997, pp. 34–7.
19. 'A pact can be defined as an explicit, but not always publicly explicated or justified agreement among a select set of actors which seeks to *define (or better, to redefine) rules governing the exercise of power . . .*', in O'Donnell and Schmitter 1986: 37 (author's emphasis).
20. See also Elster 1997: 227. Elster's observation that 'presidents may be able to stage a direct confrontation [with parliament] by mobilizing masses and crowds'

is not applicable to this case, because mass protests erupted before Stoyanov was sworn in and he was carried forward by a dynamic he did not deliberately create. Yet Elster's general point about 'positive reasons' why a popularly elected president can use his strong democratic legitimacy to get the upper hand remains valid in this context.

8

Lithuania

DAINIUS URBANAVICIUS

The Republic of Lithuania is known as a semi-presidential state. It has, of course, some basic similarities with other semi-presidential states, but these will not be explored in this chapter, since they have already been covered in Chapter 1 of this book. Instead, this chapter will introduce the main peculiarities of the Lithuanian semi-presidential regime and will describe the status of presidential power in Lithuania.

The first part of the chapter will explain the reasons why the citizens of Lithuania voted for a semi-presidential regime, while those in the other two Baltic states, namely Latvia and Estonia, preferred to adopt a parliamentary form of government where the presidency has little constitutional power. Some of the peculiarities of the Lithuanian political system will also be explained with particular reference to the historical background which had such an impact on the creation of the system. The second part will define the constitutional, or *de jure*, power of the Lithuanian presidency and clarify its relationship with the *de jure* power of the Seimas, or parliament, and the government. The third part will analyse the political 'triangle' consisting of the president, parliament, and the government. This part will also present the political realities of the last six years in Lithuania. The fourth part will focus on the personality of the president with an analysis of the period from 1993 to 1998. The conclusion will set out the main conclusions of the chapter and will also provide a prognosis for the development of the future political system in the country.

WHY SEMI-PRESIDENTIALISM?

There are various reasons for the adoption of semi-presidentialism in Lithuania. First, in the early years of the current regime (1988–92) the majority of the population, mainly Lithuanians, recalled the times when the country had been independent before the Second World War. This period was marked by a strong presidency and the influence of the person who was known in the Soviet interpretation of history as the so-called 'president of bourgeois Lithuania', Antanas Smetona. Smetona was widely regarded as a heroic president and as someone who made Lithuania a very strong state in the context of Europe as a whole. Even if his achievements were not as remarkable as many people believed, with the possible exception of agriculture, Lithuanians still emphasized his strong way of governing and his achievements in economic life. Consequently, there was a strong desire to restore a regime that could build a stable political system which was personified in the popular front movement, Sajudis, and its leaders, most notably Vytautas Landsbergis.

Secondly, the establishment of the presidency was also a reaction to the Soviet form of super-parliamentarism (Talat-Kelpsa 1996: 97). For reasons of constitutional continuity it would have been reasonable to have restored the constitution of 1938. However, this did not occur (see below). Instead, the presidency experienced a threefold transformation from the institution of the First Secretary of the Central Committee of the Soviet Socialist Republic of Lithuania, to the Chairman of the Supreme Council of the Soviet Socialist Republic of Lithuania, to the president of the Republic of Lithuania. Following each transformation, the institution maintained almost the same degree of political power.

Thirdly, the major reason, of course, for the creation of the semi-presidential regime was the political realities which followed the declaration of independence on 11 March 1990 when the Soviet Socialist Republic of Lithuania separated from the USSR. Political struggles had already begun among political groups in the Supreme Council,[1] but even at this early stage agreement had been reached on the need for a completely new constitution. The main political forces were reluctant to reintroduce the 1938 constitution, which had clearly been undemocratic (for example, Article 46 stated that the state could force people to work) and which involved a strong, even authoritarian, presidential institution. Indeed, only a few uninfluential small movements and parties supported the idea of the restoration of the 1938 constitution.

In the middle of 1991, the former communists in the Lithuanian Democratic Labour Party (LDLP) proposed a first draft of the new constitution which outlined a parliamentary regime. Indeed, it might have been easier to transform the political system into a parliamentary rather than a semi-presidential or even presidential regime as the LDLP was not as discredited as its counterparts in other countries, for example, Czechoslovakia.[2] This was at least partly due to the fact that in 1989–90 the forerunner of the LDLP, the Lithuanian Communist Party (LCP), supported the Sajudis in its fight against Moscow and Gorbachev. In this way, the LDLP maintained its political power, which it then used to protect the parliamentary regime.

At this time, the majority in the Supreme Council,[3] consisting of the members of the Sajudis, the LDLP, and other parties, had the same basic objective, the independence of Lithuania, but very different views as to how to achieve it. Because of the Soviet aggression as well as the activities of both Landsbergis and Prunskiene's grand-coalition cabinet, the Sajudis majority in the Supreme Council was slow to split into separate parties. Sajudis remained as one political force but within it there were different political groups. Cooperation was required, but there was great division between these groups which resulted in constitutional conflict.

In fact, Landsbergis was in favour of strong presidential rule. He proposed that the president should be in charge of the government's activities and should be given the right to dismiss and form a new government without parliamentary support. He also believed that the president should be given the right of legislative veto and the function of judicial review when laws seemed to be contradictory. Of course, such an idea was not totally disinterested. The Sajudis, headed by Landsbergis, then the popular Speaker of the Supreme Council, were believed to be best placed to win the presidential election.

To prepare a new draft of the constitution, the Supreme Council formed the Committee on the Revision of the Constitution which consisted of representatives from the different parties. In 1990 this committee was unable to reach an agreement because of the differences of opinion between the various protagonists. Consequently, on 10 May 1991 it merely presented the outlines for a new constitution dealing with civil rights and, thus, made no recommendations concerning the political regime.

The drafts prepared in the middle of 1991 by the LDLP and by American experts Wyman and Johnson, who worked as consultants to the Supreme Council on matters of constitutional reform, were completely at odds and reflected totally different opinions as to the direction of the future political system. Against this background, later drafts came to a more or less compromise conclusion—semi-presidentialism—in 1992. For example, the Lithuanian Liberal Party drafted a constitution in which the balance of presidential and parliamentarian systems was the closest to the constitution that Lithuania has today, even if it accorded the president even more power than he has now.

In the spring of 1992 the Sajudis majority finally split into different fractions and, thus, lost its hold over the Supreme Council. This led delegates from the Sajudis, now in a minority, and Landsbergis to try to take advantage of the situation by initiating a referendum on the presidency, having collected the necessary number of signatures from the voters. The establishment of the presidency represented its most realistic chance of staying in power and gaining a mandate to form the government. Believing that he was still very popular with the people, Landsbergis raised the question as to whether the president or the constitution should have priority. However, the people were preoccupied by economic realities and, in particular, with the negative effects of the programme of privatization. Thus, at the referendum held on 23 May 1992, a majority of people voted in favour of a strong presidency (69.5 per cent), but the participation rate was too low (57.6 per cent) for the change to be adopted (this could be achieved only if it was passed by more than 50 per cent of all those eligible to vote). The voters who disapproved of the change simply took no part in the referendum. This was a severe blow to Landsbergis's supporters. The result showed the weakness of the Sajudis, prime minister Vagnorius, and Landsbergis himself. Indeed, the results of the referendum issued a warning to them that their efforts to win the presidential election might be in vain. It also became clear that a new constitution would have to reflect a compromise.

The delegates of the political parties in the Supreme Council worked all summer and autumn trying to find an acceptable solution. There was mutual agreement that the draft of a new constitution should be finalized before the election to the Seimas in the autumn. Finally, the Supreme Council's Committee on the Revision of the Constitution prepared the final version only a few weeks before the new referendum and the first round of the parliamentary election on 25 October 1992. Because of the shortage of time (only two weeks were left prior to election) this draft was not widely discussed among the people.[4] In the end, 56.76 per cent of those eligible to vote approved this version of the constitution.

Overall, then, the constitution appeared in the context of conflict and mistrust between the main political forces in which the only solution was a balance of parliamentary and presidential forces.

SEMI-PRESIDENTIALISM IN THE CONSTITUTION

Various constitutional articles establish the role of the presidency in the political system. For example, Article 78 indicates who is eligible to hold the position of the president of Lithuania. It states:

Any person who is a citizen of the Republic of Lithuania by birth, who has lived in Lithuania for at least the past three years, who has reached the age of 40 prior to the election day, and who is eligible for election to the Seimas may be elected president of the Republic. The president of the Republic shall be elected by the citizens of the Republic of Lithuania on the basis of universal, equal, and direct suffrage by secret ballot for a term of five years.

The same person may not be elected president of the Republic of Lithuania for more than two consecutive terms.

This article was thought to eliminate potential candidates, such as Romualdas Ozolas,[5] as well as others who were younger than the required age. In addition, this article was also designed to eliminate emigrants from Lithuania from being elected president. In fact, conflict over this article sprang up in 1997 when Valdas Adamkus, an emigrant from Lithuania to the USA, made an effort to register as a candidate for the presidential election. The Central Election Committee rejected his request to register because he had not lived in Lithuania for the past three years. The Lithuanian Centre Union (LCU) filed a complaint against that decision to the Constitutional Court and was successful because, although Adamkus had not been living continually in Lithuania, he had been registered in Siauliai for more than three years and had dual citizenship.

The powers of the president in relation to the Seimas and the government are set out in Article 84.

The president of the Republic shall:

(1) settle basic foreign policy issues and, together with the Government, implement foreign policy;

(2) sign international treaties of the Republic of Lithuania and submit them to the Seimas for ratification;

(3) appoint or recall, upon the recommendation of the Government, diplomatic representatives of the Republic of Lithuania in foreign states and international organizations; receive letters of credence and recall of diplomatic representatives of foreign states; confer highest diplomatic ranks and special titles;

In this respect, then, the power of the president is skewed towards international issues which require a strong personality who is capable of making decisions, taking responsibility, and ensuring continuity of

office. The ability to make decisions in the field of international relations has come to be one of the most significant presidential powers. It
must be noted, though, that the president must work in tandem with the
government, since the Ministry of Foreign Affairs is also involved in
determining foreign policy.

In addition, the president can also issue decrees which have the force
of law. However, presidential decrees are valid only if they bear the
signature of the prime minister or the appropriate minister. Responsibility for such decrees, therefore, lies with the prime minister or the
minister who signs them. In this way, the Seimas attempted to control
the president's activities by way of the government.

Article 84 goes on to state that the president shall:

(4) appoint, upon approval of the Seimas, the Prime Minister, charge him or
her to form the Government, and approve its composition;
(5) remove, upon approval of the Seimas, the Prime Minister from office;
(6) accept the powers returned by the Government upon the election of a new
Seimas, and charge it to exercise its functions until a new Government is
formed;
(7) accept resignations of the Government and, as necessary, charge it to
continue exercising its functions or charge one of the Ministers to exercise the
functions of the Prime Minister until a new Government is formed; accept resignations of individual Ministers and commission them to continue in office
until a new Minister is appointed;
(8) submit to the Seimas, upon the resignation of the Government or after the
return of its powers and no later than within 15 days, the candidature of a new
Prime Minister for consideration;
(9) appoint or dismiss individual Ministers upon the recommendation of the
Prime Minister;

The constitution conceded that the president had the right to make a
direct impact on the government's work. This can be seen, for example,
in the president's ability to appoint the prime minister who then forms
the government. However, the Seimas also has the right to approve or
reject the president's candidate as prime minister and so it is the Seimas
which, therefore, makes the final decision. Moreover, the Seimas has the
right to approve not only the president's candidate as prime minister
but also the government's programme. If on two occasions the Seimas
does not approve the government's programme, then it can force the
government to resign. The Seimas also has the right to pass a vote of
no confidence in the prime minister, any individual minister, or the
government as a whole. Therefore, the government's position is directly
dependent on the Seimas. Part 9 of this article implies that the power

of the president is even stronger by virtue of the right to appoint or dismiss individual ministers, although this can only occur on the recommendation of the prime minister who, as noted above, is himself/ herself responsible to the Seimas.

Overall, the constitution indicates that the president is the head of state and also has a direct relationship with the government. However, it also suggests that the president is not responsible for the implementation of government policy. The president has the right to make decisions regarding foreign policy, to issue decrees with appropriate prime ministerial or ministerial approval, and to take actions in time of war. The president is not the head of the government and does not lead the government. Indeed, he is eliminated from the implementation of government policy with the exception of foreign policy.

That said, the position of the presidency changed following a judicial ruling on 10 January 1998. At this time the Constitutional Court of the Republic of Lithuania reinterpreted the constitution and issued a judgment that reduced the president's powers. It did so by declaring that the president was unable to bring about a change of government following the presidential election.

The Court's decision dealt mainly with Articles 92 and 101. Article 92 states that:

The Government shall issue its resignation to the president of the Republic after the election of the Seimas or upon the election of the president of the Republic.

Article 101 then describes the cases in which the Government must resign.

(. . .) When more than half of the Ministers are changed, the Government must be reinvested with authority by the Seimas. Otherwise, the Government must resign.

The Government must also resign if:

(1) the Seimas disapproves of the programme of the newly-formed Government two times in succession;
(2) the majority of all the Seimas deputies expresses a lack of confidence in the Government or in the Prime Minister in a secret ballot vote;
(3) the Prime Minister resigns or dies; or
(4) after Seimas elections, when a new Government is formed.

A Minister must resign if more than a half of all the Seimas members express, in a secret ballot vote, a lack of confidence in him or her. The president of the Republic shall accept the resignations of the Government or individual Ministers.

In addition, Article 84 does not invest the president with the power, after the presidential election, either to request the Seimas to reconsider the candidature of the prime minister or to approve the government.

The Court ruled that the Seimas, by approving the government's programme, gives the government a mandate to act, whereas the president does not. This is because in the process of forming the government the president simply participates as a head of state, executing the functions delegated to him by the constitution. By contrast, the Seimas participates as a representative body of the nation and the government is responsible to it. In this context, the main task of the president is merely to guarantee the interaction between the various state institutions. Crucial to the Court's decision was the ruling that a distinction be made between the two different constitutional terms 'returning its powers' and 'resigning'. It ruled that after the Seimas election the government's mandate disappears. The outgoing government should, thus, 'return its powers' to the president who then proposes the name of a new prime minister to form the government within the period of fifteen days. Only when the new government is formed does the old one 'resign'. However, after the presidential election the government's mandate is maintained. This accounts for the reason why on these occasions the government merely returns its powers to the president and does not resign. It is still the case, though, that the president can present the Seimas with a vote of no confidence in the government and if the Seimas passes the vote of no confidence, then the government must resign.

In short, the Constitutional Court's decision was politically motivated and was decided in advance. After Landsbergis, then the Chairman of the Seimas and the Chairman of the right-wing Homeland Union/ Conservatives of Lithuania party (HU/CL), had lost in the first round of the 1997 presidential election, the mainly HU/CL government was in a politically dangerous position by virtue of the fact that the new president did not approve of the government's policy. Thus, the HU/CL eliminated this threat by proposing that the Constitutional Court reinterpret the constitution in favour of the Seimas regardless of the fact that the constitution apparently invested the Seimas and the president, as noted above, with almost equal rights. The Court duly did so. It should be noted, however, that, despite the Court's decision, Lithuania, according to Maurice Duverger's definition, is still a semi-presidential state. Indeed, the Constitutional Court completed its judgment by stating that: 'according to the authority and competence of the state institution established by the Constitution of the Republic of Lithuania, Lithuania's model of government is typical of that attributed to a parliamentary regime. However, it must be emphasised that our State has some typical characteristics associated with a semi-presidential system.'

In terms of the rest of the president's powers, Article 84 goes on to state that the president shall:

(10) appoint or dismiss, according to the established procedure, state officers provided by law;

(11) propose Supreme Court candidates to the Seimas, and, upon the appointment of all the Supreme Court judges, recommend from among them a Supreme Court Chairperson to the Seimas; appoint, with the approval of the Seimas, Court of Appeal judges, and from among them, the Court of Appeal Chairperson; appoint judges and chairpersons of district and local district courts, and change their places of office; in cases provided by law, propose the dismissal of judges to the Seimas;

(12) propose to the Seimas the candidatures of three Constitutional Court judges, and, upon appointing all the judges of the Constitutional Court, propose, from among them, a candidate for Constitutional Court Chairperson to the Seimas;

Some of these articles increase the president's power, since they allow the head of state to influence the legal system by proposing judicial candidates. Given that the whole of the judicial system in Lithuania is currently being reformed, the power to make judicial appointments is of great value to the president. However, to date, the president's decisions have not rescued the declining reputation of the system. According to opinion polls, only 25 per cent of Lithuanians have confidence in the courts which puts them in the tenth position after the church (second place, 65 per cent) and the police (ninth place, 27 per cent) but ahead of the commercial banks (twelfth place, 7 per cent).

Article 84 further states that the president shall:

(13) propose to the Seimas candidates for State Controller and Chairperson of the Board of the Bank of Lithuania; if necessary, propose to the Seimas to express non-confidence in said officials;

[In reality these officials are proposed in advance by the Government or the Seimas to the president and the president makes the formality by presenting these officials to the Seimas for the approval.]

(14) appoint or dismiss, upon the approval of the Seimas, the chief commander of the Army and the head of the Security Service;

(15) confer highest military ranks;

(16) adopt, in the event of an armed attack which threatens State sovereignty or territorial integrity, decisions concerning defence against such armed aggression, the imposition of martial law, and mobilisation, and submit these decisions to the next sitting of the Seimas for approval;

(17) declare states of emergency according to the procedures and situations established by law, and submit these decisions to the next sitting of the Seimas for approval;

(18) make annual reports in the Seimas about the situation in Lithuania and the domestic and foreign policies of the Republic of Lithuania;

(19) call, in cases provided in the Constitution, extraordinary sessions of the Seimas;

(20) announce regular elections to the Seimas, and, in cases set forth in part 2 of Article 58 of the Constitution, announce pre-term elections to the Seimas;

This last part requires special attention and needs to be explained more explicitly. Article 58 states that:

Pre-term elections to the Seimas may be held on the decision of the Seimas adopted by three-fifths majority vote of all the Seimas members.

The president of the Republic of Lithuania may also announce pre-term elections to the Seimas:

(1) if the Seimas fails to adopt a decision on the new programme of the Government within 30 days of its presentation, or if the Seimas twice in succession disapproves of the Government programme within 60 days of its initial presentation; or

(2) on the proposal of the Government, if the Seimas expresses direct non-confidence in the Government.

On these occasions, the president has the right to defend the government against the Seimas and hold pre-term parliamentary elections. In this way, the president can prevent the breakdown of the government's programme in the case of conflict within the Seimas.

The president of the Republic may not announce pre-term elections to the Seimas if the term of office of the president of the Republic expires within less than six months, or if six months have not passed since the pre-term elections to the Seimas.

The day of elections to the new Seimas shall be specified in the resolution of the Seimas or in the decree of the president of the Republic concerning the pre-term elections to the Seimas. The election to the new Seimas must be organised within three months from the adoption of the decision on the pre-term elections.

The main objective of the Lithuanian political system, as mentioned above, is political stability. For this reason, the president cannot hold the pre-term election to the Seimas if the president's term of office expires within less than six months, or if six months have not passed since the pre-term election to the Seimas. And yet, the Seimas can force a pre-term presidential election under the conditions set out in Article 87:

When, in cases specified in part 2 of Article 58 of the Constitution, the president of the Republic announces pre-term elections to the Seimas, the newly-elected Seimas may, by three-fifths majority vote of all the Seimas members and within 30 days of the first sitting, announce a pre-term election of the president of the Republic.

If the president of the Republic wishes to compete in the election, he or she shall immediately be registered as a candidate.

If the president of the Republic is re-elected in such an election, he or she shall be deemed elected for a second term, provided that more than three years of the first term had expired prior to the election. If the expired period of the first term is less than three years, the president of the Republic shall only be elected for the remainder of the first term, which shall not be considered a second term.

If a pre-term election for the president of the Republic is announced during the president's second term, the current president of the Republic may only be elected for the remainder of the second term.

If there were not a limit to the number of terms of office a president may serve, the president might become too predominant. Therefore, the LDLP influenced the Seimas to limit the number of times the president can be elected.

In relation to the remainder of the president's substantive powers, Article 84 states that the president shall:

(21) grant citizenship of the Republic of Lithuania according to the procedure established by law;
(22) confer State awards;
(23) grant pardons to sentenced persons; and
(24) sign and promulgate laws enacted by the Seimas or refer them back to the Seimas according to the procedure provided for in Article 71 of the Constitution.

The president's veto in reality does not serve to make the Seimas change its decisions, but it does mean that accidental mistakes which occur in the process of legislation can be corrected afterwards. One benefit is that a returned law has to have a formal reason for being referred back to the Seimas. Thus, the Seimas can take these into account when voting for the blocked law.

In addition to Article 84, Articles 71 and 72 state:

Article 71

Within ten days of receiving a law passed by the Seimas, the president of the Republic shall either sign and officially promulgate the said law, or shall refer it back to the Seimas together with relevant reasons for reconsideration.

In the event that the law enacted by the Seimas is not referred back or signed by the president of the Republic within the established period, the law shall become effective upon the signing and official promulgation thereof by the Chairperson of the Seimas.

The president of the Republic must, within five days, sign and officially promulgate laws and other acts adopted by referendum.

In the event that the president of the Republic does not sign and promulgate such laws within the established period, said laws shall become effective upon being signed and officially promulgated by the Chairperson of the Seimas.

Article 72

The Seimas may reconsider and enact laws which have been referred back by the president of the Republic.

After reconsideration by the Seimas, a law shall be deemed enacted if the amendments and supplements submitted by the president of the Republic were adopted, or if more than half of all the Seimas members vote in the affirmative, and if it is a constitutional law—if at least three-fifths of all the Seimas members vote in the affirmative.

The president of the Republic must, within three days, sign and forthwith officially promulgate laws re-enacted by the Seimas.

The term of election is another factor that should be noted. The president's term of office is five years, while elections to the Seimas are held every four years. Thus, as in France, the relationship is asymmetric. This means that in theory the date of elections to the Seimas and presidential election coincide only every twenty years, without taking into consideration the possibility of having pre-term elections. In turn, this means that the Lithuanian political system has the potential to become destabilized. It is possible that efforts will be made to make the system more stable by restricting the president from announcing pre-term elections if the term of office of the president expires within less than six months, or if six months have not passed since the pre-term elections to the Seimas.

All told, on the one hand, it is reasonable to assert that any powers which might in the long run serve to strengthen the position of the president are being taken away from the office. For example, the Lithuanian president has no right to hold a referendum, while the president of Latvia, the supposedly 'pure' parliamentary president, does indeed have such a right. On the other hand, the Lithuanian president does have a considerable degree of authority which enables him or her to react, albeit within strict limits, to the actions of both the government and the political majority in the Seimas. Thus, despite the transition towards a parliamentary political system, the current regime is still constitutionally balanced between the president and the government.

THE 'TRIANGLE': THE RELATIONSHIP
BETWEEN THE SEIMAS, THE PRESIDENT,
AND THE GOVERNMENT

According to Maurice Duverger's schema, in semi-presidential regimes the *de jure* and *de facto* powers of the head of the state are very different. This difference is born out in the relationship between the president and the Seimas.

The election of the first president of Lithuania after the Second World War was held on 14 February 1993. There were only two candidates, namely the right-wing candidate, Stasys Lozoraitis, and the left-wing candidate, Algirdas Brazauskas. Brazauskas won the election with a 60 per cent vote. Vytautas Landsbergis, after the LDLP's success in the election to the Seimas and after his loss in the referendum in May 1992, decided not to participate as the third candidate and asked the voters who supported him to vote instead for Lozoraitis. However, this decision did not rescue Lozoraitis from losing the election and it still remains unclear whether Landsbergis's decision helped or hindered his campaign. Lozoraitis was an emigrant from Lithuania to the US but he had lived all the time in the Lithuanian embassy there. This explains why he was treated as if he had been constantly living in the territory of the Republic of Lithuania and so was eligible to stand. However, the voters voted not so much for the candidates, but against them and, therefore, Brazauskas, as the 'local' leader, received more votes than Lozoraitis.

It is clear that until the governmental crisis from December 1995 to February 1996 (see below) the president exercised only those powers which were available to him by the constitution. However, this crisis showed that the president was 'stronger' than the constitutional situation would suggest. He initiated the procedure which removed the Minister of Internal Affairs from office and started the campaign that attempted to change the prime minister, Adolfas Slezevicius, even though the prime minister and government were responsible only to the Seimas. This meant that the president exceeded his *de jure* powers (Talat-Kelpsa 1996: 100).

However, the Lithuanian case deviates from one interpretation of Duverger's model in the sense that the president is only an informal party leader and is by no means an omnipotent head of state. From 1992–6 the LDLP enjoyed an absolute majority in the Seimas and Algirdas Brazauskas, the leader of the LDLP before the presidential election and the first president of Lithuania after 1990, was in office from 1993 1998.[6] During this period, though, the president did not become a powerful head of the state who was in a position to initiate and control government policy. This was because of political in-fighting within the LDLP as well as because of the personality of the president himself. President Brazauskas chose not to assume even an informal leadership role, but to 'live together' with the government and the Seimas majority.

During Brazauskas's term of office, the government changed three times. (For a list of presidents since 1993 and prime ministers since 1990, see Figure 8.1.)

The first government that was eventually formed on 10 March 1993 was headed by Adolfas Slezevicius who took over as the leader of the LDLP. Slezevicius held that position until the governmental crisis in December 1995 which was brought about by problems faced by the two main commercial banks in Lithuania and with which he was allegedly connected.[7] During his time in office, though, Slezevicius won the title of 'the internal leader of the State', with the consequence that the majority in the Seimas practically turned into a 'voting machine' (Talat-Kelpsa 1997: 134).

This situation had an impact on the political stability of the state. First, the president, relying upon the prime minister and his strong position in the Seimas, did not interfere in the domestic life of the state. Secondly, the powers of the president were implemented in the way provided for by the constitution. In the conflict that ensued between the president and the prime minister, the majority in the Seimas decided to support the head of government. This could have severely destabilized the political situation, because the Seimas and the president could both

President (since direct election)	Prime minister
A. Brauzaskas (Feb. 1993–Feb. 1998) V. Adamkus (Feb. 1998–)	K. Prunskiene (Mar. 1990–Jan. 1991) A. Simenas (Jan. 1991–Jan. 1991) G. Vagnorius (Jan. 1991–July 1992) A. Abisala (July 1992–Dec. 1992) B. Lubys (Dec. 1992–Mar. 1993) A. Slezevicius (Mar. 1993–Feb. 1996) M. Stankevicius (Feb. 1996–Dec. 1996) G. Vagnorius (Dec. 1996–)

FIG. 8.1. Presidents and prime ministers in Lithuania, 1990–1998

claim a mandate from the people of Lithuania. However, the president managed to win back the support of LDLP and the Seimas majority from the prime minister. This was possible chiefly due to the strength of the president's personality which will be discussed in the next part of this chapter.

As noted above, the president has the right of 'suspensive veto' and can refer laws back to the Seimas. In this case, the president's veto can be overturned by a simple majority in the Seimas. From 1993–5, the president used this veto 16 times which was a reflection of the relationship between the Seimas and the head of state—the more times the president uses the 'suspensive veto', the more we can assume that there is a disagreement between the two institutions. And yet, the views of the president and those of the LDLP should not have been so very different, given the convergence of opinion at the beginning of 1993. This suggests that Brazauskas refused to assert himself as the central figure of both the LDLP and the political system as a whole (Talat-Kelpsa 1996: 103). Brazauskas preferred not to negotiate and compromise with the LDLP but to adopt a passive role using just the 'suspensive veto'.

On 15 February 1996, the president proposed, and the LDLP approved, the new prime minister, Mindaugas Stankevicius. He was the Minister of Government Reforms and Local Government Affairs in the Cabinet of Adolfas Slezevicius. In reality, his task was to smooth over the scandal that had kept the LDLP's popularity low and to manage the government's business until the next Seimas election in seven months' time. Stankevicius was the right person to undertake such a task. He was not a main figure in the LDLP and he usually kept the president and the leaders of the LDLP aware of the government's policies. In this situation, president Brazauskas was given a second chance to take the initiative and assume the role of a powerful head of the state, but, again, he did not seize this opportunity.

On 20 October 1996, the new Seimas was elected. The LDLP lost its majority in the Seimas. Instead, the HU/CL received the largest number of votes and formed a coalition with the Lithuanian Christian Democratic Party (LCDP) and two representatives the Lithuanian Centre Union (LCU). The government had an absolute majority in the Seimas. On 28 November 1996, the Seimas approved Gediminas Vagnorius as prime minister. Vagnorius, as was mentioned before, had already served as prime minister in 1991–2. Vagnorius was a strong personality and as one of the most important leaders of the HU/CL (the head of the HU/CL board) had strong support in the Seimas. After this time the president did little of significance. Moreover, the Chairman of the Seimas and the Chairman of the HU/CL, Vytautas Landsbergis, took over some of the president's main duties and played an active part in foreign affairs. Landsbergis was the person whom the world knew as being mainly responsible for Lithuanian independence. So, having regained a powerful position, he allowed himself a number of important official foreign visits, including one to the US. By contrast, Brazauskas remained passive, simply waiting for his mandate to end. However, at the end of his term of office he did make two major public speeches. The first, on 6 October 1997, was a farewell speech in which he blamed the political majority in the Seimas, the government, and the irresponsible actions of his political competitors. He looked tired and exhausted and announced that he would not stand for a second term of office. The second was shorter and important in that the president made it clear whom he would like to see as his successor. Brazauskas nominated ex-Procurator General, Arturas Paulauskas. This was very important by virtue of the fact that Brazauskas was still very popular with the people. Indeed, after his farewell speech his popularity increased even more.[8]

Seven candidates took part in the first round of the elections for the presidency in 1997–8.[9] It was clear from the beginning that the main competition would be between three candidates: Valdas Adamkus, Vytautas Landsbergis, and Arturas Paulauskas. Landsbergis, representing the political majority in the Seimas, was eliminated after the first round. The LCU supported Adamkus in the first round, but with Landsbergis's elimination the HU/CL decided to cooperate with the Lithuanian Centre Union and supported Valdas Adamkus. Paulauskas was supported by the LDLP and the Lithuanian Liberal Union (LLU) from the very beginning of the campaign. Paulauskas won the first round in December 1997 by a big margin, receiving 45.28 per cent of the votes cast. His nearest rival, Adamkus, received only 27.90 per cent of the vote, Landsbergis 15.92 per cent, and Vytenis Andriukaitis 5.72 per cent. However, in the second round of the campaign, after the co-operation between the LCU and the HU/CL, Andriukaitis, a member of the Lithuanian Social Democratic Party, personally declared that Adamkus's programme was closer to his own than the one proposed by Paulauskas. Since Andriukaitis was a young candidate and Paulauskas campaigned as the representative of a new generation, it is conceivable that Andriukaitis's votes may have passed to Paulauskas. Thus, under these circumstances Adamkus won the second round of the presidential election on 4 January 1998, receiving 50.37 per cent of the votes cast.

Adamkus received only 14,256 more votes than Paulauskas in a total turnout of 1,921,806 voters.

This election was different from the previous one in that people voted for the candidates rather against them. There were seven people with very different programmes and personal experience from which to choose. Regardless of the cooperation between the HU/CL and the LCU in the second round of the presidential elections, Adamkus is more inclined towards the LCU, but the LCU has only 14 seats of the 141 seats in the Seimas. He is not a radical, like the HU/CL, but, for example, he did declare in his programme that he would like to change the taxation system. However, if he tries to do so, then he will clash with the majority in the Seimas. It is clear that he will neither change the prime minister nor Brazauskas's foreign policy and he is unlikely to become the main governing force in the near future because of the relationship with the political majority in the Seimas. As the 'newcomer' to the political elite, he needs some time to adapt to the circumstances of the political realities in Lithuania. In the case of a governmental crisis he is hardly likely to be in a position to stabilize the political situation.

PERSONALITY FACTORS

As noted above, Algirdas Brazauskas did not avail himself of the various possibilities that were open to him to become an 'all-powerful' head of state. This indicated that he lacked strong political ambition. This was the reason why, despite the approval of the political majority in the Seimas and his charismatic popularity in the society, he refused to play an active part in political life with the exception of foreign policy and state defence. All in all, such a course of action was determined by his political background.

Brazauskas emerged as a political leader between 1988 and 1990 during the time of the national movement for independence. As the leader of the Lithuanian Communist Party he was in conflict with the radicalism of Sajudis, on the one side, and the CPSU, on the other. He had to manoeuvre between these two forces and moderate their extremism. In this context, he developed the role of peacemaker and mediator. Thus, Brazauskas became a responsible leader, one who was good at finding ways out of crisis situations, but one who also avoided responsibility for routine situations. This was demonstrated by his actions in the governmental crisis of 1996. After the presidential election in 1993, there was no pressure on him to act from the Seimas and he adopted a passive role. He did not have the initiative necessary for the consolidation of power and retreated from political life for a short period of time. Thus, the conditions for active participation in political life were lost leaving prime minister Slezevicius to take advantage of the situation and become the central figure. Brazauskas was not a good public speaker and did not create a populist image. His speeches were neutral and even created the impression of abstract retelling (Bielinis 1995: 78). In short, he felt better in the role of a technocratic politician.

After the 1996 Seimas election, Brazauskas was unable to profit from the political support of the LDLP, as the party itself was too weak. Without this support, he avoided an open conflict with the political majority. He did not oppose the appointment of Vagnorius as prime minister. Instead, he wanted to secure for himself the role of a symbolic president with a large influence in foreign affairs. However, when the political situation became unstable, he did consider it his duty to intervene in the conflict (Talat-Kelpsa 1996: 108).

Valdas Adamkus differs greatly from Brazauskas. Although at the time of writing he has only been in office for a short period, he has already carried out many official engagements in Lithuania and has made a number of decisions in the area of foreign affairs. He is also the most popular politician in Lithuania with a support rating of 81 per cent, having won over many of those who voted for Arturas Paulaskas in the presidential election. Moreover, he is not afraid to confront the majority in the Seimas. Indeed, during his first six months in office he refused to sign seven pieces of parliamentary legislation and used his 'suspensive veto' on three occasions. All told, he is a very active president.

CONCLUSION

It is obvious that, despite the efforts of the Seimas majority to decrease the *de jure* powers of the president at the beginning of 1998, Lithuania still has a semi-presidential system. However, it is also clear that the regime is still under construction and that the presence of a president who is not drawn from the parliamentary majority may bring about further changes in the political system in the future. That said, the constitution does allow political leaders certain room for manoeuvre in which to exercise *de facto* powers. This is the reason why the system operated with a weak presidency during the term of office of Algirdas Brazauskas, whereas now there is a strong presidency under the incumbency of Valdas Adamkus.

NOTES

1. There was, contrary to some Western opinion, no confrontation between the Lithuanian Democratic Labour Party (LDLP) and the Sajudis, headed by Vytautas Landsbergis, after 1990. It is a myth that Landsbergis used to advertise himself as a fighter for independence 'against the enemies that had been all around him'. In fact, in 1991, Sajudis was not strong at all. The leaders of the Sajudis candidates elected to the Supreme Council decided that the members of the Seimas could not be the members of the popular front. Almost all the delegates supported by the Sajudis were elected to the Supreme Council of Lithuania, which was the reason the Sajudis lost its power as a separate organization. Moreover, the leader of the LDLP, Algirdas Brazauskas, had been the vice-prime minister in the first government of Lithuania in 1990–1 and had worked together in the government formed by the Sajudis. The LDLP's victory in the 1992 Seimas elections was absolutely unexpected and it showed not the strength of this party, but the weakness of the others.
2. In 1989 the Lithuanian Communist Party (LCP) separated from the Communist Party of the Soviet Union (CPSU). In 1990 the LCP transformed itself into the LDLP. However, in 1989 not all CPSU members passed into the LCP. A group of people, most of them Russian-speakers, remained in the CPSU. They called themselves Yedinstvo, but after a number of acts of aggression against the Republic of Lithuania they were outlawed soon afterwards.
3. Before 25 October 1992, the main legislative institution was called the Supreme Council. After the implementation of the new constitution, parliament was called the Seimas. The title, Seimas, has a long historical tradition dating back to the sixteenth century.
4. Seven constitutional drafts were proposed by different parties and groups from 1990 to 1992, but these drafts were either unrepresentative or were prepared by small groups which had no influence on the process. Each draft set out a completely different presidential institution, ranging from a purely presidential regime to a totally parliamentary regime. None of them, though, completely eliminated the institution of president.
5. Romualdas Ozolas played an active part in political life from the very beginning of the restoration of independence. He was one of the intellectuals who had no previous relations with the communist party, unlike, for example, Vytautas Landsbergis. He was also the leader of the Lithuanian Centre Union and was in a position to win the presidential election.
6. The president of Lithuania cannot be a member of any political party, but usually every candidate originates from a party or is supported by one. In this sense, Algirdas Brazauskas can be deemed to be an LDLP president and the current incumbent, Valdas Adamkus, an LCU and HU/CL president as these parties supported him in the second round of the election.
7. A large number of people lost their savings as a result of the banking crisis. Slezevicius himself allegedly withdrew money from one of the banks before information about the crisis became public.

8. The percentage of the population that claimed to have confidence in him reached 26.2 per cent, while only 14.4 per cent had confidence in Paulauskas, 13.2 per cent in Adamkus, and 11.2 per cent in Landsbergis.
9. These were: Valdas Adamkus, Vytenis Andriukaitis, Kazys Bobelis, Vytautas Landsbergis, Arturas Paulauskas, Rolandas Pavilionis, and Rimantas Smetona. Most of these candidates declared that they would change the government, which was the reason why the majority in the Seimas decided to appeal to the Constitutional Court (see above).

9

Poland

ANIA VAN DER MEER KROK-PASZKOWSKA

The eight years of post-communist democratic rule in Poland have been marked by a struggle between rival constitutional agendas. The institutional set-up has remained the same as under the 1989 Roundtable Agreement, i.e. a dual executive and a dual legislature, but the formal competencies and effective powers of these institutions have changed over time. There were two stages in the constitution-making process: the round table negotiations leading to constitutional amendments and the regular constitution-making process (Elster 1993). The transition to democracy was to have been gradual and controlled with a new constitution being passed before the first fully competitive parliamentary elections in 1993. Instead, democratic institutions emerged in a stepwise and piecemeal manner with political events overtaking constitutional initiatives. Minor amendments were made to the 1952 constitution in anticipation of a completely new constitution being passed relatively quickly. When it became clear that the two houses of parliament would be unable to agree on a common draft and as differences emerged on what rights and freedoms should or should not be guaranteed in the constitution, a stop-gap constitution was passed which dealt only with executive-legislative relations. The often ambiguous provisions of the 1992 Little Constitution[1] were interpreted by various political forces in ways which bolstered their respective institutional powers. The passing of the Little Constitution did not, as was hoped, lead to a less heated debate between those who wanted a 'governing' president and those who favoured a figurehead president with weak powers. The constitution-making process was formally completed in the summer of 1997 with the passing of the full constitution by a legislature dominated by parties with roots in the former communist regime. Its confirmation by referendum was by a narrow majority (52.7 per cent) in the context of a low

This is part of a larger study on the transition to parliamentary democracy and its institutionalization in contemporary Poland.

turnout (42.9 per cent). The numerous political parties and organizations which were not represented in the 1993–7 legislature have vowed to reopen negotiations on certain constitutional provisions in the next parliamentary term. It remains to be seen whether they will want or, more important, be able to do so given that any amendments require a two-thirds majority. What does seem clear though is that any changes are more likely to be in the ideological sphere than in the institutional framework. A semi-presidential system is in place, but its nature has been the source of institutional squabbles throughout the period under consideration (1989–97).

Since 1990 when popular elections for the president were introduced, presidents have been faced with four parliaments[2] elected under three different electoral laws. (For a list of presidents and prime ministers, see Figure 9.1.) Presidential elections were held halfway through two of these legislative terms. The pattern of political leadership has been affected by both the composition of parliament and the relationship of the president to the parliamentary majority. At least four different situations can be identified. Prior to the 1991 parliamentary elections, the president was strong due to his electoral legitimacy vis-à-vis a legislature made up largely of deputies who had not been exposed to fully competitive elections. Between October 1991 and mid-September 1993, the president faced unstable and shifting coalitions. Successive governments were weak with undependable parliamentary support. Following the 1993 parliamentary elections, the president confronted a larger and more cohesive parliamentary majority, moreover one he was opposed to. The power of the prime minister was strengthened by the size of the majority, and the president had only a precarious foothold in parliament. Throughout his term of office (1990–5), the president tried to increase his powers and dominate prime ministers. Throughout, parliament tried to prevent him from doing so. Following presidential elections in late 1995, two successive prime ministers, backed by large parliamentary majorities, have cooperated with a president who had previously been their parliamentary leader. In autumn 1997, this president will be faced with a governing coalition opposed to him.

The nature of the transition, the protracted constitution-writing process, the different style and authority of successive presidents, significant differences in the composition of successive parliaments, and the frequently changing relations between president and parliamentary majority are all factors which make for a system in which the conventions of political practice are still fluid and emerging. The dual executive proved useful in the transition from authoritarian rule to democracy,

Presidents	Prime ministers
Wojciech Jaruzelski (PZPR, later non-party) July 1989–Oct. 1990	Tadeusz Mazowiecki (Solidarity) Aug. 1989–Dec. 1990 Solidarity coalition with PSL, SD, and PZPR
Lech Wałęsa (Solidarity, non-party) Oct. 1990–Nov. 1995	Jan Krzysztof Bielecki (KLD) Jan. 1991–Nov. 1991 KLD, PC, ZChN, and non-party coalition
	Jan Olszewski (PC) Dec. 1991–June 1992 PC, ZChN, and PL coalition
	Hanna Suchocka (UD) July 1992–May 1993 UD, KLD, ZChN, PChD, SLCh, PPG, and PL coalition
	Waldemar Pawlak (PSL) Nov. 1993–June 1995 SLD, PSL coalition
Aleksander Kwaśniewski (SLD, later non-party) Dec. 1995–	Józef Oleksy (SLD) June 1995–Dec. 1995 SLD, PSL coalition
	Włodzimierz Cimoszewicz (SLD) Jan. 1996–Sept. 1997 SLD, PSL coalition
	Jerzy Buzek (AWS) Oct. 1997– AWS, UW coalition
PZPR Polish United Workers' Party SLD Democratic Left Alliance PSL Polish Peasant Party SD Democratic Party UD Democratic Union; since 1994 UW Union of Freedom KLD Liberal Democratic Congress	PC Centre Alliance ZChN Christian National Union PL Peasant Alliance PChD Party of Christian Democrats SLCh Christian-Peasant Party PPG Polish Economic Programme AWS Solidarity Electoral Action

FIG. 9.1. Presidents and prime ministers in Poland, 1989–1998

providing the possibility to share power between old and new elites. However, the lack of stable and disciplined parties, proportional electoral systems and a conflictual rather than consensual political culture may mean that the system will not necessarily provide the political stability that it has in the French Fifth Republic.

HISTORICAL CONTEXT

In Poland, institutional relations were devised within the framework of a negotiated agreement providing for a gradual transition to democracy. The negotiators thought in terms of liberalization, in the sense of limited concessions to pluralism in the short term, with full democratization held out as a probable second stage. The Roundtable Agreement provided for a strong president to be elected by parliament. The bicameral legislature was to be dominated by a communist coalition with a promise of genuinely free elections after a four-year transitional period.

The roundtable talks were held from February to April 1989. In the course of the negotiations the government side proposed non-confrontational elections to give parliament a more pluralistic character. By bringing the opposition into the confines of the political system it hoped to gain legitimacy and increased governability. One of the main dilemmas for the opposition was whether entering into a contract on elections was too high a price to pay for the legalization of Solidarity; the more so since the authorities were also pressing for the establishment of a presidency with wide-ranging powers, modelled on the French Fifth Republic.

In the end, the opposition agreed to the presidency in exchange for a 100-member freely elected Senate. The distribution of the 460 seats in the so-called 'contractual' Sejm, which, unlike the Senate, was only partially freely elected, was fixed at 65 per cent guaranteed seats for the PZPR (Polish United Workers' Party) and its allies, 35 per cent open to free competition. The composition of Sejm and Senate together was important given that the president was to be elected for a six-year term by a majority of votes at a joint session of the two chambers. The president would have the right of legislative initiative and veto (with a two-thirds Sejm override). Further powers included the sole right to nominate the prime minister, as well as of being consulted on the names of candidates for the remaining cabinet posts, and the right to dissolve parliament if its decisions impinged upon the president's ability to carry out his constitutional prerogatives. The president also had special responsibility over the army, internal affairs, and foreign affairs. Both sides understood that the president would be from the PZPR and most probably Wojciech Jaruzelski, and would provide continuity and a guarantee of gradual transition, retaining power even after the planned free elections in 1993. Within this time the Sejm was to have passed a new constitution. Two years later the new parliament would elect a president to replace the roundtable president. The roundtable contract was thus aimed at allowing the PZPR and its allies, ZSL (United Peasants' Party) and SD (Democratic Party) to continue to govern the country, while the opposition deputies would 'legally take on the functions of a parliamentary opposition' (Gebethner 1992: 238).

Within two months of the signing of the Roundtable Agreement, the unexpected electoral success of Solidarity had undermined this scenario. Solidarity had won 99 seats in the 100-seat Senate and all of the 161 freely contested Sejm seats. The institutional arrangements as designed under the roundtable contract were to function under circumstances which were considered only a theoretical possibility by their planners. However, Solidarity was not quite ready to take over the reins of power. Considerations of foreign policy and the uncertain role of the army and internal security forces convinced Solidarity that General Jaruzelski should be elected president. Jaruzelski's election by a joint sitting of the Sejm and Senate on 19 July 1989 was achieved by the margin of only one vote thanks to strategic voting by a number of Solidarity deputies. The 'gentleman's agreement' had been upheld in the interest of political stability. However, within a few weeks, the previously subservient 'satellite' parties, which the Communists had allowed to participate in parliament since the late 1940s, had decided to change sides and form a coalition government with Solidarity. The PZPR was left with only 37.6 per cent of seats in the Sejm and thereby lost control over ordinary legislation and over the formation of government. In September, a Solidarity prime minister, Tadeusz Mazowiecki, formed a grand coalition made up of eleven Solidarity ministers and seven ministers from the satellite Peasant and Democratic parties, with four portfolios reserved for the communists. These included defence and internal affairs—two important areas dominated by the former state apparatus and over which the democratic opposition only gradually gained control.

From the beginning, Jaruzelski's claim to legitimacy was undermined by the electoral fiasco of the communist camp. It further declined as neighbouring countries pushed through more far-reaching reforms and free parliamentary and/or presidential elections were held in Hungary,

Czechoslovakia, and Bulgaria. Jaruzelski's office on the basis of the Roundtable Agreement became redundant when one of the signatories, the PZPR, dissolved itself in January 1990 and, thus, deprived the president of parliamentary support.

Thus, the question of a new president with democratic credentials was raised. Lech Wałęsa was in many ways the obvious candidate. He had been the one to undertake negotiations to form a Solidarity-led coalition government, backing Mazowiecki as prime minister. However, within a year, Mazowiecki's slow and cautious approach to reform was criticized by Wałęsa who called for a new strategy of political and economic 'acceleration' whereby the roundtable contract could be treated as invalid because the communist partners had disappeared and the army and police were no longer under communist control. Wałęsa's aspirations to the presidency and his criticism of the government led to a backlash by the intellectuals who had advised him since 1980 and who formed the core of the government and the parliamentary civic club. This was the beginning of the so-called 'war at the top' leading to polarization between two post-Solidarity camps.

On 10 April 1990 Wałęsa publicly announced his interest in becoming president. In May the PC (Centre Alliance) put Wałęsa forward as their presidential candidate and proposed that he be elected by a joint session of both houses of parliament sometime in the autumn. PC calculated that Wałęsa had the greatest chance of winning the necessary absolute majority.[3] They urged Mazowiecki not to run for president and thereby divide the Solidarity vote. Given Wałęsa's strong potential parliamentary support and partly because they were convinced Mazowiecki would be more likely to win in direct elections,[4] Mazowiecki's supporters put forward the idea of popular elections. This despite their avowed preference for a parliamentary system. There is a twist here because the PC really favoured a directly elected president on the French model.[5] In any case, within a few months Wałęsa himself had decided that Poland needed a popularly elected president with broad competencies. The decision to introduce a directly elected presidency appears to have been based mainly on political expediency and instrumental considerations, but the legitimacy deficit of the Sejm also played a role. The election of the president by popular vote had an important symbolic value. It would mark the start of complete political and economic transformation legitimized by the electorate as opposed to adherence to an elite pact envisaging gradual progress towards full democracy.

On 21 September 1990 the Sejm passed a resolution on its early dissolution and on shortening the presidential term so that direct presidential elections could be held not later than December. Although a resolution is not legally binding, it was an important political declaration which acknowleged that the Roundtable Agreements had been overtaken by the systemic and political changes in Poland (Gebethner 1993). A few days later, on 27 September, the Sejm passed a constitutional amendment to the effect that the president would be elected by the nation through universal suffrage (*Dziennik Ustaw*, 1990, no. 67, item 397). The position of the presidency within a broader institutional framework and the powers of president in relation to the government and parliament were not debated at the time. Indeed, the presidential election was seen by some as an 'extraordinary' election which would not necessarily mean that future presidential elections would be popular ones. The constitution still had to be written after all and the matter of the shape of the presidency and relations between president, government, and parliament remained open.

From a political perspective, the amended electoral procedure allowed for a smooth and dignified departure of Jaruzelski (Sokolewicz 1992). Jaruzelski was more amenable to handing in his early resignation due to a change in the constitution and the holding of elections, rather than simply resigning and having the same parliament elect a new president. From a legal-constitutional point of view, the wide powers vested in the president under the Roundtable Agreements made the choice for a directly elected president more logical.

In practice, the nature of the presidency changed. The president was no longer the guarantor of gradual change but represented the revolutionary transformation of the system. Moreover, although the powers of the president were unchanged,[6] this time the president would be able to claim electoral legitimacy in his dealings with a parliament which was seen to lack it.

Presidential elections were held in November 1990. No candidate managed to win an outright majority in the first round. The two candidates with the most votes fought a second-round run-off, which Wałęsa won. Once Wałęsa was president, his legitimacy stemming from direct elections and his authority stemming from his past record as leader of Solidarity made for a president likely to exercise his powers to the full. However, the institutional set-up provided for a system of institutions which could mutually brake and even block each others' prerogatives (Ciemniewski 1993). Wide-reaching presidential powers were confronted by a parliament that was, in constitutional terms, 'the highest organ of state authority'. Within the executive, there was an unclear division of competences between the president and the government, particularly in the fields of internal and external security. Moreover, progress on a new constitution was hampered by a lack of cooperation between the two chambers of parliament: the freely elected Senate questioning the legitimacy of the so-called contractual Sejm to pass a constitution.

The institutional set-up continued to function on the basis of the Roundtable Agreement and amendments to the 1952 constitution, and from October 1992 on the basis of the interim Little Constitution. It was in this context that Poland's semi-presidential system evolved, with political conflict shifting to the constitutional level as president, government, and parliament tried to defend or increase their powers. Draft constitutions under consideration in the various constitutional committees between 1989 and 1997 covered a broad gamut of institutional arrangements from a unicameral parliamentary system with an indirectly elected figurehead president to a semi-presidential system giving the president the power to dismiss the cabinet and dissolve parliament at will. However, it could be argued that the longer the Little Constitution stayed in force the more likely it was that the new full constitution would not radically depart from its institutional design. In this light, attempts were made to create constitutional custom by interpeting ambiguous provisions to strengthen competencies in ways not really intended by its drafters. Political ambitions and institutional rivalries have thus remained central to the constitution-making process (Osiatyński 1994).

CONSTITUTIONAL POWERS UNDER THE LITTLE CONSTITUTION

The Little Constitution delineated the president's powers which had partly evolved in the course of political practice. The areas of conflict which emerged between parliament and president during work on the Little Constitution were the powers of the president in the area of internal and external security; and the extent to which legal acts of the president should be subject to ministerial approval.

Under the Little Constitution, the president's powers with respect to the parliament were the right to initiate legislation and the right of veto over legislation passed by parliament, although the Sejm could override the veto by a two-thirds majority. The president could also ask the Constitutional Tribunal to rule on the constitutionality of legislation. The Constitutional Tribunal's ruling was not final, however, as it could be overturned by a two-thirds majority in the Sejm. The president had the right to dissolve parliament in the following cases: (*a*) if the Sejm had passed a simple vote of no confidence in the council of ministers; (*b*) if the budget was not passed by the Sejm within three months of the submission of a draft budget; and (*c*) if no government capable of receiving the confidence of the Sejm had been formed following a complex five-step procedure in which the president and the Sejm took turns to nominate their candidate for prime minister. The president also had the right to call a national referendum, provided the Senate gave its approval, a right previously restricted to the Sejm.

The president's powers with regard to the government proved more difficult to delineate as they encompassed the degree of involvement and influence the president should have on policy-making and the degree of autonomy the government should have in view of its accountability to parliament. Under Article 38(1), the prime minister informs the president about 'fundamental matters concerning the activity of the council of ministers' and under Article 38(2) the president may preside over meetings of the council of ministers on 'matters of particular importance to the state'. However, under Article 23 it is the government and not the president that, subject to the Sejm's authorization, has the right to issue regulations having the force of law.

Powers overlapped in the sphere of defence policy as well as on internal security and foreign policy. The president exercised general supervision in the field of international relations and with respect to external and internal security. To reinforce this function, the prime minister was required to seek the president's opinion before naming the foreign, defence, and internal affairs ministers. Finally if the state was threatened by external forces, the president could declare a state of war. He could also declare a state of emergency, but for no longer than three months, during which time the Sejm could not be dissolved.

Legal acts issued by the president were to be countersigned by the prime minister or appropriate minister(s), with the exception of the powers outlined above. The president could also deliver messages to parliament and appoint certain senior officials without the requirement of countersignature.

The president thus had powers of nomination and legislative powers which were to come into play especially if the government was unstable or if there was a political crisis. His role was that of a strong arbiter. The president did not have the power to dismiss the government, a prerogative sought by Wałęsa, but he did have the right to dissolve parliament if there was a simple vote of no confidence in the government, not an option under the amended 1952 constitution. This was balanced by the possibility for the Sejm to pass a constructive vote of no confidence. The catch-all clause of being able to dissolve parliament if its decisions made it impossible for the president to fulfil his constitutional obligations was also dropped.

POLITICAL PRACTICE

The designers of the Little Constitution envisaged 'a president who would function as the government's equal and loyal partner rather than its supervisor' (Vinton 1992: 26). Political practice has shown a more conflictual relationship. Certainly in practice, the Little Constitution was interpreted in ways unforeseen by its parliamentary drafters. The following section will analyse the nature of the relationship between president and parliamentary majority under different conditions and consider how constitutional prerogatives have been interpreted in political practice. It will also outline the changes in the relationship between president, government, and parliament under the 1997 constitution.

Since the passing of the Little Constitution, the president was faced with two parliaments which were quite different in terms of composition and in terms of the constellation of power. The first Sejm was characterized by a large number of internally divided, undisciplined, and unstable parties and political groups. Government coalitions were fragile, uncertain of parliamentary support for their policies. The second Sejm was made up of six parties with a more stable membership, although towards the end of the term the smaller opposition parties largely disintegrated. Government coalitions were based on large majorities in parliament. However, the election of a new president halfway through the parliamentary term changed the nature of the relationship between president and parliamentary majority.

Wałęsa had been president for two years before the Little Constitution was passed. In 1990 Wałęsa's electoral legitimacy and the Sejm's perceived lack of it had strengthened the position of the president without any changes having been made to his constitutional powers. Moreover, Wałęsa did not want to be a passive figurehead but intended to play an active role in shaping policy. He tried to influence his yet to be defined constitutional prerogatives by setting precedents which he hoped would be accepted as political custom.

Following parliamentary elections on 27 October 1991 both president and parliament were able to claim full electoral legitimacy. In the face of a majority in the Sejm unwilling to support his candidate for prime minister, Wałęsa was forced to nominate the Sejm's preferred candidate,

Jan Olszewski. Problems between the government and the president arose with regard to presidential prerogatives on coordinating security and defence policy. Faced with an uncooperative government, Wałęsa took recourse to his right of legislative initiative. He submitted a draft constitutional law giving the president wide-ranging powers at the expense of the legislature, including the right for the president to dissolve parliament following a vote of no confidence in the government. An extraordinary parliamentary committee was formed to study the proposals, but Wałęsa, unhappy about the way the committee was amending his draft, withdrew it after two weeks. After five conflict-ridden months, the government fell following a no-confidence vote. The motion of no confidence was backed up by a letter from the president to the speaker of the Sejm calling for immediate dismissal of the government. Under the 1952 amended constitution, Wałęsa had no grounds to call for the dismissal of the government, except under the vague provision that the Sejm was making it impossible to fulfil his constitutional obligations. In political terms, however, the president's 'loss of confidence' in the government provided an important signal to the opposition showing the president's support for the motion of no confidence.

This time Wałęsa's candidate for prime minister, Waldemar Pawlak, was approved by the Sejm but proved unable to form a government despite, or perhaps due to, Wałęsa's active involvement in trying to hammer out a coalition. He resigned after a month and the Sejm proposed a new candidate, Hanna Suchocka, to lead a coalition of eight parties. One of the parties left the coalition even before the government was formed, leaving it a minority coalition of seven parties but supported by a number of small parliamentary groups. This enabled it to survive for eighteen months before it too was removed by a vote of no confidence.

Under Suchocka relations between government and president were more consensual. Suchocka accepted three key ministerial nominations Wałęsa had agreed upon with Pawlak when he had tried to form a government. The prime minister's obligation to consult with the president before appointing the three ministers, those of defence, internal, and foreign affairs, was laid down a few months later in the Little Constitution. However, the president wanted to extend his influence in other fields. In February 1993, the government's choice of a new minister of culture was effectively vetoed by the president when he refused to sign the nomination. The government complied by proposing another candidate, thus implicitly acknowledging that the president could have a say in cabinet reshuffles. The wording of Article 68(2) of the Little Constitution allowed the president's legal adviser to engage in semantics: Upon a motion by the prime minister, the president may effect changes in the office of individual ministers. The legal adviser used the word 'may' to mean 'may or may not' rather than 'shall'. Prime minister Suchocka explained her position as follows: '. . . unlike the system in Germany, where the chancellor can change ministers whenever he wants, I, in the light of the constitution, must apply to the president to effect any change. Only if a minister resigns from his office, does he offer his resignation to me' (interview in *Polityka*, 29 May 1993).

Another example of the president's attempts to increase his influence was his move to appoint a chairman of the National Broadcasting Council before parliament had had time to appoint its members. Moreover, the president had not asked the prime minister to countersign the appointment.[7] The government objected on procedural grounds. Again the prerogatives of prime minister and president were not clear-cut. Leaving aside the timing of the chairman's appointment, his appointment required the prime minister's signature since it was not included on the list of legal acts which the president could carry out autonomously. Indeed, it could not have been because the broadcasting council had not been in existence when the constitution was passed. The president responded by proposing amendments to the Little Constitution which would widen the sphere of legal acts he could perform without the countersignature of the prime minister. Although the constitution was not amended, the government accepted the nomination as a *fait accompli*.

Constitutional ambiguities and a readiness on the part of the prime minister to give him his due allowed the president to increase his influence upon ministerial and other political appointments. It should be noted that the constitution did provide a number of effective checks and balances, denying the president the opportunity to take advantage of any potential weakness of government or parliament, by not granting him the right to rule by decree, the right to dismiss the government, or to call a referendum without the approval of the Senate. In political practice, however, at least one commentator thought that the period of the Suchocka government led to a shift in powers towards a stronger presidency (Wiatr 1993).

When the Suchocka government fell through a simple vote of no confidence, the president did not accept the government's resignation, but used his new powers under the Little Constitution to dissolve parliament and call elections under a new electoral law which the Sejm had passed only days before. The 1993 electoral law introduced a number of elements aimed at reducing proportionality and favouring larger parties. Recognizing that only parties with significant electoral support would enter the next parliament, and that the largest winners would be overcompensated in terms of parliamentary seats, Wałęsa tried to convince the parties which had formed the previous coalition to go to the elections as an electoral bloc. His efforts were unsuccessful. Wałęsa then initiated a presidential alliance, the BBWR (Non-Party Reform Bloc), which he hoped would be able to gain at least 20 per cent of seats in the next parliament, thus giving him a substantial parliamentary base. When this seemed unlikely, he distanced himself from the BBWR.

Following the 1993 parliamentary elections, the relations between president, government, and parliament took on a different aspect. In a parliament in which now only six parties were represented, the president was confronted with a large parliamentary majority, only four seats short of the two-thirds majority needed for constitutional reform, formed by two post-communist parties: the SLD (Alliance of the Democratic Left) and the PSL (Polish Peasant Party). The coalition tried to achieve good relations with the president by accepting that the ministers of foreign affairs, defence, and internal affairs would be picked by Wałęsa. These three 'presidential' ministers formed an integral part of the SLD/PSL government, but at the same time stood outside it.[8] At the same time, the coalition also made it clear that the president would have little choice but to nominate their candidate for prime minister. Wałęsa had wanted to nominate a candidate of his own choice, although constrained by the fact that he or she would have to come from within the ranks of the coalition. He asked the coalition for a list of three candidates. However, the coalition parties first worked out a distribution of cabinet posts between themselves and then proposed PSL leader Waldemar Pawlak as sole prime ministerial candidate. In the absence of a credible alternative, Wałęsa was forced to nominate him.

The powers of the president under the Little Constitution did not suggest that he could effectively challenge the power of a government with a large and stable parliamentary majority. Moreover, his parliamentary support was minimal, 16 seats won by the BBWR. Thus, one would expect a balance of power in favour of the government. Yet in the course of the Pawlak government, the president consistently and often effectively challenged the coalition. The weakness of parties, the troubles within the coalition, the fact that part of the opposition had not made it into parliament all offered opportunities for the president to increase his influence. To this end, the president creatively interpreted constitutional provisions to increase his prerogatives and made full use of his legislative powers: his right to submit bills, his right of legislative veto, and his right to send bills to the Constitutional Tribunal. As will be illustrated below, he also proved adept at playing one coalition partner against the other.

As leader of the weaker coalition partner, but one with greater formal powers, prime minister Pawlak could, in his first months of office, rely on Wałęsa to support him against the SLD. In February 1994, Pawlak fired a deputy finance minister. The SLD minister of finance submitted his resignation in protest which Pawlak immediately accepted without consulting his coalition partner. Wałęsa, eager to take advantage of inter-coalition disagreements, quickly signed the resignation. Relations between the coalition partners had already been tense; the SLD pressing for market reforms and the PSL trying to delay the process. The position of finance minister remained empty for months with Wałęsa refusing to accept the coalition (SLD) candidate for the post and the SLD refusing to come up with an alternative. The coalition also wanted to introduce their candidates as secretaries of state in the three 'presidential' ministries, a move that was blocked by Wałęsa. In April, frustrated by the impasse, 16 coalition deputies submitted a private members bill to amend the Little Constitution by giving the president only seven days' time to accept or reject government candidates for a ministerial post.[9] If he failed to do so, the Sejm could push through the nomination by an absolute majority. The president reacted by threatening to find a way to dissolve parliament if it tried to change his competencies. Compromise was finally reached during a meeting of the president with the SLD parliamentary party. It was agreed not to introduce changes to the Little Constitution and not to use it as an element in the 'political game' between president and coalition. The president agreed to accept coalition deputy ministers in the presidential ministries while the SLD dropped its nominee for minister of finance and came up with a new candidate acceptable to the president.

The truce did not last long. Further controversy centred around the question of whether the chief of the general staff should be answerable to the president or to the defence minister, and the struggle for control of the National Broadcasting Council. Following a meeting of Wałęsa with military chiefs in which they expressed their lack of confidence in the defence minister, and questionable and creative interpretations of constitutional provisions to increase presidential powers,[10] the Sejm took the unprecedented step of passing an appeal to the president urging him to discontinue actions that might lead to a crisis of the state and referring to infringements upon the apolitical nature of the armed forces and upon the autonomy of the National Broadcasting Council (*Kronika Sejmow*, no. 47, 12–18 Oct. 1994).

Wałęsa had been able to have his way in a number of executive appointments by co-opting the PSL prime minister and by capitalizing on conflicts between the PSL and its larger coalition partner. When the prime minister proved less amenable to Wałęsa's wishes, the president complained that the job surpassed Pawlak's abilities and that if he had had the right to recall the prime minister he would have done so half a year ago. The 1995 budget provided the catalyst which eventually brought down the Pawlak government. The fall of the government was not only due to conflict within the governing coalition but was even more the result of institutional conflict between the parliament (and government) on one side and the president on the other.

Wałęsa had been challenging the governing coalition for months and now came up with an excuse for dissolving parliament and calling new elections. He started by sending several laws adopted by parliament to the Constitutional Tribunal, claiming they were unconstitutional. Among these were the tax law and the law on state salaries, both of which would affect the budget. He then threatened not to sign the budget, and thus have an excuse to dissolve the Sejm. The president's advisers interpreted Article 21(4) of the constitution to mean that the budget not only had to be adopted but had actually to come into force within three months. Under the Little Constitution, the president has a 30-day period in which to consider and either sign or reject the budget. If this were added to the two months already taken for parliamentary consideration of the budget, the three-month period would certainly be surpassed, especially if the president were to veto the budget on the last day he was constitutionally required to sign or reject it. If the Sejm overturned the veto, the budget would have been passed twice, but without actually coming into force until after the deadline had expired (*East European Constitutional Review*, Spring 1995). Needless to say, parliament rejected Wałęsa's interpretation of the law. But just in case, it rushed through an amendment to the Little Constitution under which if the Sejm is dissolved it would continue to work until the swearing in of the next Sejm. The legislative process could continue and control of the government would still be possible. The bill was passed almost unanimously.

A few days before the bill was passed, the SLD leadership had met in the Sejm with the speaker of the house (SLD) and representatives from the opposition UW (Freedom Union) and UP (Union of Labour) to discuss possible impeachment of the president were he to undertake any unconstitutional action against parliament. During these discussions, prime minister Pawlak was on an official visit to the United States and so could not attend. Moreover, rumours abounded about his possible backroom deals with the president with respect to possible candidates for minister of defence. Upon Pawlak's return, a stormy meeting took place with the SLD leadership during which there were calls for his resignation (*Rzeczpospolita*, 4–5, 6 Feb. 1995)

On 4 February, the Sejm adopted a statement on the situation: the growing conflict between the president and parliament constitutes a threat to the normal operation of the supreme authorities of the Republic and its economy. The Sejm hereby declares that the 1995 budget had been adopted by it in a manner and at a time consistent with the constitutional requirements and there exist no constitutional premises for the dissolution of the Sejm. In these circumstances, a dissolution of parliament by the president of the Republic of Poland, . . . will be considered illegal by the Sejm and lead to the consitutional accountability of the president of the Republic. (*Kronika Sejmowa*, no. 62, 1–7 Feb. 1995)

Two days later, on 6 February, Wałęsa presented his trump card, averting a constitutional crisis and divesting himself of Pawlak in one stroke. In televised proceedings, Wałęsa met in the Sejm with the speakers and parliamentary party leaders. Accusing Pawlak's government of incompetence, party nepotism, and slowing down reforms, the president insisted that the cabinet be restructured and headed by a new prime minister. Otherwise he would find some way to dissolve parliament. This played into the hands of the SLD who had become increasingly unhappy with Pawlak's style of leadership. The next day the coalition parties proposed Józef Oleksy (SLD), speaker of the Sejm, as their candidate.

In his confrontations with the SLD/PSL coalition, Wałęsa claimed to represent the more than 30 per cent of voters who had voted for parties which had not succeeded in crossing the parliamentary electoral thresholds of 5 per cent for parties and 8 per cent for electoral alliances. He further claimed that he had received a larger percentage of the vote in the 1990 presidential elections than the coalition parties had obtained in the 1993 parliamentary elections. This, together with his conviction that in the transitional period, given the need for far-reaching reforms and given the lack of a clearly crystallized party system, a presidential system is the best solution, was sufficient reason and motivation for challenging both government and parliament.

Wałęsa's elastic interpretations of his constitutional prerogatives and his confrontational style were not popular with a large part of the electorate, however. In November 1995 Wałęsa very narrowly lost the elections to Aleksander Kwaśniewski of the SLD.[11] When shortly thereafter prime minister Olesky (SLD) was accused of spying for the KGB, he chose to resign rather than wait for the Sejm to pass a constructive vote of no confidence in the government. This gave the new president, rather than the Sejm, the initiative to designate the next prime minister. This was illustrative of a more cooperative relationship between the new president and the governing coalition. During the cabinet formation, the so-called presidential ministeries were no longer a bone of contention between president and government: internal affairs going to the SLD, defence to PSL. The minister of foreign affairs was non-partisan but sponsored by the SLD.

In his electoral campaign Kwaśniewski had stressed the need to pass a new constitution, to continue economic reform, to move towards decentralization and to strive for EU and NATO membership. He also emphasized the need for cooperation rather than conflict between president and parliament (*Polityka*, 11 Nov. 1995). In practice, Kwaśniewski has continued to support these aims which he considers to be in the interest of the nation as a whole and above party politics. He plays an important role in foreign and defence policy through informal coordination with the government. He has occasionally participated in cabinet meetings when outlines of foreign or defence policy were being discussed. Up to the end of the second Sejm, Kwaśniewski had vetoed only two bills, although he did threaten to use his veto more often, especially when economic reform was in danger of being derailed by the PSL. In this way, the president acted as a safety net ensuring reform, with the SLD prime minister counting on the president to support him against his coalition partner. Although Kwaśniewski has no formal say on economic policy, he has undoubtedly had an influence on nominations for minister of finance. His use of legislative initiative has not been aimed at reinforcing his position or undermining the government, although it has ranged from matters military to economic as well as institutional.

Kwaśniewski's style has been quite different from that of Wałęsa. His background as leader of the successor party to the communists and as someone who had been a junior minister in the last communist government has made him eager to rise above the historical communist/Solidarity divide. Since becoming president, he has been more conciliatory towards the Catholic church's role in the state than his former party colleagues in the Sejm. But he has also been criticized by the opposition for supporting controversial legislation passed by the post-communists (on PZPR former assets, on the requirement of seven years of experience for higher positions in public administration, and on legislation said to favour so-called *nomenklatura* capitalism, links between state and business interests). On the whole though he has tried to be statespersonlike and non-confrontational, emphasizing adherence to legal and parliamentary procedures. In contrast to Wałęsa's rather belligerent, hands-on approach he has made a conscious effort to build up a different image of the presidency. Moreover, while Wałęsa wanted strong presidential powers allowing him to control the government, but did not have the parliamentary support to push this vision through, Kwaśniewski had spent the two years of Wałęsa's conflict with parliament as chairman of the constitutional committee and as leader of a party wanting to limit rather than extend presidential powers.

WRITING THE CONSTITUTION IN THE SECOND SEJM

The skirmishes between president, on the one side, and government and parliament, on the other, had an effect on drafters of the 1997 constitution. Bargaining on presidential prerogatives continued under both the Wałęsa and the Kwaśniewski presidencies. Despite many individual politicians' expressed preference for a president elected by the National Assembly, no party felt it could back this. 'Once you have given people the right to vote for president, taking this away would be a dangerous measure' is a typical comment.[12] Kwaśniewski's SLD had originally opted for a pure parliamentary model in their draft constitution; their forerunners' support for a powerful president having been an instrumental device to retain influence under the Roundtable Agreements. However, in the process of constitutional bargaining their willingness to accept direct election of the president was based not only on recognition that this solution had the greater chance of all-party acceptance, but on the realization that their candidate had a good chance of being elected the next president. Thus suggestions that the president should be elected by parliament were easily defeated. That decision made, a president with considerable powers was likely. To quote Aleksander Kwaśniewski:

A president chosen in popular elections cannot be a 'ceremonial president' such as in Germany or the Czech Republic. The president should be an element of the balance between parliament and government, to have an influence on politics. If the SdRP [Social Democracy for Poland] wants to think seriously about the presidential elections, only such a president interests us. If he is to be purely ceremonial, there is no point in taking up the cudgels.[13]

The same sort of reasoning applied to other parties. A dual executive gave them two shots at gaining influence and electoral legitimacy.

Undoubtedly political practice affected the constitutional process. In the light of Wałęsa's use of the legislative veto in his conflict with parliament,[14] the constitutional committee, under Kwaśniewski's chairmanship, decided the veto should be overridden by absolute majority. Before work on the constitution could be completed, Kwaśniewski had been elected president. Within a year of taking up office, his representative in the committee suggested reverting to a two-thirds override on the grounds that there would be no point in having a veto if the override was the same majority needed for passing any legislation in the Sejm. This was accepted by the committee, but at the last moment, as part of the package allowing PSL and UP to vote for the constitution, the override was lowered to three-fifths. The president has also lost the right to veto the budget, although he can ask the Constitutional Tribunal to rule on its conformity with the constitution. The time the president has for signing or vetoing a bill has been shortened from 30 to 21 days.

However, Kwaśniewski also managed to recoup some powers at the expense of the prime minister and parliament. The constitutional bill prepared by the constitutional committee of deputies and senators had envisaged the president, on the motion of the prime minister, appointing the Chief of Staff. This was a departure from the Little Consitution which had the president, in agreement with the minister of defence, appointing and dismissing the Army Chief of Staff. In practice, Wałęsa had controlled nominations for the minister of defence. In a situation of divided majorities this had led to friction within the government, something the drafters wanted to avoid. Kwaśniewski's proposed amendment that he would have the sole right to appoint the Army Chief of Staff and other commanders for a specified period of time was accepted by the National Assembly. Kwaśniewski's motivation was to take the decision out of the party political sphere, while at the same time bolstering his position. The president also won the right to appoint the presidents of the Supreme Court, the Supreme Administrative Court, and the Constitutional Tribunal. Under the Little Constitution they had been chosen by the Sejm and this formula had been kept on by the constitutional committee. The National Assembly accepted the president's proposal that he have the right to appoint the president of the National Bank and members of the Council for Monetary Policy without the prime minister's countersignature. All in all the number of legal acts not requiring countersignature have been increased, although much of this is due to the creation of new institutions. Other legal acts not requiring countersignature remain largely the same as under the Little Constitution. The above-mentioned proposals by the president were accepted by the National Assembly on the grounds that they did not significantly upset the balance of powers between president and government and parliament and would serve to depoliticize appointments. Kwaśniewski was also successful in winning the right to submit a motion that a member of the government be put before the State Tribunal. The constitutional committee had accorded this only to a group of at least 115 MPs. The final version of the constitution gave both president and a group of 115 MPs this right.

Political reality and vested institutional interests played a large role in ensuring that there was no dramatic departure from the arrangements under the Little Constitution. Under the 1997 constitution, the power of the prime minister in relation to the rest of the cabinet and in relation to the Sejm has been consolidated while the president's powers in relation to the government and parliament have been somewhat weakened. All in all, the executive has gained at the expense of the legislature. In comparison to the Little Constitution, the president has had to accept a lower override of his veto, he has lost the right to veto the budget, and the possibility to ask the Constitutional Tribunal to rule on a bill on which the president's veto has been overturned by the Sejm. Finally, the prime minister no longer has to consult the president about the choice of the defence, foreign, and internal ministers. The president has kept his right to designate the prime minister and shall dissolve the Sejm if it fails in three attempts to form a government or if it fails to adopt the budget bill within four months of submission. Only a constructive vote of no confidence in the government may be submitted, i.e. a new prime minister must be named simultaneously with the vote of no confidence. The possibility to propose a simple vote of confidence in the government has been dropped, although Article 159 does provide for the possibility of a vote of no confidence in an individual minister. Although not specifically spelt out, this does not apply to the prime minister, since a vote of no confidence in the prime minister would be the same as a vote of no confidence in the government. The new constitution assumes cooperation within the dual executive but only Article

133(3) referring to the field of foreign policy explicitly states that the president 'acts jointly' with the prime minister and relevant minister. Under the Little Constitution the president had exercised 'general supervision'. The president may call together a cabinet council in particularly important matters and preside over it but such a council does not have powers of the council of ministers.

CONCLUSION

To date the semi-presidential system in Poland has been influenced by uncertainty about definitive institutional solutions, by two very different styles of president, and by very different compositions of parliament. In political practice the president has been neither a figurehead nor all-powerful (Duverger 1980). The president has extensive controlling powers, but most government business is carried out without participation of the president. The intention on the part of constitution-writers has been to create a presidency which would allow the incumbent to adopt the role of a non-partisan arbiter. Such a role will depend on the president's authority and ability to convince all sides of his impartiality. Given the nature of presidential campaigns this may not be easy. Parties have seen presidential elections as a way of profiling themselves, and, especially if they are not represented in parliament, they have a chance to gain media coverage and support from outside the party. The need for each presidential candidate to gather at least 100,000 signatures in turn makes them dependent upon the organizational structure of parties. Despite Kwaśniewski's dropping of party membership, he is still seen as a partisan president by many. The ideal of a non-partisan president is one standing above party politics and day-to-day governing, but also one who is able to break through impasses. As Jacek Kuroń (UW presidential candidate) has put it: 'The government is there to govern, the president is there to achieve agreements and consensus' (in *Gazeta Wyborcza*, 17 July 1995). Such a view is not that surprising in the Polish situation where semi-presidentialism has operated in the context of an emerging democracy in which some fundamental decisions have been long in the making. Despite ethnic and religious homogeneity, there are deep divisions with respect to assessments of the past, the place of religion in the state, the pace and shape of economic reform, and even the institutional set-up.

Political practice has shown presidential prerogatives being used in negative ways in institutional conflict and in positive ways by cooperating with the government. Stephen Holmes has noted that 'when presidents are directly elected, their implied powers are notoriously difficult to constitutionalize' (1993/4: 38). Constitutional provisions as such have been aimed at providing a workable balance of powers, but it is the ambiguity of constitutional provisions, perhaps an inevitable feature of new constitutions, which has been shown up in political practice. It is this ambiguity, which, when coupled with political antagonism and cohabitation, has provoked inter-institutional rivalry. The future relationship between president, government, and parliament will depend on how the party system develops, whether majorities coincide, and on electoral outcomes as much as on actual presidential prerogatives. In the elections of 21 September 1997 Solidarity Electoral Action (AWS) won 33.8 per cent of the vote, beating SLD which won 27.1 per cent. The AWS formed a government together with the Freedom Union (UW). The nature of President Kwaśniewski's relationship with the government is bound to change now that his former party colleagues are in the opposition. Influence upon the prime minister and the rest of the government through informal cooperation both within and outside his constitutional sphere of influence in foreign and defence matters is likely to diminish, although this does not rule out cooperation in trying to attain goals on which there is cross-party consensus.

NOTES

1. Officially, the Constitutional Act of 17 October 1992 on the mutual relations between the legislative and executive institutions of the Republic of Poland and on local self-government (*Dziennik Ustaw*, 1992, no. 84, item 426).
2. In this context, I refer only to the lower house, the Sejm, because it is the only institution which has a vote of investiture for the government, which can vote a motion of no confidence in the government and which can override a presidential veto.
3. It was hoped that all freely elected members of the Sejm and Senate together with deputies from the Peasant and Democratic parties would vote for him against any candidate from the (post-)communist camp. This was the Centre Alliance's principal reason for supporting election by what they otherwise saw as a not fully legitimate or representative parliament (Gebethner 1993).
4. Opinion polls showed Mazowiecki to be more popular than Wałęsa.
5. PC leader, Kaczyński, looked to Fifth Republic France as a good model for Poland. However, he thought that decisions about a directly elected presidency should be taken only after fully competitive elections to parliament (Kaczyński 1993).

6. The only change made was to shorten the term of office from six to five years.
7. By law the Sejm appoints four of its nine members, the president three, and the Senate two. Only then does the president appoint the chairman from among the existing members.
8. When the SLD's candidate, Aleksander Kwaśniewski, won the presidential elections in November 1995, the three ministers duly handed in their resignations, despite Kwaśniewski's stated view that these three ministries should be filled by 'non-party experts'.
9. The Little Constitution made no specific mention of how much time the president may take to accept a new minister, nor for that matter whether he could refuse to appoint a minister. Article 68 simply stated: '1. A minister may resign from his office by offering his resignation to the prime minister. 2. Upon a motion by the prime minister, the president may effect changes in the office of individual ministers.'
10. The Deputy Head of the Chancellery of the President, Lech Falandysz, was particularly active in trying to strengthen the president's position. His efforts led to the coining of a new word, *falandyzacja*, meaning to interpret the law to serve one's short-term political purposes. (See Osiatyński 1994.)
11. In the second round on 19 November 1995, Kwaśniewski won 51.7 per cent against 48.3 per cent for Wałęsa.
12. Interview with Andrzej Potocki (Democratic Union) in *Rzeczpospolita*, 8 Feb. 1994.
13. Interview in *Rzeczpospolita*, 21 Nov. 1994.
14. Wałęsa vetoed 14 bills passed by the second Sejm, although the Sejm failed to override his veto only on four occasions.

10

Romania

TONY VERHEIJEN

Romania emerged from one of the darkest periods in its history in December 1989, when the regime of 'Conducator' Nicolai Ceauşescu was overthrown. Ceauşescu left Romania with a traumatized population and a devastated economy. The gradual establishment of a democratic system of government during the last seven years is a remarkable achievement, even though the process has been painful and not without setbacks.

The new institutional system established in Romania is semi-presidential in the definition used in this book; it has a directly elected fixed-term president alongside a prime minister who is responsible to parliament. The semi-presidential system of government was established gradually, initially on the basis of the Electoral Law of 14 March 1990 and the rules of procedure of parliament adopted after the May 1990 elections. The institutional provisions of the Electoral Law and the rules of procedure of parliament subsequently formed the basis of the semi-presidential system of government established under the new constitution, approved in a referendum in December 1991. The differences between the institutional provisions in the Electoral Law and the provisions in the constitution are generally marginal, except for the creation of the constitutional court.

It is important to note that there is no historical precedent for the establishment of a semi-presidential system of government in Romania. Romania was a monarchy in the period from gaining its independence in 1878 until the forced abdication of the last Romanian king in 1947. Under the monarchy a period of semi-authoritarian rule by the monarch was followed by a period of limited democratic rule in the early and mid-1920s and a period of dictatorship in the late 1930s and early 1940s. Between 1947 and 1989 Romania's institutional system initially followed the model prevalent among other central and eastern European 'People's Democracies' (see Brunner in Feldbrugge 1987: 61–74). After 1974 Romania developed into what Juan Linz classifies as a Sultanistic regime (Linz 1990): a regime in which the power of the political leader is not limited by ideological or ethical rules. All close collaborators of the leader (who are selected by him personally and are often family members) serve him/her unconditionally on the basis of personal loyalty.

The inheritance of the whole period between independence and the fall of the Ceauşescu regime generally provides an unsuitable basis for the development of a democratic system of government. Romania's unfortunate political history, the repression of the initial years under communism, and the Sultanistic regime of Ceauşescu are influences which combine to create a bad precedent for Romania's political development after 1990. The way the institutional system has operated since May 1990 provides a good indication of whether Romania is likely to break with past practice. The analysis to be carried out in this chapter is therefore also of broader relevance to the study of Romania's transition to democracy.

The chapter is divided in three main parts, organized according to the three factors identified by Duverger as determining for the leadership style in semi-presidential systems (see Ch. 1 in this volume):

- the events surrounding the formation of the system;
- the constitutional powers of the president, prime minister, and parliament;
- the nature of the parliamentary majority and the relationship between the president and the majority.

It is important, when analysing the development of semi-presidentialism in Romania, to take into consideration that the first real alternation of power in Romania since 1990 took place only in 1996. Before that time there was a relative continuity in the political orientation of the government and a high degree of similarity in political orientation between the government and president Iliescu, with the exception of short periods in early 1991 and, to a lesser extent, in the first half of 1992. In most of this period the president had a strong influence over the government. Following the November 1996 elections, there continues to be a convergence in political views between the new president and the prime minister as well as the parliamentary majority, even though the political orientation of the president, the government, and the parliamentary majority is completely different. One should therefore keep in mind that not all variants for relations between president and prime minister have so far been tested in Romania.

EVENTS SURROUNDING THE FORMATION
OF THE REGIME

The Initial Phase of the Development of the Institutional System

The new Romanian institutional system was developed gradually, starting with the adoption of the Electoral Law of 14 March 1990. This law, apart from defining the electoral process for the May 1990 elections, also set out the framework for the new institutional system in Romania. It established a semi-presidential system with a directly elected president as well as a government responsible to parliament. The constituent assembly, elected in the May 1990 elections, consisted of two chambers, the Deputies' Assembly and the Senate. The Assembly had a double mandate, to draft the new constitution and to adopt the most urgent economic reform legislation. The general institutional framework laid down in the Electoral Law was complemented by the rules and regulations of the parliament, which were adopted in June 1990.

The following process of constitution writing was dominated by the National Salvation Front (NSF), the political movement set up during the revolution of December 1989. This movement initially was a 'broad church' of new political parties and interest groups. However, in the months following the collapse of the Ceauşescu regime the NSF increasingly came under the control of a group of officials ousted from the top ranks of the Romanian Communist Party during the transformation of the party between 1974 and 1982 (Verheijen 1995: 39). The political experience of the leadership of the NSF made the movement the dominant force in the run up to the May 1990 elections. The NSF won more than two-thirds of the seats in the two chambers of parliament and had its presidential candidate, Ion Iliescu, elected with an overwhelming majority in the presidential elections. The disorganized and fragmented opposition, beaten comprehensively in the elections, had hardly any influence on the development of the institutional system. The electoral defeat and the shock caused by the violent repression of civil protest in Bucharest in June 1990 paralysed the opposition forces for a long time.[1] Only in late Autumn 1990 could the first serious attempts to coordinate the activities of the different opposition parties be observed (Shafir 1990: 13–21). The gradual rapprochement between the different elements of the fragmented opposition finally led to the formation of the Democratic Convention (DC), an umbrella organization of opposition parties which was to become the first political force to seriously challenge the hegemony of the NSF. However, the DC was to become a serious political force only after the completion of the constitution writing process.

There was relatively little debate on the institutional provisions of the Romanian constitution during the constitution drafting process. In this respect Romania is very different from most other countries in Central and Eastern Europe, in particular Poland and Slovakia, and more recently Hungary. This was due in part to the preoccupation of most politicians with the serious riots in Bucharest between 25–7 September 1991 and the subsequent resignation of the government of prime minister Petre Roman.[2] For another part the relative lack of interest in the constitutional debate can be explained by the dominant position of the NSF after the elections, which led other political parties to believe that they would have little influence on the final shape of the constitution. The deep internal divisions in the NSF, between the reformist faction, led by prime minister Petre Roman, and the conservative faction, supported by president Ion Iliescu, did not really hamper the constitution writing process. These divisions concerned mostly the economic reform strategy (Verheijen 1995: 162–5).

The draft constitution was presented to the parliament in July 1991. The parliamentary debate on the constitution took place between September and December 1991. The main points of debate concerned minority rights, the irreversibility of the republican form of government, the relations between government and parliament, in particular the provisions on decree powers, and the relations between the two chambers of parliament (Verheijen 1995: 166–7). However, no significant changes to the draft constitution were made. The constitution was finally approved by 510 against 95 votes in a joint meeting of the two chambers of the constituent assembly and adopted in a referendum on 9 December 1991 (Shafir 1992a: 54). The constitution was approved by 77 per cent of the voters participating in the referendum and by 53.5 per cent of the electorate.[3] The first presidential and parliamentary elections under the new constitution were held in September 1992, completing the development phase of the new institutional system in Romania.

The events surrounding the formation of the system might not provide much insight into the way the Romanian institutional system functions. As has been explained above, there was no precedent for the development of a semi-presidential system of government in Romania. It is also difficult to find a watertight explanation as to why this model was chosen. The close relations between Romania and

France provide one possible element of an explanation. The Romanian constitution reflects the French constitution in many ways, in particular where institutional issues are concerned. The way the system of relations between local and central government has been set up is a clear reflection of the French system, even of the system as it functioned before the 1982 Mitterrand reforms. The bicameral system, set up without a clear rationale for its creation except for the short pre-war tradition, provides another example. In this light the semi-presidential nature of the new institutional system does not really come as a surprise.

The most important deviations from the French system lie in the much more limited powers of the president. The imposition of political neutrality, the limitations on presidential powers to dissolve parliament, and the conditions imposed on the use of decree powers, in particular the fact that parliament has to approve the use of decree powers by the government in every instance, all constitute important differences with the French system. These deviations, which weaken significantly the constitutional position of the president, are a reaction to the previous institutional system. Nicolai Ceauşescu abused the unlimited powers granted to him as president under the old system. Even though the NSF controlled a large enough majority to impose a strong presidential model, the fears of the potential consequences of the adoption of such a model prevented the creation of a strong presidential office. The abuse of power under the previous regime was fresh in the memory of politicians of all political convictions and it was also obvious that the adoption of a model with a strong president was likely to be rejected by the people in the referendum. The relative restraint shown by the political forces in control of both the presidency and the two chambers of parliament should therefore be interpreted as a combination of a reaction to recent history and an anticipation of the potential reaction of the Romanian electorate.

The events surrounding the creation of the system have therefore influenced the shape of the system to the extent that the powers of the president are relatively limited, in particular if compared to the French system. This is in fact rather remarkable since Romania was one of the few countries where one political party/movement was in the position to fully dominate the constitution writing process. The most plausible explanation for the restraint shown by the movement which controlled the constitution writing process is the extent to which the country and its politicians were traumatized by the Ceauşescu regime.

CONSTITUTIONAL FACTORS

The Romanian constitution of December 1991 is a rather detailed and
rigid document, in particular as far as the relations between the state
institutions are concerned. The dominance of the NSF during the constitution writing process led to the adoption of a straightforward constitutional text in which there are relatively few ambiguities. In this
section the formal position of the main parts of the new Romanian institutional system, the president, the government, the parliament, and the
constitutional court will be discussed.

A Brief Analysis of Presidential Powers

The president is the guardian of the constitutional order in Romania
(Constitution of Romania, Articles 80.2 and 84.1). The president is
directly elected for a four-year period and cannot be a member of a political party or be active in party politics during his/her mandate. The
president must win more than 50 per cent of the vote to be elected. If
no candidate wins 50 per cent in the first round, the two candidates with
the highest number of votes contest a run-off election. The president
also has the role of mediator between the different state institutions, in
case conflicts arise between them. The main powers of the president are
the following:

- the nomination and appointment of the prime minister;
- the appointment of the judges of the Supreme Court of Justice;
- calling extraordinary sessions of the parliament;
- dissolving the parliament, but only under a limited number of
  circumstances;
- promulgation of laws;
- a special role in the development of foreign and security policy.[4]

The process of government formation is strongly influenced by the
president. Only the president can propose a candidate for the office
of prime minister. The president has to consult the leaders of parliamentary groups, but he/she decides who will be appointed as prime
minister designate, unless one party has obtained an absolute majority,
in which case the president only has to consult the leader of this
particular parliamentary group. After his nomination, the prime minister designate has ten days to win the confidence of the parliament
for the proposed government and its programme. According to Article

109.3 of the constitution, the president has to propose a new candidate for the office of prime minister if the parliament does not grant the proposed government parliamentary confidence. After the parliament has rejected two candidates proposed by the prime minister, and 60 days have passed since the president first proposed a candidate for the office of prime minister, the president can dissolve the parliament. The president can only dissolve the parliament once per year. The president does not have any general powers to dissolve parliament and call new elections and he cannot dismiss a government which has the confidence of the parliament.

The president enjoys limited decree powers. The only decrees he/she can issue without a countersignature concern appointments to public offices (Articles 99.1 and 99.2). However, the appointment of the director of the Romanian Information Services (successor of the Securitate) requires the approval of the parliament (Article 62.2(g)). Another prerogative of the president is the right to return legislation to the parliament for further consideration. However, the president does not have the right to veto legislation. The president also has the right to refer legislation to the constitutional court (Article 77). The president can propose changes in the constitution, but only on a motion of the government. Another important presidential prerogative is the right to call a referendum on issues of national interest.

Parliament can suspend the president in case he commits grave errors. A suspension must be initiated by a group of one-third of the total amount of senators and deputies and approved by absolute majority. Within 30 days of the suspension, a referendum has to be organized to confirm or reject the suspension of the president. If the president is dismissed by the people new elections for the office of president have to be held within three months. In the meantime the chairman of the Senate or the chairman of the Chamber of Deputies (in this order) serves as the interim president. An interim president cannot dissolve the parliament, call a referendum, or address the nation (Articles 95–8). The broad definition of the conditions under which a procedure for suspension of the president can be initiated provides the parliamentary majority with a realistic possibility to dismiss a president who has lost popularity with the people. The constitutional court only has the right to give an advisory opinion on a proposal for suspension of the president. This provision can provide protection against a president with authoritarian ambitions, but only if he/she does not have sufficient control over the majority of the parliament and has lost the confidence of the people.

Relations between President and Government

The constitutional provisions on the relations between the prime minister and the president are clearly defined. The president has important powers in the area of security and foreign policy, described in Articles 91 and 92 of the constitution, however, presidential powers are limited since the president has to obtain a countersignature of the prime minister for all decisions in these areas. According to Article 87 of the constitution of Romania the president can preside over meetings of the government on matters of national interest in the field of foreign policy, security, and public order. In all other policy areas the president can only preside over government meetings if the prime minister asks him to do so.

The prime minister needs the approval of the president for any cabinet reshuffle. The parliament endorses the government by means of a vote of confidence but only the authorization of the president is needed if the prime minister wants to change the composition of the government (Article 85.2). Parliament can only show its disapproval of the changes by carrying a vote of no confidence.

The formal picture of relations between the president and the prime minister is rather clear. However, in reality the relations between the two components of the executive depend on the political compatibility of the president and the prime minister. The number of policy areas for which a signature of the prime minister and the president is needed is limited, which reduces the scope for open conflict. No procedure is foreseen to resolve conflicts between the president and the prime minister over areas for which they share responsibility.

The Position of Parliament

There is hardly any difference between the competencies of the two chambers of parliament, the Chamber of Deputies and the Senate, except for the difference in the number of deputies (343) and senators (143).[5] Both senators and deputies are elected through a proportional system in multi-member constituencies. Senators are expected to keep contacts with the governing body of the district in which they are elected, but the constitution explicitly forbids imperative mandates. None of the two chambers is elected on the basis of regional representation. Minority groups which fail to obtain a seat in either the Chamber of Deputies or the Senate are automatically granted one seat in the Chamber of Deputies.

The almost identical character of the Chamber of Deputies and the Senate has led to the development of an extremely complicated and time-consuming legislative process, in particular when the two chambers fail to agree on a piece of legislation. Different legislative procedures have been defined for constitutional legislation, organic legislation, and ordinary legislation (Verheijen 1995: 169–70). For certain types of decisions, the two chambers of parliament meet in a joint session. These include decisions concerning the state budget, the social security budget, examination of reports of the supreme council of national defence and the court of auditors, the control of the Romanian Information Services and the appointment of its director, the declaration of mobilization, the declaration of war, and the suspension and termination of armed conflicts. The two chambers also meet in a joint session to discuss a motion of censure as well as any government programme, policy statement, or bill over which the government wants to assume responsibility.

There are several possible explanations why Romania has chosen a system with two chambers of parliament with almost equal powers, even though in the current situation a flexible and effective decision-making procedure would have been more appropriate. One possible reason is that Romania had a similar type of legislature in the period before 1938. A different explanation is that Romanian constitution writers looked to Italy for a model. The last possible explanation is that the writers of the constitution wanted to make sure that important decisions would not be taken in a hurry. In this line of reasoning the continued existence of a two-chamber system would provide a safeguard against impulsive actions of small majorities which could do damage to the interests of the parliamentary minority. However, the constitutional court provides sufficient guarantees against impulsive decisions of small majorities.

The government enjoys limited protection from the daily moods of parliament. The limitations imposed on motions of censure are the following. A motion of censure has to be put forward by at least one-quarter of the total number of deputies and senators. A group of parliamentarians which files a no-confidence vote cannot file another no-confidence vote during the same parliamentary session.[6] A group of one-third of the deputies and senators, however, can request an extra session of parliament at the end of each official parliamentary session.[7] An extra parliamentary session provides the opposition with an additional opportunity to move a vote of no confidence.

One controversial aspect of the relations between government and parliament is the right of parliament to give decree powers to the government. Decree powers can only be given for policy areas and decisions which are not to be regulated by means of organic legislation (Article 114). Parliament can make the use of decree powers conditional to parliamentary approval in each individual case. In an emergency situation the government can issue decrees which enter into force the moment they are submitted to the parliament. The parliament can revoke these decrees afterwards. It has often been argued that these arrangements represent a potential danger for Romanian democracy. The extensive use of decree powers by the Vacaroiu government, under questionable procedures, illustrates the fact that this is not just a theoretical question (International IDEA 1997: 79–80). The experience of the Vacaroiu government proved that a small majority in parliament can effectively govern without parliamentary control in a large number of policy areas.

The creation of a constitutional court can provide a counterweight to tendencies of politicians to interpret the constitution according to their own partisan interests, and can counteract moves towards a 'dictatorship of small majorities'.

The Romanian Constitutional Court: An Independent Arbitrator?

The constitutional court is a new institution in Romania. It guarantees the respect for the letter and the spirit of the constitution. The court consists of nine judges, appointed for nine year, non-renewable mandates. One-third of the judges is replaced every three years.[8] The judges are appointed by the president (three), the Chamber of Deputies (three), and the Senate (three). The constitutional court has six main prerogatives:

- it can review legislation before promulgation or;[9]
- it can rule on challenges of the constitutionality of the rules and regulations of parliament;[10]
- it can rule on the constitutionality of legislation after legislation has been promulgated, on request of ordinary judges.[11] A judge can request a review of legislation on his own initiative, if a question arises during a court case, or on request of a (group of) citizen(s);
- it can rule on questions regarding the constitutionality of political parties;[12]
- the constitutional court has to give its opinion on all proposals concerning the revision of the constitution. The opinion is not binding (Law on the Constitutional Court, Art. 13.1 Aa);

- the constitutional court confirms the results of parliamentary and presidential elections, and plays a role in the impeachment procedure.

The constitutional court has extensive tasks and competencies, but it is weaker than the constitutional courts in most other Central and Eastern European countries, in particular those in Hungary and Bulgaria. It has no specific task of interpreting the constitution and its powers to repeal legislation before promulgation are limited; a decision of the constitutional court[13] can be overruled if both chambers of parliament decide by a two-thirds majority not to amend the contested piece of legislation. In the context of a study of semi-presidentialism, it is the lack of powers to interpret constitutional provisions that could be particularly problematic.

Conclusion on Constitutional Factors

It is important to note that the restraint shown by the NSF while defining the powers of the president has not been consistently reflected in the attitude of the presidents who have served under the new constitution. Ion Iliescu in particular used the weak position of successive governments and his influence over the political parties supporting these governments to strengthen his real position. The current president has so far shown much less inclination to extend the powers of the president beyond what is defined explicitly in the constitution. This is due to some extent to the differences in attitude between Iliescu and Constantinescu, but can also be explained to a large degree by the third factor identified by Duverger, the nature of the parliamentary majority and the relationship between the president and the majority, which will be discussed in the next section.

THE OPERATION OF THE ROMANIAN SYSTEM SINCE 1990: A FUNCTION OF THE RELATIONS BETWEEN PRESIDENTS AND POLITICAL FORCES?

The Romanian semi-presidential system has several in-built weaknesses, as discussed above. In this section a brief analysis of the operation of the Romanian institutional system will be made to see whether those weaknesses have had a real influence on the operation of the Romanian system. The analysis will focus mainly on the relations between the president and the main political forces.

Romania has so far not had to deal with a situation of official 'cohabitation'. The four prime ministers who have served in Romania since the first free elections in May 1990 were all either members of the same party from which the president originated, or politically non-affiliated but appointed with the support of the president. The experience of the one case when serious disagreements arose between president and prime minister, even though both politicians originated in the same political movement, has set a highly negative precedent for the future.

The conflict between Prime Minister Petre Roman and President Iliescu escalated into violent conflict in Bucharest in September 1991.[14] The origin of the conflict was the strong difference of opinion between Roman and conservative forces in the NSF, supported by Iliescu, over Romania's economic reform strategy. During the early period of his government, between June 1990 and January 1991, Roman managed to start the implementation of free market reforms, much against the wish of the conservative forces.[15] After Romania regained access to the main source of international assistance, the PHARE programme, in January 1991, the tide turned against Roman. In the months that followed, the conflict between the prime minister and the conservative forces in the NSF parliamentary group escalated. Roman finally resigned during the 'miners' uprising in Bucharest in September 1991, which gave the president the necessary reason to force Roman to resign. The president's implicit backing for the conservative forces was the main reason why Roman finally failed to receive parliamentary support. The incident certainly shows that constitutional provisions that require a president to be above party politics immediately lose relevance if the president refuses to respect the spirit of the constitution.

The predominantly technocratic government of Petre Roman's successor, Theodore Stolojan, had a less complicated relationship with the president. However, Stolojan, who was a supporter of radical economic reform, faced considerable delays in trying to get his reform package through parliament, in particular because he had to build supporting coalitions on each legislative proposal (March, in *Financial Times*, 11 June 1992). No significant problems were reported in relations between the president and the government.

Romanian Politics between September 1992 and November 1996:
The Increase of Presidential Influence

The parliamentary elections of September 1992 offered Romanian voters a choice between rapid market reforms, the preservation of the status quo, and extreme nationalism. Three political parties presented themselves as the pro-market forces, the NSF, which consisted of the reformist wing of the movement, the Democratic Convention (DC), and the National Liberal Party (NLP). One party, the new party formed by the conservative wing of the NSF and called the Democratic National Salvation Front (DNSF) promised a slowdown of the economic reform process. Several extremist parties, the Party of Romanian National Union, the Greater Romania Party, and the crypto-communist Socialist Labour Party, tried to gain votes by appealing to the nationalist feelings of the Romanian voters, or by trying to use the disappointment of the Romanian population with the new political forces.

The presidential elections were a contest between the president in office, Ion Iliescu, and the candidate of the Democratic Convention, Emil Constantinescu, the rector of the University of Bucharest. Petre Roman did not stand as a candidate for the presidential elections. There were four other candidates, including the nationalist mayor of Cluj, Gheorghe Funar, and Caius Dragomir, the party ideologist of the NSF. None of them was able seriously to challenge the two main candidates.[16]

The result of the parliamentary and presidential elections mostly seemed to indicate that the Romanian voters were afraid of the consequences of more radical economic reform. The Democratic Convention did not manage to beat Iliescu's DNSF, and their candidate for the presidency, Emil Constantinescu, did not manage to seriously challenge the president in office. Iliescu got over 60 per cent of the votes in the second round of the presidential elections. The DNSF captured just enough votes to be in control of the two chambers of parliament (117 seats in the Chamber of Deputies and 49 seats in the Senate) if the party could gain the support of the extreme left, represented by the SLP, and the extreme right. The extreme right was represented by two parties, the Greater Romania Party (GRP) and the Party for Romanian National Union (PRNU).[17] The programmes of those four parties had enough in common to find a common basis to support a government. However, they had too little in common to form a real coalition government. It was not in the interest of the DNSF to form a coalition with the crypto-communists of the SLP and the staunch nationalists of the PRNU and the GRP, including xenophobic politicians such as Gheorghe Funar, the mayor of Cluj. Such a move would have damaged the reputation of the DNSF. The two reform-minded parties, NSF (43 seats in the Chamber of Deputies and 18 seats in the Senate) and DC (82 seats in the Chamber of Deputies and 34 seats in the Senate), did not get enough votes to rule together. The NLP did not manage to gain the 3 per cent of the votes necessary to pass the threshold.

After the elections of September 1992 the government formation system under the 1991 constitution was used for the first time. President Iliescu was confronted with a difficult choice. The election results had made the formation of a (stable) coalition practically impossible. The most realistic option open to Iliescu was to nominate a non-affiliated politician as prime minister. The non-affiliated candidate could either form a government which could obtain the support of the three main parties in parliament (DNSF, NSF, and DC), or he could form a government acceptable to the DNSF and the parties on the extreme left and the extreme right. Discussions between the DNSF, the DC, and the NSF on the formation of a DNSF government headed by a neutral prime minister nominated by president Iliescu, with the tacit support of the two other parties, did not lead to a positive result (Shafir 1992b: 7). When the main political parties could not reach an agreement on a government on a broad political basis, the president hardly had any other option than to nominate a prime minister who had to find the support of the DNSF, other left-wing parties, and the nationalist parties.

Ion Iliescu appointed Nicolai Vacaroiu, a non-affiliated civil servant from the Ministry of Finance, as prime minister designate. Vacaroiu proposed to the joint session of the two chambers of parliament a cabinet consisting of technocrats and DNSF members. Vacaroiu found himself in the same kind of position in which the previous prime minister, Theodore Stolojan, had been. None of the main political parties could or wanted to take political responsibility, and a non-affiliated prime minister, controlled by cabinet members of the largest political party, had to do the 'dirty work'.

The political situation after the 1992 elections was potentially dangerous for the development of democracy in Romania. Three small political parties, with a limited commitment to democracy, obtained disproportionate political influence. At the same time this situation paved the way for the president, whose democratic credentials were not beyond doubt, to increase his influence in the political system. Prime minister Vacaroiu was considered to be politically close to the president and was highly dependent on the president's leverage over the diverse coalition of parties which supported the government.

The political situation in Romania from 1993 to the elections in 1996 was characterized by continuous attacks on the government of prime minister Vacaroiu, first by the opposition and later also by some of the small nationalist parties. The opposition proved incapable of bringing down the government, while the nationalist parties started demanding an increasing price for their support for the government. The president managed to increase his influence by ensuring the survival of a government which became increasingly dependent on his support (Verheijen 1995: 184).

The prime minister had to rely on the political influence of the president over parliamentarians to secure the position of his government during the numerous times when the opposition moved no-confidence votes against the government. The prime minister also needed the president's influence over the unreliable small nationalist parties to secure their support during crucial votes. The most obvious example is Iliescu's rebuke to the leader of the Party for Romanian National Union, Gheorghe Funar, when the latter demanded the replacement of several reform-minded ministers. President Iliescu openly dismissed the requests of the PRNU and made it clear that the nationalists should not expect too much of him (Reuters News Service, 24 June 1993). The PRNU reacted by voting with the opposition on a no-confidence vote moved by the opposition in December 1993, which the government survived by a narrow margin of 13 votes, and by demanding five ministerial posts in return for further support to the government (BBC Monitoring Service, 30 December 1993).

The Vacaroiu government managed to serve out its full mandate until the November 1996 elections, increasingly relying on the political leverage of the president and the support of extremist groups in the parliament to stay in power. Finally, president Iliescu appeared to have lost considerable political support by becoming so closely involved with a government with increasingly doubtful credentials. The dismal economic record of the government and its close affiliation with extreme nationalist groups made Iliescu's close affiliation with the prime minister a political liability rather than a political asset. The last moment attempts of the party and president to rid themselves of their increasingly nationalist image by breaking with the PNRU and signing the friendship treaty with Hungary came too late to rescue the tarnished image of the president (OMRI Analytical Briefs, 3 Sept. 1996). Iliescu's defeat in the November 1996 presidential elections is generally viewed as having been largely caused by his inability to distance himself from political forces with an increasingly negative reputation.

The November 1996 Elections: The Start of a New Political Era?

During the first six years of its existence, the trend in the development of the Romanian semi-presidential system was towards a stronger president and a weaker government. The strong showing of president Iliescu in the 1990 and 1992 presidential elections and the weak general support base for the three governments which functioned in Romania between May 1990 and November 1996 were the main contributing factors to the increase in the real power of the president. The strong political connections between president and government under the Vacaroiu government even led to the opposition moving a motion for impeachment of Iliescu for allegedly not respecting the political neutrality imposed on the office by the constitution. The attempts by the opposition to force the president to function more in line with the spirit of the constitution did not yield any significant results.

The November 1996 elections were a turning point in Romanian politics. The character of the first round of the elections was very different from the 1992 elections. The entry of Petre Roman into the presidential campaign made the contest into a serious three-horse race and required the president in office to run against two serious opposition candidates. Iliescu was further handicapped by a challenge against his candidature brought to the constitutional court by the opposition (*East European Constitutional Review*, Constitution Watch, Romania, Fall 1996). The constitution stipulates that a president can serve only two periods in office. The opposition parties argued that Iliescu had already served two periods as president, while Iliescu argued that he had only served one mandate under the new constitution and that the constitution could not be applied retroactively (see also Stefoi 1993: 53). Even though the constitutional court supported the constitutional interpretation of the president (*East European Constitutional Review*, Constitution Watch, Fall 1996, 20), the case created a further dent in the already seriously damaged image of the president. Iliescu's association to the Vacaroiu government with its dismal economic record, the increased strength of the opposition candidates, and the damage caused by the above court case significantly weakened Iliescu's position.

Iliescu still managed to obtain the largest number of votes in the first round of the elections, just over 32 per cent of the vote. However, the opposition vote was split between Emil Constantinescu and Petre Roman, who together obtained some 49 per cent of the vote. In the second round of the elections Constantinescu obtained most of the votes from both Roman and Gyorgy Frunda, the candidate of the Hungarian Democratic Federation in Romania. Constantinescu won the second round of the elections with a margin of about 9 per cent. The parliamentary elections were won by the Democratic Convention, which obtained over 30 per cent of the vote. The DC and its two potential coalition parties, the Social Democratic Union (USD), the successor party of the reformist wing of the NSF led by Petre Roman, and the Hungarian Democratic Federation in Romania (HDFR) had well over 60 per cent of the vote, largely sufficient to form a coalition. President Constantinescu nominated Victor Ciorbea, the mayor of Bucharest, for the position of prime minister. Ciorbea's government, made up of ministers from the Democratic Convention, the Union of Social Democracy, and the Hungarian Democratic Federation in Romania, was sworn in on 12 December 1996, heralding the first real change in power in Romania since December 1989.

The election victory of Emil Constantinescu in the presidential elections and of the political parties which supported his candidature in the parliamentary elections was nothing less than an earthquake in Romanian politics. Even though there is continuity in the form of problematic coalition management, this time due to the recurring problems between the HDFR and the other two parties over the right of ethnic Hungarians and the generally difficult relations between the DC and the USD, there is otherwise a complete change in policy style.

Apart from the changes in policy style, there are also important changes in the way the institutional system has operated since November 1996. Even though president Constantinescu has played an important high-profile role in politics, he has refrained from intervening openly in the management of the coalition. A relatively clear division of labour has started to take shape. The prime minister has assumed responsibility for the economic reform policy, while the president has been most visible in foreign policy questions, such as Romania's bids for membership of NATO and the EU and in general with Romania's interactions with international organizations. (See also International IDEA 1997: 16.) The institutional system now shows some of the features of a 'classical' semi-presidential system, in which the president plays a prominent role in foreign and security policy while the prime minister is largely responsible for internal policy issues. This is a significant change from the situation under president Iliescu, when the president was involved in practically all aspects of policy-making, including the management of the relations between 'coalition' partners.

THE CHANGING RELEVANCE OF DUVERGER'S FACTORS

In the short period in which Romania has had a semi-presidential system of government, there have been considerable differences in the balance of power between government and parliament. The period between the May 1990 elections and the adoption of the constitution was characterized by the battle for power between president Iliescu and prime minister Roman, which culminated in the violent conflict in September 1991. This conflict showed that the relative balance in powers of president and prime minister, which normally characterizes the Romanian variant of semi-presidentialism, can be manipulated by a president who has strong ties with the security services (the Romanian Information Services) and enjoys a high level of parliamentary support. The inverse might also be true. However, it is obviously much more difficult for a prime minister to ensure the impeachment of the president than for the president to force the prime minister to resign.

Parliamentary support enjoyed by Iliescu was an important factor defining the outcome of the 1991 conflict, together with the president's control over the security services. The ability of the president to control the security services was one of the crucial elements contributing to Iliescu's victory in this conflict. The level of control the president can have over state institutions such as the security services might be considered an element of the second factor identified by Duverger, the constitutional powers of president and prime minister. Since the adoption of the new constitution, the formal powers of the president regarding the control of the security services have been somewhat curtailed by the requirement that the appointment of the director of the security services has to be approved by parliament. However, parliamentary control over the security services has remained limited and a president who has strong ties with the security services might still be able to use this against political opponents. This was affirmed by Jacques Rupnik in his contribution to the International IDEA report on the democracy in Romania, in which he stated that the security services still constitute a potential problem to the new government (International IDEA 1997: 21). One can only hope that the importance of this type of factor will decline with the gradual strengthening of democracy in Romania.

The following period, between the resignation of Roman and the September 1992 elections, was marked by a stabilization of relations between president and government. The adoption of the new constitution clarified the relations between president, government, and parliament. The influence of the president, victorious in the conflict with his political rival in September 1991, remained strong. President Iliescu kept a rather low profile, allowing the interim government of prime minister Stolojan to prepare and implement a package of economic reform measures (March, in *Financial Times*, 11 June 1992). It is clear that without Iliescu's influence over the conservative forces in the NSF, Stolojan would have been unable get parliamentary support for much of his economic reform package.

The ability of the president to influence parliamentary forces was a significant factor in the second phase of the development of Romanian semi-presidentialism, the period between the September 1992 and November 1996 elections. Even though the formal powers of the president were somewhat curtailed in the constitution, the stalemate situation which arose from the September 1992 elections allowed president Iliescu much greater influence in the day-to-day politics than one would expect on the basis of his formal position. Even though the president was not formally involved in PSDR party politics, it was clear that decisions on the coalition politics of the party were taken by the president. The fact that prime minister Vacaroiu was not politically affiliated, and therefore lacked a strong support base in parliament, made him fully dependent on the support of the president. The lack of reliability of the frequently changing coalition partners of the PSDR added further weight to the prime minster's dependence on the president. The political constellation in the Romanian parliament and the non-affiliated character of the prime minister, both of which can be classified under the third factor identified by Duverger, provide the main explanation for the leadership style and the relation between president, prime minister, and parliament during this period of development of the Romanian variant of semi-presidentialism. The formal powers of the president and the prime minister, the second factor identified by Duverger, are much less relevant to the understanding of the real powers and positions of the president and the prime minister, whereas the first factor, the events surrounding the formation of the system, appears to have lost its explanatory relevance some three years after the 1989 'revolution'.

The relative explanatory value of the three factors identified by Duverger has changed yet again with the change of government and president in November 1996. As far as it is possible to draw definitive conclusions on the current position of president and prime minister in the Romanian political system, just one year after the elections, the formal position of the president and prime minister has become much more important in explaining the character of the Romanian political system. The *de facto* division of labour, with the president being more involved in foreign and security policy and the prime minister playing a more high-profile role in internal policy, reflects more clearly the letter and the spirit of the constitution. The relatively stable majority which the government has enjoyed is obviously also a factor in the 'normalization' of the Romanian semi-presidential system. Historical factors seem to have lost relevance in explaining the leadership style in the Romanian system.

CONCLUSION

Romania has had a semi-presidential system of government since May 1990. The character of the system and the leadership style has varied significantly between presidents and governments. With the first real change of leadership in November 1996, Romania also seems to have entered a phase of political stabilization. During the turbulent two years between the first free elections in May 1990 and the first elections held under the new constitution in September 1992 there was no clear pattern of development in the relations between president, prime minister, and parliament. President Iliescu emerged victorious from his power struggle with prime minister Petre Roman, but the way in which the conflict between the two politicians was finally settled gave little hope for the development of a stable institutional system. Still, under the three governments that followed the Roman government, the Stolojan and Vacaroiu governments under president Iliescu, and the current government of prime minister Ciorbea under president Constantinescu, a gradual normalization of politics has taken place. In particular during the last year the Romanian system has started to look much more like a 'soft' variant of the French system, with the president playing a high-profile role in foreign and security policy and the prime minister leading the development of internal reform policies, backed firmly by the president. However, this 'normalization' of the Romanian institutional system should not be seen as definitive.

There are a number of reasons why the current situation is likely to be the exception rather than the rule. First of all, the Romanian political party system is likely to remain rather fragmented. Most of the political parties currently in parliament have become institutionalized over the last year, except for the Democratic Convention, which is still a rather volatile coalition of parties, which were mostly united by their wish to remove the PSDR and its allies from government. It remains to be seen whether the DC will hold together. In a best-case scenario, the party system is therefore likely to be consolidated in more or less its current form. The electoral system is a second factor which will continue to keep governing coalitions relatively weak. The relatively low threshold will allow small parties to survive. While this does not necessarily pose a threat to the stability in the political system, one should take into account that in Romania the small parties are mostly extremist forces, which are unlikely to contribute to the stabilization of Romanian politics. In view of this, it is likely that in the future the role of the president in ensuring the survival of governments might again become important, as it was under the Vacaroiu government between 1992 and 1996. This in turn will make it difficult for the office of the president to develop into an office which stands above politics, as it is intended under the constitution.

Another cause for concern about the Romanian semi-presidential system is how it will cope with a situation of 'cohabitation'. The precedent set by the conflict between Roman and Iliescu, who actually represented the same political party, raises serious questions about the viability of the system if a situation of forced 'cohabitation' would arise again in the near future. One would simply have to hope that a situation of 'cohabitation' will not occur in the near future, until democracy is more deeply rooted in Romania.

In the second part of this chapter the leadership style in the Romanian semi-presidential system was discussed, using the factors identified by Duverger. The main conclusion regarding these factors is that the three factors, the circumstances under which the system was created, the formal powers of the institutions, and the nature of the parliamentary majority, or, in the Romanian case, the composition of parliament, are quite helpful in explaining the prevailing leadership style. On the basis of the analysis of Romania, two points can be raised about the relevance of Duverger's factors. The first is that the formal powers of the president over other state institutions should be taken into account, not only the relations between the president, prime minister, and parliament. The Romanian case shows that in particular presidential control over the security forces can be an important factor in understanding the real position of the president vis-à-vis government and parliament. This might apply to a much higher degree to systems in transition than to established democracies, but is nevertheless a factor to be considered. The constitutional powers of the president should therefore, in my view, be interpreted broadly rather than narrowly. The second remark is that the importance of the three factors identified by Duverger can change significantly over time. In the case of Romania it has so far been necessary to discuss the relative importance of factors for each different government. Whereas this might change in the future, if the Romanian system really stabilizes, it would for now be impossible to come to a final conclusion as to what factor(s) are dominant in determining leadership style in Romania. The answer right now would be 'different factors at different times'. It seems to me, however, that Duverger would be hardly satisfied with an answer as inexact as this. My final conclusion, therefore, is that Duverger's method of analysis is of much less use in analysing systems in development than in analysing established semi-presidential systems. In order to obtain a more exact conclusion on leadership style in the Romanian semi-presidential system, using Duverger's analytical method, one would have to wait at least another three elections.

NOTES

1. Civil protests, mainly led by the student movement, on University Square in Bucharest were brought to a violent end by 'miners' called upon by the president to defend the government against the alleged disturbances of public order by the protestors.
2. The scenario was largely similar to the events in June 1990. Protests by miners against the Roman government, allegedly orchestrated by the security services under the control of the president, led to the resignation of Roman when the riots sparked by the protests spiralled out of control.
3. More than 30 per cent of the electorate did not vote.
4. Even though the president needs the countersignature of the prime minister to exercise most of his powers in this area, the powers that the president enjoys in these two policy areas are much more extensive than in any other policy area.
5. The number of deputies varies with each election due to two factors. First, minority organizations which fail to obtain a seat are to be granted one seat each to ensure representation (after the 1996 elections there are 15 minority seats). Secondly, the number of seats in the chamber of deputies is related to the size of the electorate and can therefore vary over time.
6. The parliament sits in two sessions per year; this means that it is mathematically almost impossible for the government to face more than two no-confidence votes per year.
7. The first session runs from February to the end of June, the second session runs from September to the end of December.
8. As an exception the judges of the current constitutional court have been appointed for different periods of time. Of each group of three judges, one is appointed the three years, one is appointed for six years, and one is appointed for nine years.
9. On the initiative of either the president, the chairman of one of the chambers of parliament, 50 deputies, or 25 senators.
10. On the request of either the chairman of one of the chambers of parliament, 50 deputies, or 25 senators.

11. On request of a regular court. This can be direct, if a judge considers a specific piece of legislation unconstitutional, or indirect; if a citizen or a group of citizens consider a piece of legislation unconstitutional, they can ask a judge to put the question to the constitutional court. It is up to the judge to decide whether this type of request is valid or not.

12. On request of the chairman of one of the chambers of parliament (in case he can persuade the chamber concerned to give him the mandate to do so) or on request of the government.

13. To be taken by an absolute majority of the judges.

14. Several sources claim that the anti-Roman wing of the NSF actually 'called' the miners to Bucharest to bring down Roman (Ionescu 1991: 18–22).

15. The reason why Roman could proceed relatively unchallenged was Romania's need to restore credibility with the international institutions after the violent clampdown on peaceful civic protests in Bucharest in June 1990.

16. Gheorghe Funar managed to obtain about 10 per cent of the votes in the first round of the presidential elections. He obtained his votes mainly in Transylvania and other areas in which a substantial percentage of the population belonged to national minorities. The Romanian population of those regions voted en masse for him.

17. All these parties together would have 176 out of 341 votes in the chamber of deputies, 74 out of 143 votes in the senate, and 250 out of 484 votes in a joint session.

11

Russia

STEPHEN WHITE

The Russian presidency is of recent origin. There was always a prime minister, or (in the Soviet period) a chairman of the Council of Ministers; indeed, Lenin was the dominant figure in the early Soviet years not as party leader, but as chairman of what was known at that time as the Council of People's Commissars. The prime minister and his colleagues were elected by the Soviet parliament, the USSR Supreme Soviet. In addition, there was a collective presidency or Presidium of the Supreme Soviet, and the chairman of that body carried out the functions of head of state. Once Leonid Brezhnev had been elected to the chairmanship of the Presidium, in 1977, it became conventional to refer to him in foreign capitals as 'President Brezhnev'. But there was still no presidency as such: Stalin, it appears, had considered but then rejected the idea in the 1930s on the grounds that there was 'no place for an individual president elected by all the people, like the Supreme Soviet, and able to challenge the Supreme Soviet', and it was considered again under Khrushchev but dropped as soon as he had been forced out of office (Lazarev 1990). In any case, neither the chairman of the Presidium nor the prime minister was accountable in any meaningful way to the parliament, or (still more so) a mass electorate; rather, decisions on matters of this kind were taken by the party leadership and routinely ratified.

All of this had begun to change in the late Soviet period. A presidency, Gorbachev had originally argued, would 'concentrate too much power in the hands of a single person', and in the first instance it was decided to create a new position, a chairmanship of the parliament, to which the party leader was duly elected (*XIX Konferentsiya*, 1988, vol. 1, p. 59, and vol. 2, pp. 129, 139). But the discussion continued: Andrei Sakharov, for instance, suggested the direct election of the parliamentary chairman in his election address in the spring of 1989, and in the draft constitution that he proposed later in the year he included a 'President of the Union of Soviet Republics of Europe and Asia' who would be elected every five years by the population at large (A. Sakharov 1994: 258–9, 272, 274). The decision to move to a presidential system was taken later the same year, as Gorbachev's advisers became convinced that only in this way would they recapture the initiative from their political opponents (Zlobin 1994; Kuznetsov 1996). A presidency was approved with some haste in March 1990, and Gorbachev was elected as its first (and last) incumbent with the support of 71 per cent of the deputies who voted. Exceptionally, the choice was made by the Congress of People's Deputies, rather than by the population as a whole, and this deprived the new Soviet president of the popular mandate that his Russian counterpart was able to claim the following year.

Boris Yeltsin had been elected chairman of the Russian parliament in May 1990, and then in June 1991 he was elected Russia's first-ever president in a direct popular election against five other candidates. The presidency, it was established by this time, was normally an elective office, and it was a position of executive authority: neither Gorbachev nor Boris Yeltsin, as former prime minister Nikolai Ryzhkov remarked, liked the idea of 'reigning like the Queen of England' (Nenashev 1993: 26). Indeed in Russia, after December 1993, it was the presidency that defined the character of the political system, as Yeltsin used his ascendancy after the dissolution of parliament to secure the adoption of a constitution that extended his already considerable powers. 'I don't deny that the powers of the president in the draft [constitution] are considerable', he told *Izvestiya*, 'but what do you expect in a country that is used to tsars and strong leaders?' (15 Nov. 1993, 4).

Developments in Russia were part of a wider trend towards executive presidencies, not only in the former republics but throughout the communist and post-communist world. The USSR itself had 'led the world' in the number of its presidents at various levels (Kunaev 1991: 39); among the republics Turkmenia had been the first to institute a position of this kind in 1990 and in 1994, with the adoption of a new constitution, Belarus became the last. Most of Eastern Europe had moved towards an executive presidency by the same time, with Albania, the Czech Republic, Hungary, and Slovakia the main exceptions (N. A. Sakharov 1994; McGregor 1994; Taras 1997*b*). At the same time the late 1980s had seen the development of a body of scholarship that 'took institutions seriously', and there were many indications, in this literature, that an executive or even a semi-presidency was unlikely to contribute towards the formation of a party system or political stability more generally (see for instance Lijphart 1992; Sartori 1994; Linz and Valenzuela 1994). Did the Russian experience, by the mid-1990s, bear out these gloomy forecasts? Had a working balance been found between an elected president, the government that he appointed, and a parliament that was also directly elected? And how did the Russian semi-presidency relate to the wider framework set out by Duverger and examined systematically in the pages of this book?

THE CONTEXT OF SEMI-PRESIDENTIALISM IN RUSSIA

Soviet rule had left a complex of legacies to its post-communist successors. In Russia particularly it had left an unresolved tension between a newly established executive presidency and a parliament that had been elected in the spring of 1990, the Congress of People's Deputies. It was 'inevitable', Yeltsin reflected later, that at the end of the Soviet period there would be a conflict between 'two systems of power' (*Izvestiya*, 10 Dec. 1994, 1). The Congress, he complained, tended 'just to reject, just to destroy'. Too many deputies engaged in 'cheap populism and open demagoguery . . . and in the final analysis, the restoration of a totalitarian Soviet-Communist system' (*Izvestiya*, 10 Dec. 1992, 1). For parliamentarians and their speaker, Ruslan Khasbulatov, the issue was a rather different one: whether government should be accountable to elected representatives, and whether a broadly representative parliament should be allowed to act as a counterbalance to what would otherwise be an overwhelmingly powerful executive. For Khasbulatov, Russian history and then Marxism-Leninism had combined to exaggerate the power of a single 'tsar'. It was essential, in these circumstances, to establish a secure division of powers and then to develop the role of parliament as a 'representative organ' of the whole society. Parliament, in particular, could serve as a 'counterweight' to the executive, exercising its influence over public spending, legislation, and the composition of government as parliaments did in other countries. And he argued more generally that a presidential republic was not appropriate to the particular circumstances of post-communist Russia, with its need to maximize consensus and public understanding (Khasbulatov 1992).

These differences, in the end, were resolved by force, when parliament was dissolved by presidential decree on 21 September 1993 and then shelled into submission by the Russian army on 4 October following an attempt by Khasbulatov, vice-president Rutskoi, and their supporters to occupy the Kremlin and establish their own authority. Yeltsin had predicted a 'decisive battle' between the supporters and opponents of his programme of reforms, and there had already been plans, the previous spring, to 'arrest the Congress' by gas and military force if it approved a vote of impeachment (Korzhakov 1997: 158–9). In the circumstances that obtained after the suppression of what Yeltsin described as a 'parliamentary insurrection' it was a more centralist draft than those that had been under discussion during the summer that was published in November 1993 and approved at a referendum the following month. There was, in fact, some doubt if the constitution was itself constitutional: under the law on the referendum a majority of the electorate, not just of voters, had to indicate their support, and there was some evidence that the turnout had in any case fallen below 50 per cent, which was the level that Yeltsin had specified in his decree (see for instance *Moskovskii komsomolets*, 11 Jan. 1994, 1). It was difficult, however, to alter any of the provisions of the document that had now become Russia's first post-communist constitution, and it appeared to have shifted Russian politics decisively towards what an *Izvestiya* journalist described as a 'superpresidential republic' (12 Oct. 1994, 4).

The man who now exercised these far-reaching powers had been born in the village of Butko in the Sverdlovsk region of western Siberia in 1931, the son of peasant parents. After completing his studies, Yeltsin had worked as a construction engineer managing a large state enterprise that specialized in prefabricated housing; in 1961 he joined the CPSU, becoming a full-time party functionary in 1968 and in 1976 first secretary of the Sverdlovsk regional party organization. In 1985, after Gorbachev had come to power, he moved to Moscow to become first secretary of the party organization in the capital, where his outspoken comments soon attracted attention. His speech at the 27th Party Congress in 1986 began with references to the 'Bolshevik spirit' and 'Leninist optimism' that prevailed at their deliberations, but went on to ask why over so many years the party had failed to eliminate social injustice and the abuse of official position. Then in October 1987 he was called to speak to the Central Committee plenum that was considering Gorbachev's draft report on the 70th anniversary of the revolution. Yeltsin wanted, he wrote later, to 'screw up [his] courage and say what [he] had to say'; his speech was no more than a few headings on a sheet of paper. It was nonetheless the decisive moment in his political career. There had been no changes in the way the party secretariat operated, Yeltsin told the delegates, or in the conduct of its head, Yegor Ligachev. More and more instructions were being issued, but they were receiving less and less attention. Meanwhile in the Politburo there had been a 'noticeable increase' in what he 'could only call adulation of the general secretary'. In 70 years, he declared in another version of the speech, they had failed to feed and clothe the people they claimed to represent, while providing for themselves abundantly. And there were criticisms of the General Secretary's wife, who was being paid for what was thought to be voluntary work and was in danger of acquiring her own 'cult of personality' (for the speech, see *Izvestiya TsK KPSS*, no. 2, 1989, 239–41, and for an unauthorized version *Le Monde*, 2 Feb. 1988, 6; his own version of events appears in El'tsin 1990: 134).

The speech, predictably, led to his dismissal as Moscow party secretary, and he was dropped from the Politburo. But the more Yeltsin was attacked by the party leadership, the more he came to be seen as a champion of ordinary citizens against an over-powerful, often corrupt establishment; and the introduction of competitive elections at the same time as his disgrace allowed him to turn this popular following to his advantage. In March 1989, standing for the Moscow national-territorial constituency, he won over 89 per cent of the vote against a party-approved competitor; his winning margin, over five million votes, was so large it entered the *Guinness Book of Records*, and it contrasted sharply with Gorbachev's decision to take one of the 100 seats that were reserved for the CPSU and for which a 100 candidates were nominated, avoiding a direct appeal to the electorate and still more so a direct confrontation with his leading opponent. A year later, in elections to the Russian parliament, Yeltsin won another popular mandate when he took over 80 per cent of the vote in his native Sverdlovsk; and he began to use his position, once he had been elected parliamentary chairman at the end of May 1990, to advance the claims of the republics and especially of Russia against the central state and its ruling party.

Yeltsin admitted in the memoirs he published in 1994 that he relied on his self-image as a 'wilfull, determined, strong politician'. But he also confessed that he was easily influenced by the opinions of people he respected; and sometimes his ideas were changed completely by 'a word said in passing or a line in a newspaper article'. There was, it seems, a decisive moment in this intellectual trajectory, in late 1989 when Yeltsin visited a Moscow bathhouse. He found himself surrounded by a crowd of about 40 naked men, all urging him to keep up his challenge to the leadership. It was, he recalled, 'quite a sight'. And it was at this moment in the banya, with everything reduced to its essentials, that he had 'changed [his] world view, realised that [he] was a communist by Soviet tradition, by inertia, by education, but not by conviction' (El'tsin 1994:

181). Yeltsin was also influenced by a visit to the United States in September 1989, his first to a capitalist country. Amazed by the array of foodstuffs that was readily available in a Houston supermarket, he commented that this disproved the 'fairy tales' about the superiority of socialism. In the view of Lev Sukhanov, one of his closest aides, it was at this time Yeltsin decided to leave the ranks of the CPSU (Sukhanov 1992: 143–50); it could in fact have seen the end of his career entirely as he chose to go swimming late at night in shark-infested waters, ignoring the public warning (Yaroshenko 1997: 32–3).

CONSTITUTIONAL POWERS

Russia was certainly an example of the significance of tradition and circumstances in the formation of a semi-presidential model of government. The longer-standing tradition was of a powerful leader, be he a tsar, a general secretary, or a president. The prime minister, by a tradition of lesser antiquity, was an executant rather than a figure of independent political authority, nominated by the ruler and accountable to him rather than (in normal circumstances) to an elected parliament, although there were occasions—as under Lenin, in the first years of the new regime, or after the death of Stalin—when it appeared that the prime minister might become the locus of real authority. There had, in fact, been some moves towards the 'checks and balances' of which Gorbachev spoke approvingly even in the Soviet period. After 1964, in particular, the prime ministerial position was separated from the party leadership in order to avoid an excessive concentration of power in the hands of a single person; and there was an emphasis upon 'collective leadership', even if the party leader was clearly the dominant figure. The early post-communist system, similarly, balanced an elected president against an elected parliament, and for some time it appeared likely that post-communist Russia would be headed by a president but one whose authority was balanced by a vice-president and by some degree of accountability to the elected parliament. In the event, the presidential coup that took place in September and October 1993 allowed the introduction of a constitution that (in the view of commentators) endowed the presidency with powers that were comparable with those of Napoleon III in nineteenth-century France (*Pravda*, 10 Dec. 1993, 3); journalists, indeed, dubbed Yeltsin a 'president-tsar' (*Nezavisimaya gazeta*, 13 Oct. 1993, 1).

In terms of the constitutional powers of president, prime minister, and parliament, the president was clearly the dominant figure (see Table 11.1). The president was head of state and guarantor of the constitution itself, which invested him with powers that could potentially be very large indeed.

It was the president who represented the Russian Federation at home and abroad, and the president who defined the 'basic directions' of foreign and domestic policy, particularly in the annual 'state of the union' address that he gave to both houses of parliament. The president was directly elected for four years by direct, equal, and secret ballot, and could not be elected for not more than two consecutive terms (unlike the American constitution, he could theoretically be re-elected after another president had served a normal term). A Russian president had to be at least 35 years old (unlike the draft, there was no upper age

TABLE 11.1. *The Russian presidency*

Under the December 1993 Constitution, the President of the Russian Federation is:

- head of state (Art. 80:1);
- guarantor of the Constitution (Art. 80:2),
  to which he swears an oath of allegiance (Art. 82:1);
- he 'defines the basic directions of the domestic and foreign policy of the state' (Art. 80:3)
  and represents the Russian Federation domestically and internationally (Art. 80:4);
- he is elected for four years by direct, equal, and secret ballot (Art. 81:1);
  he must be at least 35 years old, and have lived in the Russian Federation for at least ten years (Art. 81:2),
  and may not be elected for more than two consecutive terms (Art. 81:3);
- he 'appoints with the agreement of the State Duma the Chairman of the Government of the Russian Federation', has the right to preside at government meetings and 'takes decisions on the resignation of the Government of the Russian Federation'; he nominates candidates for the Chairmanship of the State Bank; on the recommendation of the prime minister he appoints and dismisses deputy premiers and federal ministers; he nominates candidates for the Constitutional Court, the Supreme Court, and the Procuracy General; he forms and heads the Security Council, appoints and dismisses his plenipotentiary representatives in the regions as well as the high command of the armed forces and diplomatic representatives in foreign states and international organizations (Art. 83);
- he calls elections to the State Duma, dissolves the Duma in specified circumstances, calls referendums, initiates legislation, and reports annually to the Federal Assembly on 'the situation in the country' and the 'main directions of the domestic and foreign policy of the state' (Art. 84);
- he is commander-in-chief and can declare a state of war (Art. 87)
  as well as a state of emergency (Art. 88);
  he grants pardons (Art. 89)
  and issues decrees that have the force of law throughout the territory of the Federation (Art. 90).

limit), and he had to have lived in the Russian Federation for at least ten years (this ruled out some of the émigré candidatures that had been seen in Eastern Europe; an émigré, indeed, won the Lithuanian presidency in early 1998). The president, moreover, had extensive powers of appointment: he appointed the prime minister 'with the agreement of the State Duma', he appointed and dismissed deputy premiers and ministers, and he nominated candidates for the Constitutional Court, the Supreme Court, and the Procuracy General. He could, in addition, dissolve the Duma in specified circumstances, and call referendums (a power which had previously belonged to the parliament). He could initiate legislation, and issue his own decrees that had the force of law throughout the Federation; he headed the armed forces, and could declare a state of war as well as a state of emergency (for the text, see *Konstitutsiya Rossiiskoi Federatsii. Prinyata vsenarodnym golosovaniem 12 dekabrya 1993 g*, Moscow, Yuridicheskaya literatura).

The prime minister had more limited but related powers. He was appointed by the president 'with the consent of the State Duma'; the government submitted its resignation to a new president and the president had in turn to submit his prime ministerial nomination within two weeks of taking office. But unlike parliamentary systems, there was no question of the prime minister submitting his resignation to a newly elected Duma and securing majority support for his continued tenure of office. On the contrary, prime minister Chernomyrdin made clear, after his Our Home is Russia party had secured just over 10 per cent of the popular vote in the December 1995 parliamentary election, that he would not be resigning and that he would not be changing the policies he was pursuing (*Segodnya*, 20 Dec. 1995, 1). Equally, the dramatic dismissal of the entire cabinet in March 1998 and the nomination of a new prime minister were quite unconnected with the balance of power within the Duma, still less the outcome of a new election. The Duma, for its part, did have some influence over the choice of prime minister, but it was a power of last resort. The Duma had to vote on any nomination within a week; if it rejected three such nominations the president was required and not merely empowered to dissolve the Duma and call a new election. The Duma had another power of last resort: this was its power to vote no confidence in the government as a whole. If it did so twice within a period of three months, the president had either to announce the resignation of the government, or dissolve the Duma. But these were clearly exceptional powers, which would not be used in normal circumstances and which would lead in most cases to the dissolution of the Duma itself.

It was the prime minister, in turn, who took responsibility for the ordinary business of government. He made proposals to the president for the tenure of other positions in government; he set 'guidelines' for the conduct of the government as a whole, and 'organise[d] its work'. It was the government as a whole that submitted an annual budget to the Duma, and took responsibility for a 'uniform state policy' in culture, science, education, health, social security, and the environment. The government, similarly, was responsible for public order and the rule of law; and it could issue resolutions and directives in order to carry its decisions into effect. Under the Law on the Government, which was approved in December 1997 (*Sobranie zakonodatel'stva Rossiiskoi Federatsii*, no. 51, 1997, art. 5712), a full meeting of the government took place once a month, with a smaller Presidium meeting 'as necessary'. Ministers could not be members of the Duma or of the Federation Council, they could not hold other government positions or engage in business, and in an attempt to limit the opportunities for abuse of office they had to declare their income and assets on an annual basis, and could receive no payment for their publications or speaking engagements or gifts of money or their equivalent. Given Yeltsin's indifference to detail and his extended absences, the government had a good deal of autonomy in the conduct of its business provided it retained the general confidence of the president; but when he chose to do so, as in the nomination of a young and little-known energy minister, Sergei Kirienko, to the premiership in March 1998, he could impose his wishes with little direct regard to public or parliamentary opinion.

Viktor Chernomyrdin had been appointed prime minister in December 1992, when the Congress of Deputies refused to accept Yeltsin's nomination of Yegor Gaidar, and was confirmed in his position after the 1996 presidential election. Yeltsin, however, was apparently jealous of the prominent role that Chernomyrdin had been playing in domestic and international affairs—newspaper commentaries suggested he had made the president 'almost redundant' (*Kommersant-daily*, 23 Mar. 1998, 1)—and on 23 March he unexpectedly dismissed the entire government and appointed Sergei Kirienko acting prime minister, explaining at the same time that there would be 'no change in policy' (*Rossiiskaya gazeta*, 24 Mar. 1998, 1). Kirienko, a boyish 35-year-old who had served as energy minister since the previous November, was virtually unknown to the wider public ('Sergei who?', asked *Moscow News*) but was formally nominated four days later, Yeltsin describing him as a 'technocrat, a manager, a person who has no connections with any parties or movements' (*Rossiiskaya gazeta*, 28 Mar. 1998, 1). Kirienko, it emerged, was a graduate of the Gorky Institute of Water Transport Engineering and a former Komsomol official from Nizhnii Novgorod, who had then moved into factory management and banking; as he told newsmen, he had 'a Russian mother, a Jewish father and a Ukrainian surname' (ibid., 3 Apr. 1998, 2). Kirienko was rejected on the first vote on 10 April and by a larger majority on 17 April but was finally approved a week later, many deputies aware that if they rejected his nomination a third time not simply would the Duma itself be dissolved but the president would be able to impose his own choice until a new Duma had been convened.

If this was semi-presidentialism, it was a semi-presidentialism that was weighted very heavily in the president's favour, and it was a stable dominance, modified more by the vagaries of presidential health than by the composition of the Duma or the changing views of the wider public. The prime minister could sometimes take the initiative, as when Chernomyrdin took charge of negotiations during the hostage crisis at Budennovsk in the summer of 1995; and he had an international role, for instance through the premier's institutionalized dialogue with the US vice-president, Al Gore. In the absence of a vice-president in Russia itself, it was the prime minister who took on the presidential role if the president resigned, or was impeached, or suffered from a 'continued inability to discharge the powers and the duties of the office for reasons of health'. There would be new presidential elections, in such circumstances, within six months. But it was always clear that the prime minister depended for his position upon the continued confidence of the president, and that this was true even if he had the support of a political party, and of powerful interests, and had access to individual and corporate wealth (Chernomyrdin had become one of Russia's richest men with the privatization of the gas industry, for which he had formerly been the responsible minister). Equally, it was clear that other figures within the presidential circle could often wield a lot more influence: such as the president's sometime bodyguard, Alexander Korzhakov, or his daughter and adviser, Tatyana Dyachenko, or even his tennis coach. Formal position counted for little within the court politics of the Yeltsin presidency; it was far more important to be related by geographical origin (the 'Sverdlovsk mafia'), or by family or marriage, or through the performance of essential services (such as the wealthy industrialist, Boris Berezovsky, who was close to Yeltsin's daughter and who had helped to bankroll the successful presidential campaign in 1996).

PRESIDENTS, PRIME MINISTERS,
AND PARLIAMENTS

The complex and unsatisfactory relationship between president, prime minister, and parliament was a much more general feature of presidential systems (see Baylis 1996). The December constitution had been intended to resolve any tensions of this kind in favour of the president. It certainly endowed him with extensive powers to nominate the prime minister and government, to dissolve the Duma if it repeatedly refused to endorse his choices, and to issue his own decrees with the force of law. In 1994 and 1995 alone Yeltsin put more than a hundred draft laws to parliament, and vetoed more than one-third of the draft laws that were submitted for his signature after the Federal Assembly had approved them (Okun'kov 1996: 64, 74). Indeed the president's frequent recourse to decrees, appeals, constitutional messages, and statements in the mass media made him appear a source of legislation in his own right, a clear violation of the principle of a separation of powers. Some of his decrees, moreover, including those on the basis of which he launched the war in Chechnya in December 1994, were issued in secret and without the knowledge let alone the capacity to scrutinize them of the Russian parliament (it was for reasons such as this that the US Congress in 1973 had adopted the War Powers Act, restricting the power of the president to commit US troops abroad).

At the same time there was no guarantee that the prime minister that the president nominated would reflect majority opinion in the Federal Assembly, or that the decisions of the government he headed would find favour with the deputies of either house. There were three votes, as we have seen, before Sergei Kirienko was accepted by the Duma, and for these four or five weeks there was no legitimate successor to the president in the event of death or incapacity, as Kirienko was an acting rather than fully *de jure* prime minister. The Duma, for its part, could adopt decisions entirely at odds with presidential policies, as it did in February 1994 when the conspirators of August 1991 and the parliamentary leaders of September/October 1993 were amnestied. The Duma could also pass a vote of no confidence in the government, as it did (but not by a sufficiently large majority) in October 1994. Under the provisions of Article 117 this led either to the dismissal of the government by the president, or to the dissolution of the Duma itself. But there was, again, no guarantee that future elections would resolve the crisis, and no reason for the president to accept their outcome; and there could in any case be no dissolution of the Duma on this basis within the first year of its election. The president, unlike his American counterpart, spent little time in meetings with parliamentary leaders and factions; the result was often a compromise, as in the successive budgets that were agreed by both sides, but the outcome could also be a 'cold war' between president and parliament, a deadlock that reflected the powers they had respectively been allocated under the constitution.

One of the ways in which presidents and parliaments were linked in other nations was through the party system. And this, again, was a weakness in the post-communist system, at least in Russia. Yeltsin had left the CPSU in July 1990 at its 28th Congress; later he took the view that, as an elected Russian president, he should remain independent of party affiliation. There was talk, before the December 1993 election, that he might form a 'party or movement' to promote his views; but there was no serious attempt to do so, and in the event he stood above the contest, as did prime minister Chernomyrdin. The president again took no direct part in the Duma election of December 1995, although in an eve of poll broadcast he urged voters not to choose the Communists. Parties themselves remained notoriously weak, with limited memberships and a constant tendency to divide (see Lowenhardt 1998; and Wyman, White, and Oates 1998); there were party formations in the Duma itself, but they were a very approximate reflection of the distribution of party support at the election (half the vote had gone to parties that were not represented at all; not all of the deputies joined their 'own' factions in the new Duma; there were factions that had no counterpart in a party outside parliament; and not even the Communists, in the vote on the nomination of prime minister Kirienko in 1998, were able to deliver the vote of their own deputies). The consequence was that there was no institutional mechanism that could bind president, prime minister, and parliament together within a single set of policies, ideally one that had been approved by the public at large in a national election.

Those elections themselves took place at different times, and with different electoral systems. The parliament was elected in two sections: 225 seats by plurality in single-seat constituencies, and 225 by a national party-list contest with the seats awarded on a proportional basis to all the parties or alliances that secured more than 5 per cent of the vote. The president was elected on the French pattern, with the successful candidate required to secure more than 50 per cent of the vote in the first round, or a plurality in a run-off second round against the other candidate with the largest vote (for a thorough discussion of these matters see White, Rose, and McAllister 1997). The parliamentary vote, in December 1995, gave seats to just 4 of the 43 parties and movements that put forward candidates; the largest share of the party-list vote went to the Communists, but independents won most of the single-member seats, and there was no stable majority for either government or opposition. The presidential contest, in June and July 1996, did at least deliver a clear result (see Table 11.2), but it also revealed a society that was deeply divided: between north and south, between the 'two capitals' and the rest of the country, between rich and poor, and between committed reformers and supporters of many of the egalitarian policies of the old regime.

TABLE 11.2. *The 1996 Russian presidential election*

First round: 16 June 1996	Registered electorate = 108,495,023	
Boris Yeltsin, Independent	35.3	26,665,495
Gennadii Zyuganov, Communist	32.0	24,211,686
Alexander Lebed, no party	14.5	10,974,736
Grigorii Yavlinsky, Yabloko	7.3	5,550,752
Vladimir Zhirinovsky, Liberal Democrat	5.7	4,311,479
Svyatoslav Fedorov, Workers' Self-Government	0.9	699,158
Mikhail Gorbachev, International Fund for Socioeconomic and Political Research	0.5	386,069
Martin Shakkum, Socioeconomic Reform	0.4	277,068
Yuri Vlasov, National Patriotic Party	0.2	151,282
Vladimir Bryntsalov, Russian Socialist Party	0.2	123,065
Aman-Gel'dy Tuleev, Communist (withdrew at last minute in favour of Zyuganov)	0.0	308
Against all candidates	1.5	1,163,921
Total valid vote	68.7	74,515,019
Invalid ballots	1.0	1,072,120
Total turnout	69.7	75,587,139
Second round: 3 July 1996	Registered electorate = 108,589,050	
Boris Yeltsin, Independent	53.8	40,203,948
Gennadii Zyuganov, Communist	40.3	30,102,288
Against both candidates	4.8	3,604,462
Total valid vote	68.1	73,910,698
Invalid ballots	0.7	780,592
Total turnout	68.8	74,691,290

Source: Derived from Tsentral'naya izbiratel'naya komissiya Rossiiskoi Federatsii, *Vybory Prezidenta Rossiiskoi Federatsii. 1996. Elektoral'naya statistika* (Moscow: Ves, mir, 1996), 128 and 130.

YELTSIN AND THE RUSSIAN SEMI-PRESIDENCY

All semi-presidential systems depend heavily upon the person of the president and the prime minister. The Russian system depended more than many others, in ways that went well beyond the formal prescriptions of the constitution, and in terms not simply of the president's policy choices but also his physical health and personality. The 1993 constitution added to these concerns by abolishing the position of vice-president (in the post-communist world only Bulgaria, Korea, Kazakhstan, and Kyrgyzstan retained a position of this kind (N. A. Sakharov 1994: 89)). Under the constitution, as we have seen, the president relinquishes office ahead of time in the event of his resignation, impeachment, or 'inability to perform the duties of his office for reasons of health'. In these circumstances the powers of the president pass on a temporary basis to the prime minister, and new elections have to be called within three months (Article 92). But who, asked commentators, was to decide if the president was 'totally unable to exercise his powers'? The president himself, by signing a decree? Or the prime minister? Or a special conference of doctors? Including whom? Or, perhaps, a presidential assistant—but which one? As long as there were no answers to such questions, there was a 'real possibility' that the president could be isolated from power and the country governed 'in his name' by 'powerful "backstage figures"' (*Moskovskie novosti*, no. 75, 1995, 5).

Yeltsin himself complained that 'as soon as [he went] on holiday, speculation [began] about [his] health' (*Izvestiya*, 26 Mar. 1994, 1). But there were many such absences, and several occasions on which the president's health was acknowledged to be the reason; and it was not surprising that every visit to the hospital was accompanied by 'arguments and rumours that undermine[d] his authority' (ibid., 5 July 1996, 2). In 1993 Yeltsin was confined to hospital with a nervous disorder (radiculitis) that could require strong sedation. In December 1994 he underwent an operation on his nose. In April 1995 a spring holiday was extended by a further week because of the president's high blood pressure, and in July he was rushed to hospital complaining of acute chest pains; appointments were cancelled and a scheduled visit to Norway had to be postponed. In October 1995 there was a recurrence of the same cardiac difficulties; he was in hospital for more than a month and did not return to his Kremlin desk until the end of December. There were further rumours when Yeltsin disappeared from public view between the two rounds of the presidential election in 1996, and a wooden television appeal on the eve of the decisive vote was not reassuring. The president had become a 'painted mummy', complained one of Zyuganov's supporters; 'they're suggesting we vote for a living corpse' (*The Guardian*, 2 July 1996, 2). There was a further period of uncertainty when Yeltsin underwent a multiple heart bypass operation in November 1996 and it was months before he resumed his presidential duties; in December 1997 he was back in the sanatorium as a result of what officials described as an acute respiratory infection.

Concerns about the presidential role were not allayed by repeated reports of alcoholism. The president himself admitted, in an interview in 1993, that he 'sometimes' allowed himself a glass of cognac on a Sunday evening with his family, or some beer after visiting the bathhouse (*Argumenty i fakty*, no. 16, 1993, 3). His parliamentary critics were more forthcoming. 'It's time to stop the public drunkenness of our President', a Communist deputy demanded after an unsteady performance during the president's first visit to the United States. 'When he's shown on television, he can't stand up without support' (*Nezavisimaya gazeta*, 16 May 1992, 2). There was further criticism in early 1993 when the president, defending himself against impeachment, spoke uncertainly before the Russian parliament and had to be assisted from the hall (deputies agreed he had 'created a strange impression'), and later in the year when Russian troops withdrawing from Germany were treated to a 'stirring rendition of Kalinka' under the impromptu conductorship of the president (*The Guardian*, 29 Mar. 1993, 18, and 9 Sept. 1994, 12). A number of advisers who expressed their concern at his performance while in Germany were simply left at home on the president's next foreign trip, which concluded with his controversial non-appearance at Shannon airport to take part in discussions with the Irish prime minister. Yeltsin, his staff explained, had simply overslept; subsequent testimony made clear that he had suffered a serious stroke, and was not allowed to leave the plane by his staff (Korzhakov 1997: 209–10), but his political opponents took a less charitable view and accused him subsequently of being in a 'permanent state of visiting Ireland' (Rutskoi in *Lipetskaya pravda*, 2 Mar. 1995, 2).

The Soviet system had maintained an effective form of government by monopolizing political power in the hands of the Communist Party and, within the party, by concentrating authority in the hands of the leadership. The partly reformed system that existed after 1988 was an uneasy combination of party direction 'from above' and electoral control 'from below', a tension that was eventually resolved in favour of the voters. The post-communist system, however, introduced a new source of tension with the separate election of an executive president and a working parliament. The tension between the two led to a governmental impasse throughout 1992 and 1993; but the constitution that was introduced in December 1993 provided no long-term solution, and there were continued calls for its amendment. For a start, presidential and parliamentary elections might take place on the same date, so as to maximize the chance that they would have a common programme of government; and there were more far-reaching calls for a conventional parliamentary system as in Britain or Scandinavia, with government led by a prime minister accountable to a directly elected assembly rather than a president (*Izvestiya*, 15 Mar. 1994, 1, 4). The Communist opposition was particularly hostile to the presidency, and party leader Zyuganov called for it to be abolished altogether as 'one of the first actions of a new president, if one is elected from the opposition' (Zyuganov 1994: 188–9); the same view was pressed by former prime minister Nikolai Ryzhkov (*Pravda*, 8 Feb. 1995, 1) and the chairman of the Duma, who saw Russia 'in the long term' as a parliamentary republic (*Izvestiya*, 11 Apr. 1996, 1). The chairman of the upper house, Yegor Stroev, called for the Duma to be given at least the ability to influence the choice of key ministers, if not the government as a whole (*Argumenty i fakty*, no. 3, 1997, 3).

A workable system, it seemed clear, would require a move to a more fully semi-presidential 'French' system in which the President enjoyed a popular mandate but the government or at least its key ministers required the support of a parliamentary majority. The Russian tradition was strong in its attention to centralized direction; its future was likely to depend upon the extent to which it could incorporate other, more Western traditions of accountability and popular consent.

12

Slovenia

MIRO CERAR

DOES SLOVENIA HAVE A PARLIAMENTARY OR A SEMI-PRESIDENTIAL SYSTEM?

In Slovenia the power of the state is divided along classical lines into a legislature, an executive, and a judiciary.[1] Legislative power is exercised by the parliament, comprising a National Assembly, which is the general representative house, and a National Council, which is a body representing various interests and has very limited powers.[2] Executive power is divided between the president and the government. Judicial power is exercised by the ordinary courts and the Constitutional Court, which rules on the conformity of legal enactments with the constitution and the law and decides constitutional complaints and certain other matters.[3]

In Slovenia it is generally accepted, both in professional and political circles as well as among the general public, that Slovenia has a parliamentary system in which the focus of political decision-making lies with the parliament and the government. As in other Central and East European countries in transition (with certain exceptions, notably Russia), in Slovenia the formal powers of parliament remain very strong, for the legislators proved to be more reluctant to curb their own powers vis-à-vis the powers of the executive branch (Zielonka 1994: 90). But, unlike the pure parliamentarism which certain countries opted for (Albania, Belarus, the Czech Republic, Estonia, Hungary, Latvia, and Slovakia), the Slovene arrangements belong more to a group which could be characterized as 'parliamentarism with a directly elected president' (ibid.), also including countries such as Bulgaria, Lithuania, Poland, Romania, and Ukraine, although the role of the directly elected president in Slovenia is relatively small. This applies mainly to the president's *de jure* powers because, as in Bulgaria for example, his power in practice may be greater than it appears on paper (Bugarič 1997: 138).

In Slovenia the president of the republic is the head of state, whose function or powers are mainly of a representative, initiative, and proto-col nature. Yet because it has a popularly elected fixed-term president, Slovenia can be classified as a semi-presidential regime following the definition in Chapter 1, although this is obviously only a formal definition. And, as Elgie himself points out in Chapter 1, various definitions of semi-presidentialism exist, none of which alone can ac-curately reflect the characteristics of an individual regime. Hence, in the rest of this chapter I will focus less on questions of appropriate classification—although I will give this some attention—than on the actual nature and features of the position and role of the president in the context of the constitutional and political system of the Republic of Slovenia.

NATIONAL INDEPENDENCE AND THE ESTABLISHMENT OF THE FIRST PRESIDENT OF THE REPUBLIC, PARLIAMENT, AND GOVERNMENT

Slovenia only became an independent state in 1991[4] and in the same year adopted a new constitution which laid the foundations for an entirely new political system and a remodelling of the state institutions. Therefore, the working of the new institutions of power, such as the president, the government, and the National Assembly, can only be judged over a relatively brief period of time—the first government was formed with the adoption of the constitution, while the first National Assembly and president of the republic were not elected until December 1992. Previously, an entirely different system had applied in Slovenia, based on the assembly system of power and the political monopoly of the Communist Party. Legislative power in Slovenia then fell within the jurisdiction of an assembly, and executive power was in the hands of an executive council and the collective presidency of the Slovene Federal Republic. In practice, though, all branches of power were essentially guided by Communist Party policy (although it must be said that one-party dictatorship in the latter decades of socialist Yugoslavia and in Slovenia was considerably more benign than in other East European communist countries). Moreover, in the most im-portant matters the Slovene authorities were subordinate to the federal Yugoslav authorities (the federal assembly, the federal executive council, the president, and later the presidency of Yugoslavia). Slovenia is now in the initial period of establishing its new institutional structure, and so the legal framework and the rules of the political game which are now taking shape between the president, the parliament, and the government will probably be quite decisive in determining the future workings of and relationships between these actors. The five-year term of office of the first president of the Republic of Slovenia expired in December 1997, the National Assembly was elected for a second time at the end of 1996, and so far there have been three governments. As far as the president is concerned, his constitutional powers under normal circumstances have indeed proved to be relatively weak and are primarily, but not exclusively, of a representative and protocol nature. But at the same time the incumbent president, Milan Kučan, has succeeded over the past five years on an informal level in preserving and expanding his political influence (in areas such as political life, economics, and the media), as well as his relatively high level of popularity among the Slovene public. One of the factors that has contributed to this situation is that because of his weak constitutional powers the president does not bear any direct responsibility for most of the more important political decisions and, hence, there is that much less opportunity to criticize his actions. The electorate's critical attitude towards the political institutions, which is generally very strong during times of transition, for specific and objective reasons, is mainly targeted at the government and the parliament, and especially at the political parties.

An international comparison of trust in institutions carried out in 1995 revealed that the citizens of Central and East European countries have, in general, a significantly lower level of trust in their institutions than the populations of West European countries (quoted by Toš 1996: 649–50). And this is especially true of trust in the political institutions. Nevertheless, in Slovenia trust in the government, parliament, and the president is, on average, markedly higher than in the other countries in this group,[5] although there was a steady decline in trust in the political institutions in Slovenia from 1991 to 1996. This negative trend is particularly strong with regard to the political parties, and also the National Assembly and the government, but less so as far as the president is concerned.[6] Despite a fall in trust in the president of the republic over the past six years, he still commands the highest level of trust among all the political and state institutions.

The National Assembly is clearly the strongest political player in Slovenia, something which proceeds directly from its constitutional position and powers, and is probably also a reflection of the genuine enthusiasm for the new parliamentary democracy, in which the representative body of the people was supposed to be the most important regulatory force (Zajc 1997: 14). As will become clear, there is also an element here of a hangover from the previous assembly system. It could even be said that Slovenia's current parliamentary model presupposes a weak government and in the delimitation of policy-making powers this tends to favour the National Assembly, which attempts to be the supreme regulator of the state in an operational sense as well (ibid. 13–14 and 22–3). As solid as this argument may be, there is nevertheless also a tendency in Slovenia towards a strengthening of the executive branch of power at the expense of the legislature, which in individual matters the government is able to achieve primarily with the support of its coalition in parliament. Additionally, the National Assembly may pass a vote of no confidence in the prime minister—a mechanism which the Slovene constitution adopted from the German constitutional arrangements—but only if it simultaneously elects a new prime minister by absolute majority. In general, this mechanism of constructive vote of no confidence prevents a government crisis as such and helps to reinforce the position of the government.

In this initial phase of the establishing of democracy, i.e. since 1992, there have been no extraordinary circumstances or situations in Slovenia which would permit and require the use of the extraordinary powers of the president (such as the issuing of decrees with the binding force and effect of statute), or which would require the replacement of any of the holders of senior political office (the president of the republic, the president of the National Assembly, or the prime minister). But in the circumstances that followed the parliamentary elections in November 1996 when there was a stalemate in the 90-member National Assembly (the deputies were split 45 : 45 over the forming of a government coalition) and it was not possible to form a government for several months, the role of the president was highlighted as he had the power to propose the first candidate for prime minister. And the president's chosen candidate was elected to office by the National Assembly at the second attempt.[7] But as we will see, this is the only real 'power' of the president as regards the forming of a new government.

The president has no significant formal role in the legislative process or the policy-making process, all of which is within the jurisdiction of the National Assembly and the government. For the time being this 'limited' role of the president is not causing any concern among the general public or among experts, demonstrating that in this respect the constitutional concept has so far proven to be a generally acceptable solution. Yet at the same time, because of its weak political powers the office of president has become, to a certain extent, less interesting to the political parties, which direct most of their energy at elections into obtaining seats in parliament and potentially in government. But, of course, no serious political party in Slovenia renounces in advance its aspirations to occupy the position of president, because his informal influence can be great.

HISTORICAL FACTORS AND THE EVENTS SURROUNDING THE FORMATION OF THE REGIME

Historical Factors and Influences on the Birth and Development of the Republic

Throughout its history Slovenia was never an independent political state before 1991. Nevertheless, as a part of wider state entities it did develop its own representative institutions. The various ups and downs notwithstanding, it is fair to say that by the beginning of the twentieth century Slovenia already enjoyed a rich tradition of representative systems and democratic experience, and that fluctuations in its political development matched the general progress of representative systems elsewhere in Europe (Vilfan 1995: 22).

Slovenia's first state president was elected in 1992. In the time when Slovenia was a province under the Austro-Hungarian Crown (until the end of the First World War), during the Slovenes' subsequent incorporation in the State of Slovenes, Croats, and Serbs and later the Kingdom of Serbs, Croats, and Slovenes (both in 1918), and then during communist Yugoslavia after the Second World War, there was no opportunity to establish the institution of a head of a sovereign (i.e. independent) Slovene state. Throughout this period Slovenia was mainly governed from distant centres of power, where although it had representatives it had no real opportunity to exert any decisive political influence.

In a sense the origin of the head of a Slovene state dates back to the collective executive committee of the Liberation Front, founded in 1941 as the executive arm of the Slovene National Liberation Committee, which was the organization set up to lead the struggle against the German and Italian occupiers (see Ribičič 1996a: 137). In communist Yugoslavia, of which Slovenia became a federal unit after the Second World War, Slovenia acquired its first 'head of state', the presidium of the people's assembly of Slovenia, which, along the lines of the Soviet model, was not merely a collective 'head of state' but also acted as the leader of the people's assembly, and in periods between sessions of the assembly was the body responsible for supervising the work of the government. Naturally, all these Slovene organs of power were subordinated to the federal Yugoslav organs. The presidium comprised a president, one or two deputy presidents, and no more than twenty other members.

In 1957 the presidium was abolished in Slovenia, but it was not replaced with an individual 'head of state' as happened at the federal level. After 1963 the role of the head of the Slovene federal unit was gradually taken over by the presidency of the assembly of the Republic of Slovenia, established in accordance with the standing orders of the assembly. But it was not until 1974 that Slovenia acquired a 'head of state', in the form of the collective presidency of the Socialist Republic of Slovenia, which represented the Slovene republic (then still a federal unit of socialist Yugoslavia) and had significant powers in the areas of defence and international relations as well as certain other important political issues.

Gradual constitutional development led in 1989 to the abolition of automatic membership of the presidency of the republic (previously, two seats were reserved in this eight-member presidency for senior Party officials) and the number of members was reduced to four plus the so-called president of the presidency; furthermore, direct elections were introduced for the president and members of the presidency (ibid. 138–40). Direct elections to the presidency came about chiefly due to the strong public pressure and the efforts of the civil society, within which numerous intellectuals and other opponents had already formed a fairly strong political opposition to the ruling Communist Party by the end of the 1980s.

The transition to the current system with an individual president acting as head of state was part of the process of gaining independence and the associated democratization of Slovenia. This marked a radical break with the previous system, in which the 'head of state' was a collective body having a fundamentally different function. Moreover, up until 1989 the collective presidency had no democratic legitimacy. The most important difference is obviously that the current president of the republic is the head of an independent and internationally recognized state, while the previous Slovene presidencies and other 'state' organs were subordinated to the federal Yugoslav authorities, and of course in a political sense to the Communist Party.

And clearly this transition to a political system with a president of the republic did not mark a direct break with the monarchist tradition of which the country was once part (under Austria and then Yugoslavia). This had come much earlier, at the time when the first Yugoslav republic was formed after the First World War.

The Constitutional Debate—A Semi-Presidential or a Parliamentary System?

In the constitutional debates a basic dilemma facing all the Central and East European countries in transition from communism to Western-type democracy was the choice between a parliamentary and a semi-presidential model of state power (see Marko 1991: 45–50; Trócsányi 1995: 19–21; Kaučič, 1992: 737). In Slovenia, too, this question was a feature of the initial phase of the debate on the new constitution. The working draft of the constitution, drawn up by a group of experts working under a constitutional commission, offered two alternatives for political debate. Under a semi-presidential model, the popularly elected president of the republic was to have, among his powers, a decisive influence on the formation of the government, since he would appoint the prime minister and, at the prime minister's proposal, the other ministers. Under the parliamentary model, the prime minister was to be elected by the National Assembly, while the president would have only a limited representative and protocol role (see Jambrek 1992: 316–24). Even in this initial phase of the constitutional debate a consensus was soon reached on the greater suitability for Slovenia of the parliamentary model,[8] which was substantiated primarily by the danger that during the transition, and subsequently, an individual holding the office of a strong president could be too strong a counterweight to the other organs of state or even prevail over them. Particularly from the point of view of supervising the government, the parliamentary system was judged more democratic than a (semi-)presidential system (Krivic 1990: 1186), although this was a contemporary view that, even in theory, is generally open to dispute. Nevertheless, certain characteristics of a semi-presidential regime as defined in Chapter 1 were built into Slovenia's constitutional system.

The Direct Election of the President and the First Presidential Term

In the constitutional debate the position prevailed that the president of the republic should be directly elected. This somewhat contradictory solution (a popularly elected president with weak powers), which Elster, for instance, even claims 'goes against the grain of constitutional thinking' (1993: 197), was chiefly a result of public pressure. In the initial phase of the transition, i.e. in the late 1980s and at the start of the 1990s, there was a clearly expressed desire among the public to elect the president of the republic by direct ballot.[9] But at the time the voters probably expected that a popularly elected president would have a stronger political influence and a more relevant role. It was only in subsequent years that the public became aware of the actual constitutional position of the president. At the beginning of the transition people were generally poorly informed as to the powers of the then still collective presidency, and of the powers of the assembly and its executive council. Even when the first election was held for the president of the republic under the new constitution, the majority of voters were not fully aware of the constitutionally defined powers of the president. This relatively widespread ignorance of the function of the various institutions at the time was mostly a result of the complicated formal structure of authority under the previous communist regime, when there had been a significant degree of public apathy towards politics in general, and the failure to provide organized and intensive public information on the new constitutional institutions through the media.

At the time when the new constitution was being drawn up, it is fair to say that the institution of president of the republic was, to a great extent, adapted to suit the then president of the presidency and now president of the Republic of Slovenia, Milan Kučan, who had previously been the leader of the League of Communists of Slovenia for several years. For his highly successful reformist leadership of the League of Communists in the 1980s, Kučan won enormous respect among the people of Slovenia, particularly during the time when the Slovene League of Communists was fighting against the centralist and hegemonic tendencies of the pro-Serbian Yugoslav League of Communists. Kučan's popularity meant that the parliamentary parties, most of which were against his election as president of the republic (either because of his communist past or for reasons stemming from various rivalries),[10] were fully aware that he would indeed win a direct ballot. But in the face of undeniable public support for direct presidential elections, the parliamentary parties were unable to get their proposal for parliament to elect the president into the constitution. Had they been able to do so then Kučan would almost certainly not have been elected. Given this situation, the parliamentary parties sought to reduce the influence of 'president-to-be' Kučan by opting for relatively minor presidential powers. Predictions that Kučan would win proved to be wholly accurate. At the election in December 1992 he won a large majority of the votes

(63.8 per cent) at the first round, beating the other seven candidates who had been put forward by the leading political parties, and thus becoming the first president of Slovenia. In 1997 he was re-elected winning 55.54 per cent of the vote at the first ballot.[11]

In 1992 Kučan's election was also partly due to his fairly moderate political stance and modest public manner, since the Slovene public generally are quite dismissive and distrustful of charismatic leaders (Markič 1992: 752; Tomc 1993: 152), especially if they represent an extreme political line. This was another reason why in the constitutional debate a consensus was quickly achieved in favour of establishing a parliamentary system and rejecting the kind of semi-presidential system which certain experts would have fashioned along the lines of the French model. This moderate mentality prevailing among the citizens of Slovenia also clearly distinguishes this country from some of the other former Yugoslav republics, such as Serbia and Croatia, where 'heroic' leaders were retained or subsequently emerged (Markič 1992: 752).

The office of president is thus not encumbered with important political powers and consequently the president's representative role is strengthened. In addition to carrying out obligations of state protocol, initiative, and representation, the president also attends numerous events at the micro level and in so doing establishes an identification between the people and the state (Lukšič 1993: 23). And this function of the president is very important in terms of consolidating the stability of the political system; through 'minor politics the president ensures the conditions for major politics', while not having any great decision-making powers when it comes to major politics (ibid.).

Elements of the Assembly System

One of the major factors influencing the new constitutional set-up governing the president and the other branches of power was the legacy of the previous system. Over a period of decades in communist Yugoslavia an assembly system had been established. This was a system of unity of powers in which the position of the executive was essentially more subordinated to the assembly, as the supreme political and legislative organ, than is characteristic in a parliamentary or (semi-)presidential system. An example of the legacy of the assembly mentality is the fact that under the constitution ministers are appointed and dismissed by the National Assembly at the proposal of the prime minister, which is very different from the approach taken in almost all other parliamentary systems. Also, particular elements of the assembly system are present in some of the laws and in the provisions of the National Assembly's standing orders, which tend to place the government in a position that is highly subordinate in formal terms to the National Assembly (Grad 1995: 461 and 466–7).

In the past this assemblyism had gradually become ingrained in the mentality of the Slovenes, and still today is evident in a distinct mistrust of individuals bearing strong political authority. Not only does the president have weak powers and, as mentioned, the prime minister is restricted in his selection of ministers, but the president of the National Assembly also has relatively small powers as far as the running of the National Assembly is concerned. In Slovenia there is a strong desire for important political matters to be decided collectively. Even if they do have a certain charisma, individuals can only establish themselves as strong leaders within a particular political party, with the support of its members and followers. And at the level of state institutions this charisma is lost, which forces the most visible state officials to act with moderation and caution in public. We can presume that this, too, is a reflection of the collectivist political nature of the Slovenes, which can only be fundamentally changed by exceptional or crisis situations.

These, then, are some of the basic assumptions on which the current position and role of the Slovene president are founded, assumptions which reflect historical development and the events that directly influenced the formation of the new constitutional system in Slovenia. Only the future development of the president of the republic as a constitutional institution will reveal whether the semi-presidential elements will gradually lead to strong presidencies—within the framework of the system as it exists, of course—or whether the role of the president will remain largely symbolic and marginal compared to that of the parliament and the government.

THE CONSTITUTIONAL POWERS OF THE PRESIDENT, PRIME MINISTER, AND PARLIAMENT

The basic function of the president is to represent the Republic of Slovenia and to act as the supreme commander of the defence forces, as well as to carry out certain other tasks (mainly of a protocol nature) which the president performs in accordance with the constitution.

The office of president is incompatible with any other public office or employment. Since, under the constitution, Slovenia does not have a vice-president, in the event of the president being permanently incapacitated, or in the event of his death, resignation, or termination of office for any other reason, the duties of the president of the republic are taken over by the president of the National Assembly until the election of a new president of the republic. In this case the vote to elect a new president must be called within 15 days of the termination of office of the former president. The constitution does not determine who stands in for the president of the republic if the president of the National Assembly is unable to do so.

In Slovenia the parliament has less of an influence on the position of the president than is typical in most other parliamentary systems, while the president has comparatively little opportunity to influence the position and workings of parliament (Grad 1995: 464). Moreover, the role of the president in the formation of the government is significantly less important in the Slovene system than in most other parliamentary systems (ibid. 462).

The Election of the President of the Republic

The president is elected at a direct, general election conducted by secret ballot. This popular election gives the president an important integrative role in the country (Rupnik, Cijan, and Grafenauer 1994: 193). A presidential election is called by the president of the National Assembly. Presidential candidates may be proposed by any of the following: (1) a group of at least ten deputies of the National Assembly; (2) a political party backed by the signatures of at least three deputies or 3,000 voters; (3) at least 5,000 voters. Each deputy or voter may only give their signature in support of a candidacy once. The law provides that no one may simultaneously stand as candidate for president and for member of the National Assembly or National Council.

The candidate with a majority of valid votes cast is elected president. The president is elected for a term of five years and may serve no more than two consecutive terms. Only Slovene citizens may be elected president. Unlike most other systems, the constitution sets no special age restrictions on presidential candidates. Under constitutional and legal rules therefore in Slovenia each citizen who has attained the age of 18 years and whose legal capacity has not been withdrawn is eligible to vote for and to stand for election as president.[12]

The Powers of the President in the Procedure to Elect the Government

In Slovenia, along the lines of the German model, after parliamentary elections have been held the president proposes to the National

Assembly a candidate for prime minister, but unlike the German system the president plays no role in the appointment of ministers. Before proposing a candidate for prime minister, the president must hold consultations with the leaders of the parliamentary groups, but is not bound by their opinions and proposals. If the prime ministerial candidate does not obtain the required support in the National Assembly, which is an absolute majority of the votes, the president may propose another candidate, or the same candidate again, within 14 days and after holding renewed consultations. However, in this 'second round' candidates may also be proposed by the parliamentary groups themselves or any group of at least ten deputies. If several candidates are proposed within the 14-day period, each is voted on separately, with the candidate proposed by the president being voted on first and then, if that candidate is not elected, the other candidates are voted on in the order in which they were proposed.

If no candidate is elected the president must dissolve the National Assembly and call fresh parliamentary elections unless within 48 hours the National Assembly resolves to conduct a further vote for the office of prime minister, when an ordinary majority of the votes will suffice (in this case a minority government may be formed). At this ballot a vote is held in respect of the individual candidates in the order of the number of votes they received in previous ballots, and then new candidates are put to the vote, with any candidate put forward by the president again having precedence. If no candidate manages to secure the required majority of votes at this ballot the president dissolves the National Assembly and calls new elections.

Besides this case, the constitution envisages only one other circumstance in which the National Assembly may be dissolved, which is when the government fails to carry a vote of confidence. The prime minister may require a vote by the National Assembly on a motion of confidence in the government. If this vote of confidence is not carried by a majority of all elected deputies, the National Assembly must, within 30 days, either elect a new prime minister or express its confidence in the incumbent prime minister in a fresh vote, otherwise the president dissolves the National Assembly and calls new elections. The constitution envisages no other possibility for a dissolution of the National Assembly, which means that constitutionally the National Assembly is unable to dissolve itself. The president may not make an independent decision on whether or not to dissolve the National Assembly but must do so in both cases outlined above.

After the National Assembly and the government have been formed following elections the president maintains a certain cooperation with them, but no longer has any powers that would enable him to intervene directly in their operations. The only exception is the situation where the National Assembly is unable to convene owing to a state of emergency or war. In such exceptional circumstances the president may, at the proposal of the government, issue decrees with the force of statute.

The Powers of the President in a State of Emergency or War

The National Assembly decides on the declaration of a state of emergency or a state of war, and on urgent measures in such situations, at the proposal of the government. The National Assembly also decides on the use of the defence forces. If, however, the National Assembly is unable to convene, the president is empowered by the constitution to proclaim a state of emergency or a state of war at the proposal of the government, and to decree the introduction of urgent measures and the use of the armed forces. In a state of emergency or war, the president may, at the proposal of the government, issue decrees relating to defence with the binding force of statute, decide on the use of the Slovene army, on the introduction of work and material duties, and on a general mobilization during a state of emergency. The president must submit any such decision to the National Assembly for confirmation as soon as it is able to convene.

By issuing decrees with the binding force of law in a state of emergency the president may also, as an exception, restrict certain human rights and fundamental freedoms, except for some of these rights which protect the most important human values.[13] However, extraordinary measures based on such decrees may not cause inequality based only on certain personal characteristics of an individual. From this it is clear that a presidential decree with the force of statute may have not only statutory power but also constitutional power, since it may temporarily restrict or cancel certain constitutionally determined basic rights.

While the president must submit a decree with the force of statute to the National Assembly for confirmation as soon as it convenes, the constitution does not determine what happens in the case where the National Assembly does not confirm a presidential decree of this nature. In such a case, not only does the decree cease to be valid but some writers claim that if the decree is not ratified the president may be charged by the National Assembly before the Constitutional Court with a violation of the constitution (see Kaučič 1995: 267). The right of the president to issue decrees with the force of statute is therefore only an extraordinary and temporary power which cannot be taken to permit autocratic or arbitrary behaviour of any sort.

The Role of the President in the Legislative Process and the Opportunity for the President to Influence the Work of the National Assembly

In the legislative process the president's only power is to promulgate laws. The president has no formal right of statutory initiative, nor does he have the possibility to directly participate in the legislative procedure. He is not able to submit a veto in respect of laws or any other enactments and may not demand a legislative referendum. The only influence the president may have on the legislative process and other parliamentary procedures is through his opinions and suggestions, which are not binding on the National Assembly (see Ribarič 1996: 80–1). Additionally, the president may demand that an extraordinary session of the National Assembly be called, which gives him the opportunity to put his opinions and suggestions directly to parliament.[14]

The president must promulgate a law within eight days of its enactment. In Slovene constitutional theory he cannot refuse to do so because the promulgation of laws is a constitutional duty of the president. If the president were to refuse to promulgate a law, theorists have proposed that this duty of his should be taken over by the president of the National Assembly, who signs laws in any case, and who stands in for the president when he is unable to carry out his official duties (Kaučič 1995: 264).

Unlike certain other parliamentary systems, the Slovene constitution does not permit the president to issue acts for the implementation of laws (such as decrees), let alone acts having the nature or force of a law, other than, as explained earlier, in the exceptional circumstances of a state of war or a state of emergency, and then only at the proposal of the government.

The standing orders of the National Assembly contain provisions ensuring that the president is kept informed of everything happening in the National Assembly (he is notified of sessions taking place and of the receipt of material relating to matters on the Assembly's order of business). If the president conveys his opinion on a particular matter to the National Assembly without being requested to do so, the president of the National Assembly must forward that opinion to all deputies and to the relevant working body, but the opinion does not bind any of the deputies to anything. The president also has the right to explain his opinions and positions on specific matters directly at a session of the National Assembly. And under the constitution the National Assembly may require the president to express an opinion on a particular matter. In practice such formal communication between the president and the National Assembly has been minimal. The president has so far not exercised the right to give a presentation of his opinion in person to the National Assembly, while the National Assembly has only twice called upon the president to provide an opinion (see Ribarič 1996: 81).

Charges against the President, the Prime Minister, or Ministers before the Constitutional Court

Like the prime minister and the ministers, the president does not enjoy immunity and so may be criminally liable for his actions under generally valid regulations. In addition, the constitution separately regulates the so-called 'impeachment' of the president. If, in the course of carrying out his duties of office, the president acts in a manner contrary to the constitution or commits a serious breach of the law, he may be charged before the Constitutional Court upon the proposal of the National Assembly. The Constitutional Court either upholds the charge or acquits the accused president. With a two-thirds majority of the votes of all nine judges, the Constitutional Court may also decide to dismiss the president from office. After the Constitutional Court has received a resolution from the National Assembly on an impeachment of the president, it may decide that the president must temporarily cease to hold office until it rules on the charge.

Impeachment hearings against the president are held in public and the president himself is invited. If the president resigns during the proceedings or if his term of office ends, the Constitutional Court terminates the proceedings. However, even in this situation the Constitutional Court must continue the proceedings if specifically requested to do so by the National Assembly or by the president himself.

The National Assembly may also bring charges against the prime minister or other ministers before the Constitutional Court if it believes that they have violated the constitution or broken the law in the course of carrying out their duties of office. The Constitutional Court deals with a charge of this nature in the same way as it does an impeachment of the president. If a proposal is submitted to charge the prime minister, the president must, at the request of the National Assembly, give his opinion on it, and the prime minister must give an opinion on a proposal to charge any individual minister.

Parliamentary Inquiry into the Actions of the President and Other Holders of Public Office

As far as the accountability of the president is concerned, and also that of the prime minister and other ministers, it should be added that in accordance with the constitution and the law, they, like every other holder of political office (such as deputies of the National Assembly or members of the National Council), may be subject to a parliamentary inquiry to determine their political responsibility. A parliamentary inquiry is held in respect of matters which do not involve a direct violation of the constitution or the law, and hence they do not fall within the jurisdiction of the ordinary courts or within the framework of an impeachment, but do involve actions on the part of public officials which are inappropriate and damaging, politically or otherwise (Ribarič 1995: 277–85).

Other Powers of the President

The president is also responsible for numerous other matters which do not have any major direct political impact. Other duties of the president are:

- to call elections to the National Assembly and to call the first session of a new National Assembly;
- to accredit and revoke the accreditation of Slovene ambassadors and envoys and to accept the credentials of foreign diplomatic representatives;
- to publish ratification documents;
- to grant pardons;
- to confer decorations and honorary titles;
- in the procedure to ratify an international treaty, to propose to the Constitutional Court that it express an opinion on the treaty's conformity with the constitution;
- to propose to the National Assembly the election of Constitutional Court judges and five (of the 11) members of the Judicial Council;
- to appoint public officials where so determined by law (currently the relevant laws provide that the president only proposes to the National Assembly the appointment of the Human Rights Ombudsman, nine members of the Court of Auditors, and six members of the Bank of Slovenia Council plus its governor).

It should be noted that the constitution does not prescribe the countersignature of the prime minister or individual ministers to acts passed by the president, which reflects the constitutionally restricted powers of the president (Kaučič 1995: 272). So far this has not caused any problems in practice or any theoretical reconsideration, although the idea of countersignature in principle would not be incompatible with the general concept of the Slovene constitution (Ribarič 1997: 47).

The Relationship Between the National Assembly and the Government

The relationship between the National Assembly and the government is one that is basically quite typical of a parliamentary system, although there are certain exceptions which call to mind the assembly system. The National Assembly elects the prime minister and appoints the ministers, and also directs the work of the government, primarily through legislation. The constitution stipulates that the government is independent and the individual ministers are independent within the scope of their particular portfolios, and that the government and ministers are accountable to the National Assembly. The prime minister is responsible for the unity, direction, and administrative programme of the government and for coordinating the work of the various ministers. The ministers are collectively responsible for the work of the government and each minister is separately responsible for the work of his own ministry.

As the organ of executive power and the highest body of state administration, the government determines, directs, and coordinates national policy in accordance with the constitution, the laws, and other general acts of the National Assembly. To this end the government issues various executive regulations and other acts, and adopts political, economic, financial, and other measures which are important for the country's development. The government proposes to the National Assembly the adoption of laws, the national budget, national programmes, and other general acts which lay down the principles of long-term policy in individual areas. In carrying out its functions, the government is independent, but obviously within the constitutional and statutory framework and within the scope of the national budget, and the policy principles and long-term orientations of the National Assembly. On matters concerning the directing of national policy, the implementation of laws and other regulations passed by the National Assembly, and the overall administrative functioning of the state, the government is accountable to the National Assembly.

The primary powers of the National Assembly are:

- to enact and proclaim amendments to the constitution;
- to adopt laws, the national budget, and the final account of the national budget;
- to ratify international treaties;
- to adopt its own standing orders;
- to adopt national programmes, declarations, resolutions, recommendations, positions, and decisions;
- to commission a parliamentary inquiry;
- to call a referendum (constitutional, legislative, or consultative);
- to vote on a motion of confidence or no confidence in the government;
- to decide on the lodging of impeachment charges against the president, the prime minister, or any other minister before the Constitutional Court;
- to decide on the immunity of deputies, judges, and Constitutional Court judges;
- to decide on the declaration of a state of war or a state of emergency;
- to decide on the use of the defence forces.

In addition, the National Assembly has the power to elect, appoint, and dismiss the prime minister, other ministers, the president and deputy president of the National Assembly and other officials in the National Assembly, members of permanent delegations of the National Assembly to international organizations, judges, Constitutional Court judges, five members of the Judicial Council, the governor of the central bank, the members of the Court of Auditors, and other holders of public office as determined by statute.

The National Assembly is able to supervise the work of the government and establish its responsibility chiefly through its working bodies, parliamentary questions, interpellations (where after a parliamentary question and debate the deputies may require a vote on a motion of no confidence in the government or an individual minister), a constructive vote of no confidence, or by lodging impeachment charges against the prime minister or an individual minister before the Constitutional Court. The government, for its part, is able to influence the work of the National Assembly primarily through its position as a proposer of laws and other acts. The prime minister may also require the National Assembly to vote on a motion of confidence in the government. Such a vote may be tied to the passage of a particular law or some other decision in the National Assembly. And if the decision is not adopted in the National Assembly, in other words if the Assembly fails to express its confidence in the government, then the National Assembly must, within 30 days, elect a new prime minister or express its confidence in the incumbent prime minister in a fresh vote, otherwise the president, as explained earlier, must dissolve the National Assembly and call new elections.

Jurisdictional Disputes between the President, the National Assembly, and the Government

The constitution determines that disputes over jurisdiction between the National Assembly, the president, and the government are decided by the Constitutional Court. In accordance with the law, the Constitutional Court begins proceedings at the instigation of any of the three which believes that one of the others has encroached upon or assumed matters within their own competence. The Constitutional Court delivers a ruling to determine which of the three is competent, and may abrogate or set aside any regulation found in its deliberation to be unconstitutional or unlawful.

THE NATURE OF THE PARLIAMENTARY MAJORITY AND THE RELATIONSHIP BETWEEN THE PRESIDENT AND THE MAJORITY

The Influence of the President on the Formation of the Government

In general terms the strength of the president depends of course on the relative strengths or weaknesses of the competing branches of power. Where parliaments are highly fragmented, the governing coalitions unstable, and the courts inexperienced, even a president with weak powers can have a decisive influence (Holmes 1993/4: 36). Despite the fact that the political situation in Slovenia is not yet sufficiently consolidated, no situation has yet emerged in practice which would directly and transparently give the president a dominant political influence.

Deputies of the National Assembly are elected under a proportional system, which means that immediately after a general election intensive negotiations proceed on the formation of a government coalition.[15] The participation of the president in these negotiations takes the form of consultation with the representatives of the parliamentary groups, more than once if necessary, in order to determine which candidate for the post of prime minister has the greatest possibility of attracting majority support in the National Assembly. As mentioned earlier, the president does formally enjoy the right to propose a prime ministerial candidate independently, but is obviously restricted in this by the distribution of power within the National Assembly.

If a clear and solid coalition emerges among the parliamentary parties after an election, then the president will generally propose the candidate from this coalition as prime minister. In no way can consultations with the president override the deciding role of parliament (Ribarič 1992*b*: 692), but in circumstances where several coalition options emerge the president's role in proposing a candidate may be much more important. This, however, only applies to cases such as that which followed the 1996 general elections, when, with the 90-member National Assembly symmetrically polarized (45:45), the defection of a single member of parliament from one group of parties to another meant that the candidate proposed by the president was elected. Under different circumstances, where the process of negotiation and election of a prime minister may involve a larger 'redistribution' of party votes, after a first unsuccessful round of voting a candidate representing another option opposing the president's choice may be proposed by an individual parliamentary group or an ad hoc group of at least ten deputies.

It should be said that ever since the first democratic elections in 1990 no clear, typical way of forming coalitions has established itself. The new and modernized parties have formed quite diverse coalitions—from the Demos coalition based on principles, to the so-called 'small coalition' at the end of the term of the first democratically elected Slovene Assembly (in 1992), to the 'grand coalition' of three quite different parties in the National Assembly's first term (1992–6), and the current 'pragmatic coalition' of the Liberal Democratic Party and the Slovene People's Party (see Zajc 1997: 15). Such development would suggest that with the current proportional electoral system the political scene in Slovenia at least for the next few years will remain rather unpredictable and, hence, each governing coalition in parliament will largely be a result of the prevailing balance of forces between the parliamentary parties. Nevertheless, over the long term we can expect that this situation will gradually calm down and lead to two or three stronger political blocs emerging, with a greater transparency developing in the relations between them. This will indirectly be helped by party discipline, which is increasing all the time, and especially among the parliamentary parties.

If the success of the parliamentary system depends on conditions or factors such as: (*a*) relatively disciplined parties, (*b*) a level of party loyalty, (*c*) the capacity of parties to work together, and (*d*) the absence or isolation of anti-system parties (Linz 1994: 62), then in general it can be said of Slovenia that it already meets the last condition, and that it is gradually moving towards fulfilment of the first two conditions, while it is still some way from meeting the condition under point (*c*).

The President and the Parliamentary Coalition

In view of the electoral system and the dynamics of party life in Slovenia, it is inevitable that after elections the National Assembly will be composed of several parties, among which major compromises will be required in order for a government coalition to be formed.[16] If the president is a member or an adherent of any of the parliamentary parties, this does not generally mean he has majority support in parliament because with the current proportional electoral system it is highly unlikely that any single party could gain a predominant position in the National Assembly. An individual party can only be a relative winner of the elections. Of course, it is possible for the governing coalition to be so closely related, politically and otherwise, that at presidential elections it proposes a joint candidate, or that its fundamental principles coincide with the views of the incumbent president, without it having had a direct influence on his election.

In formal terms any alliance or opposition between the governing coalition and the president is only of minor relevance, i.e. only within the scope of their limited influence on each other and the limited powers of the president (e.g. concerning appointments and elections). Nevertheless, despite the limited powers of the president such alliances should not be underestimated, for if the president and the government coalition are tuned into the same frequency then they can exert an extremely powerful influence on public opinion, which this 'symbiosis' can more easily guide towards support for the policies of the government, thus improving the coalition's chances of remaining in power. And of course the support of the coalition significantly boosts the president's chances of re-election.

In general, the head of state can play the role of adviser or arbiter by bringing party leaders together and facilitating the flow of information among them (see Linz 1994: 47). In Slovenia this is only possible if the president enjoys the respect and confidence of the political parties and their leaders, because his meagre constitutional powers give the president very little opportunity to force this role on the parties. Given the satisfactory mechanisms for constituting parliament and the relationship between parliament and government that exists in Slovenia, the absence of the president or his minimal presence in the role of mediator or adviser to the parliamentary parties would not, as a rule, have any significant impact on the functioning of the system. But in a state of emergency the situation would be quite different; not only does the president enjoy greater formal powers in such circumstances but the fact that the president is directly elected by the people would take on a much greater significance. This could also be an important factor in the case where the president, under normal circumstances, were to use his publicly expressed views to increase the pressure on the political parties in parliament. But it is difficult to predict what kind of importance Slovene public opinion, which is quite strongly polarized along party or ideological lines, would attach to the president in such case because so far the president has avoided making any public statements that would increase the pressure on a specific political party to decide in a particular way.

Party Affiliation of the President

As a representative of the state, the president must operate on a level which is above party politics, which means, among other things, that he does not favour or discriminate against any party, but it does not mean that he has no personal stance on social and political values or that he does not express them in public (Ribarič 1996: 93). Moreover, the Slovene constitution does not prohibit the president from having formal party membership while in office.

When he began his term as president, a position for which he stood merely on the basis of popular backing and not party support, Milan Kučan suspended his party membership. Formally he has remained a member of the Renewed Party of Communists but during his period in office he has withdrawn from membership and from any activities in the administrative bodies of the party, thus symbolically and partly also in fact demonstrating that he wishes to be the president of all Slovenes. Nevertheless, such manoeuvres by individual presidents cannot realistically disguise their political allegiance or orientation, which in any case is apparent from their work. But this move by Kučan was in line with developments in most of the post-communist countries, where presidents are not tied to a particular party. In Bulgaria, Romania, and Lithuania the presidents are even legally obliged to relinquish party membership before taking office (Zielonka 1994: 98).

And so during the previous four-year term of the National Assembly and the first year of its current term, a period covering the five-year term of office of the incumbent president, Milan Kučan, it could be said that a cohabitation has existed between the president and the prime minister, and at the same time between the president and the governing coalition in parliament. But of course this cohabitation, because of the sharp separation of powers between the president, on the one hand, and the parliament and government, on the other, as well as the weak powers of the president, has had hardly any relevant effect on policy-making.

The President and the Continuity of State Authority

Whereas the National Assembly has a four-year term, the president of the republic serves a term of five years, which is intended to secure continuity of state authority. The course of time, early elections to the National Assembly, or the president ceasing to hold office before his term has expired could lead to parliamentary and presidential elections being held simultaneously, but the chances are fairly small.

The continuity of state authority embodied in the president during parliamentary elections, and during the time immediately following elections before the National Assembly is constituted, is important and contains the potential for real power on the part of the president to act as a temporary substitute for the National Assembly in a state of emergency.

CONCLUSION

With the aid of Duverger's formal classification of semi-presidential systems we can conclude that Slovenia does not have a French-style all-powerful presidency, nor a balanced presidency and government, as in Finland or Portugal, for example, but rather a figurehead presidency (see Duverger 1980: 167–77). Presidencies in this category are characterized according to Duverger by the fact that the presidents are directly elected pursuant to the constitution, but the state's political practice is parliamentary, which means that the power of the president is relatively small.

Shugart proposes five basic types of constitutional system: pure presidential, premier-presidential, president-parliamentary, parliamentary with president, and pure parliamentary (see Shugart 1993: 30–1). Under this classification, the Slovene arrangements would have to be described as 'parliamentary with president'. Slovenia has a parliamentary system in which the president is directly elected (unlike a pure parliamentary system where the president is elected by parliament) but has a weak position because he has no power to decide independently on the composition of the government or to dissolve parliament, and furthermore has no power to decide independently on the adoption or implementation of laws (ibid. 31). By comparison with the constitutionally prescribed powers of the president in other former communist countries of Central and Eastern Europe, the powers of the Slovene president are among the weakest (see Lucky 1993/4: 81–94).

Elster (1993: 196) argues that the power of a president in general depends upon his capacity (i.e. his constitutional powers) to do the following: (1) conduct national defence and foreign policy; (2) call a state of emergency or introduce martial law; (3) call a referendum; (4) exercise legislative initiative; (5) exercise legislative veto; (6) appoint the government; (7) remove the government; (8) appoint and remove individual ministers; (9) dissolve parliament; (10) appoint state officials without the countersignature of parliament. Looking at Elster's criteria and the full range of possible powers enjoyed by presidents throughout the world (see Shugart and Carey 1992: 148–58), we see that the Slovene president does not have most of these powers (of Elster's criteria the Slovene president only has, to a limited extent, the powers under points 1, 2, and 9). This merely confirms the formal classification of his position and underlines the assertion that the Slovene system can only be designated semi-presidential in a formal sense, because as far as the distribution of political powers is concerned Slovenia's system can only be described as parliamentary.

In conclusion, we can summarize that, while the role of the Slovene president is weak in the formal sense, this does not prevent a particular individual as president from having a strong political influence on the other branches of power and on the public through his informal activities. But because the institution of a state president in Slovenia is still in its very early stages, it is difficult to give any reliable appraisal yet of all the more important aspects. So far the constitutional position and role of the president have not given rise to any serious concern among the public, and so we cannot really expect any changes at least over the next few years, regarding the constitutional regulation of the institution of president of the republic. But of course it is only future presidents and developments in the Slovene political arena that will really demonstrate the frameworks within which the president can act and establish himself as a political player.

NOTES

1. The Slovene constitutional system is based on the principle of the separation of powers, although as far as the relationship between parliament and the government is concerned, it is more of a power-sharing arrangement which is characteristic of parliamentary systems (see Sartori 1997: 101). Moreover, the position and activities of the president are to a great extent separated from parliament and the government.

2. The National Council is a corporative body comprising 40 representatives of local interests and the interests of employers, employees, farmers, small business people, independent professionals, and non-profit-making organizations. Unlike the National Assembly which is directly elected on the principle of one person one vote, the National Council is indirectly elected, with each area of interest electing its own representative. The powers of the National Council relate almost exclusively to participation in the legislative process, although the Council has no power to make final decisions. In individual legislative debates the National Council may only transmit its opinion to the National Assembly; and following the adoption of a law it may lodge a so-called suspensory veto or require the calling of a legislative referendum. The National Council has no special relationship with the president, and indeed only has a very limited relationship with the government, which must submit to the National Council any material or information which is important for the work of the Council. In addition, representatives of the government may be invited to take part in sessions of the National Council, where they present the positions of the government.

3. For a description of the basic characteristics of these branches of power, and the relationship between them in the Republic of Slovenia, see Grad, Kaučič, Ribičič, and Kristan 1996: 91–239; Rupnik, Cijan, and Grafenauer 1994: 117–228, 243–59, and 293–308; Grad 1992: 137–49; Ribičič 1992: 173–83; Ribarič 1992*a*: 184–8; and Krivic 1992: 189–201.

4. Slovenia declared independence on 25 June 1991, when it adopted a Basic Constitutional Charter on the Independence and Sovereignty of the Republic of Slovenia. This was followed by a ten-day war in which the army of the former Socialist Federal Republic of Yugoslavia failed to prevent Slovenia from leaving the federation. Even before the end of 1991 the rest of the world was gradually beginning to recognize Slovene independence, a process which continued with increasing intensity through 1992, before culminating in acceptance into the United Nations on 22 May 1992.

5. Among the Central and East European countries, trust in the government is highest in Slovenia (43 per cent) and the Czech Republic (43 per cent), followed by Bulgaria (36 per cent), Croatia (36 per cent), Slovakia (30 per cent), Romania

(26 per cent), Poland (21 per cent), Hungary (18 per cent), Belarus (15 per cent), and Ukraine (15 per cent)—average 28 per cent. Trust in parliament is highest in Croatia (30 per cent), followed by Slovenia (27 per cent), Bulgaria (26 per cent), Slovakia (25 per cent), Romania (25 per cent), Poland (24 per cent), the Czech Republic (23 per cent), Hungary (22 per cent), Belarus (13 per cent), and Ukraine (11 per cent)—average 22 per cent. The highest level of trust in the president is in Slovenia (58 per cent), followed by Croatia (51 per cent), Romania (48 per cent), Belarus (38 per cent), Bulgaria (38 per cent), Hungary (37 per cent), the Czech Republic (36 per cent), Ukraine (31 per cent), Poland (29 per cent), and Slovakia (26 per cent)—average 39 per cent (Toš 1996: 649–50).

6. From 1991 to 1996, trust in political parties in Slovenia fell from 12 per cent to just 4 per cent, while trust in the National Assembly over the same period fell from 27 per cent to 11 per cent, trust in the government from 43 per cent to 29 per cent, and trust in the president from 68 per cent to 40 per cent (see Toš 1996: 651–4).

7. The parliamentary elections in 1996 were followed by a government crisis which lasted several months. The so-called parties of the Slovene Spring (the Slovene People's Party, the Social Democratic Party of Slovenia, and the Slovene Christian Democrats) together had 45 deputies, exactly the same as the remainder of parliament, which supported Janez Drnovšek, the prime ministerial candidate of the Liberal Democratic Party, which had the largest number of seats. President Milan Kučan decided to propose Drnovšek to the National Assembly, and because he was not elected at the first ballot, Kučan proposed him again in the second vote, since the alternative was the candidate of the right-wing coalition of the 'spring parties', who was far less acceptable for the left-leaning Kučan. However, just before the second vote one of the deputies in the right-wing group, a Christian Democrat, declared that he was prepared to cast his vote for Drnovšek in order to prevent the perpetuation of the government crisis. This meant that when it came to the vote the president's chosen candidate was elected prime minister by the narrowest of margins, and after subsequent negotiations the strongest party of the right, the Slovene People's Party, joined the Liberal Democratic Party in government.

8. For a presentation of this model in the context of the draft of the new Slovene constitution, see Cerar 1991: 130–3.

9. In an opinion poll carried out in 1989 some 86.7 per cent of respondents were in favour of a directly elected president, 4.4 per cent believed the president should be elected by the assembly of the Slovene republic, 4.1 per cent were in favour of the municipal assemblies electing the president, and 4.8 per cent were undecided (*Slovensko javno mnenje* 1989). A 1990 opinion poll revealed 82.3 per cent in favour of the direct election of the president, 7.8 per cent were in favour of the president being elected by the assembly with a two-thirds majority, 4.5 per cent thought the assembly should elect the president with an ordinary majority, and 5.4 per cent were undecided. In the same poll 30.8 per cent of respondents believed it sufficient for a presidential candidate merely to be an adult, 29.8 per cent thought a candidate ought to be older than 30, 33.2 per

cent thought a candidate ought to be older than 40, and 6.6 per cent were undecided. Regarding the possible powers of the president, it is interesting to note
that as many as 71.3 per cent of respondents thought that the president should
call sessions of the government, and 69.9 per cent believed that the president
should even preside over sessions of the government (*Stališča Slovencev ob novi
ustavi* 1992). Thus, the constitutional system eventually arrived at departs from
public opinion chiefly in that there is no minimum age stipulation for a presidential candidate (a candidate need only be at least 18 years old) and the president was granted no powers to influence the work of the government. However,
it is highly likely that at this time the respondents did not clearly differentiate
between the institutions of president and government in a parliamentary or
semi-presidential system.

10. At the time of the presidential elections in 1992 public opinion polls showed
    that even those parties whose voters had mostly supported the candidacy of
    Milan Kučan put forward their own candidates to oppose him (see Ribičič
    1996*b*: 288).

11. On 23 Nov. 1997 the incumbent president, Milan Kučan, received 55.54 per cent
    of the total vote and, thus, won the presidential elction at the first round.
    Other candidates were unsuccessful: Janez Podobnik (Slovene People's Party)
    received 18.39 per cent of the vote, Jozef Bernik (joint candidate of the Social
    Democratic Party and the Slovene Christian Democrats) 9.50 per cent, Marjan
    Cerar (independent) 7.04 per cent, Marjan Poljsak (independent) 3.21 per cent,
    Anton Persak (Democratic Party) 2.70 per cent, and Franc Miklavcic (Slovene
    Christian Socialists) 0.55 per cent.

12. By comparison, a presidential candidate in the US, Austria, and Portugal must
    be at least 35, in Germany, Bulgaria, Turkey, and Macedonia at least 40, and in
    Italy as much as 50 years old.

13. Under the constitution there is no circumstance in which it is permitted to tem-
    porarily cancel or restrict the rights guaranteed under the following articles:
    Article 17 (the inviolability of human life); Article 18 (the prohibition against
    torture); Article 21 (the protection of human personality and dignity in legal
    proceedings); Article 27 (the presumption of innocence); Article 28 (the prin-
    ciple of legality in the criminal law); Article 29 (legal guarantees in criminal pro-
    ceedings); and Article 41 (freedom of conscience).

14. An extraordinary session may be convened outside the period of the regular
    sittings of the National Assembly or during the period of the regular sittings in
    the absence of the conditions for convening an ordinary session. Extraordinary
    sessions are not only convened because of extraordinary circumstances but also
    in cases involving ordinary legislative or other procedures needing to be dealt
    with urgently. If the president of the National Assembly does not call an extra-
    ordinary session when requested to do so by the president, then the president
    may call the session himself.

15. Parliamentary seats are allocated in accordance with a proportional system with
    certain corrective elements. Special features of this system are: (1) voting takes
    place on individual candidates in constituencies; (2) a threshold of three seats
    (3.33 per cent) is set for entry into the National Assembly. This second correc-

tive element is a direct component of the majority system. For more on elections to the National Assembly, see Grad 1996: 119–20.

16. At the 1992 elections eight parties gained seats in the National Assembly, and seven parties at the 1996 elections. In 1992 the distribution of seats was as follows: Liberal Democratic Party (22), Slovene Christian Democrats (15), Associated List (14), Slovene National Party (12), Slovene People's Party (10), Democratic Party (6), Greens of Slovenia (5), Social Democratic Party of Slovenia (4). And at the 1996 elections the distribution of seats was: Liberal Democratic Party (25), Slovene People's Party (19), Social Democratic Party (16), Associated List of Social Democrats (9), Slovene Christian Democrats (10), Democratic Party of Pensioners of Slovenia (5), Slovene National Party (4). Two seats in the 90-member National Assembly are permanently reserved for representatives of the Hungarian and Italian ethnic communities.

13

Ukraine

ANDREW WILSON

Ukraine can be said to have a semi-presidential system insofar as it has direct presidential elections combined with a prime minister and a government answerable to both president and parliament.[1] Since winning independence in 1991, Ukraine has also gained a reputation for political gridlock. Both of the presidents elected since independence—Leonid Kravchuk (1991–4) and Leonid Kuchma (1994–)—disappointed the initial hopes of their supporters, building up an impressive array of powers on paper, but proving unable to match this in practice. Conflict between presidents, prime ministers, and the chairmen of parliament has been an endemic feature of Ukrainian politics, as have the frustrations of a weak and fractious post-communist party system. Kuchma faces an uphill struggle to be re-elected on schedule in October 1999.

This chapter seeks to explain why semi-presidentialism has nevertheless provided an attractive form of political compromise in Ukraine's ethnically, linguistically, and regionally divided society, despite the problems of political stasis that it has both reflected and helped to promote. There is no space here to discuss the underlying historical reasons for these divisions in Ukrainian society—interested readers may look elsewhere (Wilson 1997a). Instead, our aim is to explain why circumstances have made it difficult for Ukraine to choose any other regime type, despite the residual enthusiasm of the Ukrainian left for a Soviet, i.e. parliamentary, republic. We follow the pattern established in previous chapters by first examining how semi-presidentialism was established in Ukraine and then looking at Duverger's other key criteria: the constitutional powers of the key political actors, the nature of the parliamentary majority, and the relations between the president and that majority.

THE INITIAL SETTLEMENT

Ukraine's constitutional system emerged in two distinct bursts of activity: the first in the turbulent months before and after independence was won from the USSR in August/December 1991; the second in the intense debates surrounding the passing of a temporary Constitutional Agreement in June 1995, followed by the final introduction after six years of discussion of a new post-Soviet constitution a year later in June 1996. Arguably, the regime has therefore been founded twice, but in practice the constitutional settlement of 1995–6 did not mark as sharp a break with previous politics as many commentators had expected or hoped for (Wilson 1997*b*).

The presidency was originally established by the law of July 1991, when the USSR was still in existence and Ukraine was one of its fifteen constituent republics. At the time, Mikhail Gorbachev's reforms had allowed the republics to seize more powers, but he was still trying to keep them in the Union. Ukraine, unlike the Baltic republics, Georgia, or Armenia, was in theory still persuadable. A minority of Ukrainian politicians looked forward to independence, but most were prepared to negotiate with Moscow and saw a Ukrainian president as a means of strengthening their position in this bargaining process. Ukraine was also copying the example of Russia, where, for similar reasons, Boris Yeltsin had just (on 12 June) been elected president of the Russian Federation—also one of the constituent republics of the USSR—as a rival to Gorbachev as Soviet president.

It was therefore not originally envisaged that the new Ukrainian president would act as a head of state; his function would be to protect Ukrainian law and institutions from Moscow's interference. Significantly, the assumed main candidate for the presidency was Leonid Kravchuk, then the chairman of the Ukrainian parliament, known by its Ukrainian name of Verkhovna Rada (Supreme Council or Supreme Soviet). The 1991 Act said little about how the Ukrainian president would actually relate to Ukrainian institutions. As a separate Ukrainian state then seemed a distant prospect, Ukrainian law-makers simply grafted the presidency onto the already existing parliamentary (soviet) system without really considering the consequences this would have in institutionalizing conflict between the various branches of power once the latter began to act with real independence.

Some members of the then opposition did propose that Ukraine go further and adopt an executive presidency, but the Communist Party was implacably opposed, and in 1991 was still powerful enough to block the suggestion (left-wing opposition to any expansion of presidential power has been a persistent feature of Ukrainian politics ever since).[2]

However, the law had only been on the statute book for one month (first elections were pencilled in for December 1991), when the failed Moscow coup of August 1991 brought about the destruction of the USSR and radically changed political circumstances. On 24 August the Ukrainian parliament declared independence and on 30 August the local Communist Party was banned. Newly independent Ukraine now needed a head of state, and the institution of the presidency was to be an important means of symbolizing and personifying that independence and emphasizing the break with Moscow. With the main traditional channels of governance disabled, Ukraine also badly needed any kind of political leadership.

Moreover, although parliament had adopted the Declaration of Independence by 346 votes to 1, Ukrainian leaders were well aware that elite consensus was potentially fragile and that the underlying ethnic, linguistic, and regional divisions that had dictated Ukraine's relatively cautious approach before August were still in existence. Ukraine's 11.4 million Russian minority, concentrated in the cities of the east and south, had to be reconciled to the break with Russia. Ukrainian leaders were also sensitive to the historical and religious divides between those parts of the country which had long-standing connections with Russia/the USSR, where millions of Ukrainians spoke Russian as a first language, and the western territories that had only become part of Soviet Ukraine in the 1940s.[3] As late as March 1991, 70.5 per cent of Ukrainian voters had backed Gorbachev's referendum on the preservation of the USSR, with only west Ukraine voting solidly against, and Ukrainian elites were anxious to win maximum support in a new referendum to confirm parliament's Declaration of Independence to be held on the same day as the presidential election. The predicted economic benefits of independence and Kravchuk's 'safety first' campaign stressing experience and continuity were therefore presented to voters as a package.

Ukrainian leaders were also concerned to avoid opening up the political system to nascent outsider competition (Easter 1997), and the presidency seemed a good way of shielding existing power-holders from the amorphous and unpredictable parliament (Protsyk 1995). Most of the 346 deputies who voted for independence were former Communist apparatchiks, and it was informally understood that they would be allowed to remain in power so long as their new-found enthusiasm for the national cause remained solid.[4] A consensus of support for a somewhat stronger presidency therefore began to develop, on the assumption that the office would be shaped by the personality and political style of Kravchuk, in particular his characteristic preference for governing through brokered compromise between elites.

This was reflected in the choice of constitutional changes made in early 1992,[5] after the popular vote on 1 December 1991 had safely confirmed Kravchuk as president (61.6 per cent) and Ukraine as an independent state (90.3 per cent). The president was now described as 'the head of state and head of the executive power in Ukraine', and granted the power to appoint the prime minister and other leading ministers, subject to parliamentary approval. The government (Cabinet of Ministers) was now described as being 'subordinate to the president', whom it was envisaged would now exercise considerable executive functions. Kravchuk was even granted limited powers to rule by decree.

However, the underlying assumption of collective elite responsibility left relations between the president and the rest of the executive still seriously underdefined. Kravchuk was reluctant to take responsibility for any programme of real change, and was happy to share power and, more importantly perhaps, responsibility. Although other constitutional innovations included creating a series of extra-parliamentary structures, such as a presidential *Duma* (advisory council) and a system of *predstavnyky* (prefects) in the provinces, their real purpose was to bind all central and regional elites to the independence project rather than to introduce one-man rule.[6] Kravchuk's decree powers were confined to the area of economic reform, where he remained cautious and inactive, before relinquishing the power after only a few months in October 1992.

Significantly, the president gave an annual report to parliament, but only the prime minister was 'accountable' to it for his actions. On the other hand, Kravchuk failed to establish a lasting working relationship with any of his prime ministers, who were frequently dumped when political circumstances required. Kravchuk's rolling cycle of elite appeasement led to him appointing and dismissing four prime ministers in his two and a half years in office: Vitol'd Fokin (to October 1992), Leonid Kuchma (October 1992 to September 1993), Yukhym Zviahil's'kyi (September 1993 to May 1994), and Vitalii Masol (May 1994 to February 1995).

Moreover, Ukraine retained certain key features of the institutional design of the communist era. In particular, the chairman of parliament was also a significant figure, to the extent that Ukraine was almost governed by a triumvirate. Once elected by a caucus vote of deputies, he directed debate and procedure in the manner of the speaker of the American House of Representatives, as well as chairing the powerful presidium of parliament and its network of committees. Moreover, the system of local soviets, in a direct hangover from the communist era, was under his control as chairman of parliament, the 'Supreme Soviet' of Ukraine. Kravchuk had held the post before 1991 and his successor, Ivan Pliushch, used it to launch an ultimately unsuccessful bid for the presidency in 1994. Kravchuk's successor, Leonid Kuchma, also had difficult relations with Pliushch's successor, Oleksandr Moroz, the head of the Socialist Party of Ukraine.

Kravchuk's defenders have argued that the new president, sensing the fragility of the state, was not prepared to risk political stability by embarking on any radical reform project. Ukraine had to rely on old political institutions or risk a power vacuum. Moreover, the delicate balance of Ukraine's ethno-linguistically and regionally divided society could supposedly only be preserved if existing elites were left in power (Motyl 1995). This meant, however, that Kravchuk was unable to fight on a record of governmental activism when he was forced into an early election in the summer of 1994 (Arel and Wilson 1994*b*; Litvin 1997; Lytvyn 1994). His economic record (output down some 40 per cent, inflation at 10,200 per cent in 1993 alone) was truly awful. Instead, Kravchuk sought to mobilize a constituency of nationalist support by standing on the achievement of Ukrainian statehood and depicting his main rival, former prime minister Leonid Kuchma, as a dangerous Russophile who would undermine state independence.

Kravchuk lost by 45.1 per cent to 52.1 per cent in the second round, as, in an election polarized between Ukrainian-speakers and Russian-speakers (the population is divided approximately equally between the two), Kuchma's pragmatic defence of Russian-speaking culture and greater emphasis on economic reform proved popular in the east and south. On the other hand, support for Kravchuk amongst Ukrainian nationalists was eroded by the parlous state of the economy. Kravchuk won every oblast west of the river Dnipro (Dnieper), bar one (Kirovohrad); Kuchma won every oblast to the east and south (Arel and Wilson 1994*b*; Khmelko and Wilson 1998). Kravchuk had, however, at least created the circumstances in which voters felt it was safe to remove him from office without threatening Ukrainian independence.

REFOUNDATION, 1995–6

New president Kuchma was temperamentally inclined to push some of the issues that Kravchuk had let lie (Lukanov 1996). Moreover, the economy at least was at crisis point. Once Kuchma launched Ukraine's first serious economic reform programme in October 1994 he presented his drive to increase presidential power as a means of forcing it through the left-dominated legislature (the left parties in fact only controlled about 40 per cent of the seats after the spring 1994 elections to parliament). Others suspected he saw it as an end in itself. Whatever the case, Kuchma developed a wide-ranging agenda for constitutional reform within a few months of taking office, concentrating in particular on his inability to dissolve parliament, his lack of an effective veto over its often unpredictable legislative output,[7] and the difficulty of controlling local elites and enforcing reform implementation in the Ukrainian regions. Kuchma therefore proposed a Law on Power to revamp the constitution, at the same time as taking a series of unilateral measures, such as granting himself expanded decree powers and the right to dismiss local elected officials. Kuchma also created a Council of the Regions as a means of binding regional elites to his administration (Wolczuk 1998).

Significantly, however, Kuchma continued Kravchuk's habit of hiding behind the prime ministerial 'shield', even, bizarrely, keeping the left-wing hangover Vitalii Masol in office during the belated launch of Ukraine's economic reform programme in October 1994, as Kuchma presumably judged he had not yet soaked up maximum unpopularity. Thereafter, Kuchma went through prime ministers as rapidly as Kravchuk. After Masol came Yevhen Marchuk (March 1995 to May 1996), Pavlo Lazarenko (May 1996 to July 1997), and Valerii Pustovoitenko (July 1997–). Kuchma also had to continue working with the left-wing chairman of parliament, Oleksander Moroz, whom he was unable to force out of office until after the 1998 parliamentary elections.

Parliament not surprisingly refused to give Kuchma's proposed Law on Power a constitutional majority (two-thirds of all deputies). However, in the spring of 1995 Kuchma's threat to appeal over deputies' heads and utilize his still fresh mandate by holding a national confidence referendum to test the relative popularity of president and parliament led to political compromise. Ukraine backed away from the possibility of repeating the October 1993 confrontation in Russia, when Yeltsin had bombed parliament into submission, and in June president and parliament signed a Constitutional Agreement to delimit authority between them (*Konstytutsiinyi dohovir*, 1995). Nevertheless, 81 deputies, mainly leftists, voted against and the Agreement had to be watered down to secure the support of the 240 who voted in favour, Kuchma having accepted that the two-thirds majority necessary to amend the constitution in line with the Agreement was unobtainable.

The Constitutional Agreement led to a considerable expansion in the powers of the presidency, largely at the expense of parliament, but not to the extent originally sought by Kuchma. Although the president was now described as 'exercising his power as head of the state executive power through heading the government', the existing balance of power between the various branches of state was not radically altered. The most important change was the introduction of a proper presidential veto power, which now required a constitutional majority (two-thirds of deputies) to overturn. The president's decree powers were also considerably extended. As under Kravchuk, Kuchma could now issue decrees on questions of economic reform, but in theory the power now extended to any area of his competence where there was no existing law. Such decrees would have the force of law until confirmed or overturned by relevant legislation. The president's appointment powers were also extended and parliament's functions of executive oversight reduced.

The Constitutional Agreement was to last for one year only and committed its signatories (president and parliament) to achieving a more long-term solution by devising a new constitution within the same period. Although the method was not specified and parliament once again dragged its feet, the uncertain outcome of the Russian presidential election in June 1996 helped to concentrate minds, and a new constitution was finally passed by 315 votes to 36 after an all-night sitting on 27/28 June (Het'man 1996)—only a few days late. Once again, the document was a compromise. The opposition of the left, many of whom still wanted to abolish the presidency altogether, was only overcome by including a long list of socio-economic rights (to work, welfare, free education, etc.) and by accepting more constraints on presidential power than Kuchma would have preferred.

THE NEW CONFIGURATION OF POWERS

Five years of piecemeal change had seemingly culminated in a lasting settlement. Nevertheless, in essentials the new constitution was little different from the 1995 Constitutional Agreement. The president lost certain powers of appointment, but gained the benefit of tougher impeachment procedures. The latter now had to be initiated by a majority of deputies. 'A decision on accusation' required a two-thirds vote, and the final vote itself a three-quarters majority. Moreover, the newly created Constitutional Court had to accept that proper constitutional grounds for impeachment (state treason or other crime) had been proved (Article 111). A farcical call for Kuchma's impeachment that rapidly petered out in September 1997 showed how difficult this would be.

The president's power to force through economic reform by decree was extended to the end of his term—edicts would now automatically became law if parliament failed to block them within thirty days. Moreover, the president's right of legislative initiative was strengthened by the stipulation that his proposals could be considered out of turn by parliament—granting the presidential programme a form of priority (Article 93). Crucially, however, despite a long and persistent campaign Kuchma was unable to win the power of dissolution (in sharp contrast to Yeltsin in Russia, neither Kravchuk nor Kuchma were ever able to free themselves of their troubles with parliament by the use of such a power). The president could only dissolve parliament in the unlikely circumstances of it failing to assemble within thirty days of the beginning of a normal session (Article 90). This provision had little effect in practice, although it did make prolonged boycotts of parliament by right or left (in order to prevent sessions formally beginning) much less likely. Kuchma dropped a proposal for a bicameral parliament, as existing deputies suspected he would have too much power over the upper house.

Nor was Kuchma able to win the other key power he coveted, namely the ability to bypass parliament through the use of referenda (his threat to do so in 1995 was unconstitutional but effective, as parliament then assumed he would easily have won any popularity contest). Article 72 of the constitution allowed for the possibility of 'an all-Ukrainian referendum ... to be designated by the Verkhovna Rada or by the president of Ukraine', but at the same time confirmed the previous situation that referenda could be called on popular initiative on the request of no less than three million citizens of Ukraine (i.e. by petition). Three million (out of a total population of 51 million) was a very high number and had effectively prevented, again in contrast to Russia, the use of referenda since December 1991.[8] Referenda could not be held on issues of taxes, the budget, and amnesty, but would be compulsory for any proposal to alter the territory of Ukraine (Articles 74 and 73). Amendments to the core principles of the constitution would also have to be confirmed by referendum (Article 156). In practice, this meant that the president could organize a referendum if he really wanted to, but that civic initiatives on controversial subjects like the status of the Russian language or relations with Russia (which the Communists campaigned for after they argued Kuchma had reneged on his 1994 campaign promises) were likely to fail.

The new constitution conferred considerable appointment powers on the president, including the right to designate ambassadors, and 'on the submission of the prime minister of Ukraine, members of the Cabinet of Ministers of Ukraine, chief officers of other central bodies of executive power, and also the heads of local state administrations, and terminate their authority in these positions' (Article 106). The latter power was particularly significant, as heads of local authorities were directly elected in Ukraine in 1994 and were often local power-brokers in their own right. The president also had the power to appoint the procurator general, one-third of the members of the new Constitutional Court, one-half of the members of the Council of the National Bank and the National Council on Television and Radio Broadcasting, and the heads of the latter, the State Property Fund (the body in charge of privatization), and the Anti-monopoly Committee (Article 106). In Ukraine's semi-reformed economy, still dominated in most spheres by state monopolies, presidential control of the commanding heights of the mass media and the privatization process was of massive importance.[9]

Parliament had to confirm some, but not all, of these appointments, namely that of prime minister (but not other ministers), procurator general, and the heads of the Anti-monopoly, State Property Fund, and Broadcasting Committees.[10] The power to appoint the head of the National Bank, granted to Kuchma by the 1995 Constitutional Agreement, was restored to parliament by the 1996 constitution. In any case, Viktor Yushchenko, head of the National Bank since 1993, was by now a powerful independent figure in his own right.

The constitution also confirmed the president's special powers over the troublesome Republic of Crimea that Kuchma had first introduced in 1995. (The Crimean peninsula was placed under Ukrainian jurisdiction in 1954 during the period of Soviet rule, but was the only part of Ukraine with an ethnic Russian majority, 62 per cent as of 1993. Crimea was made an Autonomous Republic within Ukraine even before independence in 1991. After the election of a separatist Crimean president, Yurii Meshkov, and local assembly in 1994, Kuchma dismissed Meshkov, abolished the office of Crimean 'president', and took special powers to control the Crimean government, that is the local Council of Ministers.)

According to the 1996 constitution, the head of the Crimean Council of Ministers, now effectively the highest remaining political figure in

Crimea, could only be appointed and dismissed from office by the Supreme Council of the Autonomous Republic of Crimea with the consent of the president of Ukraine (Article 136). Kuchma was usually able to place a supporter in the post—on two occasions since 1994 his son-in-law Anatolii Franchuk—although he also kept local feelings in mind. The Ukrainian president also had the power to suspend any law passed by the Crimean assembly, while making 'a simultaneous appeal to the Constitutional Court of Ukraine in regard to their constitutionality' (Article 137). The constitution also stated, somewhat confusingly, that the Ukrainian president could 'revoke . . . acts of the Council of Ministers of the Autonomous Republic of Crimea' (Article 106) without making any such appeal to the Constitutional Court.

The 1996 Ukrainian constitution also institutionalized key potential extra-parliamentary bases of presidential power, in particular the Council of National Security and Defence first established by Kravchuk (Article 107), although no mention was made of the Council of Regions created by Kuchma in 1994. The Ukrainian president was also Commander-in-Chief of the Armed Forces and responsible for senior military appointments. As such, the president had the power to 'forward a submission . . . on the declaration of war' to parliament, and could declare a state of national or local emergency or 'ecological emergency', 'with subsequent confirmation of these decisions by the Verkhovna Rada [parliament] of Ukraine' (Article 106). Internal security forces were also under his control.

In summary, the 1995–6 settlement did much to define the evolving nature of the Ukrainian version of semi-presidentialism, but many aspects of that system remained *sui generis*. Moreover, the settlement rested on a new constitution that was often unclear or contradictory, or that failed to achieve what it sought to do. It was also far from clear how the new constitution would operate in practice, or if it would indeed determine political practice rather than vice versa. One leading commentator argued that the settlement was best described as a truce between clans, akin to the 1215 Magna Carta, rather than a definitive resolution of all outstanding political problems (Zolotor'ov 1997).

WEAKNESSES AND CRITICISMS OF THE 1996 CONSTITUTION

A first obvious problem was that the 1996 constitution aimed towards a classic separation of powers, but did not fully establish it. The president's power to issue decrees and the stipulation that the Cabinet of Ministers must follow all 'acts of the president' (Article 114) gave the head of state some quasi-legislative functions. His power to overturn acts of the Cabinet of Ministers, decisions of local authorities, and acts of the Council of Ministers of the Crimean Republic (Articles 106 and 118) usurped some of the functions of a Constitutional Court (Zolotor'ov 1997; see also Tatsii *et al.* 1996; and Bilous 1997). Moreover, the president also had the ability to create and to liquidate central organs of executive power (Article 106), in effect the kind of power to shape the political system normally reserved for founding assemblies.

On the other hand, there was no real provision, as there is in France, for the president to preside at meetings of the Cabinet of Ministers,[11] or for the president to countersign ministerial acts. Nor was it clear exactly how the Cabinet of Ministers was supposed to carry out the acts of the president (Articles 113 and 116). Both Kravchuk and Kuchma developed large presidential administrations of their own, but practical coordination of the activities of president and government remained difficult.

The position of the government, sandwiched between parliament and president, was also problematical. It had neither the strength and coherence provided by representing the parliamentary majority, nor the direction imposed by being truly a creature of the president. Successive governments were too often politically opaque, organizationally passive, and lacking in any stimulus to action. There was no reward for taking positive action, only the threat of losing parliament's confidence and/or the president's support. Too many Ukrainian prime ministers have therefore been unaffiliated technocrats with short-term and fragile mandates (Protsyk 1995). Inaction, however, inevitably led to declining public confidence and a rapid turnover of prime ministers—Ukraine averaged one a year after independence, in marked contrast to Chernomyrdin's long service as Russian prime minister.

Nevertheless, despite president and parliament sharing 'dual control' over the government, the advantage lay with the president. A particularly controversial aspect of the new constitution was the stipulation that the prime minister was accountable to the president rather than to the parliamentary majority (Article 114). Elections that changed the composition of parliament need not necessarily change the composition of the government, whereas the election of a new president automatically led to the resignation of the whole government (Article 115). Significantly, the new parliament elected in March 1998, although little different in composition from its predecessor, began a campaign to change this clause almost immediately.

The president could dismiss the prime minister and the government at any time (Article 115), but a parliamentary vote to censure the government required the support of one-third of deputies to initiate and a majority of all deputies, not just of those present and voting, to succeed. The constitution also limited parliament's power over the government through the provision that 'the issue of responsibility of the Cabinet of Ministers . . . shall not be considered by the Verkhovna Rada of Ukraine [parliament] more than once during one regular session' (Article 87). In other words, a vote of no confidence could only be proposed once a session, not passed. If it failed to pass, deputies could not try again. Moreover, in order to try to avoid the kind of constant parliamentary harassment of government that left-wing deputies engaged in after the launch of Ukraine's economic reform programme in October 1994, the same article of the constitution stipulated that once deputies voted to approve the programme of the Cabinet of Ministers a confidence motion could not be proposed for a year thereafter. Taken together, the two provisions were supposed to resemble a Ukrainian equivalent of the constructive vote of no confidence required in the German Bundestag, according to which deputies cannot just vote a government out of office but must already have another to put in its place. Finally, a degree of confusion was added by the requirement that the final resignation of the prime minister and his government must be accepted by the president, with the as yet untested implication that the president could order the government to remain in post even after a successful parliamentary vote of no confidence (Article 115).

All seven Ukrainian prime ministers since 1991 have technically been removed by the president rather than parliament, although in practice of course the president was often responding to political pressure from outside. Vitol'd Fokin, for example, was removed in October 1992 after an earlier vote of no confidence in July (the vote received a plurality but not a majority), Pavlo Lazarenko was removed in July 1997 after criticism at the congress of the main centre party, the People's Democratic Party. Kuchma haughtily declared before the 1998 parliamentary elections that he saw no reason why they should effect his existing choice of prime minister.

The contradictions and confusions in the constitution were not helped by the fact that the position of the Constitutional Court as a constitutional guardian and arbiter and policer of the separation of powers had still to be established. Despite several attempts, Ukraine was unable to elect a Constitutional Court until the winter of 1996/7, and the line the

Court took in its first decisions would have a crucial long-term effect on the political system. Unfortunately, Ukraine's general legal system had no well-established tradition of freedom from political interference. Most judges were still political appointees from the Soviet era. One-third of the Court's members were appointed by the president, one-third by parliament, and one-third by a Congress of Judges of Ukraine (six each). The Court itself elected its chair by secret ballot, but only for one three-year term (Article 148).

IN SEARCH OF A PARLIAMENTARY MAJORITY

The Ukrainian president's apparent relative advantage in terms of constitutional powers has, however, been offset in practice by problematical relations with the parliamentary majority, or, more precisely, by the absence of such a majority.

Neither Ukrainian president has ever enjoyed a position of stable control over parliament. The main reason for this situation, equally apparent in both the 1990–4 and 1994–8 parliaments, has been Ukraine's weakly developed party system. As in all post-communist states, the amorphous and embryonic nature of civil society has made party formation difficult, but in Ukraine the process has also been hindered by the sub-national divisions that hinder the formation of truly all-Ukrainian parties (see below) and by political and legal barriers.

As regards the latter, the 1990 elections were in effect held simultaneously with the abolition of the Communist Party's long-standing monopoly on party politics. Although an embryonic umbrella opposition movement was able to secure some representation (see below), the process of party formation in effect began after the elections (Wilson and Bilous 1993). The 1994 elections were held under a law which handicapped party development by retaining the Soviet-era system of workplace nominations and majority voting in individual territorial constituencies. National parties could not nominate candidates, only their local branches. As a result, some three-quarters of all candidates were non-party, as were around a half of those originally elected (Arel and Wilson 1994a). The majority of non-party deputies joined parties or factions after the elections, after parliamentary rules were changed to privilege factions in debate and in committee and delegation membership, but many of the new parties were therefore top-down structures, created by ambitious deputies with no real grass-roots organization.

The 1998 elections were held using a mixed voting system, with 50 per cent of the seats elected from territorial constituencies and 50 per cent from national party lists, as in the 1993 and 1995 elections to the Russian Duma. Ukraine introduced a 4 per cent barrier for parties to secure representation on the party list, lower than Russia's 5 per cent, but still a formidable hurdle in the Ukrainian context. The new system was designed to accelerate processes of party development and consolidation and increase the long-term possibility of alignment between presidential and parliamentary party coalitions. Nevertheless, eight parties were successful, although their combined vote of only 65.8 per cent led to the exclusion of the 22 other parties and blocks on the list. The proportion of deputies originally elected as independents (114 out of 450, or 25 per cent) was, however, significantly lower than in 1994.

Underlying problems remained, however. The most important was that, even after several sets of national elections, there was still no real consolidated national Ukrainian party system as such, only a series of overlapping regional party systems. Paradoxically or not, this has meant a certain stability in Ukrainian politics. The sum-total of the regional party systems tends to be a result that is quite predictable overall, as it is so difficult for parties to cross regional barriers (Arel and Wilson 1994*a*; Birch 1998). In the west of Ukraine, the historical heartland of Ukrainian nationalism, party competition is largely a contest between different brands of that nationalism. In central Ukraine moderate nationalists compete with the parties of the left and sometimes the centre, whereas in the largely Russian-speaking east and south the nationalists are shut out and the left and centre parties are the main contestants. In most places local parties compete with national alternatives and rural contests are very different from urban. Crimea has its own unique party system.

It has therefore proved impossible to date for any single party to speak for a 'majority' in Ukraine. This was of course one further factor increasing the importance of the president as the one figure with a national mandate (Shugart and Carey 1992). However, practical realities of coalition-building in Ukraine have meant that likely candidates for the presidency have had to emerge from the amorphous middle ground, both ideologically and geographically. It is unlikely that any candidate could win the presidency from either extreme—either a Communist or a Ukrainian nationalist.[12] Ukraine's most radical nationalist region, Galicia in west Ukraine, only contains about 10 per cent of the electorate. Its polar opposites, the east Ukrainian left-wing stronghold of the Donbas (Donets'k and Luhans'k) account for only 16 per cent and Russian nationalist Crimea only 5 per cent. Kravchuk came from Volhynia, north of Galicia in west Ukraine, but was strongly associated with the political elite in Kiev (Kyyiv) and did not run as a nationalist in 1991. Kuchma's political base was in the central-eastern city of Dnipropetrovs'k, an archetypal centre of Russian-speaking Ukrainian culture.

On the other hand, Ukraine's best-organized parties are concentrated on the left and on the right, while centre parties remain weak and divided. Although centrist voters are numerically dominant at election time, the amorphous identity of Ukraine's central regions and Ukraine's 'central', i.e. Russian-speaking Ukrainian, voters makes party formation and political mobilization of centrist forces relatively difficult between times (Smith and Wilson 1997). Electoral realities may have forced both Kravchuk and Kuchma to try to govern from the centre, but neither has found much consolidated support there.

The 450 members of the parliament elected in 1990 were originally divided more or less clearly between the Communist 'Group of 239' and their would-be nemesis, the national-democratic opposition umbrella movement, whose 122 deputies dubbed themselves the 'People's Council'. A further 28 deputies belonged to the 'Democratic Platform', a centrist splinter group from the Communist Party (see Table 13.1). Initially the Communists functioned as a majority caucus, albeit with increasing indiscipline, but by the time the presidential system was set up in late 1991 the USSR had collapsed and the Communist Party had been banned. Furthermore, the People's Council, deprived of its original *raison d'être*, had split into several factions.

In the latter years of the parliament, between 1992 and 1994, no single group or faction could therefore command more than fifty or sixty seats. The main successor group to the People's Council, *Rukh* (the

TABLE 13.1. *Main groups in the Ukrainian parliament, initial balance of forces*

Groups	1990	1994	1998
Left	239 (53%)	147 (43%)	177 (39%)
Centre	28 (6%)	49 (14%)	106 (24%)
Independents	61 (14%)	50 (15%)	114 (25%)
Right	122 (27%)	92 (27%)	49 (11%)
TOTAL	450	338	450

Sources: Wilson 1997*a*: 121; Arel and Wilson 1994*a*: 12–13.

Ukrainian for 'movement') had 50 deputies, the refoundation Communists (technically the For Social Justice faction created in spring 1993) approximately forty. In any case, consolidation of an effective majority was rendered difficult by the damaging provision that deputies could belong to any two factions. Politics was dominated by the amorphous middle ground, mainly former Communists, but with a sprinkling of moderates and centrists from the People's Council.

In the next set of parliamentary elections in 1994 only 338 out of 450 seats were originally filled.[13] Of these, 147 belonged to the Left Block (Communists, Socialists, and Agrarians) and 92 were on the right, including *Rukh*, which had twenty-seven. The rest belonged to a shifting kaleidoscope of centrist or independent factions. Apart from *Rukh* and the Communists, none of the 15 parties represented in parliament had more than 20 seats (25 deputies were necessary to form a faction, so most were non-party or coalitions of parties). Moreover, Kuchma's election in July 1994 came after the parliamentary elections in March (as with Kravchuk in 1991). He was therefore unable to shift the parliamentary arithmetic in his favour through any coat-tails effect. (As so often in semi-presidential systems, the failure to synchronize presidential and parliamentary elections has increased the chances of estrangement between different coalitions of political forces backing the two.)

The left parties secured the election of Oleksandr Moroz, leader of the Socialist Party, as chairman of parliament (and successfully resisted periodic attempts to oust him after 1994), and won control of the more important parliamentary committees. However, they were unable significantly to restructure the government, which remained amorphous and largely non-party. Moreover, with a plurality not a majority of the seats, the left could be outvoted if the right and centre joined together,[14] especially as the three left parties were increasingly prone to divisions both between and within themselves. In effect therefore the left began to act as a 'disloyal opposition'; they had the power to block many presidential initiatives, but were unable to form a decisive parliamentary majority of their own (Wilson 1997c).

In the 1998 elections the Communists won even more seats, 121 out of 450, but the overall balance of forces was little changed. The left parties had 177 seats in total (39 per cent), the centre 106 (24 per cent), the right 49 (11 per cent), and independents 114 (25 per cent). The parties themselves, however, emerged from the elections somewhat stronger, and it was likely that they would gradually absorb the independents, most of whom seemed likely to gravitate towards the centre parties. Nor was there a presidential 'party' in any parliament. Both presidents emerged from the amorphous parliamentary middle ground. Kravchuk never aligned himself openly with any political force. He was a 'national communist' renegade in 1990–1 and briefly flirted with *Rukh* in 1992, but neither group was a secure enough platform for his political ambitions (Wilson 1997*a* and 1997*b*; Litvin 1997). Kravchuk's re-election campaign in 1994 was backed by most nationalists and Ukrainophile centrists, but was resolutely non-party.

Kuchma's natural supporters, east Ukrainian centrists, controlled less than 50 seats after the 1994 elections. Moreover, although Kuchma made a tactical pitch for the support of leftist voters in eastern and southern Ukraine in July 1994, his adoption of a radical programme of economic reform in October quickly alienated the left parties and explains the bitterness of their subsequent hostility to his administration. Thereafter, Kuchma was forced to rely on attempts to build broader coalitions of support in the centre and/or centre-right, but the former remained difficult to consolidate and the latter insufficient in itself.

Various attempts were made to consolidate the political centre and launch a series of 'parties of power' in 1995–7, including the Popular Democrats, the party of many leading ministers, a relaunched Social Democratic party with Kravchuk as a leading member, and a state-supported Agrarian party to rival the leftist version. Former prime minister Pavlo Lazarenko took over the *Hromada* (Community) party in 1997. Kuchma also attempted to split the left by wooing the relatively moderate Moroz away from the Communists. However, the new parties competed amongst themselves and Kuchma could not risk associating himself with any one of them alone. In the 1998 elections Kuchma declined to back any single party and urged electors to vote against the left. His supporters fanned out amongst several parties, many of whom failed to make it into parliament, while the closest party to the president, the Popular Democrats, won only 4.99 per cent of the list vote and only 30 out of 450 seats.

Significantly, Kuchma was largely unable and/or unwilling to adopt a more active role after winning wider powers in 1995–6. He has never sought to bypass parliament or resort to government by decree to the extent practised by Yeltsin after 1993. In part this was because Ukraine entered a prolonged pre-election period after 1996, with the parliamentary elections in March 1998 closely followed by the presidential election in 1999 (Kuchma *de facto* announced his intention to run for re-election as early as Autumn 1996). However, it was also because Kuchma, well aware of the narrowness of his political base and the relative stability of Ukrainian political geography, was reluctant to brow-beat parliament with constitutional powers alone, especially after the 1998 elections left the parliamentary arithmetic little changed and his own position considerably weakened.

In Ukraine, therefore, there has been no real alternation between shifting parliamentary majorities, or between 'presidential' and 'parliamentary' phases of government. In the paradigmatic case of the latter cycle, Fifth Republican France, such alterations have been due either to presidents being forced to appoint prime ministers who head an incoming anti-presidential parliamentary majority (1986, 1993, 1997) or, conversely, to a new president dissolving parliament in the attempt to align parliamentary arithmetic to his own newly created majority (1981, 1988). In Ukraine, neither scenario is likely as yet. Neither president nor prime minister has ever really enjoyed a majority in parliament in the true sense, so such a cycle has been impossible.

The lack of clear-cut majorities in parliament also affects the position of Ukrainian prime ministers. Prime ministers have to be confirmed by an arithmetical majority in parliament, but have never been leaders of the majority. Presidents tend to consult with faction leaders before making their choice of premier, but even if the latter were to edge towards a common recommendation it would be unlikely to be a partisan choice—the number of factions was simply too many. Most prime ministers, like Ukraine's presidents, have emerged from the amorphous centre ground. Even when a left-wing premier was deliberately chosen by Kravchuk after the left-wing parties won a plurality of seats in the spring 1994 elections, Kravchuk managed to find one (Vitalii Masol) who was not formally affiliated to any party. In the immediate aftermath of the 1998 elections, Kuchma declared his loyalty to Pustovoitenko, even though his party, the Popular Democrats, had won only 5 per cent of the vote.

The balance of power between president and prime minister has therefore also depended on the personality of Ukraine's numerous premiers and the party and clan politics that surround them. Kravchuk's first prime minister, Vitol'd Fokin, was a weak figure handicapped by the fact that he was a carry-over from the Soviet era, who became prime minister only in virtue of his previous office (Chairman of the Council of Ministers) having been converted into the premiership. Fokin's successor, Kuchma, in contrast, was a powerful figure in his own right, backed by Ukraine's industrial elite, who was initially able to force Kravchuk to take a back seat once he was appointed prime minister in October 1992. Kuchma's successor, Zviahil's'kyi, was a regional boss from Donets'k in east Ukraine, appointed after strikes in the region in the summer of 1993, with a limited mandate to keep the region quiet. Of Kuchma's prime ministers, Marchuk and Lazarenko were more assertive than Masol, who was handicapped by having originally been Kravchuk's choice. Marchuk was a former head of the security service, Lazarenko an ally of Kuchma from Dnipropetrovs'k, but both were dismissed when they developed political ambitions of their own (arguably the non-party status of Ukrainian prime ministers encourages the development of presidential aspirations—as Kuchma himself did under Kravchuk; if prime ministers were members of the president's party they would perhaps be easier to discipline). Pustovoitenko was widely seen as a stop-gap, appointed to prepare Kuchma's re-election campaign rather than enact any real programme of reform.

CONCLUSION

The Ukrainian system is characterized not so much by the alternation of presidential and parliamentary phases around a semi-presidential mean (Linz 1994), as by the coexistence of a potentially authoritarian but rarely activist presidency with an unaccountable and populist parliament (see also Pritzel 1997). The president's constitutional position is formidable, but his position in parliament has always been weak. The division of labour could not be said to have had productive consequences, at least in terms of regularized policy outputs (Linz 1997). It has, however, helped contribute to social stability by discouraging winner-takes-all majoritarianism. The dangerous polarization that emerged in the 1994 presidential election has rightly led Ukrainians to fear the consequences of such a system. It also explains why Ukraine, often attentive to Russian example in other respects, has refrained from creating a more purely presidential system along the lines consolidated by Yeltsin after 1993.

However, Ukraine's semi-presidential system still lacks a certain internal logic. Relations between president, prime minister, and parliament remain problematical. Instead of the president directly answering to parliament for his or her policy, it is the government which is actually responsible to parliament, despite the president's considerable range of executive functions. Parliament confirms the president's appointments of prime ministers (and certain other senior appointments) and votes on approval of the general programme of the Cabinet of Ministers, but is not forced to take on any more positive responsibility. The legislature is therefore encouraged to be free-floating and to criticize all and sundry, making it even more difficult for a permanent consolidated majority to emerge. On the other hand, the president, as argued above, tends to hide behind the government and the prime ministerial 'shield'. Prime ministers tend to be given just enough authority to make their later dismissal worthwhile, but not sufficient to actually govern.

The main reason for the absence of clear fields of responsibility is the lack of strong political parties to give some backbone to the system and to help align its various parts. The 1998 elections produced some limited progress towards party consolidation, but stronger parties are unlikely to be created by constitutional engineering alone. They will also have to bridge the underlying social divisions that remain a more fundamental reason why the Ukrainian political system is diffuse and difficult to coordinate and why political leadership is such a difficult art.

NOTES

1. In terms of Shugart and Carey's schema (1992), the Ukrainian system can be considered 'president-parliamentary' (Wilson 1997*b*).
2. The left has sought to preserve the characteristic constitutional features of 'Soviet power', in particular the traditional hierarchy of 'people's assemblies' supposedly responsible to local communities but also capable of disciplined defence of 'socialist achievements'.
3. Kiev and the eastern (Right) Bank of the river Dnipro (Dnieper) were first linked with Russia in 1654; eastern and southern Ukraine were absorbed by Russia in the late eighteenth century. Russian-speakers predominate throughout the region. Central Ukraine west of the Dnipro, including the province of Volhynia, was annexed by Russia during the final Partitions of the old Polish Commonwealth in 1793–5. The rest of west Ukraine (the three sub-regions of Galicia, Bukovyna, and Transcarpathia) was only joined to the Ukrainian Republic, then a part of the USSR, during the Second World War. Ukrainian-speakers predominate west of the Dnipro, especially in the far west. In terms of religion, most Ukrainians are Orthodox, although since 1991 there have been at least three branches of the Church (the Moscow Patriarchy, Kievan Patriarchy, and the Autocephalous). Ukrainians in the western regions of Galicia and Transcarpathia have since 1596/1649 mainly belonged to the Greek Catholic Church.
4. The former opposition in fact split on the issue of whether to cooperate with Communists-turned-nationalists, but most regarded the mere fact of independence as sufficient to overcome their doubts.
5. Until 1996, the 1978 Soviet-era constitution remained in force, as periodically amended by parliament.

6. Both the *Duma* (after barely a year) and the *predstavnyky* (in 1994) were quickly abolished, demonstrating the difficulty of institutionalizing the new Ukrainian political system.
7. Before 1995 the president had no real veto, only had the power to return legislation. Should he do so, parliament could enact any proposal as law by passing it again by a simple majority.
8. Ukrainian elites were rightly wary of the effect that referenda could have in Ukraine's divided society. In particular, they worried that local leaders in Crimea or the Russian-speaking east might add questions to the ballot that could compromise Ukrainian statehood.
9. During the 1998 parliamentary elections, a strong negative campaign against former prime minister Lazarenko and his *Hromada* party was organized through the state mass media.
10. In 1997 Kuchma kept the controversial liberal, Volodymyr Lanovyi, in his position as head of the State Property Committee despite parliament's repeated refusal to confirm him in office.
11. The president often attended meetings of the Cabinet of Ministers, Kuchma more so than Kravchuk, but there was no constitutional provision for this to be regularized.
12. All elections from 1990–8 showed a similar coalition of nationalist support, concentrated in the west and amongst the central Ukrainian intelligentsia, producing a maximum of around 25 per cent of the vote (for example, in the 1991 presidential election, Kravchuk's main nationalist opponent, V'iacheslav Chornovil, won 23.3 per cent). At the opposite end of the spectrum, the Communists are the largest single party in Ukraine (in the 1998 elections they won 24.7 per cent), but even when united with the other parties of the left had a maximum support level of just over 40 per cent. The only feasible presidential strategy for the left was to form an alliance with some of the centre parties (Wilson 1997*c*).
13. The election law for 1994 imposed two distinct requirements for elections to be valid. A majority in any given constituency had to vote, and a candidate had to receive a majority of the votes cast. Originally, most elections were sabotaged by the latter provision, as Ukraine preserved the Soviet system of negative voting. Voters crossed off the names of all but their chosen candidate, but 4–5 per cent of voters might cross off every name, meaning that 50 per cent was difficult to achieve in a tight race (positive voting was introduced in 1998). When elections were rerun in the empty seats, however, voters were reluctant to turn out. Parliament was therefore handicapped by both provisions. As late as 1997, 35 seats were still without an elected deputy.
14. The key to the formation of 'situational majorities' was the centre factions. Their support (and that of moderate leftists) secured the passing of the 1996 constitution; their indifference and/or lack of voting coherence frequently led to the loss of economic reform measures.

14

Semi-Presidentialism and Comparative Institutional Engineering

ROBERT ELGIE

The recent process of democratization in Central and Eastern Europe and the former USSR has generated a considerable amount of interest in the subject of constitution-building and institutional engineering. A large number of newly democratized states have had to adopt a new constitution and choose a particular set of political institutions. Indeed, similar choices have been put before decision-makers elsewhere in Europe, notably in Italy, where profound constitutional change has been on the political agenda for a number of years now. In all of these states political leaders have been faced with the issue of whether or not there is an optimum constitutional arrangement that should be adopted. Are certain constitutional provisions better than others? One aspect of this issue concerns the question of executive/legislative relations. What regime type should a country adopt? In this respect, it is argued by some writers, most notably Linz, that the virtues of parliamentary regimes outweigh the perils of presidential regimes (Linz 1994). By contrast, it is argued by others, for example Mainwaring and Shugart, that presidential systems can be designed to function quite effectively (Mainwaring and Shugart 1997).

Needless to say, the concept of semi-presidentialism is entirely germane to these discussions and in two ways. First, many countries have, as it were, voted with their feet and actually adopted semi-presidential regimes. For example, in the countries of Central and Eastern Europe and the former USSR there are now 17 semi-presidential regimes (see Chapter 1, Figure 1.1), whereas there are only a handful of parliamentary regimes (including Albania, Estonia, the Czech Republic, Hungary, Latvia, and Slovakia) and an even smaller number of presidential regimes (Georgia, Tadjikistan, and Turkmenistan). Secondly, over and above what constitution-builders have actually decided, academics have debated the pros and cons of adopting semi-presidential structures. So,

Duverger has argued that semi-presidentialism has 'become the most effective means of transition from dictatorship towards democracy in Eastern Europe and the former Soviet Union' (1997: 137). Sartori, too, has asserted that in certain circumstances it can be appropriate for a country to opt for a semi-presidential system (1997: 135–7). By contrast, other writers have argued that semi-presidential regimes contain inherent institutional dangers. For example, Linz writes that 'as much or more than a pure presidential system, a dual executive system depends on the personality and abilities of the president . . .' and goes on to add that 'responsibility becomes diffuse and additional conflicts are possible and even likely . . .' (1994: 52).

The academic debate is the focus of this chapter. Having said that, this chapter is not concerned with the normative aspect of this debate. It does not aim to demonstrate that semi-presidentialism is either a better or worse form of government than presidentialism or parliamentarism. It is not written with the intention of establishing a definitive list of the advantages and disadvantages of semi-presidential regimes. Instead, this chapter is concerned with the terms of this debate. It aims to show that as it currently stands the debate about the pros and cons of the various regime types is fundamentally flawed. Its goal is to show that the assumptions which underlie the contemporary debate need to be reconsidered before meaningful conclusions about the true advantages and disadvantages of these regime types can be drawn.

Drawing on the country studies in the previous chapters, the first part of this chapter identifies the diverse patterns of leadership to be found in European semi-presidential regimes.[1] The second part returns to Duverger's framework for the study of semi-presidentialism and considers the importance of historical, constitutional, party political, and other factors in determining why these leadership patterns should vary so much. Finally, the third part indicates what the experience of European semi-presidentialism tells us about the issue of comparative institutional engineering.

PATTERNS OF SEMI-PRESIDENTIAL LEADERSHIP

Semi-presidential regimes demonstrate a variety of political practices. This is not a new point. Indeed, Duverger began his classic study of semi-presidentialism with the observation that in the seven countries with which he was concerned (Austria, Finland, France, Iceland, Ireland, Portugal, and the Weimar Republic) political practice varied tremendously (1980: 167). To the extent that five of these seven countries have been studied in this book and that an additional seven newly democratized countries have also been considered, it is not surprising to discover that Duverger's observation is still accurate. There is indeed a great diversity of political practice across the set of semi-presidential regimes. However, if Duverger's observation about the variety of semi-presidential practices can be confirmed, his classification of the types of leadership to be found in these regimes needs to be reconsidered. In his 1980 article Duverger asserted that there were three main types of semi-presidential practices: some countries had a figurehead presidency; other countries had an all-powerful presidency; and in another set of countries the president shared authority with the prime minister (ibid.). By drawing on the observations made in the preceding chapters plus the Portuguese experience, it can be demonstrated that Duverger's threefold classification not only fails to capture the transformation of certain semi-presidential regimes over time, it also fails to capture the essential diversity of leadership patterns that currently exist. The rest of this section will identify the basic patterns of leadership that can be found in European semi-presidential regimes.

Three points can be made about political practice in semi-presidential countries. Some countries have experienced one dominant pattern of leadership since the creation of the semi-presidential regime. Other countries have experienced a shift from one dominant pattern of leadership to another. A further set of countries have failed to experience any dominant form of leadership and continue to experience a variety of political practices.

In one set of countries there has been a single dominant pattern of leadership since the outset of semi-presidentialism. This was the case in six of the twelve countries that were examined: Austria, Bulgaria, Iceland, Ireland, Russia, and Slovenia. Two points, though, must immediately be noted. First, in the case of Bulgaria, Russia, and Slovenia, the democratic system is still comparatively young. In this sense, the pattern of political leadership may yet be a transitional one. Nevertheless, without the benefit of hindsight, it is quite reasonable to assert that there has to date still only been one dominant pattern of leadership. Secondly, in all six countries there have undoubtedly been variations over time in the relationship between the different political actors. So, for example, in Austria President Klestil has used his power to refuse government appointments more publicly than his predecessors. Similarly, in Bulgaria the Zhelev and Stoyanov presidencies have shown a number of dissimilarities. Even in Ireland, President Robinson was more active than most of her predecessors. In this sense, then, Ganev is right to imply that there are dangers in generalizing about presidential/prime ministerial relations in semi-presidential regimes. However, to the extent that generalizations are an essential element of comparative politics, then we can justifiably contend that these six countries have indeed experienced one dominant pattern of leadership since the onset of semi-presidentialism.

In terms of the actual pattern of leadership that these six countries have experienced, there is a degree of difference between them. In five of the six, the presidency has in practice demonstrated only limited powers and there has been prime ministerial leadership of the executive. This is the case for Austria, Bulgaria, Iceland, Ireland, and Slovenia. For the most part, then, presidents in these five countries can be classed, *à la* Duverger, as figurehead institutions, although at times the Bulgarian presidency may have shown itself to be more closely involved in the decision-making process than heads of state elsewhere. In Russia, though, the presidency has demonstrated considerable powers. Indeed, as White points out, in practice Russia has been deemed by some to have a superpresidential system. This means that to date the Russian presidency comes under Duverger's (somewhat exaggerated) heading of an all-powerful institution. All told, what is clear from the experience of these countries is that semi-presidential regimes can experience dominant forms of leadership but that the dominant form may be either prime ministerial or presidential.

In other European semi-presidential countries there has been a shift over time from one dominant pattern of political leadership to another. This is particularly the case for Finland, although it also applies to Portugal. In Finland, Arter insists that there has been a move from a president-dominated system of government, particularly during the long Kekkonen presidency, to a system of prime ministerial pre-eminence by the 1990s. By contrast, in Portugal there has been a shift from a presidential/prime ministerial balance, notably during the years immediately following the transition to democracy in 1976, to a system of prime ministerial government, particularly after 1982. As before, the usual disclaimers apply. First, in the case of Portugal the early years of the regime may be considered to be exceptional. Indeed, there is certainly an argument to be made that the 1982 constitutional amendments effectively refounded the regime and that ever since there has been only one dominant pattern of leadership. This implies that Portugal should really be placed alongside Austria, Bulgaria, and so on in the previous category of semi-presidential regimes. That said, on the assumption that

Portuguese semi-presidentialism began in 1976, then there is no doubt that there has been a shift from one dominant pattern of political leadership to another. Secondly, particularly in the case of the long-established Finnish regime there have clearly been variations within each of the dominant patterns of political leadership. Most notably, perhaps, Arter indicates that it was not until 1940 that the presidency began to take charge of foreign policy-making, thus deploying the full *de jure* powers of the office. Again, though, within this context it is still reasonable to argue that Finland and Portugal have both, generally speaking, experienced a transformation from one basic pattern of political leadership to another. Indeed, this is a fundamental point to be learned from the Finnish and Portuguese patterns of semi-presidential government.

In a final set of countries there is no dominant form of leadership. This is the case in France, Lithuania, Poland, Romania, and Ukraine. For example, in Poland there have been periods of presidential, prime ministerial, and shared government since the first free elections. Similarly, in Romania there was considerable presidential influence in the period immediately after free elections, since when the relationship between the president and the prime minister has become more balanced. Equally, in Ukraine the presidency has tried to be activist but has never benefited from a secure parliamentary majority, which has led to shifting alliances between president, prime ministers, and parliaments. At the risk of repetition, in all three cases, and Lithuania as well, it might be argued that the leadership pattern has not yet 'settled down' and that in the future a dominant form of leadership may emerge. As yet, though, this has not been the case and so these three countries belong more to this category of semi-presidential regimes than any other. Finally, the French case is potentially problematic. In the period immediately following the 1962 constitutional amendment the presidency was strong. However, since the mid-1980s periods of presidential government have regularly been followed by periods of prime ministerial government.[2] In this sense, it might conceivably be argued that France has moved from one dominant form of leadership (presidential) to another (alternating presidential/prime ministerial) and so belongs in the previous category of countries alongside Finland and Portugal. However, to the extent that strong presidentialism can still occur, that the presidential influence had weakened by the mid-1970s and that alternations between presidential and prime ministerial government have occurred relatively regularly since the mid-1980s, then it is best to classify France as a country in which there is no fixed pattern. Overall, what we can glean from the

French, Lithuanian, Polish, Romanian, and Ukrainian experiences is that in some semi-presidential countries there are no single dominant forms of leadership.

All of this confirms that there is a great degree of diversity in semi-presidential practices. (This diversity is captured in Figure 14.1.) Indeed, it suggests that the degree of diversity is even greater than was indicated in Duverger's original schema (1980: 167). Needless to say, this is caused by the fact that almost 20 years have passed since Duverger's research and because the experience of a new set of semi-presidential regimes has been included in the present study.[3] Therefore, having identified the diverse patterns of semi-presidential leadership, it is now necessary to explore the reasons for the diversity. Why is it that countries which operate within the same basic constitutional structure exhibit so many different forms of political practice?

EXPLAINING THE DIVERSITY OF SEMI-PRESIDENTIAL LEADERSHIP

The Founding Context

In all cases there is a clear correlation between the context in which a country adopted a semi-presidential form of government and the

One dominant form of leadership since start of regime		Shift from one dominant form to another		No dominant form of leadership
Prime ministerial	Presidential	president to prime minister	president/prime minister to prime minister	
Austria Bulgaria Iceland Ireland Slovenia	Russia	Finland	(Portugal)	France[a] Lithuania[b] Poland[c] Romania[d] Ukraine[b]

[a] president and prime minister
[b] president, prime minister, parliament
[c] president, prime minister, and president/prime minister
[d] president and president/prime minister

FIG. 14.1. Patterns of leadership in semi-presidential regimes

pattern of leadership that emerged immediately thereafter. Indeed, there is a particularly clear correlation in the case where dominant forms of leadership, be it prime ministerial or presidential, have emerged and where multiple patterns of presidential, prime ministerial, and parliamentary leadership have occurred.

In Austria, Iceland, and Ireland the founding context helps to explain why these countries have experienced a figurehead presidency. In Austria semi-presidentialism was introduced in 1929 after almost a decade of parliamentary government in which the head of state already played a largely symbolic role. Thus, the precedent for this type of system was already in place. This also meant that when the country returned to semi-presidentialism in 1945, this was effectively the condition under which the system was reintroduced. In Iceland and Ireland the situation was slightly different. Here, adoption of semi-presidentialism was a largely symbolic act. It was not designed to provide either an individual or the executive with the capacity for strong leadership. Instead, it was motivated by the desire to affirm the democratic credentials of the regime. This was significant because in both the Icelandic and Irish cases the former colonial power, Denmark and Britain respectively, was ruled by a monarch. Thus, the creation of a directly elected presidency was a clear sign of the legitimacy of the independent regime when compared with the previous situation. So, in Iceland, as Kristinsson argues, the directly elected presidency was not designed to create a new locus of power or to upset the existing balance of power which was by then already clearly tilted towards the head of government. In Ireland the same situation applied. Indeed, the choice of the first Irish president, an agreed non-political candidate, was also significant in that it cemented the leadership position of the government as the president assumed a passive role. In both cases, then, the founding context of the regime helped to set the scene for weak presidencies.

In two cases, Bulgaria and Slovenia, the founding context also helps partly to explain the presence of a figurehead presidency but for different reasons. In Austria, Iceland, and Ireland, semi-presidentialism was adopted after a number of years of democratic government. By contrast, in Bulgaria and Slovenia semi-presidentialism was adopted as part of the process of democratization itself in the period immediately following authoritarian rule. Two main motivations were present in these countries during this period. First, there was the desire to maximize the democratic elements of the system so as to mark a clear break with the past. This encouraged the installation of a new regime with a directly elected president. Secondly, there was also the desire to avoid the prospect of authoritarian rule in the future. Thus, the presidency was conceived right from the outset as a weak institution, even if in Slovenia, as Cerar notes, the public believed that a directly elected president might turn out to be more than just a figurehead. Be that as it may, the founding context again helps to explain why a dominant form of extremely limited presidential government emerged.

In two cases, France and Russia, the founding context is also relevant but this time in explaining why a strong presidency emerged. In the case of France, the 1962 constitutional amendment occurred at a time when de Gaulle was already in office and when the tradition of strong, president-dominated executive government had been established. Thus, the direct election of the presidency strengthened de Gaulle's legitimacy, and that of his immediate successors, but it also merely confirmed the existing practice of presidential leadership. In Russia the presidency was established in the context of a system which expected the executive to be a strategic actor. In contrast to the Bulgarian and Slovenian cases the Russian president was impelled to act as a modern-day tsar. Indeed, this trend was reinforced in 1993 when president Yeltsin took firm action to prevent the October coup. Thus, in both France and Russia circumstances conspired to encourage strong presidential government.

Finally, in the case of four countries, Finland, Lithuania, Poland, Romania, and Ukraine, a mixed set of conditions applied at the founding of the regime which, it might be argued, helps to account for the rather varied forms of leadership in these countries. In Finland, semi-presidentialism was a compromise between republicans and former monarchists. The result was a situation in which the president's legitimacy was questioned by one part of the political elite and yet was championed by another. The result, as Arter point outs, was a situation in which presidential, prime ministerial, and parliamentary relations were initially written in a form which allowed for many different interpretations. In Lithuania and Ukraine a similar situation applied in the sense that there was no consensus as to what role the presidency should play. As a consequence, the period following independence was, as Wilson observes about the Ukrainian case, marked by institutional conflict between the various branches of government. In Poland, the patterns of semi-presidentialism government are tied up with the collapse of the 1989 Roundtable Agreement, the ambiguities of the interim Little Constitution, and the long-standing debate as to the most appropriate role for the presidency. Again, the situation was one in which there was the opportunity for multiple forms of leadership to occur. Finally, in Romania the motivation for semi-presidentialism seems quite confused as if decision-makers wanted to maximize the legitimacy of the country's political institutions but stumbled upon the French model, or at least a particular view of it, rather by accident. In this case, too, there was ample opportunity for different patterns of governmental relations to emerge.

Constitutional Powers

Just as there is a correlation in many cases between the founding context and patterns of semi-presidential leadership so in some cases there is also a correlation between constitutional powers and leadership practices. It should immediately be noted, though, that constitutions are sometimes weak predictors of political practice. As Duverger noted in his classic article, '[a]lthough the constitution plays a certain part in the application of presidential powers, this role remains secondary compared to that of . . . other parameters . . .' (1980: 179). As might be expected, the chapters in this book confirm Duverger's observation. In some cases, there is little or no relationship between the president's *de jure* powers and the president's actual role. This is particularly the case for Iceland, where the president has some important constitutional prerogatives that have never been used, and to a lesser extent it is also the case for Austria, where, again, certain presidential powers have remained dormant. In three sets of cases, though, the correlation between presidential powers and political practice is stronger. This is not to say that the constitutional situation is necessarily the cause of the prevailing pattern of leadership. It is simply to say that the extent of the president's constitutional powers and the institution's actual powers largely coincides.

In the case of Bulgaria, Ireland, Portugal after 1982, and Slovenia, presidents who are constitutionally weak also wield few practical powers. It should be noted that in the Bulgarian case there is, however, a degree of disagreement in the literature. McGregor classes the constitutional powers of the Bulgarian presidency as amongst the strongest in Central and Eastern Europe (1994: 29). By contrast, Shugart and Carey consider the Bulgarian presidency to be one of the weakest of all presidential institutions (1992: 155),[4] which is a judgement that Ganev seems to endorse. While acknowledging this apparent difference of opinion, it seems reasonable to conclude that the relatively modest constitutional role of the Bulgarian presidency is reflected in the office's generally limited influence in practice. This is certainly the case for Ireland, post-reform Portugal, and Slovenia. In these cases the role of the president is mainly ceremonial. The opportunity for presidential leadership is constitutionally absent, even if in all cases there are still residual opportunities for presidential influence to be asserted. Thus, if the absence of presidential powers is not the only cause of limited presidentialism it is certainly a not inconsiderable institutional impediment to presidential leadership.

In Russia the opposite situation applies. The president is strong both constitutionally and in practice. The constitution is weighted heavily in favour of the president in terms of appointments, legislative powers, and the right of independent initiative. Again, the constitutional position is not the only cause of Russia's powerful presidency, but at times it has certainly bolstered the president in his dealings with the other institutions of the state.

In Finland, France, Lithuania, Poland, Romania, and Ukraine a more complicated situation can be discerned. In these countries the constitution is not skewed unequivocally in favour of one political actor or another. Instead, power is either shared or distributed ambiguously. At the same time, the pattern of leadership in these countries is for the most part mixed. Thus, it might be argued that the constitutional situation at least partly causes and certainly reflects actual political practice. In Finland, this has been most noticeable in the realm of foreign affairs where Article 33 of the 1919 constitution states that Finland's relations with foreign powers 'shall be determined by the president' but also goes on to state that the management of foreign affairs belongs to the foreign minister. This creates the conditions for various interpretations of presidential power in this domain. The same is true in France both in this area and more widely. So, even during periods of 'cohabitation' when the prime minister has been the dominant actor the president has managed to maintain a hold on foreign and defence policy-making. In Poland it was noted that the president's powers with regard to the government have proved difficult to delineate, again providing the potential for different interpretations of presidential power in varying circumstances. In Romania the constitutional division of powers is more rigid but again neither the president nor the prime minister is in a dominant position. Finally, in Ukraine the relations between the presidency and the executive were for a long time, as Wilson notes, seriously underdefined. Even then, the 1995/6 settlement merely confirmed that the Ukrainian version of semi-presidentialism was to a large extent *sui generis* and that the many of the provisions of the new constitution were either unclear or contradictory. As with the other cases, this has provided the opportunity for multiple forms of leadership rather than a single dominant form. As such, this example, like the others, confirms the correlation between constitutional powers and patterns of semi-presidential leadership.

Party Politics

In his study of semi-presidentialism, Duverger was keen to emphasize the importance of party politics in determining the nature of political leadership. In fact, he implied that this was the most important factor in this respect (1980: 182). In particular, he argued that party politics explained the discrepancies between constitutional powers and actual practice. He stated that in countries without a parliamentary majority there was likely to be the greatest coincidence between the constitution and practice, resulting in the situation where presidents and prime ministers shared powers (ibid.). He also stated that in countries with a stable parliamentary majority there was likely to be a disparity between the constitution and practice, creating in some cases a symbolic presidency and in others an all-powerful institution (ibid.).

The evidence in this book does indeed suggest that party politics can be an important factor in determining the practice of semi-presidential leadership. However, the evidence also suggests that Duverger's particular line of argument is somewhat misleading. In short, the relationship between parliamentary politics and presidential power is rather more complex than Duverger originally indicated and is not always the most important factor in explaining the diversity of semi-presidential politics. In this respect, it is useful to make three observations. In some countries, the complexion of the parliamentary majority is largely irrelevant to the functioning of the system. In other countries, the complexion of the majority is relevant and helps to explain why multiple patterns of leadership have occurred. Elsewhere, the complexion of the majority is again relevant and accounts in part for why there has been a transformation of leadership patterns over time.

In Austria, Bulgaria, Iceland, Ireland, Russia, and Slovenia the party political complexion of the parliamentary majority has had little or no effect on the pattern of leadership. This is most apparent in Ireland where the result of the presidential election has scarcely impacted upon the process of governmental politics and where changes in government have hardly affected the role of the president. In Ireland, the presidency has always been weak. In Iceland, the same point applies, although, as Kristinsson argues *à la* Duverger, this may be because the party system has been able to produce stable rather than fragmented majorities. In

Austria and Slovenia, too, the make-up of the parliamentary majority
has been of only marginal importance in determining the president's
role. So, in Austria President Klestil may have been able to prolong the
agreement between the coalition partners and prevent an election in
1995, but overall the powers of the presidency have not been particularly sensitive to the changing configuration of governmental and parliamentary majorities. Equally, in Slovenia the president's position has
not been significantly affected by the pattern of party politics, even when
government and opposition parties had exactly the same number of
deputies in the National Assembly in 1996. In both countries, therefore,
the presidency has remained weak whatever the party political situation. In Russia the opposite point is true. The presidency has remained
strong whatever the party situation, although in March 1998 Yeltsin did
find it difficult to appoint his first-choice prime minister because of
opposition in the Duma. Finally, in Bulgaria there is at least some evidence to suggest that the president's relationship with the parliamentary majority has influenced the leadership potential of the office.
However, the Bulgarian presidency still remains a relatively weak institution when compared with equivalent institutions in other countries.
We can conclude, then, that in the case of figurehead or 'all-powerful'
presidents the role of the parliamentary majority is largely irrelevant to
the role of the president. In all of these cases historical, cultural, and
constitutional factors are more important than party political reasons in
determining the dominant pattern of leadership.

By contrast, in France, Lithuania, Poland, Romania, and Ukraine the
relationship between the president and the parliamentary majority does
help to explain why multiple patterns of leadership have occurred. This
is perhaps most notably the case in Ukraine where the absence of a parliamentary majority has been the prime cause of the country's shifting
pattern of executive leadership. In Romania, Verheijen argues that in
the case of prime minister Vacaroiu the fact that he lacked a strong base
in parliament meant that he looked to the president for support. This
helped to maintain a degree of influence for the head of state. In Poland,
the president has had to face radically different parliamentary majorities at particular times and this has resulted in a variety of presiden-
tial/prime ministerial relationships. Finally, in France the presence of a
loyal presidential majority from 1962–74 meant that presidential power
was at its strongest during this period. By contrast, the incidence of
majorities opposed to the president after 1986 has caused periods of
'cohabitation' to occur during which time the powers of the president
have been weakened. In all of these cases, therefore, the nature of party

politics combines with other factors to reinforce the trend towards shifting patterns of political leadership.

Finally, in Finland the complexion of the majority is one reason why there has been a transformation of leadership patterns over time. In the first two post-war decades the fragmented nature of the party system meant that the president was obliged to intervene in the process of coalition-building. This was one of the factors which reinforced the position of the head of state within the system. From 1966 onwards, as Arter notes, the party system has been able regularly to deliver stable majority coalitions. By the late 1980s, this factor combined with others to weaken the president's role and to bring about a shift from quasi-presidential government to a less dominant presidency.

Other Factors

In addition to the importance of historical, constitutional, and party political reasons, there are other factors which help to account for the particular patterns of semi-presidential leadership that were previously observed. It would, however, be a rather fruitless exercise to try to provide a full and comprehensive list of these factors. This is because there would little or no heuristic value to any such list. As soon as it was applied to countries other than those examined in the present study then a new set of particularistic factors would emerge. As a result, all that can usefully be achieved at this juncture is to identify some of the factors that have clearly emerged during the course of the chapters to date so as to give an indication of the sort of areas which need to be considered.

In a number of chapters the personal element was important in determining the functioning of the political system. There is no doubt that if the circumstances are right individuals can shape the nature of the political process. This was particularly noticeable in the case where strong personalities were involved. So, in Finland the presidency was for a long time shaped by Kekkonen and his vision of the role that the institution should play. Similarly, de Gaulle clearly shaped the popular image of the French presidency. He created the expectation that there should be presidential leadership. At the same time, though, the political system can also be shaped by figures who have a less forceful vision of their place in the system. In this vein, Cerar points out that the Slovenian presidency was adapted to suit the first incumbent, Milan Kučan. This is at least one reason why Slovenia is an example of a symbolic presidency. Equally, Urbanavicius points out that in Lithuania president Brazauskas chose not to assume even an informal leadership role and preferred to leave the problems of governing to the prime minister and parliament. Again, this at least partly accounts for the reason why the powers of the Lithuanian president have perhaps not yet been fully mobilized. Finally, in some cases the impact of personality was important in establishing mixed forms of leadership. As such, the Polish situation was to a certain extent shaped by the rather different ambitions of president Wałeşa and then president Kwasniewski. Equally, the Romanian case was affected by first president Iliescu and then president Constantinescu, both of whom had their own policy styles. All told, it is clear that individuals operate within particular historical and cultural contexts, in the framework of a set institutional structure and with the support or otherwise of an array of party forces. And yet, on occasions, there is still the opportunity for the personal element to shape the running of the system as a whole.

Whereas the personality factor was generally influential across a number of countries, the experience of the Finnish case illustrated how a variety of different elements can be important in shaping the leadership context in a single country. In Finland, the role of the presidency was at least partly shaped by the geo-political location of the state. The need to maintain amicable relations with the Kremlin following two defeats by the Red Army between 1939 and 1944 prompted the president personally to take charge of Finno-Soviet relations, thus increasing the influence of the office. However, when the Soviet Union collapsed so too did one of the foundations of presidential power, so helping the country shift towards a more prime ministerial form of government. At the same time, the country's membership of the European Union meant that the role of the prime minister was further strengthened by virtue of, for example, the head of government's presence at European Council meetings. Thus, constitutional amendments, party system changes and personality factors have all helped to bring about a shift in Finnish leadership styles, but so too has the impact of country-specific external events.

SEMI-PRESIDENTIALISM AND COMPARATIVE INSTITUTIONAL ENGINEERING

To date this study has generated two key observations about semi-presidential politics. The first is that semi-presidential regimes are characterized by a wide variety of political practice. This variety was clearly noted in Duverger's initial study of semi-presidentialism. However, the present study has shown that the diversity of political practice is even greater than Duverger indicated. Indeed, it is reasonable to suggest that if the focus of study were to be widened so as to include semi-presidential regimes in South and South-East Asia, Africa, the Americas, and so on, then the diversity of leadership patterns would be shown to be even greater still. The second observation is that the diversity of semi-presidential leadership can only be explained by reference to a wide variety of factors. Again, the most important of these factors were identified in Duverger's classic study. However, the present study has placed a rather different emphasis on these factors than was previously the case. Indeed, it has done so both generally and in the case of individual countries.

In the last section of the book, it will be argued that these observations reflect not just upon the politics of semi-presidentialism in isolation but also upon the wider academic debate about comparative constitutional engineering in general. Most notably, they call into question the current terms of this debate. They do so in two ways. First, the diversity of semi-presidential practice illustrates the importance of how regime types are defined and how writers go about classifying different countries as examples of particular regime types. Secondly, the fact that only a wide variety of factors can explain the diversity of semi-presidential politics demonstrates that arguments about the advantages and disadvantages of particular regimes types must be made with reference to such factors. Each point will be examined in turn.

The first point concerns the choice of regime types and the classification of countries as examples of particular regime types. In Chapter 1 a semi-presidential regime was defined as the situation where a popularly elected fixed-term president exists alongside a prime minister and cabinet who are responsible to parliament. On the basis of this definition a large number of semi-presidential countries was identified and diverse patterns of European semi-presidential leadership were then illustrated in the chapters which followed. In Chapter 1, however, it was also noted that many of the writers who are currently engaged in the debate about comparative constitutional engineering adopt different definitions of semi-presidentialism and/or classify a different set of countries as examples of semi-presidential regimes. In these cases, the number of semi-presidential countries is usually much smaller and the patterns of leadership with which these countries are associated are often deemed to be much more homogenous.

The difference between these two approaches is highly significant. In the present study the definition of semi-presidentialism and the list of semi-presidential regimes illustrated the diversity of political practices in countries with the same basic constitutional structure. However, in many of the studies of comparative constitutional engineering the definition of semi-presidentialism and the list of semi-presidential regimes are often chosen so as to illustrate the similarity of political practices in countries with the same basic constitutional structure. This second approach, it might be argued, is problematic. For example, Linz seemingly restricts his set of semi-presidential regimes to Finland, France, pre-1982 Portugal, and the Weimar Republic (Linz 1994: 48–9). Needless to say, by excluding the experience of countries like Austria, Iceland, and Ireland from the list, this choice of countries leads to the natural conclusion that semi-presidential regimes are all characterized by dual executives, presidential/prime ministerial conflict, mixed forms of leadership and so on. In this way, Linz's analysis comes very close to being a self-fulfilling prophecy. The same point applies to some of the proponents of semi-presidentialism. For example, Sartori also excludes Austria, Iceland, and Ireland from his list of semi-presidential regimes and he only considers Portugal to have been semi-presidential from 1976–82 (Sartori 1997: 127–9). Again, therefore, this approach leads to a set of countries which operate, by definition, in a relatively similar way. This naturally leads Sartori to conclude that, despite the attractions of semi-presidentialism, the 'split majority problem still haunts . . . the semi-presidential experience' (ibid. 137). And yet of course it does so precisely because countries which have never experienced this problem are excluded from Sartori's list. Sartori rightly argues that the choice of definition is crucial because 'erroneous inclusions inevitably distort the grasp of a specimen' (ibid. 127). However, it might equally be argued that erroneous exclusions also distort the grasp of a specimen as well. Finally, the same point applies to Shugart and Carey. They eschew the concept of semi-presidentialism, but their alternative formulations (premier-presidentialism, president-parliamentarism, and so on) are drawn up on the basis of the same logic and so their conclusions about the pros and cons of these formulations are subject to the same criticism.[5]

It is clear, then, that both the choice of definitions and the classi-fication of countries on the basis of those definitions cannot help but predetermine the conclusions that will eventually be reached about the regimes types in question. Bearing this in mind, though, it might be argued that the most appropriate way of defining semi-presidentialism and the most appropriate way of classifying semi-presidential regimes is one which was adopted in this book. In this case, the definition of semi-presidentialism was provided in Chapter 1 by virtue of a theoretical analysis. Only then was there an examination of how the various semi-presidential systems, thus defined, were seen to operate in practice. Following this examination, conclusions about the politics of semi-presidentialism were then derived. As such, this methodology minimized the extent to which the conclusions of the book were prejudged. In other cases, though, it appears as if the first point of reference is how countries actually operate: does the prime minister dominate, does the president dominate, is there a sharing of executive powers? Once this is established, the definition of particular regime types is then asserted: often parliamentarism, presidentialism, and semi-presidentialism, respectively. The pros and cons of each regime type are then discussed and it is often concluded that semi-presidentialism results in a confusion of executive powers. However, in cases like this, writers are bound to conclude that semi-presidentialism runs the risk of producing executive conflict because the only countries which are deemed to be semi-presidential are ones in which such conflict has already been identified in the first place. All told, therefore, this methodology puts the proverbial cart before the horse and maximizes the chances of producing self-fulfilling prophecies.

This study, therefore, has demonstrated that there are problems not necessarily with the arguments about the actual pros and cons of semi-presidentialism, presidentialism, parliamentarism, and so on (after all, it has been shown that semi-presidentialism can produce a confusion of executive powers, even if this is not necessarily the case) but that there are certainly problems with the way in which regime types are defined and countries are classified as examples of such. In this way, it has demonstrated that there are worries regarding how the current debate about comparative constitutional engineering is being conducted.

The second point concerns the factors which explain the politics of regime types. This point follows on the previous one and can be stated quite briefly. In this chapter it was shown that the diversity of semi-presidential politics can only be explained with reference to a variety of factors. This finding, though, itself followed on from the definition of semi-presidentialism that was given in Chapter 1 and from the studies of the various semi-presidential regimes that were then undertaken on the basis of this definition. In other studies, though, where semi-presidentialism is defined differently and where the set of semi-presidential regimes contains a more restricted number of similar-functioning, usually mixed-leadership, countries, it also follows that the factors explaining the politics of these systems are likely to vary as well.

Again, the difference between these two approaches is significant. In the present study the list of semi-presidential regimes included countries which are normally excluded from any such list, such as Austria, Bulgaria, Iceland, Ireland, Russia, and Slovenia. In this case, it was quite reasonably concluded that historical, cultural, party political, and institutional factors were all salient in explaining how this set of countries actually functioned in practice. In other studies, though, where the list of semi-presidential regimes includes only those countries where there are mixed forms of leadership, such as the ones cited by Linz above, then there is a natural tendency to emphasize the role played by institutional arrangements at the expense of these other factors.[6] This is because the argument is primarily concerned with the issue of divided government, 'cohabitation', presidential/prime ministerial relations, and so forth. Again, therefore, the choice of countries is bound at least partly to predetermine the sorts of conclusions that will be reached. However, given that, it is better to adopt an approach which minimizes this issue, as in this book, rather than an approach which compounds this problem, as in certain other studies.

As before, then, this point does not necessarily imply that the arguments currently made about the advantages or disadvantages of particular regime types are incorrect (institutional features are clearly important), nor does it suggest that other writers simply ignore extra-institutional factors. However, it does suggest that there are dangers inherent in the way in which some writers go about making their arguments. Once again, therefore, doubt is cast on the terms of the current debate about comparative constitutional engineering.

CONCLUSION

Semi-presidentialism has always been and will continue to remain a contested regime type. This book, though, has taken the study of semi-presidentialism one stage further. It has examined the concept of semi-presidentialism and the practice of semi-presidentialism in a range of European countries. In itself, this marks a significant innovation and adds considerably to the sum of knowledge about this aspect of comparative politics. There is, however, a considerable way to go. There is a great need to examine the politics of semi-presidential regimes outside the European arena. There is a need to compare more rigorously the politics of semi-presidentialism with the politics of presidentialism, parliamentarism, and so on. Finally, there is a need to explore the theoretical implications of the concept and its alternatives in more detail. In this sense, this study merely provides a modest contribution to the study of semi-presidentialism and the politics of semi-presidential regimes.

NOTES

1. The usual disclaimer applies. This chapter is the responsibility of the author and not the other contributors to this book.
2. As argued in Ch. 1, this does not mean that there have been alternations between presidential and parliamentary regimes (as some authors imply), but rather that there have been alternations between strong presidential powers and strong prime ministerial powers within the same semi-presidential regime.
3. Of course, it might be argued that the inclusion of the newly democratized countries creates an in-built bias towards the finding that political practice is highly diverse. After all, such countries are likely to experience a period of political turbulence before they 'settle down'. At the same time, though, there are still important lessons to be learnt from their, albeit limited, experience. So, while the problems of generalizing from events in recently established semi-presidential countries must be acknowledged, evidence from these systems can legitimately be called upon to illustrate more general points.
4. It should be noted, though, Shugart and Carey's study is not, strictly speaking, a study of constitutional powers alone (see below). Instead, it is a combination of constitutional and actual powers.
5. A similar criticism applies to studies which undertake a statistical examination of the success or otherwise of different regime types. For example, Stepan and Skach identify only three semi-presidential regimes from amongst the list of countries which became independent in the period from 1945–79 and which were continuously democratic from 1980–9 (1993, pp. 14–15). They do so because they classify countries such as Guyana and Sri Lanka as examples of parliamentary regimes and countries such as Cape Verde, Madagascar, Mali, and South Korea as examples of presidential regimes. As a result, though, the figures for the longevity of these regime types and the percentage of democratic years in which the executive had a legislative majority are skewed.
6. As noted in Ch. 1, writers such as Linz and Sartori emphasize that non-institutional factors affect the way regimes function. However, the conclusions that they draw about the advantages and disadvantages of regimes types invariably focus on the institutional arrangements of the various countries in question.

BIBLIOGRAPHY

XIX Konferentsiya (1988), *XIX Vsesoyuznaya konferentsiya KPSS 28 iyunya–1 iyulya 1988g.: Stenograficheskii otchet*, 2 vols. (Moscow: Politizdat).

AHO, ESKO (1993), 'Presidentti ja hallitus', in Keijo Immonen (ed.), *Pitkä Linja. Mauno Koivisto. Valtiomies ja vaikuttaja* (Helsinki: Kirjayhtymä), 83–98.

ANCKAR, DAG (1992), 'Finland: Dualism and Consensual Rule', in Erik Damgaard (ed.), *Parliamentary Change in the Nordic Countries* (Oslo: Scandinavian University Press), 151–90.

ARDANT, PHILIPPE (1987), 'L'Article 5 et la fonction présidentielle', *Pouvoirs*, no. 41: 37–62.

AREL, D., and WILSON, A. (1994*a*), 'The Ukrainian Parliamentary Elections', *RFE/RL Research Report*, 3 (26): 6–17.

——— (1994*b*), 'Ukraine under Kuchma: Back to Eurasia?', *RFE/RL Research Report*, 3 (32): 1–12.

ARTER, DAVID (1981), 'Kekkonen's Finland: Enlightened Despotism or Consensual Democracy?', *West European Politics*, 4 (3): 219–34.

—— (1987), *Politics and Policy-Making in Finland* (Brighton: Wheatsheaf).

BAHRO, HORST, and VESER, ERNST (1995), 'Das semipräsidentielle System—"Bastard" oder Regierungsform sui generis?', *Zeitschrift für Parlamentsfragen*, no. 3: 471–85.

BARTOLINI, STEFANO (1984), 'Sistema partitico ed elezione diretta del capo dello stato in Europa', *Rivista Italiana di Scienza Politica*, 14 (2): 223–43.

BAYLIS, THOMAS A. (1996), 'Presidents versus Prime Ministers: Shaping Executive Authority in Eastern Europe', *World Politics*, 48 (Apr.): 297–323.

BENEDIKTSSON, B. (1965), in *Land og lydveldi*, i (Reykjavik: Almenna bokafelagid).

BERCHTOLD, KLAUS (1978) (ed.), *Die Verfassungsreform von 1929* (Vienna: Braumüller).

BERGMAN, TORBJÖRN (1993), 'Formation Rules and Minority Governments', *European Journal of Political Research*, 23 (1): 55–66.

BEUVE-MÉRY, HUBERT (1987), 'De la dictature temporaire au régime semi-présidentiel', in *Droit, institutions et systèmes politiques. Mélanges en hommage à Maurice Duverger* (Paris: Presses Universitaires de France), 533–40.

BIELINIS, L. (1995), 'Ivardziai politiniame tekste ir politiko nuostatos', *Politologija*, 6 (1): 73–82.

BILOUS, A. O. (1997), *Polityko-pravovi systemy: svit i Ukraïna* (Kiev: AMUPP).

BIRCH, S. (1998), 'An Aggregate-Level Analysis of Voting Behaviour in the Ukrainian Parliamentary Elections of 1994', in T. Kuzio (ed.), *Contemporary Ukraine: Dynamics of Post-Soviet Transformation* (New York: M. E. Sharpe).

BOLAND, KEVIN (1977), *Up Dev!* (Rathcoole, Co. Dublin: Kevin Boland).

BROWN, J. F. (1994), *Hopes and Shadows: Eastern Europe after Communism* (Durham, NC: Duke University Press).

BUGARIČ, BOJAN (1997), 'From Plan to Market: One Way or Alternative Paths? A Critique of Institutional Reforms in Central and Eastern Europe', Ph.D. thesis (University of Wisconsin).

CASEY, JAMES (1992), *Constitutional Law in Ireland*, 2nd edn. (London: Sweet and Maxwell).

CERAR, MIRO (1991), 'Die Verfassungsrechtlichen Grundlagen der Konstitu-ierung des Staates Slowenien', in J. Marko and T. Borić (eds.), *Slowenien—Kroatien—Serbien, Die neuen Verfassungen* (Wien–Köln–Graz: Böhlau Verlag), 100–40.

CHUBB, BASIL (1978), *The Constitution and Constitutional Change in Ireland* (Dublin: Institute of Public Administration).

CIEMNIEWSKI, JERZY (1993), 'Podział władz w "małej konstytucji"', in Maria Kruk (ed.), *'Mała konstytucja' w procesie przemian ustrojowych w Polsce* (Warsaw: Wyd. Sejmowe), 19–41.

COAKLEY, JOHN, and GALLAGHER, MICHAEL (1996) (eds.), *Politics in the Republic of Ireland*, 2nd edn. (Limerick: PSAI Press).

COHENDET, MARIE-ANNE (1993), *La Cohabitation: Leçons d'une expérience* (Paris: Presses Universitaires de France).

COLLINS, STEPHEN (1996), *The Cosgrave Legacy* (Dublin: Blackwater Press).

CONAC, GÉRARD (1992), 'Le Présidentialisme', in Olivier Duhamel and Yves Mény (eds.), *Dictionnaire constitutionnel* (Paris: Presses Universitaires de France), 812–21.

Constitution Review Group (1996), *Report of the Constitution Review Group* (Dublin: Stationery Office).

COOGAN, TIM PAT (1993), *De Valera: Long Fellow, Long Shadow* (London: Hutchinson).

CRAMPTON, R. J. (1997), *A Concise History of Bulgaria* (Cambridge: Cambridge University Press).

DE BAECQUE, FRANCIS (1976), *Qui gouverne la France?* (Paris: Presses Univer-sitaires de France).

——(1986), 'Le Partage des moyens entre la présidence de la République et le premier ministre', in Jean-Louis Seurin (ed.), *La Présidence en France et aux Etats-Unis* (Paris: Economica), 282–306.

DÉCAUMONT, FRANÇOISE (1979), *La Présidence de Georges Pompidou: Essai sur le régime présidentialiste français* (Paris: Economica).

DUHAMEL, ALAIN (1980), *La République giscardienne* (Paris: Grasset).

DUHAMEL, OLIVIER (1993), *Les Démocraties. Régimes, histoire, exigences* (Paris: Seuil).

——(1995), 'Président, premier ministre, gouvernement. Les différents cas de figure', in Nicholas Wahl and Jean-Louis Quermonne (eds.), *La France prési-dentielle. L'Influence du suffrage universel sur la vie politique* (Paris: Presses de la FNSP), 121–37.

DUIGNAN, SEÁN (1995). *One Spin on the Merry-Go-Round* (Dublin: Blackwater Press).

DUNLEAVY, JANET EGLESON, and DUNLEAVY, GARETH W. (1991), *Douglas Hyde: A Maker of Modern Ireland* (Berkeley: University of California Press).

DUVERGER, MAURICE (1970), *Institutions politiques et droit constitutionnel*, 11th edn. (Paris: Presses Universitaires de France).

——(1971), *Institutions politiques et droit constitutionnel*, 12th edn. (Paris: Presses Universitaires de France).

——(1974), *La Monarchie républicaine* (Paris: Robert Laffont).

——(1978), *Echec au roi* (Paris: Albin Michel).

——(1980), 'A New Political System Model: Semi-Presidential Government', *European Journal of Political Research*, 8: 165–87.

——(1982), *La République des citoyens* (Paris: Ramsay).

——(1984), 'Presidential Elections and the Party System in Europe', in Richard L. McCormack (ed.), *Political Parties and the Modern State* (New Brunswick, NJ: Rutgers University Press), 87–107.

——(1986*a*), 'Duverger's Law: Forty Years Later', in Bernard Grofman and Arend Lijphart (eds.), *Electoral Laws and their Political Consequences* (New York: Agathon Press), 69–84.

——ed. (1986*b*), *Les Régimes semi-présidentiels* (Paris: Presses Universitaires de France).

——(1986*c*), 'Système présidentiel et système semi-présidentiel', in Jean-Louis Seurin (ed.), *La Présidence en France et aux Etats-Unis* (Paris: Economica), 347–58.

——(1986*d*), 'Le Concept de régime semi-présidentiel', in Maurice Duverger (ed.), *Les Régimes semi-présidentiels* (Paris: Presses Universitaires de France), 7–17.

——(1991), *Les Constitutions de la France*, 12th edn. (Paris: Presses Universitaires de France).

——(1992), 'Régime semi-présidentiel', in Olivier Duhamel and Yves Mény (eds.), *Dictionnaire constitutionnel* (Paris: Presses Universitaires de France), 901–4.

——(1996*a*), *Le Système politique français*, 21st edn. (Paris: Presses Universitaires de France).

——(1996*b*), 'Les Monarchies républicaines', *Pouvoirs*, no. 78: 107–20.

——(1997), 'The Political System of the European Union', *European Journal of Political Research*, 31: 137–46.

DWYER, T. RYLE (1980), *Eamon de Valera* (Dublin: Gill and Macmillan).

EASTER, G. M. (1997), 'Preference for Presidentialism: Postcommunist Regime Change in Russia and the NIS', *World Politics*, 49 (2): 184–211.

ELGIE, ROBERT (1993), *The Role of the Prime Minister in France, 1981–91* (London: Macmillan).

——(1996), 'The French Presidency—Conceptualizing Presidential Power in the Fifth Republic', *Public Administration*, 74 (2): 275–91.

——(1998), 'The Classification of Democratic Regime Types: Conceptual Ambiguity and Contestable Assumptions', *European Journal of Political Research*, 33 (2): 219–38.

—— and WRIGHT, VINCENT (1996), 'The French Presidency: The Changing Public Policy Environment', in Robert Elgie (ed.), *Electing the French President: The 1995 Presidential Election* (London: Macmillan), 172–94.

ELSTER, JON (1993), 'Constitution-Making in Eastern Europe: Rebuilding the Boat in the Open Sea', *Public Administration*, 71 (1–2): 169–217.

——(1993/4), 'Miscalculations in the Design of the East European Presidencies', *East European Constitutional Review*, 2 (4)/3 (1): 95–8.

——(1997), 'Afterword: The Making of Postcommunist Presidencies', in Ray Taras (ed.), *Postcommunist Presidents* (Cambridge: Cambridge University Press), 225–37.

EL'TSIN, B. N. (1990), *Ispoved' na zadannuyu temu* (Leningrad: Chas pik).

——(1994), *Zapiski Prezidenta* (Moscow: Ogonek).

ENGELMANN, FREDERICK C. (1962), 'Haggling for the Equilibrium: The Renegotiation of the Austrian Coalition', *American Political Science Review*, 56: 651–62.

FARRELL, BRIAN (1988), 'From First Dáil through Irish Free State', in Brian Farrell (ed.), *De Valera's Constitution and Ours* (Dublin: Gill and Macmillan), 18–32.

——(1996), 'The Government', in John Coakley and Michael Gallagher (eds.), *Politics in the Republic of Ireland*, 2nd edn. (Limerick: PSAI Press), 167–89.

FARRELL, DAVID M. (1997), *Comparing Electoral Systems* (Hemel Hempstead: Prentice Hall).

FELDBRUGGE, F. J. M. (1987), *The Distinctiveness of Soviet Law* (Dordrecht: Martinus Nijhoff Publishers).

FISCHER, HEINZ (1993), *Die Kreisky Jahre 1967–1983* (Vienna: Löcker).

FITZGERALD, GARRET (1991), *All in a Life* (Dublin: Gill and Macmillan).

GALLAGHER, MICHAEL (1988), 'The President, the People and the Constitution', in Brian Farrell (ed.), *De Valera's Constitution and Ours* (Dublin: Gill and Macmillan), 75–92.

——(1996), 'Parliament', in John Coakley and Michael Gallagher (eds.), *Politics in the Republic of Ireland*, 2nd edn. (Limerick: PSAI Press), 126–49.

—— and MARSH, MICHAEL (1993), 'The 1990 Presidential Elections: Implications for the Future', in Ronald J. Hill and Michael Marsh (eds.), *Modern Irish Democracy: Essays in Honour of Basil Chubb* (Dublin: Irish Academic Press), 62–81.

GANEV, VENELIN I. (1993/4), 'The Bulgarian Presidency II', *East European Constitutional Review*, 2 (4)/3 (1): 62–4.

——(1995), 'The Mysterious Politics of Bulgaria's "Movement for Rights and Freedoms"', *East European Constitutional Review*, 4 (1): 49–53.

——(1997*a*), 'Emergency Power Provisions in the New East European Constitutions', *American Journal of Comparative Law*, 45 (3): 585–612.

GANEV, VENELIN I. (1997*b*), 'Bulgaria's Symphony of Hope', *Journal of Democracy*, 8 (4): 125–39.

——(forthcoming), 'Bulgaria: The (Ir)Relevance of Postcommunist Constitutionalism', in Jan Zielonka (ed.), *Constitutional Engineering in Eastern Europe* (Florence: European University Institute Press).

GARRY, JOHN (1995), 'The Demise of the Fianna Fáil/Labour "Partnership" Government and the Rise of the "Rainbow" Coalition', *Irish Political Studies*, 10: 192–9.

GEBETHNER, STANISŁAW (1992), 'Political Institutions in the Process of Transition to a Postsocialist Formation', in Walter D. Connor and Piotr Ploszajski (eds.), *Escape from Socialism: The Polish Route* (Warsaw: IFiS Publishers), 232–54.

——(1993), 'Geneza i tło polityczno-ustrojowe wyborów prezydenckich 1990 r.', in Stanisław Gebethner and Krzysztof Jasiewicz (eds.), *Dlaczego tak głosowano. Wybory prezydenckie '90* (Warsaw: ISP), 10–60.

GEDDES, BARBARA (1995), *The Politician's Dilemma* (Berkeley: University of California Press).

GEHLER, MICHAEL (1995) ' "... eine grotesk überzogene Dämonisierung eines Mannes ..." Die Waldheim-Affäre 1986–1992', in Michael Gehler and Hubert Sickinger (eds.), *Politische Affären und Skandale in Österreich* (Thaur: Kulturverlag), 614–65.

GISLASON, G. TH. (1945), 'Lydraedi og stjornfesta', *Helgafell*, 4: 114–23.

GOLDINGER, WALTER (1982), 'Wilhelm Miklas', in Friedrich Weissensteiner (ed.), *Die österreichischen Bundespräsidenten* (Vienna: Österreichischer Bundesverlag), 81–120.

GRAD, FRANC (1992), 'Parlament', in *Nova ustavna ureditev* (Ljubljana: University of Ljubljana Law Faculty), 137–49.

——(1995), 'Nekatere značilnosti razmerij med državnim zborom, državnim svetom, predsednikom republike in vlado', in *Javna uprava*, no. 4 (Ljubljana: Institute of Public Administration), 457–76.

——(1996), *Volitve in volilni sistemi* (Ljubljana: Institute of Public Administration).

——KAUČIČ, IGOR, RIBIČIČ, CIRIL, and KRISTAN, IVAN (1996), *Državna ureditev Slovenije* (Ljubljana: ČZ Official Gazette).

GURKOVSKA, JULIA (1996), *Presidentut i presidentsvoto* (Sofia: Centre for Liberal Strategies, Occasional Paper).

HÄMÄLÄINEN, UNTO (1997), 'Ahti Karjalaisen ja Nikolai Patolitshevin yhteinen salaisuus', in *Helsingin Sanomat. Kuukausiliite*, 37–9.

HARDARSON, O. (1997), 'Kjor thjodhofdingja: geta Islendingar laert af Irum?', in *Islensk felagsrit*, 87–99.

HET'MAN, V. P. (1996), *Yak pryimalas' konstytutsiia Ukrainy* (Kiev: Yanko).

HOFFMAN, STANLEY H. (1959), 'The French Constitution of 1958: I. The Final Text and its Prospects', *American Political Science Review*, 53 (2): 332–57.

HOGAN, GERARD, and WHYTE, GERRY (1994), *The Irish Constitution*, 3rd edn. (London: Butterworths).

HOLMES, STEPHEN (1993/4), 'The Postcommunist Presidency', *East European Constitutional Review*, 2 (4)/3 (1): 36–9.

HORGAN, JOHN (1997), *Seán Lemass: The Enigmatic Patriot* (Dublin: Gill and Macmillan).

HOWORTH, JOLYON (1993), 'The President's Special Role in Foreign and Defence Policy', in Jack Hayward (ed.), *De Gaulle to Mitterrand: Presidential Power in France* (London: Hurst), 150–89.

IERACI, GIUSEPPE (1994), 'Presidenzialismo e parlamentarismo nelle "democrazie difficili" ', *Quaderni di Scienza Politica*, 1 (1): 35–90.

International IDEA (1997), *Democracy in Romania* (Stockholm: Capacity Building Series, no. 1).

IONESCU, DAN (1991), 'Riots Topple Petre Roman's Cabinet', *Report on Eastern Europe*, 2 (42): 18–22.

JAHNEL, DIETMAR (1987), 'Die Mitwirkung des Bundespräsidenten an der Bundesgesetzgebung', *Juristische Blätter*, 109: 633–40.

JAMBREK, PETER (1992), *Ustavna demokracija (Graditev slovenske demokracije, države in ustave)* (Ljubljana: Državna založba Slovenije).

JOHANNESSON, O. (1954), 'Althingi og framkvaemdavaldid', *Timarit logfraedinga*, 1: 4–27.

JUSSILA, OSMO, HENTILÄ, SEPPO, and NEVAKIVI, JUKKA (1995), *Suomen poliittinen historia 1809–1995* (Porvoo–Helsinki–Juva: Werner Söderström).

JYRÄNKI, ANTERO (1971), *Valta ja vallan siirto* (Helsinki: Kirjayhtymä).

——(1981), *Presidentti. Tutkimus valtiopäämiehen asemasta Suomessa vuosina 1919–1976* (Porvoo–Helsinki–Juva: Werner Söderström).

KACZYŃSKI, JAROSŁAW (1993), *Czas na zmiany. Z Jarosławem Kaczyńskim rozmawiają Michał Bichniewicz i Piotr M. Rudnicki* (Warsaw: Editions Spotkania).

KALELA, JAAKKO (1993), 'Mauno Koivisto ja 90-luvun ulkopolitiikan puitteet', in Keijo Immonen (ed.), *Pitkä Linja. Mauno Koivisto. Valtiomies ja vaikuttaja* (Helsinki: Kirjayhtymä), 221–53.

——(1996), 'Demokratia ja ulkopolitiikka', *Ulkopolitiikka*, 3: 42–3.

KASTARI, PAAVO (1977), *Suomen valtiosääntö* (Helsinki: Suomalaisen lakimiesyhdistys: B-sarja, 179).

KAUČIČ, IGOR (1992), 'Volitve predsednika republike', *Teorija in praksa*, nos. 7–8: 737–41.

——(1995), 'Funkcija predsednika republike in državni zbor', in *Expert Meeting of Lawyers in the Field of Public Law* (Brdo pri Kranju: Institute of Public Administration), 257–72.

KEELER, JOHN T. S., and SCHAIN, MARTIN A. (1996), 'Presidents, Premiers and Models of Democracy in France', in John T. S. Keeler and Martin A. Schain (eds.), *Chirac's Challenge: Liberalization, Europeanization, and Malaise in France* (London: Macmillan), 23–52.

KEOGH, DERMOT (1994), *Twentieth-Century Ireland: Nation and State* (Dublin: Gill and Macmillan).

Kerrigan, Gene (1983), 'First Citizen: A Portrait of Patrick J. Hillery as President', *Magill*, June: 49–55.

Khasbulatov, Ruslan (1992), 'Kakaya vlast' nuzhna Rossii?', in *Narodnyi deputat*, no. 12: 7–14 (part 1), and no. 13: 7–14 (part 2).

Khmelko, V., and Wilson, A. (1998), 'Regionalism and Ethnic and Linguistic Cleavages in Ukraine', in T. Kuzio (ed.), *Contemporary Ukraine: Dynamics of Post-Soviet Transformation* (New York: M. E. Sharpe), 60–80.

Kirchheimer, Otto (1967), 'Decree Powers and Constitutional Law in France under the Third Republic', in Otto Kirchheimer, *Politics, Law and Social Change: Selected Essays of Otto Kirchheimer* (New York: Columbia University Press), 110–30.

Kirchschläger, Rudolf (1992), 'Zwölf Jahre im Amt des Bundespräsidenten—ein Rückblick', in B.-Ch. Funk *et al.* (eds.), *Staatsrecht und Staatswissenschaft in Zeiten des Wandels* (Vienna: Springer), 202–9.

Kjuranov, Deyan, and Kristev, Ivan (1996), *Politichesko nastojashte 1995–1996* (Sofia: Centre for Liberal Strategies).

Koja, Friedrich (1993), 'Wer vertritt die Republik nach außen?', *Juristische Blätter*, 115: 622–31.

——(1994), 'Die rechtlichen und politischen Möglichkeiten des Bundespräsidenten bei der Ernennung der Bundesregierung', *Journal für Rechtspolitik*, 2: 175–9.

——(1997), 'Der Bundespräsident und das Heer', *Journal für Rechtspolitik*, 5: 15–21.

Kolarova, Dimitar, and Dimitrov, Rumyana (1996), 'The Roundtable Talks in Bulgaria', in Jon Elster (ed.), *The Roundtable Talks and the Breakdown of Communism* (Chicago: University of Chicago Press), 172–213.

Kollmann, Eric C. (1965), 'The Austrian Presidency, 1918–1958', *Austrian History Yearbook*, 1: 90–117.

——(1973), *Theodor Körner. Militär und Politik* (Vienna: Verlag für Geschichte und Politik).

Komitea mietintö (1994), *Valtiosääntökomitea 1992:n mietintö*, 4.

Konstitutsiia Ukraïny (1996), Kiev, Secretariat of the Supreme Council of Ukraine.

Korinek, Karl (1990), 'Die Beurkundung der Bundesgesetze durch den Bundespräsidenten', in Alois Mock and Herbert Schambeck (eds.), *Verantwortung in unserer Zeit. Festschrift für Rudolf Kirchschläger* (Vienna: Österreichische Staatsdruckerei), 121–6.

Korzhakov, Aleksandr (1997), *Boris El'tsin: ot rassveta do zakata* (Moscow: Interbuk).

Kravchuk, L., and Kychyhin, S. (1994), *Leonid Kravchuk: ostanni dni imperiï... Pershi roky nadii* (Kiev: Dovira).

Kreisky, Bruno (1986), *Zwischen den Zeiten* (Berlin: Sieder).

——(1988), *Im Strom der Politik* (Berlin: Sieder).

Kristev, Ivan (1996), 'Konstitutsijata kato politicheska istoriaja', in *The President and the Constitution* (Sofia: Centre for Liberal Strategies).

——(1997), 'Predizvikatelstvoto: predvaritelni izbori', in Antonii Todorov *et al.* (eds.), *Bulgarskite izbori 1990–1996* (Sofia: Demetra).

KRISTINSSON, GUNNAR HELGI (1994), *Throun islensku stjornarskrarinnar* (Reykjavik: Felagsvisindastofnun).

——(1996), 'Parties, States and Patronage', *West European Politics*, 19 (3): 433–57.

KRIVIC, MATEVŽ (1990), 'Parlamentarni sistem z reprezentativno vlogo šefa države in s stabilno vlado', *Teorija in praksa*, nos. 10–11: 1185–90.

——(1992), 'Vlada', in *Nova ustavna ureditev* (Ljubljana: University of Ljubljana Law Faculty), 189–201.

KUNAEV, D. (1991), 'O moem vremeni', *Prostor*, no. 12: 2–44.

KUZNETSOV, E. L. (1996), 'Iz istorii sozdaniya instituta Prezidenta SSSR', *Gosudarstvo i pravo*, no. 5: 95–104.

LAGROYE, JACQUES (1992), 'Le Conflit de l'automne 1962. Dispersions et convergences dans la formalisation du rôle', in Bernard Lacroix and Jacques Lagroye (eds.), *Le Président de la République. Usage et genèses d'une institution* (Paris: Presses de la FNSP), 161–93.

LAURILA, JUHANI (1995), 'Finnish-Soviet Clearing Trade and Payment System: History and Lessons', in *Bank of Finland Studies* (A:94; Helsinki: Trio-Offset).

LAZAREV, B. M. (1990), 'Prezident SSSR', *Sovetskoe gosudarstvo i pravo*, no. 7: 3–14.

LEE, J. J. (1989), *Ireland 1912–1985: Politics and Society* (Cambridge: Cambridge University Press).

LIJPHART, AREND (1992*a*) (ed.), *Parliamentary versus Presidential Government* (Oxford: Oxford University Press).

——(1992*b*), 'Introduction', in Arend Lijphart (ed.), *Parliamentary versus Presidential Government* (Oxford: Oxford University Press), 1–27.

——(1994), 'Presidentialism and Majoritarian Democracy: Theoretical Observations', in Juan J. Linz and Arturo Valenzuela (eds.), *The Failure of Presidential Democracy: Comparative Perspectives* (Baltimore: Johns Hopkins University Press), 91–105.

——(1997), 'Trichotomy or Dichotomy?', *European Journal of Political Research*, 31: 125–8.

LINDAL, S. (1992), 'Stjornskipuleg stada forseta Islands', *Skirnir*, 166 (Autumn): 425–39.

LINZ, J. L. (1990), 'Transitions to Democracy', *Washington Quarterly*, 13 (3): 153–64.

LINZ, JUAN J. (1994), 'Presidential or Parliamentary Democracy: Does It Make a Difference?', in Juan J. Linz and Arturo Valenzuela (eds.), *The Failure of Presidential Democracy* (Baltimore: Johns Hopkins University Press), 3–87.

——(1997), 'Introduction: Some Thoughts on Presidentialism in Post-Communist Europe', in Ray Taras (ed.), *Postcommunist Presidents* (Cambridge: Cambridge University Press), 1–14.

LINZ, JUAN J., and VALENZUELA, ARTURO (1994) (eds.), *The Failure of Presidential Democracy* (Baltimore: Johns Hopkins University Press).

LITVIN, V. M. (1997), *Ukraina: politika, politiki, vlast'. Na fone politicheskogo portreta L. Kravchuka* (Kiev: Al'ternatyvy).

LOWENHARDT, JOHN (1998) (ed.), *Party Politics in Post-Communist Russia* (London: Frank Cass).

LUCKY, CHRISTIAN (1993/4), 'Table of Presidential Powers in Eastern Europe', *East European Constitutional Review*, Fall/Winter: 81–94.

LUDWIKOWSKI, R. (1996), *Constitution-Making in the Region of Former Soviet Dominance* (London: Duke University Press).

LUKANOV, Y. (1996), *Tretii prezydent: politychnyi portret Leonida Kuchmy* (Kiev: Taki spravy).

LUKŠIČ, IGOR (1993), 'Zmagovalci in poraženci volitev 1992', in *Volitve in politika po Slovensko* (Ljubljana: Zbornik ocen, razprav in napovedi, Znanstveno in publicistično središče, 13–28.

LYTVYN, V. M. (1994), *Politychna arena Ukraïny: diiovi osoby ta vykonavtsi* (Kiev: Abrys).

McGREGOR, JAMES (1994), 'The Presidency in East Central Europe', *RFE/RL Research Report*, 3 (2), 14 Jan.: 23–31.

MAINWARING, SCOTT (1993), 'Presidentialism, Multipartism, and Democracy: The Difficult Combination', *Comparative Political Studies*, 26 (2): 198–228.

—— and SHUGART, MATTHEW S. (1997), 'Juan Linz, Presidentialism and Democracy', *Comparative Politics*, 29 (4): 449–71.

MARKIČ, BOŠTJAN (1992), 'Politične stranke, volilna kultura, volilni sistem', *Teorija in praksa*, no. 29: 748–52.

MARKO, JOSEPH (1991), 'Die neuen Verfassungen: Slowenien–Kroatien–Serbien. Ein Vergleich', in J. Marko and T. Borić (eds.), *Slowenien–Kroatien–Serbien, Die neuen Verfassungen* (Wien–Köln–Graz: Böhlau Verlag), 1–50.

MARSH, MICHAEL (1999), 'The Making of the Eighth President', in Michael Marsh and Paul Mitchell (eds.), *How Ireland Voted 1997* (Boulder, Colo.: Westview Press).

—— and WILFORD, RICK (1991), 'Irish Political Data, 1990', *Irish Political Studies*, 6: 125–49.

—— —— KING, SIMON, and McELROY, GAIL (1996), 'Irish Political Data, 1995', *Irish Political Studies*, 11: 213–308.

MASSOT, JEAN (1993), *Chef de l'état et chef du gouvernement. Dyarchie et hiérarchie* (Paris: La Documentation Française).

MATZKA, MANFRED (1985), 'Sozialdemokratie und Verfassung', in Manfred Matzka (ed.), *Sozialdemokratie und Verfassung* (Vienna: Europaverlag), 9–155.

MOTYL, A. J. (1995), 'The Conceptual President: Leonid Kravchuk and the Politics of Surrealism', in Colton, T. J. and R. C. Tucker (eds.), *Patterns in Post-Soviet Leadership* (Boulder, Colo.: Westview Press), 103–21.

MÜLLER, WOLFGANG C. (1995), 'Adolf Schärf', in Herbert Dachs, Peter Gerlich, and Wolfgang C. Müller (eds.), *Die Politiker* (Vienna: Manz), 502–12.

——(1996), 'Political Institutions', in Volkmar Lauber (ed.), *Contemporary Austrian Politics* (Boulder, Colo.: Westview Press), 23–57.

——(1997), 'Österreich: Festgefügte Koalitionen und stabile Regierungen', in Wolfgang C. Müller and Kaare Strøm (eds.), *Koalitionsregierungen in Westeuropa* (Vienna: Signum).

NENASHEV, M. F. (1993), *Poslednee pravitel'stvo SSSR* (Moscow: Krom).

NOGUEIRA ALCALÁ, HUMBERTO (1986), *El Regimen Semipresidencial. Una Nueva Forma de Gobierno Democrático?* (Santiago: Andante).

O'DONNELL, GUILLERMO (1996), 'Delegative Democracy', in Larry Diamond and Marc Plattner (eds.), *The Global Resurgence of Democracy* (Baltimore: Johns Hopkins University Press).

——and SCHMITTER, PHILIPPE C. (1986), *Transitions from Authoritarian Rule: Tentative Conclusions about Uncertain Democracies* (Baltimore: Johns Hopkins University Press).

OKUN'KOV, L. A. (1996), *Prezident Rossiiskoi Federatsii: Konstititsiya i politicheskaya praktika* (Moscow: Infra-M/Norma).

O'LEARY, BRENDAN (1991), 'An Taoiseach: The Irish Prime Minister', *West European Politics*, 14 (2): 133–62.

O'NEILL, PATRICK (1993), 'Presidential Power in Post-Communist Europe: The Hungarian Case in Comparative Perspective', *Journal of Communist Studies*, 9 (3): 177–201.

——(1997), 'Hungary: Political Transition and Executive Conflict: The Balance or Fragmentation of Power?', in Ray Taras (ed.), *Postcommunist Presidents* (Cambridge: Cambridge University Press), 195–224.

O'REILLY, EMILY (1991), *Candidate: The Truth behind the Presidential Campaign* (Dublin: Attic Press).

OSIATYŃSKI, WIKTOR (1994), 'Poland's Constitutional Ordeal', *East European Constitutional Review*, Spring: 29–38.

O'SULLIVAN, EOIN (1991), 'The 1990 Presidential Election in the Republic of Ireland', *Irish Political Studies*, 6: 85–98.

PACTET, PIERRE (1995), *Institutions politiques. Droit constitutionnel*, 14th edn. (Paris: Masson/Armand Colin).

PASQUINO, GIANFRANCO (1995), *Mandato popolare e governo* (Bologna: il Mulino).

——(1997), 'Semi-Presidentialism: A Political Model at Work', *European Journal of Political Research*, 31: 128–37.

PEEVA, RALITSA (1997), 'The Bulgarian Round Table Talks: A Case of Negotiated Transition?', unpublished manuscript, New York, New York School for Social Research.

PELINKA, ANTON (1995), 'Kurt Waldheim', in Herbert Dachs, Peter Gerlich, and Wolfgang C. Müller (eds.), *Die Politiker* (Vienna: Manz), 586–93.

PELINKA, ANTON, and WELAN, MANFRIED (1971), *Demokratie und Verfassung in Österreich* (Vienna: Europa Verlag).

PETER, FRIEDRICH (1986), '30 Jahre Freiheitliche Partei Österreichs', in *30 Jahre Freiheitliche Partei Österreichs* (Vienna: Freiheitliches Bildungswerk), 23–80.

PIRINGER, KURT (1982), *Die Geschichte der Freiheitlichen* (Vienna: Orac Pietsch).

POPOV, STEFAN (1996), *Prezidentut: modelirane na administratsijata* (Sofia: Centre for Liberal Strategies, Occasional Paper).

PRITZEL, I. (1997), 'Ukraine between Proto-Democracy and "Soft" Authoritarianism', in K. Dawisha and B. Parrott (eds.), *Democratic Changes and Authoritarian Reactions in Russia, Ukraine, Belarus, and Moldova* (Cambridge: Cambridge University Press), 330–69.

PROTSYK, O. (1995), 'Do Institutions Matter? Semi-Presidentialism in Ukraine and France', MA thesis (Central European University, Budapest).

RHODES, R. A. W. (1996), 'The New Governance: Governing without Government', *Political Studies*, 44 (4): 652–67.

RIBARIČ, MIHA (1992*a*), 'Funkcije in pristojnosti predsednika republike', in *Nove ustavna ureditev* (Ljubljana: University of Ljubljana Law Faculty), 184–8.

——(1992*b*), 'Predsednik republike in človekove pravice', *Teorija in praksa*, nos. 7–8: 687–93.

——(1995), 'Uveljavljanje odgovornosti predsednika republike', in *Expert Meeting of Lawyers in the Field of Public Law* (Brdo pri Kranju: Institute of Public Administration), 273–85.

——(1996), 'Predsednik republike v procesu političnega odločanja', in *Expert Meeting of Lawyers in the Field of Public Law* (Rogaška Slatina: Institute of Public Administration), 79–94.

——(1997), 'Odnos med Predsednikom Republike Slovenije in vlado', in *Demokracija—vladanje in uprava v Sloveniji* (Ljubljana: Slovene Political Science Society), 39–53.

RIBIČIČ, CIRIL (1992), 'Ustavni položaj predsednika republike', in *Nova ustavna ureditev* (Ljubljana: University of Ljubljana Law Faculty), 173–83.

——(1996*a*), 'Predsednik republike', in F. Grad, I. Kaučič, C. Ribičič, and I. Kristan (eds.), *Državna ureditev Slovenije* (Ljubljana: ČZ Official Gazette), 133–47.

——(1996*b*), 'Volilni sistem v Sloveniji—Osebnost kandidatov in sorazmerna zastopanost strank', in *Volilni sistemi* (Ljubljana: Knjižna zbirka Krt), 283–303.

RINGHOFER, KURT (1977) (ed.), *Die österreichische Bundesverfassung* (Vienna: Verlag des Österreichischen Gewerkschaftsbundes).

ROSE, RICHARD (1980), 'British Government: The Job at the Top', in Richard Rose and Ezra Suleiman (eds.), *Presidents and Prime Ministers* (Washington, DC: American Enterprise Institute), 1–49.

RUDELLE, ODILE (1984), 'Le Général de Gaulle et l'élection directe du Président de la République. Étapes d'un processus stratégique', in *Revue Française de Science Politique*, 34 (4–5): 687–710.

RUMPUNEN, KAUKO (1997), *Aikoja ja tapauksia Ahti Karjalaisen elämästä* (Helsinki: WSOY).

RUPNIK, JANKO, CIJAN, RAFAEL, and GRAFENAUER, BOŽO (1994), *Ustavno pravo Republike Slovenije* (Maribor: University of Maribor Law Faculty).

SAKHAROV, ANDREI (1994), *Trevoga i nadezhda* (Moscow: Interverso).

SAKHAROV, N. A. (1994), *Institut prezidentstva v sovremennom mire* (Moscow: Yuridicheskaya literatura).

SALMINEN, ESKO (1996), *Vaikeneva valtiomahti? Neuvostoliitto/Venäjä Suomen lehdistössä 1968–1991* (Helsinki: Edita).

SARTORI, GIOVANNI (1994), 'Neither Presidentialism nor Parliamentarism', in Juan J. Linz and Arturo Valenzuela (eds.), *The Failure of Presidential Democracy: Comparative Perspectives* (Baltimore: Johns Hopkins University Press), 106–18.

——(1997), *Comparative Constitutional Engineering: An Inquiry into Structures, Incentives and Outcomes*, 2nd edn. (London: Macmillan).

SCHÄRF, ADOLF (1955), *Österreichs Erneuerung 1945–1955* (Vienna: Verlag der Wiener Volksbuchhandlung).

——(n.d.), 'Österreich wieder in Freiheit 1955–1957', unpublished manuscript, Vienna, Verein für Geschichte der Arbeiterbewegung.

SCHAUSBERGER, FRANZ (1982), 'Franz Jonas', in Friedrich Weissensteiner (ed.), *Die österreichischen Bundespräsidenten* (Vienna: Österreichischer Bundesverlag), 257–312.

SCHRAM, G. G., and JOHANNESSON, O. (1994), *Stjornskipun Islands* (Reykjavik: Haskolautgafan).

SCHUMPETER, JOSEPH (1950), *Capitalism, Socialism and Democracy* (New York: Harper and Row).

SEIPEL, IGNAZ (1930), *Der Kampf um die österreichische Verfassung* (Vienna: Braumüller).

SEXTON, BRENDAN (1989), *Ireland and the Crown, 1922–1936: The Governor-Generalship of the Irish Free State* (Dublin: Irish Academic Press).

SHAFIR, MICHAEL (1990), 'Oppositional Regrouping, the Democratic Anti-Totalitarian Forum and the Civic Alliance', *Report on Eastern Europe*, 1 (50): 13–21.

——(1992a), 'Constitution Approved in Referendum', *RFE/RL Research Report*, 1 (2): 53–6.

——(1992b), 'Romania's Elections: More Change than Meets the Eye', *RFE/RL Research Report*, 1 (44): 7–11.

SHUGART, MATTHEW S. (1993), 'Of Presidents and Parliaments', *East European Constitutional Review*, 2 (1): 30–2.

——and CAREY, JOHN M. (1992), *Presidents and Assemblies: Constitutional Design and Electoral Dynamics* (Cambridge: Cambridge University Press).

SHUGART, MATTHEW S., and MAINWARING, SCOTT (1997), 'Presidentialism and Democracy in Latin America: Rethinking the Terms of the Debate', in Scott Mainwaring and Matthew Soberg Shugart (eds.), *Presidentialism and Democracy in Latin America* (Cambridge: Cambridge University Press), 12–54.

SIGGINS, LORNA (1997), *Mary Robinson: The Woman Who Took Power in the Park* (London: Mainstream).

Slovensko javno mnenje (1989), Ljubljana, Research Institute, Faculty of Sociology, Political Science and Journalism, June.

SMITH, G., and WILSON, A. (1997), 'Rethinking Russia's Post-Soviet Diaspora: The Potential for Political Mobilisation in Eastern Ukraine and North-East Estonia', *Europe–Asia Studies*, 49 (5): 845–64.

SOKOLEWICZ, WOJCIECH (1992), 'The Legal–Constitutional Bases of Democratisation in Poland: Systemic and Constitutional Change', in George Sanford (ed.), *Democratisation in Poland, 1988–90* (New York: St Martin's Press), 69–97.

STADLER, KARL R. (1982), *Adolf Schärf. Mensch–Politiker–Staatsmann* (Vienna: Europaverlag).

Stališča Slovencev ob novi ustavi, Slovensko javno mnenje 1990/2 (1992), Ljubljana, Centre for Research into Public Opinion and Mass Communication, Faculty of Sociology, Political Science and Journalism, Dec.

STEFFANI, WINFRIED (1995), 'Semi-Präsidentialismus: ein eigenständiger Systemtyp? Zur Unterscheidung von Legislative und Parlament', *Zeitschrift für Parlamentsfragen*, no. 4: 621–41.

STEFOI, ELENA (1993/4), 'Ion Iliescu, Profile and Interview', *East European Constitutional Review*, 2 (4)/3 (1): 51–8.

STEINER, KURT (1972), *Politics in Austria* (Boston: Little, Brown and Co.).

STEPAN, ALFRED, and SKACH, CINDY (1993), 'Constitutional Frameworks and Democratic Consolidation: Parliamentarianism versus Presidentialism', *World Politics*, 46 (Oct.): 1–22.

——(1994), 'Presidentialism and Parliamentarism in Comparative Perspective', in Juan J. Linz and Arturo Valenzuela (eds.), *The Failure of Presidential Democracy: Comparative Perspectives* (Baltimore: Johns Hopkins University Press), 119–36.

——and SULEIMAN, EZRA N. (1995), 'The French Fifth Republic: A Model for Import? Reflections on Poland and Brazil', in H. E. Chehabi and Alfred Stepan (eds.), *Politics, Society, and Democracy: Comparative Studies* (Boulder, Colo.: Westview Press), 393–414.

STONE, ALEC (1992), *The Birth of Judicial Politics in France* (New York: Oxford University Press).

SUKHANOV, LEV (1992), *Tri goda s Elítsinym* (Riga: Vaga).

SULEIMAN, EZRA N. (1994), 'Presidentialism and Political Stability in France', in Juan J. Linz and Arturo Valenzuela (eds.), *The Failure of Presidential Democracy* (Baltimore: Johns Hopkins University Press), 137–62.

SUOMI, JUHANI (1996), *Taistelu puolueettomuudesta* (Keuruu: Otava).

SYKES, PATRICIA LEE (1997), 'Iron Ladies, Green Goddesses, the Mouth of Marilyn Monroe: When Women of Conviction Enter the Politics of Consensus', *Current World Leaders*, 40 (6): 50–71.

TALAT-KELPSA, LAIMONAS (1996), 'Pusiau prezidentalizmo link', *Politologija*, 7 (1): 93–111.

——(1997), 'Prezidentas ir parlamentas: reiksme valstybës politiiam stabilumui', *Politologija*, 9 (1): 133–41.

TARAS, RAY (1997*a*), 'Separating Power: Keeping Presidents in Check', in Ray Taras (ed.), *Postcommunist Presidents* (Cambridge: Cambridge University Press), 15–37.

——(1997*b*) (ed.), *Postcommunist Presidents* (Cambridge: Cambridge University Press).

TATSII, V., *et al.* (1996), *Konstytutsiia Ukraïny—osnova reformuvannia suspil'stva* (Kharkiv: Pravo).

TETLOCK, PHILIP E., and BELKIN, AARON (1996) (eds.), *Counterfactual Thought Experiments in World Politics* (Princeton: Princeton University Press).

TIILIKAINEN, TEIJA (1993), 'Om Finlands förhållande till utlänska makter bestämmer presidenten', *Politiikka*, 35 (4): 283–91.

TOINET, MARIE-FRANCE (1996), 'The Limits of Malaise in France', in John T. S. Keeler and Martin A. Schain (eds.), *Chirac's Challenge: Liberalization, Europeanization, and Malaise in France* (London: Macmillan), 279–98.

TOMC, GREGOR (1993), 'Slovenci o politiki in politikih', in *Volitve in politika po Slovensko* (Ljubljana: Zbornik ocen, razprav in napovedi, Znanstveno in publicistično središče), 138–55.

Toš, NIKO (1996), 'Zaupanje v demokratični sistem', *Teorija in praksa*, no. 4: 631–72.

TRÓCSÁNYI, LÁSZLÓ (1995), 'Constitutionnalisme et changement du régime politique en Europe Centrale et Europe de l'Est', in *System Transformation and Constitutional Developments in Central and Eastern Europe* (Kecskemét-Szeged), 7–23.

VARES, VESA (1993), *Konservatiivi ja murrosvuodet. Lauri Ingman ja hänen poliittinen toimintansa vuoteen 1922* (Helsinki: Suomen Historiallinen Seura).

VARGOVA, MARIELA (1997) (ed.), *Konstitutsionen sud—1991–1996* (Sofia: Otvoreno obshtestvo).

VERHEIJEN, TONY (1995), *Constitutional Pillars for New Democracies* (Leiden: DSWO Press).

——(1997), 'System Transformation and the Role of Constitutions: A Comparative Analysis of Central and Eastern European Countries', in J. J. Hesse and T. A. J. Toonen (eds.), *Yearbook of Comparative Government and Public Administration* (Berlin: Nomos Verlag), 395–419.

VILFAN, SERGIJ (1995), 'The History of Slovene Popular Representation, Pre-20th Century', in *The National Assembly of the Republic of Slovenia* (Ljubljana: National Assembly of the Republic of Slovenia), 13–22.

VILHJALMSSON, TH. (1994), 'Synjunarvald forsetans', in *Afmaelisrit—Gaukur Jorundsson sextugur* (Reykjavik: Bokautgafa Orators).

VINTON, LOUISA (1992), 'Poland's "Little Constitution" Clarifies Walesa's Powers', *RFE/RL Research Report*, 1 (4 Sept.).

VIRKKUNEN, SAKARI (1978), *Ståhlberg. Suomen ensimmäinen presidentti* (Helsinki: Otava).

WALDHEIM, KURT (1996), *Die Antwort* (Vienna: Amalthea).

WARD, ALAN J. (1994), *The Irish Constitutional Tradition: Responsible Government and Modern Ireland, 1782–1992* (Blackrock: Irish Academic Press).

——(1996), 'The Constitution Review Group and the "Executive State" in Ireland', *Administration*, 44 (4): 42–63.

WEISSENSTEINER, FRIEDRICH (1982), 'Michael Hainisch', in Friedrich Weissensteiner (ed.), *Die österreichischen Bundespräsidenten* (Vienna: Österreichischer Bundesverlag), 46–80.

WELAN, MANFRIED (1986), *Das österreichische Staatsoberhaupt* (Vienna: Verlag für Geschichte und Politik).

——(1992), *Der Bundespräsident. Kein Kaiser in der Republik* (Vienna: Böhlau).

——(1995*a*), 'Der Bundespräsident im System der österreichischen Bundesverfassung', in Günther Schefbeck (ed.), *75 Jahre Bundesverfassung* (Vienna: Verlag Österreich), 483–99.

——(1995*b*), 'Rudolf Kirchschläger', in Herbert Dachs, Peter Gerlich, and Wolfgang C. Müller (eds.), *Die Politiker* (Vienna: Manz), 289–98.

——(1997), *Das österreichische Staatsoberhaupt*, 3rd edn. (Vienna: Verlag für Geschichte und Politik).

WHITE, STEPHEN, ROSE, RICHARD, and MCALLISTER, IAN (1997), *How Russia Votes* (Chatham House, NJ: Chatham House).

WIATR, JERZY (1993), *Krótki Sejm* (Warsaw: BGW).

WILLIAMS, PHILIP (1968), *The French Parliament 1958–67* (London: George Allen & Unwin).

WILSON, A. (1997*a*), *Ukrainian Nationalism in the 1990s: A Minority Faith* (Cambridge: Cambridge University Press).

——(1997*b*), 'Two Presidents and their Powers', in Ray Taras (ed.), *Post-Communist Presidents* (Cambridge: Cambridge University Press), 67–105.

——(1997*c*), 'The Ukrainian Left: In Transition to Social Democracy or Still in Thrall to the USSR?', *Europe–Asia Studies*, 49 (7): 1293–1316.

——and BILOUS, A. (1993), 'Political Parties in Ukraine', *Europe–Asia Studies*, 45 (4): 693–703.

WOLCZUK, KATARYNA (1998), 'The Politics of Constitution Making in Ukraine', in T. Kuzion (ed.), *Contemporary Ukraine: Dynamics of Post-Soviet Transformation* (New York: M. E. Sharpe), 118–38.

WRIGHT, VINCENT (1989), *The Government and Politics of France*, 3rd edn. (London: Unwin Hyman).

WYMAN, MATTHEW, WHITE, STEPHEN, and OATES, SARAH (1998) (eds.), *Elections and Voters in Postcommunist Russia* (Cheltenham: Edward Elgar).

YAROSHENKO, VIKTOR (1997), *El'tsin: ya otvechu za vse* (Moscow: Vokrug sveta).

YOUNG, JOHN (1985), *Erskine H. Childers, President of Ireland: A Biography* (Gerrards Cross: Colin Smythe).

ZAJC, DRAGO (1997), 'Moč in nemoč slovenske parlamentarne demokracije', in *Demokracija—vladanje in uprava v Sloveniji* (Ljubljana: Slovene Political Science Society), 9–25.

ZHELEV, ZHELYU (1995), *Inteligentsija i politika* (Sofia: Literaturen forum).

ZIELONKA, JAN (1994), 'New Institutions in the Old East Bloc', *Journal of Democracy*, 5 (2): 87–104.

ZLOBIN, NIKOLAI (1994), 'From the Archives', *Demokratizatsiya*, 2 (2): 316–31.

ZOLOTOR'OV, V. (1997), 'Osnovnyi Zakon Ukraïny z pozytsii konstytutsional-izmu', in O. Haran' and V. Kulyk (eds.), *Stanovlennia vladnykh struktur v Ukraïni* (Kiev: Den'), 89–113.

ZYUGANOV, GENNADII (1994), *Derzhava*, 2nd edn. (Moscow: Informpechat').

INDEX